# Building an Efí Cybersecurity Program

## 2nd Edition

## Tari Schreider

**C|CISO, CRISC, ITIL® Foundation, MCRP, SSCP**

**Kristen Noakes-Fry, ABCI, Editor**

ISBN 9781944480530 PRINT
ISBN 9781944480554 PDF
ISBN 9781944480547 EPUB

A Division of Rothstein Associates Inc.

203.740.7400

info@rothstein.com
www.rothstein.com

**Keep informed about Rothstein Publishing:**

 www.facebook.com/RothsteinPublishing

 www.linkedin.com/company/rothsteinpublishing

 www.twitter.com/rothsteinpub

ISBN 9781944480530 PRINT

ISBN 9781944480554 PDF

ISBN 9781944480547 EPUB

**Brookfield, Connecticut USA**

**203.740.7400**

info@rothstein.com
www.rothstein.com
www.rothsteinpublishing.com

# Dedication

For my daughters, Vanessa and Whitney – my greatest fans and the ones who always keep me humble. They were always understanding during the times I was away helping others improve their cybersecurity programs.

# Acknowledgments

To Thomas Caulfield, former publisher of *Systems User Magazine*. Tom mentored me in writing and published my first article over 30 years ago. He set the bar for doing the right thing, being a gentleman, and always having humility. I only wish he were still with us to see this book published.

# Preface

Few companies today could survive without the Internet; either you are part of the digital economy, or you are reliant upon those who are. I am hard-pressed to find someone today who does not interact with some aspect of the Internet to perform all or some of his or her work duties. IT professionals and managers alike need to be cybersecurity-savvy to compete in today's job market. You must accept that you are or will be working for an organization that takes cybersecurity seriously. To ensure you do not become one of those managers you read about who lets the cyber aggressors in the backdoor, you must also take cybersecurity seriously as well.

Whether you are a new manager, or a current manager involved in your organization's cybersecurity program, I am confident this book will answer many questions you have about what is involved in building a program. You will be able to get up to speed quickly on program development practices and have a roadmap to follow in building or improving your organization's cybersecurity program.

- Even if you are new to cybersecurity, in the short period of time it will take you to read this book, you can be the smartest person in the room grasping the complexities of your organization's cybersecurity program.
- If you are already involved in your organization's cybersecurity program, you have much to gain from reading this book. This book will become your go-to field manual to guide or affirm your program decisions.

After 30 years of experience in the trenches, designing and building cybersecurity programs throughout the world, I wrote this book to help the process go more smoothly for you. In creating this roadmap for you, I was motivated by what I see as a systemic lack of experience and resources in those tasked with designing and building cybersecurity programs.

First, many managers have never had to build a cybersecurity program from the ground up, resulting in cybersecurity programs based on insular opinions guiding program development rather than sound architecture and design principles.

- Managers involved in cybersecurity can expect an average tenure in their role of approximately two years, which means they are inheriting cybersecurity programs serially throughout their careers. This leaves little time to forge experience gained through building a program of their own design.
- In addition, few of these managers graduated from a cybersecurity degree program that teaches architecture and design.

Second, we do not have a generation of managers equipped to build cybersecurity programs.

- By many accounts, there are over one million cybersecurity jobs open in the US. According to the US Bureau of Labor Statistics, this industry will grow by 37% through 2022. Who will fill these roles? Only the recently graduated or certified are available to fill these open positions, but neither group has the experience necessary to build a cybersecurity program.
- Certifications and degrees may not always be a true measure of the skills required to build today's programs, since there is no substitute for experience.

Third, inexperienced managers have difficulty separating fact from what I call "security theater."

- A multibillion-dollar industry of thousands of cybersecurity vendors and consultants driven by their own self-interest can easily lead managers astray. Managers with little experience can fall under their spell, succumbing to their cybersecurity technologies and becoming locked into proprietary program maturity models.
- I have seen many led down a perilous path of cybersecurity programs crammed with technologies that promise to protect their information and assets from hackers but offer little in the way of basic blocking and tackling.

This book is intended to give you the knowledge and guidance that will allow you to choose wisely and avoid the pitfalls I have described above.

My experience working with hundreds of companies will serve as your roadmap to step you through building your own cybersecurity program. In writing this book, I analyzed over 150 cybersecurity architectures, frameworks, models, etc., so that you would not have to. I have called out those that I felt were great examples to assist you along your journey. This alone will save you hundreds of hours attempting to conduct the research necessary to identify all the components of a cybersecurity program.

My best wishes as you follow the roadmap to create an effective cybersecurity program for your organization!

*Tari Schreider*

Atlanta, Georgia
September 2019

# Why a Second Edition?

When I was writing the first edition of this book, I knew that certain aspects of it would become dated owing to rapid changes in the cybersecurity industry, threat landscape and providers. Two years later I take full measure of all that has evolved in the cybersecurity world. Increasing zero-day attacks, growth of state-sponsored adversaries and consolidation of cybersecurity products and services all converged to shape where we are today. We have also witnessed some of the world's largest data breach events, increasingly destructive ransomware attacks and changes in legal and regulatory statutes.

Aside from substantial updates of standards, source links and cybersecurity products here is what's new in the second edition:

- 50+ callout boxes highlighting cyberattacks and important resources.
- 60 self-study questions to hone your knowledge.
- 25 overviews of cybersecurity technologies.
- Expanded coverage of the intersection of cybersecurity and privacy.
- Expanded coverage of security training strategies.
- A new security talent development section.
- Discussion of cyber insurance policies.
- A new security testing strategies section.
- New adversary profiles.
- Expansion of attack surface discussion.
- Inclusion of new threat frameworks.

- Inclusion of a service management catalog.
- Introduction to emerging cybersecurity technologies.
- 17 powerful templates to document your cybersecurity program.

I have always envisioned keeping this book regularly updated to ensure you would have a reliable cybersecurity reference source. I see this book as a forum to express my views on protecting assets and information. I also see it as a way to share what I learn through teaching Chief Information Security Officers (CISOs). Teaching affords me a platform to learn how some of the largest companies in the world address cybersecurity. I look forward to sharing future updates with you.

*Tari Schreider*

# Foreword

First off, let me start by saying that I've worked with Tari Schreider for over 10 years. During this time, we have developed a friendship based on a shared passion for Information Security. Tari has been a key part of helping me build Information Security programs, and I have been able to take that body of knowledge with me wherever I go as I help other companies build their security programs.

After I took on security leadership for an organization early in my career, Tari and I worked together to develop the Information Security program using the ISO 27001 framework. With Tari's help, I was able to perform a gap analysis of our existing program, align our current policies, standards, and controls, and build a multi-year roadmap for addressing the greatest threats and highest risks to the organization and closing program gaps. Using the ISO 27001 framework and the concepts that Tari outlines in this book, I could demonstrate to senior management, the Board, and our regulators that our program was organized and comprehensive.

Since that time, I have used that experience to build security programs for several companies where I led security teams. Much has evolved with organizations since we first worked together. Companies have become more risk aware, have integrated security into software development, and have started to use artificial intelligence to assist in analyzing user behavior.

Tari's book is like a compendium of his knowledge that he's imparted on me and many others in the industry over the years. It's based on established frameworks and models and, more importantly, practical experience. While I wish I had this book when I first started, I was fortunate to able to work directly with Tari. However, I know that for those who won't be so lucky, I plan to make this one of the books I gift to my staff and security friends.

This book truly is a go-to field guide for designing, building, and maintaining an Information Security program. It's perfect both for someone new to the field and the seasoned professional alike. I know it's a book that I'll be referencing often, and I think that you will, too.

*Michael Speas*

VP, Chief Information Security Officer
Western & Southern Life
August 2019

# Contents

# Introduction

Think about building your organization's cybersecurity program as a journey. Do you know what you will need to bring? As with any trip, your purpose can be for either business or pleasure. If it is for business, then there's a good chance you are inheriting someone else's program and problems. If it is for pleasure, then you will be able to build your own program from the ground up. In any case, if you are reading this book, there's a good chance that your purpose is business, and your boss has already told you your next destination – cybersecurity land. A cybersecurity program will represent the completion of your journey.

All trips have one thing in common. You need to prepare. Trips require a roadmap and a guide or Sherpa to make the journey as smooth as possible. Before you begin your trip, at the very least, you look at a map and some travel brochures. The map shows you how to get to your destination, and the brochures point out interesting sites along the way. Even if you find yourself a passenger on your trip to cybersecurity land (HR manager, attorney, etc.), you can still add value to the trip by using this book to ask the right questions.

For our journey in this book, we will follow a map, and I will be your Sherpa. Each chapter will be a stop on your journey to creating a cybersecurity program, providing important references to help you along the way. Your journey will look something like the winding road in the diagram below.

- Your first stop will have you designing your cybersecurity program, after which you will proceed to establishing principles and policies for how your program should be managed.
- The midpoint of your journey involves identifying the highway robbers or hackers and other threats you want your program to protect against.
- Stop four shows you how to assess and manage risk.
- Nearing the end of your journey, your fifth stop will have you define defensive measures required to protect your organization's assets and information.

- The next to the last stop shows you how to operate your program and ensure you have the right staff doing the right things.
- In the final stop I show you how to unpack all that you have learned.

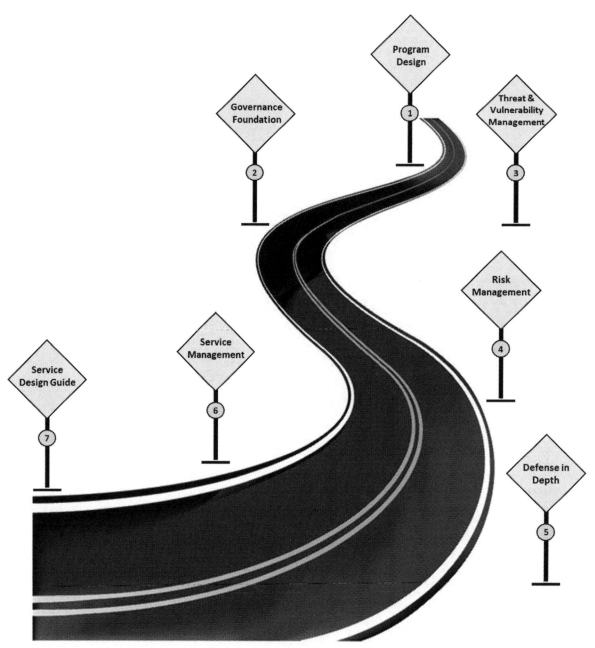

*Figure 0.1*

**Chapter 1: Designing a Cybersecurity Program** – Whenever you begin a journey, it is best to have your destination in sight. A blueprint does just that, it lets all involved in the program's construction know what it should look like once completed. To begin your cybersecurity program, you will need a blueprint that outlines the program's general structure as well as its supporting components. In this chapter, I offer an ideal state example of a cybersecurity program blueprint as well as introduce you to industry leading cybersecurity frameworks. I will also introduce you to leading cybersecurity technologies you should consider adding to your program.

**Chapter 2: Establishing a Foundation of Governance** – The way your company is controlled by the people who run it, is called governance. The way your cybersecurity program is controlled is also governance. Governance is all about making the right decisions for the benefit of the organization. For a cybersecurity program to stand the test of time, it must benefit from proper governance. Governance ensures the program adheres to its design principles. In this chapter, I explain what constitutes a governance program as well as the proper governance of a cybersecurity program. An overview of the top information governance frameworks and models will provide you with an understanding of resources available to mature your cybersecurity program's governance foundation. You will also learn how to automate your governance foundation. I will also discuss how to treat your top cybersecurity talent.

**Chapter 3: Building a Threat, Vulnerability Detection and Intelligence Capability** – Your next step is to determine what is most important to your organization. This includes classifying your organization's assets and information by importance and identifying the types of threats and vulnerabilities to which they are exposed. Next, this chapter shows you how to identify the different points of entry an attacker can use to steal your sensitive information. All these points of entry make up your attack surface, as this is what you will be protecting with your program. I will show you how to create a threat intelligence function that leverages your threat inventory and vulnerability detection systems to reduce the exposure to your attack surface. You will also learn how to acquire threat intelligence and how to make it actionable. To ensure everything works, I will walk you through various methods of testing a cybersecurity program.

**Chapter 4: Building a Cyber Risk Management Capability** – Now that you know the threats and vulnerabilities your organization is exposed; a *risk profile* can be determined. Your risk profile is your organization's willingness to take risks in comparison to the threats faced. In this chapter, I show you how to leverage industry-leading risk assessment frameworks and calculators to derive your organization's risk score. I will show you how to organize and manage your risks with a *risk register*. A register is an inventory of your organization's risk by order of criticality. Each risk is assigned an owner and a corresponding plan to mitigate or manage the risk. Importantly, the topic of risk extends past your organization to third-parties, allowing you to close an often-exploited loophole that could allow unauthorized access to your organization's critical information.

**Chapter 5: Implementing a Defense-in-Depth Strategy** – Up to this point in the journey your focus has been building the foundation and structure of the cybersecurity program. Now that's done, we must populate our program with services and in order to readily find and manage those services we need to put them in a central place, a catalog. The countermeasures service catalog is a repository with a parking space for every one of your program services. Each parking space will include the documents, controls, artifacts and product descriptions that describe the purpose and benefit of each service. The catalog is where you will go to make service enhancements, add new services or retire old services.

**Chapter 6: Applying Service Management to Cybersecurity Programs** – Your next stop of your journey shows you everything that you will need to do to operate your program according to its design and governance principles. Many reported security breaches occurred when organizations did not implement their cybersecurity countermeasures properly. These breaches take place because many managers stop just short of their destination. They fail to implement their program's countermeasures to ensure they operate efficiently and effectively. In this chapter, I show you how to deliver and support your cybersecurity countermeasures, managing them in a continuous improvement lifecycle. I will give real-world examples of best practices for service management.

**Chapter 7: Cybersecurity Program Design Toolkit** – Your last stop on the journey is the creation of your cybersecurity program design guide. Here I provide templates for baselining your existing program, designing the new or revised program and documenting how your program is built. How you complete these templates is covered in the previous chapters. Through these forms, I show you how to determine what is usable in a current program, what can be saved as well as what should be improved to provide maximum protection of information and assets.

Cybersecurity programs are complex, requiring a methodical approach to their design and construction. When setting out on a journey to build a cybersecurity program, my advice is to start at the beginning, resist hopscotching stops, and stay true to the journey. This book is a process, emphasizing the benefits of basic preparatory steps that are often overlooked. Your journey begins with creating a blueprint of what you are going to build, and it will end with ensuring your program operates as a mature service organization.

> *This book makes extensive use of hyperlinks to aid the reader in finding supportive external information. Links have been verified up to the publication date; however, some links may be changed at their source or restricted by certain browsers. In the event of a broken link, you can either paste the URL in a browser or search on the associated link name.*

# Chapter 1

# Designing a Cybersecurity Program

My experience has shown that most cybersecurity programs do not originate from a comprehensive design. Rather, they tend to evolve based on disparate opinions of stakeholders who often change strategies and approaches without considering or addressing fundamental design problems. Your organization's success in defending against internal and external bad actors will hinge on the completeness of your cybersecurity program. As a manager involved in cybersecurity within your organization, how can you ensure that you have all the right pieces of cybersecurity in place to close any gaps that might serve as hidden passages of attack? The answer is to follow a prescriptive design approach that blends experience-based guidance with authoritatively sourced resources. Adopting this approach not only identifies the gaps, but it leads to the development of cyber-gates to block intruder passages.

Cybersecurity program design will require you to know a little something about systems architecture, including blueprints, frameworks, and models. This chapter allows you to go to the front of the line, bypassing years of training and working in the field. Your pass to the front of the design line comes from my sharing of approaches and years of practical application of cybersecurity strategies in designing cybersecurity programs that have served me well over the years.

***This chapter will help you to:***

- Learn that investing the time and effort to properly design your cybersecurity program is tantamount to its success.
- Create a properly structured cybersecurity program.
- Leverage good practices to improve your cybersecurity program design.

## Chapter 1 Roadmap

In this chapter, well heck, all the chapters, I throw a lot of content your way and some would even say an overwhelming amount of content. At first, it may seem difficult to dimension all this data in the context of building a cybersecurity program, but don't worry, I have your back. This chapter, along with successive chapters includes reference architectures or a map that you can follow to answer the questions "what should I tackle first?" or "where should I focus my attention?"

The end of each chapter provides you with a checklist to ensure you check all the design boxes on your program. This map, however, separates essential background knowledge from outcomes necessary to build your cybersecurity program. I caution you not to skip the background or foundational content as it provides the knowledge necessary on how and why outcomes are achieved.

The outcome of this chapter is that you will have created your cybersecurity program design guide. The design guide serves as your "as built" documentation or owner's manual. In a single place, you can describe the architecture of your cybersecurity program. This document should be referenced often and kept up to date through document management to trace from origin to current state how information and assets are protected within your organization.

Figure 1.0 shows a reference map of how the cybersecurity program would look when you follow the program design checklist at the end of the chapter. It is an abstraction view where program detail grows as your program increases in maturity. The components in gray are outcome-based.

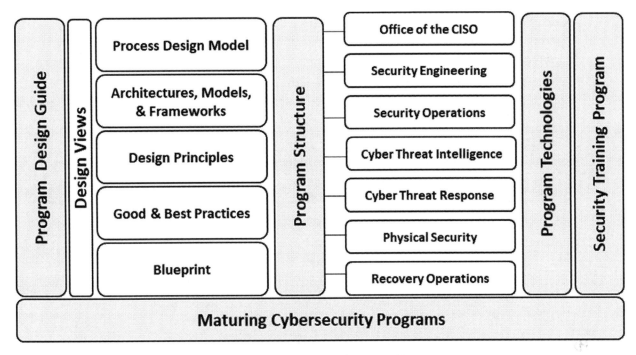

*Figure 1.0. Program Design Reference Architecture*

Each component and sub-component of the reference architecture is covered in more detail later in the chapter.

As this is the first stop on your journey, it is important that you get it right as it will set the tone for your entire trip. To help you with this as well as focus your energies, I will outline the outcome-based steps required to creating the program design guide. The other content presented in the chapter is more reference, foundational or background oriented used to help you build out the outcomes.

- **Step 1: Create Your Program Design Guide** – This guide brings together all the elements of design for your cybersecurity program. Whether the guide takes shape as a three-ring binder or in digital form stored, for example, in a SharePoint portal, it will contain your design views, models, et al, principles, practices and your program blueprint. In this step you consolidate your essential design documents into a book that describes how your cybersecurity program was designed and built.
- **Step 2: Define Your Program Structure** – The program structure is the organizational construct of your cybersecurity program. It scales to the size of your staff and defines the roles and responsibilities of the organization. In this step, you will select the cybersecurity framework declared in your design guide (ISO, NIST, etc.) that will influence your overall program design. You could almost think about it as an organization chart for your cybersecurity program design.

- **Step 3: Identify Your Program Technologies** – Supporting each of the domains of program structure are program technologies. With literally thousands of technology choices, it is important to identify the right ones to support your cybersecurity program. Knowing which ones to select is principally driven by the risk treatment requirements of your cybersecurity program. In this step you consider from twenty-five of the most essential cybersecurity technology categories which ones are necessary to protect your information and assets.
- **Step 4: Create Your Security Training Program** – The first line of defense is the security awareness and security culture of your organization. To accomplish this an effective security training program is required. The program must be a balance between education and testing where users develop the necessary muscle memory to serve as human firewalls, stopping threats before they have a chance to take hold. In this step you will design effective user training programs.
- **Step 5: Mature Your Cybersecurity Program** – Cybersecurity programs are not a one-size-fits-all proposition. Each organization has its own unique risk profile, business constraints, and investment appetite. Also, not every aspect of a cybersecurity program needs to have the same level of maturity. In this step, you will need to select a maturity model and follow its guidance to further define your cybersecurity program.

A question that I am often asked is "what if I don't have the time or the resources to do everything you presented in this book?" "What should my priorities be, and which activities are the most critical to protect information and assets?" These are excellent questions. For example, if your company had very little resources and could only invest in one disaster recovery control, I might recommend backup power. My rational would be that power outages were the most common cause of datacenter disruptions. So, following that rational, here are what I believe are the minimum activities you should undertake to start your cybersecurity program:

- **Adopt a Cybersecurity Framework** – Select either ISO 27001 or NIST SP 800-53 as your cybersecurity program framework. These two standards represent the two most popular cybersecurity frameworks in the world, and you can't go wrong selecting either one.
- **Identify Legal and Regulatory Requirements** – Use the Compliance Requirement template in Chapter 7 to identify the top-5 laws and regulations with which your organization must comply. You will want to ensure you don't unwittingly violate any statues while you're building your cybersecurity program. In the event you experience a breach of security, you can claim some high ground in stating you were following legal and regulatory requirements to maintain privacy of information.
- **Inventory Existing Cybersecurity Program Technologies** – Use the Service Design Package (SDP) in Chapter 7 to document the current capabilities of your organization's information and asset protection technologies. The SDP helps you understand how you are protecting information and assets and whether they are sufficiently protected.

- **Provide Security Awareness Training to Users** – Train users in the expected practices and proper treatment of assets and information. Focus on showing them how not to fall victim to ransomware and phishing attacks.

Please don't interpret completing these five critical steps as one-and-done. Focusing only on these five activities is not sustainable in the long run and eventually you will need to go back through this chapter and fill in the blanks.

# 1.1 Cybersecurity Program Design Methodology

Over the course of my career, I have either developed or assessed over one hundred comprehensive cybersecurity programs. Going by Malcolm Gladwell's 10,000-hour rule, I qualify as an outlier on *assessing* cybersecurity programs. This experience has granted me the insight that there are certain common denominators of the most successful programs; these are the focus of this chapter. I will share with you the good practices I observed across the many cybersecurity projects I have been involved with. Depending on the size of your organization and scope of your program, you may wish to eliminate or combine some of the components I present. I begin with components that address the overall management of the cybersecurity program and end with components that address the daily management of program countermeasures.

### Did You Know?

For each cybersecurity opening, there was a pool of only 2.3 employed cybersecurity workers for employers to recruit. That is almost exactly the same ratio of openings-to-employed workers as in 2015-16. By comparison, there are 5.8 employed workers per job opening across the economy in general. Even with the expansion of cybersecurity programs, supply has not kept up with demand.

*Do you have difficulty finding top cybersecurity talent?*

**Source:** https://www.burning-glass.com/research-project/cybersecurity/

## 1.1.1 Need for a Design to Attract the Best Personnel

Cybersecurity programs rely on talented contributors and their retention. A properly organized program enables personnel to see how they contribute to the program's vision and mission. To help you achieve the proper program structure, I provide what I believe is an ideal state blueprint. Trust me when I say that in today's highly competitive cybersecurity jobs market, attracting and maintaining personnel will be a challenge. If you build a program that is disorganized and messy, it will be difficult for you to attract anyone to *man the ship*.

If you look at the various security architecture and design books available, most will be hundreds upon hundreds of pages that I know most of you simply do not have the time to read. This book is much different; it focuses on just what you need to know. This chapter sets your journey in motion by discussing the basic design considerations of building a cybersecurity program. When building anything, it is best to have a methodology to follow. Dozens of methodologies exist by many names, but their message is the same: There is a sequence to follow when building something if you want it done right. What I learned quickly was that unless you follow a design methodology, the results of your efforts will be unpredictable. For example, if you wait to align your program with the business, you risk facing an expensive program redo when your stakeholders inform you that you have managed only to create an inhibitor to their business. Cybersecurity program staffing and personnel issues are discussed in Chapter 6.

## 1.1.2 A Recommended Design Approach: ADDIOI Model™

After doing my first dozen or so programs, I realized that the approaches I had been using lacked an emphasis on services and processes. They aligned more with building a physical product. I needed an approach which would accommodate building something that was service oriented. Figure 1-1 is what I refer to as the ADDIOI Model™ (align, design, develop, implement, operate, and improve). It has proved quite useful over the years.

I arrived at my methodology by adopting phases of the ADDIE Model (analysis, design, development, implementation, and evaluation). ADDIE, originally developed in 1975 for the US Army by what was previously known as the Center for Educational Technology at Florida State University (Forest, 2014), provided about 80% of what I was looking for in clarifying my approach. ADDIE has since been adopted and modified by hundreds of consulting companies throughout the world.

Starting with the ADDIE Model, I made subtle but important changes in constructing my ADDIOI Model (align, design, develop, implement, operate and improve) methodology. The first difference is that I declare *analysis* as a process within the *align* phase to emphasize alignment to the business from the start. I added *operate* as a phase to emphasize the design was oriented toward processes and services. While my phase that I call *improve* is the same as *evaluate* in the ADDIE Model, I named the phase *improve* to emphasize continuous service improvement and that action is required to correct inefficiencies. Figure 1-1 shows a representation of the ADDIOI Model's phases as a continuous improvement circle.

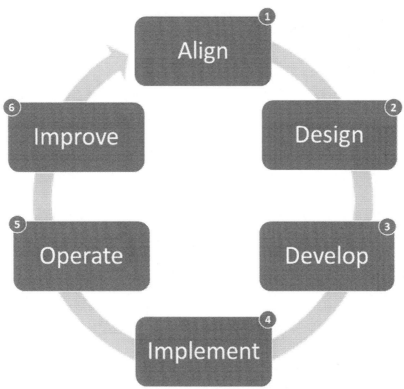

*Figure 1-1. ADDIOI Model™. (By Tari Schreider, licensed under a Creative Commons Attribution-NonCommercial-NoDerivatives 4.0 International License)*

### 1.1.3 The Six Phases of the ADDIOI Model™

The phases of the model include:

1. **Align** – This phase is where you identify your organization's business goals and align them to the capabilities of the cybersecurity program. Always remember the business is your benefactor paying for all your cybersecurity gizmos, so alignment is crucial. You must show the value of your program by demonstrating how it reduces operational risk. A key outcome will be program design requirements. The align phase is an ongoing process and supports the improve phase.
2. **Design** – This phase is what this chapter predominately addresses – designing the structure of your cybersecurity program. Here you create your program blueprint to show stakeholders the vision of the final product and validate alignment to the business in a concrete manner. For example, if one of your business goals is to maintain regulatory compliance, compliance capability should be reflected in your design.
3. **Develop** – This phase is where you configure and test the cybersecurity countermeasures called out within the design requirements. The develop phase may also include creating or modifying application code to support cybersecurity countermeasures. For example, integrating an access authentication or single sign-on solution will require application integration. Countermeasure testing provides the basis to create experience-based

11

implementation plans and acceptance criteria to move countermeasures from test to production. Information technology (IT) infrastructure is locked down (hardened) in this phase, making it resilient to cyberattack. Developing and customizing cybersecurity services and technologies are the primary activities of this phase.

4. **Implement** – This phase is the execution of implementation plans to "go live" with your cybersecurity countermeasures and services developed in the previous phase. You should strive to create a culture of security with your training program, instilling the human firewall philosophy, your first line and many times your last line of defense. This is the phase where you will organize cybersecurity program staff around the program's components. Onboarding security service providers occurs within this phase as well. Deployment and training are the primary activities of the implement phase.

5. **Operate** – This phase is where the day-to-day management and operations of the cybersecurity countermeasures occur. Most commonly referred to as security operations (SecOps), security tools administration, threat monitoring, and the security service desk are located here as well. The service desk is an IT function that serves as a single point of contact for customers to resolve their computing or applications issues. Other parts of the cybersecurity program such as cyber threat intelligence may use security tools; however, SecOps generally handles their daily administration. Program sustainability is the primary focus of the operate phase.

6. **Improve** – This phase is the process of continuous improvement. Most cybersecurity programs operate as a good practice but moving to a best practice requires continuous improvement. I discuss the difference between good and best practices later in the chapter. Key performance metrics and regular assessments are used to baseline the program, and a maturity model is used to guide program improvements. You will read more about maturity models at the end of this chapter. Continuous improvement is the primary activity of this phase.

At this point, you should have some idea of what methodology you will use in setting up your cybersecurity program. There is a very good chance your organization has adopted a development methodology. The keepers of your methodology are likely the program management office (PMO) or system development lifecycle (SDLC) group. If you do choose to adopt an existing in-house approach, be careful that it is fit for purpose and not intended for only software development. If you start hearing words like Agile or SCRUM, take caution, since those approaches will not lead you down the development path you desire. Agile and SCRUM are software development approaches that security attaches, rather than development approaches for creating cybersecurity program. This may seem like a subtle distinction, but it's a rather important distinction for you to note.

## 1.2 Defining Architectures, Frameworks, and Models

Now that you have selected your design methodology, it is time to sort through the sea of cybersecurity architectures, frameworks, and models that you will need to reference in your design. I have spent many an hour debating and researching the differences between architectures, frameworks, and models only to find there are no universal definitions. Perhaps my thoughts will spare you substantial frustration and confusion trying to figure out the varied definitions and inaccuracies. Much of the confusion originates with some standards bodies who call their model a "framework," when, in actuality, it is a model or vice versa. Adding to the confusion are organizations that now use terms like *architecture framework* or *model framework*.

You are probably asking: Why are there no standard industry definitions for *architectures*, *frameworks*, or *models*? The answer is there are simply too many competing architectures, frameworks, and models. Case in point, according to the Survey of Architecture Frameworks, there are presently 75 IT-related architectures and frameworks alone. Check some of them out at http://www.iso-architecture.org/ieee-1471/afs/frameworks-table.html. Virtually all 75 include at least a subcomponent that addresses cybersecurity. In speaking with several associations about their frameworks and models over the course of writing this book, I found they all had their own valid reasons not to align on a standard nomenclature. Reasons ranged from seeking a differential advantage, to member preference, to "we were here first."

Where does this leave us in trying to land on a standard and meaningful cybersecurity design vocabulary? As crazy as this may sound, you must declare your organization's own cybersecurity design terminology. I am not saying to avoid completely guidance from one or more of the examples I provide throughout the book, but rather focus on terminologies and definitions that your organization can agree upon and support. To help you, I have provided my definitions of *architectures*, *frameworks*, and *models* in Table 1-1. I have found these general enough to meet the design requirements of just about any cybersecurity program.

**Table 1-1. Definitions of Architectures, Frameworks, and Models**

| Attribute | Architecture | Framework | Model |
|---|---|---|---|
| **Definition** | Overall design of a cybersecurity program depicting its essential components, interrelationships, and design principles and guidelines. | Broad overview of a cybersecurity program depicted as a skeletal or framework diagram. Components are interlinked to show how components support your information and asset protection approach. | A graphical or mathematical representation or abstraction of essential aspects of a cybersecurity program process, system, or solution within a component. |
| **Purpose** | Serves as a representation of what the cybersecurity program will resemble when completed including defining the various components and their interactions. | Guides the development of a cybersecurity program ensuring that supporting components adhere to design principles and guidelines. | Facilitates understanding of the complex through an essentials-only view of your cybersecurity practices, methods, or approaches. |
| **Characteristics** | • Visionary.<br>• Business outcome focused.<br>• Layer approach.<br>• Standards-based.<br>• Design requirements. | • Descriptive.<br>• Deliverable-focused.<br>• Structure, skeleton, or outline.<br>• Foundation.<br>• Pre-defined functions. | • Prescriptive.<br>• Process focused.<br>• Solves a problem. |
| **ADDIOI Model™ alignment** | Align and design. | Develop and implement. | Operate and improve. |
| **Example** | | | |
| **Reference material** | • DOE IT Security Architecture.<br>• Open Enterprise Security Architecture (O-ESA).<br>• Sherwood Applied Business Security Architecture (SABSA).<br>• TOGAF® and SABSA® Integration. | • Cyber Kill Chain® Framework.<br>• NIST Cybersecurity Framework.<br>• Risk Management Framework (RMF) for DoD Information Technology (IT).<br>• Software Security Framework (SSF).<br>• Zachman Framework.™ | • Information Governance Reference Model (IGRM).<br>• National Initiative for Cybersecurity Education (NICE) Capability Maturity Model.<br>• Reference Model of Information Assurance & Security (RMIAS). |

*Note: Links contained in the table are current as of September 22, 2019.*

14

It can be very easy to become overwhelmed if you start overthinking architectures, frameworks, and models. I have seen near-Hatfield and McCoy feud-like arguments break out over deciding on design definitions, especially if you have a few enterprise architects in the room. I cannot think of a better example of why language matters. Just as diplomats' vet language tirelessly to prevent diplomatic incidents, so should you.

Before you begin designing your first control of your cybersecurity program, negotiate and publish the definitions of *architecture*, *framework*, and *model* in your program design guide. Document approvals of key stakeholders, architects, and other influencers within your design guide. Use change control to document any modifications to these definitions. Use the definitions to create templates of architectures, frameworks, and models to ensure design consistency and conformity to approved definitions.

## 1.2.1 Program Design Guide

One of the fundamental tools that you as an architect will require in order to build your cybersecurity program is a design guide. A design guide sets out the key principles, standards, and requirements necessary to ensure a cybersecurity program properly aligns to your business and your program is of the highest quality. Beginning a project without a design guide, almost with all certainty, will result in gaps small and large in your cybersecurity program. Every architectural course or standard I have ever read states categorically that a design guide is a minimum requirement. Yet, many of my customers believe that it is a luxury and an unneeded expense. I couldn't disagree more, and I encourage you to fight the resistance you may encounter and be steadfast in the use of a design guide.

The design guide is the repository for all your declared cybersecurity architectures, frameworks, models, blueprints, and regulatory and technology standards. The guide also documents all the notice of decisions (NoDs) that were made to decide on technologies, security event feeds, encryption algorithms, and many other critical defining parameters of your cybersecurity program. Without a design guide for all those involved in building your cybersecurity program, many individual decisions could be made that may not be in the best interest of the program overall. At a minimum, your design guide should address:
- Scope of protection based on attack surface scale.
- Declared industry standards the program is based.
- Data classification levels that countermeasures would be defined.
- Strategy for defense-in-depth adoption.
- Investment parameters for acquiring cybersecurity technology.
- Functional requirements of the cybersecurity program.
- Access and authentication approach for all classes of users.
- Information privacy and protection legal requirements.
- Definition of service management inclusion.
- Declaration of cybersecurity controls baseline.

- Target maturity levels and roadmap.
- Risk treatment philosophy.

Check out Chapter 7 Architectural Tool Kit for examples of cybersecurity program design templates.

## 1.3 Design Principles

Establishing guiding principles when embarking on an architectural project will eliminate many design debates before, they begin. Principles are general rules and guidelines, intended to be enduring and seldom amended, that inform and support the way in which you set about creating your cybersecurity program. They serve as a litmus test to answer the questions, "Should we be doing this?" or "Does this belong in our design?" Over the years, I have read many elaborate design principles; however, many were just statements and not really principles. The following are a set of cybersecurity program design principles that I have used in my program designs:

- **Principle 1:** The cybersecurity program exists to protect organization assets and information.
- **Principle 2:** The cybersecurity program's investments in practices, methods, and technologies will be commensurate with the value of the assets and information at risk.
- **Principle 3:** The cybersecurity program's services will benefit from service management practices.
- **Principle 4:** The cybersecurity program's approach to protecting assets and information will comply with all legal and regulatory statutes.
- **Principle 5:** The cybersecurity program will be an enabler to the business aligning to stakeholder requirements.
- **Principle 6:** The cybersecurity program will address real and likely threats in a risk management driven approach.
- **Principle 7:** The cybersecurity program will leverage internationally accepted cybersecurity standards and good practices.

## 1.4 Intersection of Privacy and Cybersecurity

Cybersecurity programs do not typically encompass the domain of privacy; however, they do include privacy protecting technologies. You don't need to look any further for evidence of this then by examining the roles of a Chief Privacy Officer (CPO) and Chief Information Security Officer (CISO). CPOs are concerned with defining the use and privacy of data through policies whereas CISOs are concerned with preventing the theft of data through the application of privacy preserving technologies.

A cybersecurity program must be concerned with ensuring the security of employee and customer data as prescribed by a company's data privacy policies. The introduction of big data and move toward comingling disparate data types into shared data pools requires a change in data protection strategy. This strategy must be co-authored by the CPO and CISO in acceptance of the intersection of data privacy and cybersecurity. The protection of data is where privacy and cybersecurity cross paths. A comprehensive data protection strategy leverages privacy policies and data safeguards to ensure a unified approach in meeting data privacy rules and regulations. Organizations with an expectation of preventing data breaches can only succeed in this goal by bringing data protection and privacy together through the realization that data privacy cannot be achieved without privacy preserving technologies.

> **Did You Know?**
>
> In November 2018, Marriott disclosed that hackers accessed the Starwood guest reservation database since 2014 stealing 383 million hotel guest records. Under the General Data Protection Regulation (GDPR), the UK's Information Commissioner's Office (ICO) intends to impose a fine of $123,705,870. The ICO claims Marriott violated the privacy provisions of the GDPR.
>
> *Have you stress tested your cybersecurity program against the provisions of the GDPR?*
>
> **Source:**
> https://www.zdnet.com/article/marriott-faces-123-million-gdpr-fine-in-the-uk-for-last-years-data-breach/

## 1.5 Good Practice vs. Best Practice

Now that you have your design methodology determined and you have arrived at your architectural terms definitions, it is time to sort out one last area of confusion you undoubtedly will face sooner rather than later – your understanding of the difference between a good and a best practice. For years, standards bodies and consulting firms used the term *best practice* as a way to state that their approach was superior based on supporting data from a sample set of customers. In reality, standards bodies and consulting firms could not provide a large enough sample size to support a best practice claim. It is almost impossible within the context of cybersecurity to produce a body of evidence large enough of organizations carrying out the same task to make objective points of comparisons. Many consulting companies have invested millions of dollars in methodologies to benchmark organizations to catalog best practices. This effort began to fade when people started to take a hard look at how best practices were determined. Many of us simply were not convinced the best practice data supported the best practice claims.

- The term *best practice* implies a superior practice or approach that results in a level of performance exceeding that of peer organizations. To accomplish assurance of such superiority, you would need to accumulate data from very similar organizations doing very similar cybersecurity functions. You may be able to find some similarities; but, as a whole, no two organizations (let alone hundreds) operate their cybersecurity program in a uniform, consistent manner. In addition, best practices require that organizations openly share what works and what does not work. Needless to say, sharing information about cybersecurity programs has never been popular.
- On the other hand, a *good practice* is achievable and, more importantly, measurable. Good practices simply require that you carry out your cybersecurity program functions according to recommended or approved security codes of practice. To ensure that you are adhering to good practices, you must respond positively to these questions:
  - Are you following a generally accepted code of security practice such as those published by the National Institute of Standards and Technology (NIST) Special Publication (SP) 800-53 Revision 5 located at https://csrc.nist.gov/CSRC/media/Publications/sp/800-53/rev-5/draft/documents/sp800-53r5-draft.pdf or International Organization for Standardization ISO/IEC 27001 located at https://www.iso.org/isoiec-27001-information-security.html?
  - Do you document, enforce, and report your adherence?

If you still want to pursue best practices, rather than simply adhering to good practices, there is nothing to stop you. Once you have established your good practices, repeatedly ask yourself what works, how it works, and why is works well. Keep asking and answering those questions over time, continuously improving your good practices into best practices within your organization. If you are lucky enough to find other organizations doing the same thing, compare notes.

## 1.6 Adjust Your Design Perspective

At this point, I am asking you to adjust your thinking based on my experience and allow me to guide you toward a higher-level of understanding about your own approach to designing a cybersecurity program. I believe such an adjustment will help you clarify in your mind some of the confusing aspects of what you will encounter. The change is not that dramatic, but nonetheless it is important. I want you to think of all of this as architecture and yourself as an architect. Once you make this change in your mind, it is that simple. You will view the world of design with the same clarity that I did when I made the shift.

The word *architecture* has come to mean so many things in the cybersecurity world that it now convolutes the narrative of design. I want you to think in terms of what *architecture* was meant

18

to mean. When people say *architecture*, I think of the actual role of an architect and his or her outcome. For example, when someone says the name <u>Frank Lloyd Wright,</u> the iconic nature of his architecture immediately comes to mind. You know what to expect when you see one of his designs. Similarly, I want your management to know what to expect when they see your design for a cybersecurity program. Begin your journey of design believing you are an architect and your tradecraft is architecture. You use blueprints, frameworks, and models to build your architecture. You need to think like an architect to be an architect.

The simple visual in Figure 1-2 shows you how I view cybersecurity architecture as a schema. The balance of the chapter discusses blueprints, frameworks, and models, which are the tools of your architecture trade.

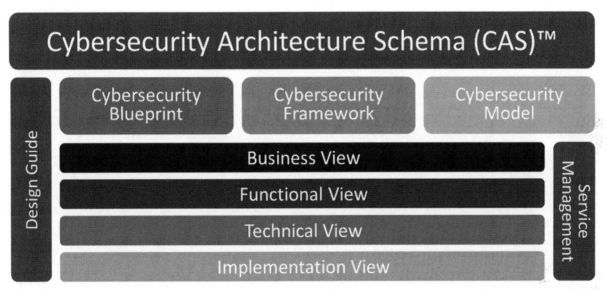

*Figure 1-2. Cybersecurity Architecture Schema (CAS)™. (By Tari Schreider, licensed under a Creative Commons Attribution-NonCommercial-NoDerivatives 4.0 International License)*

## 1.7 Architectural Views

It is often difficult to show an entire blueprint or architecture to someone and hope it all sinks in. Designs are generally too complex to be consumed by stakeholders in one fell swoop. One reason for this is that few people will be interested in the entire architecture and will only want to see that portion which applies directly to them. To facilitate this, the architecture community uses views or layers of the whole design to represent areas of the design specific to certain stakeholders. The combination of the views constitutes the entire design. If you were building a house you would have separate architectural views for the frame, plumbing, electrical, etc. Views have been a mainstay of IT architecture for over 30 years. I highly recommend the ISO/IEC/IEEE 42010 website located at <u>http://www.iso-architecture.org/ieee-1471/index.html</u> to learn more about architectural views and all things IT architecture. For my purposes, I have identified four views that I have used consistently in my cybersecurity program designs for their relevance, simplicity, and effectiveness. These views are: business, functional, technical, and implementation.

- **Business view – the why:** The business view answers the question, "Why are we doing this?" This view addresses requirements and concerns of the users from their business perspective. Here you define what the cybersecurity program is intended to accomplish, what basic functionality it should have, and the type of usability envisioned. This is where you align the cybersecurity program to key business drivers. For example, the business may want more speed and agility which can be accomplished by empowering customers to perform some security functions themselves.

- **Functional view – the what:** The functional view answers the question, "What should it do?" This view is concerned with the required capabilities of the cybersecurity program. For example, speed and agility would require the program to provide self-service capabilities for customer password resets. In this view, we are not concerned with how that would be performed, just that the program should provide that functionality.

- **Technical view – the how:** The technical view answers the question, "How should it be done?" This view establishes the preferred approach to provide key capabilities. In the functional view, we stated that password self-service would provide the improved speed and agility that the business requires for customers. The how would be using a single sign-on solution or an identity and access management (IDAM) provisioning system, both of which support password resets. This view is not concerned with the specific product that would be used.

- **Implementation view – with what:** The implementation view answers the question, "What will we use?" This view is concerned with the detail of the actual products and solutions that are required to implement the technical view. Staying with our previous example, we would select a product that provides single sign-on and IDAM to allow password resets. The technology is the last layer of the design to ensure you don't acquire products before all the requirements are met in the design.

If you go through any of the architectures located in 1.2 Survey of Architecture Frameworks, you will find these four views commonly used in many of the listed architectures.

## 1.8 Cybersecurity Program Blueprint

Before construction begins on a new home, homeowners and contractors must agree on what the house will look like as well as the number of rooms and their sizes when finished. Building a cybersecurity program should be no different. You may be surprised at the number of cybersecurity programs built, costing many hundreds of thousands or millions of dollars more than a home, without a basic blueprint. I have found no rational explanation for why this practice occurs.

In the many cybersecurity programs, I have been involved with, I have asked managers for their program blueprint, framework, or architecture, but I have never received a single document. I was often told that they follow ISO 27001 family – Information security management systems or NIST SP 800-53, etc., but not one company could provide a diagram or drawing of their cybersecurity program. I have also been offered a dizzying array of PowerPoints, but all fall short of an architectural document. Imagine buying a house and the builder saying in response to a request for a blueprint, "Just look at page 20 in *Better Homes and Gardens* magazine to see what your house will look like."

> **TIP:** If I have one piece of advice for you, it is this: Never be that person who is unable to provide me with a blueprint of your cybersecurity program!

So exactly what do I mean by *blueprint*? A blueprint is simply a guide for making something, consisting of drawings, pictures, and instructions. Its purpose is to communicate to everyone involved in the construction of that something what it looks like.

In the context of a cybersecurity program, an architect uses a blueprint to communicate the vision of the program without committing specific implementation details. An example would be a situation in which the architect identifies the need for a cybersecurity operations center (C-SOC) but leaves the specifications of the C-SOC open for stakeholders to decide. Stakeholders may choose to build out a C-SOC or contract for C-SOC services from a managed security services provider (MSSP).

A blueprint serves as the master plan identifying the structure and components of your program. It provides you with a model of the finished product. When I buy a product that requires assembling, I place the product packaging with its picture prominently displayed right in front of me so I can see what the finished product should look like. Using a blueprint in building a cybersecurity program is no different. I prefer to use a Euler diagram for presenting my cybersecurity program blueprints. A Euler diagram is a method used to represent sets and their relationships, often overlapping shapes to suggest scale and relationship. Learn more about Euler diagrams at https://creately.com/blog/diagrams/venn-diagrams-vs-euler-diagrams/. Figure 1-3 shows an example of a cybersecurity program blueprint that I have used and refined over many years. You will also note that I have overlaid the ADDIOI Model on the blueprint to illustrate the intersection and importance of a development methodology in the design of a cybersecurity program.

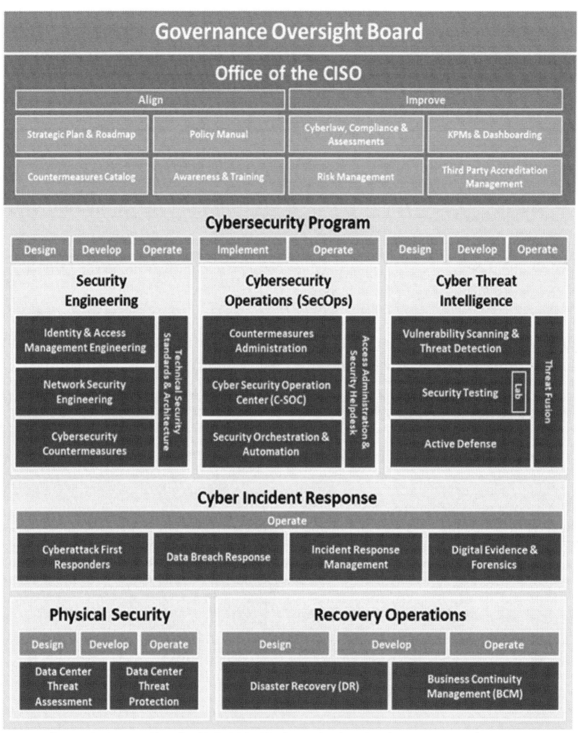

*Figure 1-3. Cybersecurity Program Blueprint. (By Tari Schreider, licensed under a Creative Commons Attribution-NonCommercial-NoDerivatives 4.0 International License)*

22

**TIP:** Create a placemat of your cybersecurity program blueprint. Print a high-quality color version of your blueprint and laminate it like a placemat. Carry this with you always and use to educate stakeholders in one-on-one sessions. Use a grease marker to elaborate points or draw attention to program components. You will find this is a simple yet highly effective communications medium.

So why do I use the term *blueprint* rather than the more commonly used terms *architecture*, *framework*, or *model* to describe cybersecurity programs? By training and trade, I am an architect; subsequently, I follow the professional nomenclature used by architects, in which a blueprint is a primary outcome of an architect's work. The fact that I design cybersecurity solutions does not diminish the need to follow architectural standards including terminology. Therefore, for purposes of this book, I subscribe to the notion that architecture is a process and your role in creating a cybersecurity program is that of an architect.

# 1.9 Program Structure

The blueprint shows us the structure of the cybersecurity program. Arriving at the right structure for a cybersecurity program is no easy task. It is very much like the chicken and the egg argument: Which came first? Here the argument centers on whether the cybersecurity staff or the program came first. There are two decidedly different camps when it comes to creating a cybersecurity program structure. In one camp, we have organizations that first create an organization chart, hire staff, and then define the departments of their program. In the other camp, we have organizations that define their cybersecurity departments first and then find the best personnel to staff those functions. I belong to the latter camp. I have always advocated that a sound cybersecurity program structure cannot be based on the NFL approach were coaches build a team around a few star players. Organizations that take this approach soon find that when their stars become injured or leave, they are left with an unpredictable team. It is best to begin with a solid program foundation. A strong, well-conceived program will enhance the abilities of all cybersecurity personnel, turning your "B" players into "A" players. Think about the adage that a rising tide lifts all boats. I have seen many cybersecurity programs rely too much on star players.

Cybersecurity blueprints should not contain the detail of the entirety of your program. The purpose is to provide an abstract view that communicates the structure of your cybersecurity program succinctly and effectively. The top of the blueprint indicates a governance oversight board which is discussed in Chapter 2.

## 1.9.1 Office of the CISO

As shown in Figure 1-3, it is no longer effective for the role of Chief Information Security Officer (CISO) to be an individual person. In recognition of the role having become strategic and focused on enterprise security management, the CISO role is evolving into the Office of the

CISO. Establishing the roles and responsibilities of a CISO within an office elevates its value to the organization, acknowledges it is a business function, and bridges any gaps between the business and the cybersecurity program. The Office of the CISO subcomponents include:

- **Strategic plan and roadmap:** Strategic plans comprise your vision for protecting information and assets, a mission statement for accomplishing that vision, and guiding principles. The Office of the CISO needs to establish the vision and mission of the program to set the tone of the program's strategy.
  - o The vision is a declaration of the organization's cybersecurity objectives aligned to business objectives.
  - o The mission statement communicates the purpose of the cybersecurity program.
  - o The strategic plan lays out where your cybersecurity program is currently, where you want the program to grow, and how you will arrive at the future vision of the program.
  - o A roadmap highlights the steps necessary to work through the program to achieve the future vision. This component includes a maturity model that guides the roadmap trajectory.
- **Policy manual:** A policy manual is a compendium of the organization's cybersecurity policies. Policies should be concise and have longevity, not subject to the dynamics of organizational change. Policies support laws and regulations and outline the required behavior of employees, contractors, and customers. Policies need to be enforceable and their purpose is to contribute directly to the protection of information and assets.
- **Cyberlaw, compliance, and assessments:** The cybersecurity program has a duty to maintain a state of compliance with applicable laws and regulations. Accomplishing compliance is through the application of controls and risk treatments to protect the information and assets prescribed by legal and regulatory statutes. Compliance within the cybersecurity program rolls up to corporate compliance. It is important for you to understand that you play a supporting role and your program's lack of compliance may adversely affect your organization's overall compliance posture. Assessments reside within this subcomponent. They can include technical compliance checking against policies or gap analysis against security regulations and standards.
- **Performance measures (KPM / KPI) and dashboarding:** Key Performance Metrics (KPM) and Key Performance Indicators (KPI) are only second to security policies as an effective way to drive the correct behavior of your cybersecurity program. A KPI explains what is measured and a KPM is a numeric value of the measure (metric) itself. They establish a baseline for each aspect of your program and present the positive or negative achievement of the operational margins of a cybersecurity program. Performance measures are effective at demonstrating transparency of a cybersecurity program and highlighting areas requiring attention. You will want to avoid creating more metrics than can be reasonably monitored and measured. It is better to have a few good actionable KPMs than dozens that simply produce voluminous reports that provide little to no real value.

Dashboarding is the process of streaming your performance results to a series of graphical representations such as heat maps, bar and pie charts, or scorecards. Dashboard views provide a single-pane-of-glass view into your entire cybersecurity program. I will cover dashboarding more in Chapter 2. You will find sample KPMs in Appendix A.

- **Countermeasures catalog:** Countermeasures deserve a level of documentation like how a retail organization presents its products to customers in a consumer catalog. Service owners should complete a standardized template ensuring a uniform approach to managing countermeasures. Countermeasure descriptions should include a service overview, standard features, provisioning instructions, performance measures, compliance mapping, cost, service ownership, support information, and other pertinent service descriptive information. The service catalog organization should follow the structure of the program's components with a secondary organization by subcomponents if required.

- **Awareness and training:** Ideally, awareness and training perform best when operated as a continuous cycle. Users of the organization's information and assets are the first line of defense. This subcomponent includes application security training, anti-phishing training, and security awareness. Awareness and training should have the goal of creating a culture of security populated with human firewalls. All security training should exist in one place.

- **Risk management:** During a review of threats and vulnerabilities, you will have a continuous process of identifying, analyzing, evaluating, and treating the loss exposures that you find. The process of risk management includes maintaining an inventory of risks and associated risk treatment plans. The cybersecurity programs must be risk-based where deployed countermeasures work to reduce an organization's risk profile.

- **Third-party accreditation management:** Your strategic partner relationship management will ensure compliance with program policies. The office should examine ISO 27001, NIST SP 800-53 or Cloud Security Alliance (CSA) - https://cloudsecurityalliance.org/about/ standards' compliance of third-parties to determine if partners introduce risk to the organization. I provide more detail on third-party risk management in Chapter 4.

The next layer of the blueprint shown in Figure 1-3 is the cybersecurity program. Here I have defined six main components consisting of security engineering, cybersecurity operations, cyber threat intelligence and cyber incident response, physical security, and recovery operations.

## 1.9.2 Security Engineering

Security engineering involves the architecture and design of a secure network and operating environment. Staffed by subject matter experts with deep technical knowledge in key cybersecurity domains consisting of cloud protection, cryptography, network security, operating system hardening, and identity and access management. The installation, resiliency, and maintenance of cybersecurity technologies (such as firewalls, data loss prevention, and anti-malware systems) are the responsibility of this component. Security engineering subcomponents include:

- **Identity and access management (IDAM) engineering:** This subcomponent is concerned with designing and developing the connectors and feeds to identity management, provisioning, and access control solutions. The provisioning of network resources, application and database access, and endpoints through in-house or cloud based IDAM, is the responsibility of IDAM engineering. Connecting and synchronizing all these moving pieces are largely technical functions requiring application and infrastructure engineers and developers.

- **Network security engineering:** This subcomponent is concerned with the design of a secure network architecture consisting of network segmentation, secure zones, and security technology placement. Engineers are responsible for secure network device configurations, traffic routing, threat detection and containment, denial of service attacks, and deployment of security policies to network devices. This function is responsible for encryption technology, certificate life cycle management, and WiFi/RF security.

- **Cybersecurity countermeasures:** This subcomponent is concerned with the selection, testing, deployment, and upgrades of cybersecurity countermeasures that can detect, prevent, and recover from the effects of a threat. Threats can be internal or external as well as malicious, incidental, or accidental. The organization's defense-in-depth model discussed in Chapter 5 is located within this function. The engineers positioned here are experts in vender or solution technologies, ensuring the products are properly configured and deployed. They are not involved in daily operations; however, they provide troubleshooting support and backup for administrative support. They will also select and provision cloud security solutions in conjunction with security engineering.

- **Technical security standards and architecture:** This subcomponent establishes, maintains, and implements the technical security architecture of the organization. It enforces technology standards and configurations of security products. One of its more critical functions is the design and testing of infrastructure hardening standards. Personnel of this function have a deep understanding of cybersecurity standards and practices, often sitting on or collaborating with standards committees.

Security engineering turns over operational responsibility to security operations for the administration and daily operations of security technology.

## 1.9.3 Security Operations

Security operations (SecOps) involves the daily operations and support of the cybersecurity program. Once security engineering has designed and built the cybersecurity countermeasures, SecOps takes over to operate and manage. This component includes security product administrators, the security operations center, security orchestration, automation and response, and the security support aspects of the service desk. SecOps subcomponents include:

26

- **Countermeasures administration:** This subcomponent provides the daily administration of the security products in production. This group manages the policies, filters, rules, and configuration changes. Personnel manage log and audit files and perform regular product health checks. The resiliency and uptime of the security products are also of concern. Custom reporting and performance measurements relating to security technology reside in this group.
- **Cybersecurity operations center (C-SOC):** The C-SOC is a physical, virtual center or hybrid dedicated to monitoring an organization's applications, databases, network, servers, IoT devices, and endpoints to detect security events and defend against cyberattacks. Here, analysis of blended security incident and event management data occurs to detect network anomalies and other harbingers of cyberattack. Organizations often outsource this function to a managed security service provider (MSSP). If you outsource this function, my advice is to manage it as if it were an in-house function. (See Chapter 6 for more information on C-SOCs).
- **Security orchestration and automation:** SecOps maintains its own infrastructure engineers to ensure that underlying host technology of the security products deploys and operates correctly within the IT enterprise. Here, countermeasures form their own interconnected ecosystem producing logs and event data. For example, two separate security technologies, one for detecting vulnerabilities and one for patching vulnerabilities, become one seamless and continuous vulnerability detection and patching cycle. In larger organizations, the amount of technology required to support the cybersecurity program's countermeasures is equivalent to a data center of a small to midsize company.
- **Access administration and security service desk:** Service desk (formerly known as help desk) personnel handle email-related security issues such as SPAM, phishing attacks, and suspicious attachments. They are also the first line of defense for endpoint malware outbreaks. The service desk is responsible for password resets and other access-related issues.

---

**Did You Know?**

A December 2018 report from the US House of Representatives' Oversight and Government Reform Committee was quite critical of Equifax's poor security practices. In particular, Equifax's security patching program was admonished for not following up on 8,500 vulnerabilities discovered in 2015 after the release of their patch management policy. Equifax also failed to implement committed automated patching tools and remediate over 1,000 flaws found on externally facing systems.

*How well patched are your critical systems?*

**Source:**
https://www.securityweek.com/equifax-was-aware-cybersecurity-weaknesses-years-senate-report-says

Security personnel can reside with other service desk staff or within their own organization with security calls routed directly to them.

## 1.9.4 Cyber Threat Intelligence

Cyber threat intelligence is the driver of your cybersecurity program. The intelligence gathered directs the deployment and/or adjustment of countermeasures to address threats. Intelligence arrives in either strategic or tactical format. Strategic intelligence is information that presents a high-level abstract of risk not yet tactically quantified, but nonetheless merits monitoring. For example, an organization that may move into a new business area that historically has been the target of activist organizations will require intelligence to monitor the threat. Intelligence suggests that where activists go, hacktivists follow. Tactical intelligence includes the gathering of application, device, and network logs for analysis to detect indicators of compromise. Tactical intelligence focuses on the hacker's tactics, techniques and procedures (TTP). Sophisticated security incident and event management (SIEM) solutions or services determine threats through analysis of the raw data. Cyber threat intelligence subcomponents include:

- **Vulnerability scanning and detection:** This subcomponent is concerned with scanning every aspect of the IT enterprise to detect vulnerabilities. Various scanning technology designed specifically for applications, databases, operating systems, networks, and other IT-connected devices seeks vulnerabilities requiring patching or remediation. The detection of vulnerabilities provides notice of exploits within the enterprise that left unchecked, pose a security risk. An analysis of vulnerability scan results determines whether a risk is present and to what level of criticality. High-level threats require a risk treatment plan, a step-by-step program that determines how an organization addresses risk.
- **Security testing:** Testing of cybersecurity countermeasures and applications ensures that vulnerable code and configurations do not permeate the IT infrastructure. Three tiers of security testing exist.
  - Tier 1 involves risk-based testing or analysis of risk according to a profile or questionnaire applied to the application, solution, or third party. The score from this type of testing determines how rigorous the next tier should be.
  - Tier 2 is vulnerability testing. This type of testing involves analyzing the software or application to identify weaknesses in code or design. The focus here is to determine the application's exploit potential.

- Tier 3 is actual penetration testing or ethical hacking. Exploiting weaknesses to estimate the damage or harm that could arise from an attack is the prime focus. This subcomponent is where the security-testing lab is located.
- Tier 4 is threat hunting. Here the TTP of hackers are used to identify if a compromise has already occurred. Threat hunting is also effective when used to validate a SOC's current threat detection capabilities.

- **Active defense:** Active defense is the next step beyond vulnerability scanning and threat detection. This proactive capability searches for hidden attackers with the intent to eradicate their presence within your enterprise. Threat hunting is one example of an active defense. You must accept that some level of malicious activity is always going on within your network. History and events prove penetrations can occur within virtually any network. SOCs primarily focus on catching visible threats; active defense focuses on the unseen threat. Active defense is all about understanding what is normal about your IT enterprise and creating a baseline. Abnormal behavior is the optics for catching the threat actors or those that pose harm to your information and assets. Think of active defense as a form of military mission of seek and destroy the enemy. Missions rely on intelligence to guide hunting activities.

- **Threat fusion:** Protecting today's IT enterprise must accept the premise that threats can originate from numerous sources, obvious and not so obvious. The purpose of threat fusion is to take multiple sources of threat intelligence and fuse them into a cohesive, actionable, picture of threat. Fusion can be manual, semi-automated, or fully automated using a commercial fusion platform. The types of data that should feed threat fusion consist of email, social media, web pages, Microsoft Office documents, PDFs, logs, analyst reports, news feeds, etc. The object is to mine the data looking for harbingers of attacks, behavior anomalies of the operating environment, and indicators of compromise. Appendix A provides a list of threat fusion platforms. Threat fusion is commonly built upon a threat intelligence platform (TIP).

### 1.9.5 Cyber Incident Response

Cyber incident response is concerned with the coordination of response and restoration efforts related to cyberattacks or disruptions to the cybersecurity program itself. This capability maintains dedicated personnel for daily management, rehearsals, and improvement; however, during times of incidents, personnel from other components staff specific roles as a force multiplier to handle the increased workload. Cyber incident response subcomponents include:

- **Cyberattack first responders:** This subcomponent is a SWAT-like team that maintains its own special cyber-weapons and tactics to thwart an active attack. Separate from incident response, personnel here are focused on "pulling the plug" on a cyberattack using all means available including disconnecting the organization from the Internet. This emergency response team is comprised of highly trained personnel from within the cybersecurity program and is on call around the clock. External cyber response companies can also buttress this team.

- **Data breach response:** This is a specific plan to address the regulatory and practical requirements of responding to a data breach. The legal complexities of a data breach require a focused effort on this event alone. The incident response subcomponent handles all other types of cyber incidents. Data breach planning occurs here with regular testing and simulations of breaches. This capability has dedicated staff with force multiplication from other parts of the organization during an actual data breach. This group has interfaces to many parts of the organization (legal, public relations, etc.) to assist in data breach events.

- **Incident response management:** Incident response is concerned with addressing and managing the aftermath of a security breach in an orderly manner. The objective is to limit damage and return to normal as soon as possible. The focus also includes the identification of the vulnerabilities that led to the compromise and the creation and execution of a remediation plan to prevent future occurrences.

- **Digital evidence and forensics:** This subcomponent are concerned with the legally admissible gathering of digital evidence and forensic investigation of cybercrimes. Personnel are highly skilled with substantial experience in forensics. In some instances, this capability requires licensed private detectives or licensed forensic investigators. Personnel are responsible for controlling access to evidence chain of custody, evidence preservation, and forensics tools. I cover this topic is detail in *The Manager's Guide to Cybersecurity Law*.

## 1.9.6 Physical Security

Physical security within the context of our program structure is focused on protecting the data center that houses the cybersecurity program assets. Countermeasures protect assets and personnel from natural and manmade threats consisting of fires, floods, storms, utility failures, etc. Physical security subcomponents include:

- **Data center threat assessment:** Like a risk assessment, a data center-based threat assessment seeks to uncover the manmade and natural incidents that could render the data center either inaccessible or uninhabitable. The same practices and methods used for risk management apply here; however, the context is physical damage, theft, illegal access, or prevention of use of the data center housing the data center.

- **Data center protection:** This subcomponent is focused on providing preventative measures to manage or mitigate the effects of physical events. Protecting the data center begins with barriers to prevent unauthorized access or terrorist attacks, continues with surveillance and notification of illegal access, and ends with continuity of essential resources and utilities required to keep the data center operating despite a physical event. Minimum protective measures include fire suppression, water diversion and alerting, power continuity, and access control and monitoring.

## 1.9.7 Recovery Operations

When all else fails, the cybersecurity program will require a means to resume operations either temporarily or permanently. This component is increasingly coming under the control of the cybersecurity program due in great part to the similarity of resources required to perform recovery operations. Additionally, organizations are more likely to experience an outage related to a cyber event than a physical event. Recovery operations subcomponents include:

> **Did You Know?**
>
> A February 2019 fire in a Wells Fargo data center in Shoreview, Minnesota caused disruptions to online, mobile banking as well as other services nationwide including ATMs.
>
> *Can your data center survive a fire?*
>
> **Source:**
> https://www.usnews.com/news/best-states/california/articles/2019-02-07/fire-causes-wells-fargo-customers-to-lose-access-to-accounts

- **Disaster recovery (DR):** Cyberattacks can be a leading cause of impacts to an organization like natural disasters are. However, in most cases, no harm comes to the physical assets and facilities; but critical business functions are still nonetheless affected. The unique nature of cyber-rated disasters requires a disaster recovery plan equally unique. The plan also must address the recovery of cybersecurity operations in the event of a conventional disaster. In this example, the recovery would be a team or function within the overall IT recovery plan.
- **Business continuity management (BCM):** During the time that IT operations or the cybersecurity program is in recovery mode, the organization must continue to provide critical business functions. These functions can continue using third parties or semi-manual approaches. In extreme cases, the organization can invoke a temporary cessation of activities. The goal of this subcomponent is to make the organization resilient to disaster events.
  - **Recovery point objective (RPO)** is the interval of time that could pass during a disruption before the quantity of data lost during that period exceeds the BCM plan's maximum allowable threshold.

- o **Recovery time objective (RTO)** is the duration of time or service level within which a business process must be restored after a disaster to avoid unacceptable consequences associated with a disruption to continuity of critical business operations.

**Note:** The related DR/BCM activity of business impact analysis is covered in Chapter 4.

## 1.10 Cybersecurity Program Frameworks and Models

Now that I have provided you with what I believe is an ideal state blueprint that outlines the organizational structure for your cybersecurity program, it is time to start adding some detail. Each of the subcomponents call out a specific cybersecurity discipline; however, you must define what occurs within each domain. I will use identity and access management engineering as an example. Based on the knowledge of your organization, select passages from one of more frameworks to fill in the detail. Staying with our identity and access management engineering, I selected, from the NIST Cybersecurity Framework, the category of access control. The Framework guides me toward the supporting NIST SP 800-53 document that provides substantial guidance for this security discipline. It is as simple as that. Locate an authoritative source of your security disciplines from the following frameworks or models presented in this chapter.

> **TIP:** Create a cybersecurity program blueprint that best fits your organization; then select either NIST, ISO, etc. to map their respective control constructs for alignment with your program. Such an alignment provides you with a contemporary visual of your program validated with the good practices of NIST, ISO or both.

When reviewing cybersecurity frameworks and models, you will find that this will be a bit like the adage "all roads lead to Rome." Only in this case, all roads lead to NIST SP 800-83 or ISO/IEC 27001/27002. You will start to notice that many have their origin in either ISO or NIST. Which is why I have seen many cybersecurity programs base their programs on either ISO or NIST. Although both frameworks are well documented and fit for purpose in designing your cybersecurity program, they do not present as a modern cybersecurity organization or visual in my opinion. Therefore, I provided you with an ideal state blueprint in Figure 1-3. Table 1-2 provides a high-level side-by-side comparison of the frameworks discussed in this chapter.

**Table 1-2. Cybersecurity Framework Comparison**

| Criteria | HITRUST | ISF | ISO 27001 | NIST CSF |
|---|---|---|---|---|
| Full Title | Health Information Trust Alliance | Information Security Forum | International Organization of Standards | National Institute of Standards and Technology Cybersecurity Framework |
| Cost | Free to members | Free to members | Yes | Free to all |
| Certifiable | Yes | No | Yes | No |
| Current version | v9.2 | 2018 | 27001:2017 | 1.1 |
| Industry focus | Healthcare | Any | Any | Any |
| ISO-based | Yes | No | Yes | No |
| Cross mapping to other control standards | Yes | Yes | No | Yes |
| NIST integration | Yes | Yes | No | Yes |
| Maturity levels | Yes | Yes | No | Yes |
| Controls inventory | Yes | Yes | Yes | Yes |
| Risk model | Yes | Yes | Yes | Yes |

My selection and presentation of frameworks does not constitute an endorsement for any framework. I selected these frameworks based on my personal knowledge of working with each of them at various client engagements over the years. I have found that certain frameworks just seem to be a better fit for some organizations. Only you can be the judge of which framework will work best in your cybersecurity program.

To provide equal billing to each framework I list them in alphabetical order providing an overview of the sponsoring organization, links to learn more, and an analysis where I discuss their strengths, weaknesses, and my bottom-line opinion.

## 1.10.1 HITRUST® CSF®

The Health Information Trust Alliance (HITRUST) Common Security Framework (CSF) is a comprehensive cybersecurity and privacy framework originally intended for healthcare organizations. HITRUST CSF became the most widely adopted security framework in the US healthcare industry in 2010 (HITRUST, 2010) and has not lost that designation since. Here is the first example of all roads lead to Rome. HITRUST CSF leverages the International Organization of Standards (ISO) and the International Electrotechnical Commission (IEC) standards 27001 and 27002. This design element alone makes it suitable for organizations outside of the healthcare field.

One of the key aspects of HITRUST CSF is that it has been cross mapped with widely used security standards that you may wish to include in your cybersecurity program. Major standards (mentioned throughout this book) mapped in CSF include:

- Center for Internet Security (CIS) Critical Security Controls.
- Cloud Security Alliance Cloud Controls Matrix.
- Control Objectives for Information and Related Technology (COBIT) - 2019.
- Health Insurance Portability and Accountability Act (HIPAA) Security Rule.
- ISO/IEC 27001:2013 Information technology – Security techniques – Information security management systems – Requirements.
- ISO/IEC 27002:2013 Information technology – Security techniques – Code of practice for information security controls.
- NIST Special Publication (SP) 800-37 Revision 2, Risk Management Framework for Information Systems and Organizations: A System Life Cycle Approach for Security and Privacy - R2.
- Payment Card Industry (PCI) Data Security Standard (DSS).

**Note**: Links above are current as of June 22, 2019.

The organization of HITRUST CSF includes 14 control categories, which contain 45 control objectives and 149 control specifications based on ISO/IEC 27001 and 27002. In addition to the ISO/IEC 27001 and 27002 baseline, HITRUST CSF includes three additional categories (domains): Information Security Management System (ISMS), Risk Management, and Privacy Practices. What makes HITRUST CSF unique is that each control consists of up to three implementation levels applied to healthcare organizations according to specific organizational, system, and regulatory factors. You can read all about HITRUST CSF at their website https://hitrustalliance.net/hitrust-csf/. Figure 1-4 is a representation of the HITRUST CSF framework presenting CSF's control and objectives categories.

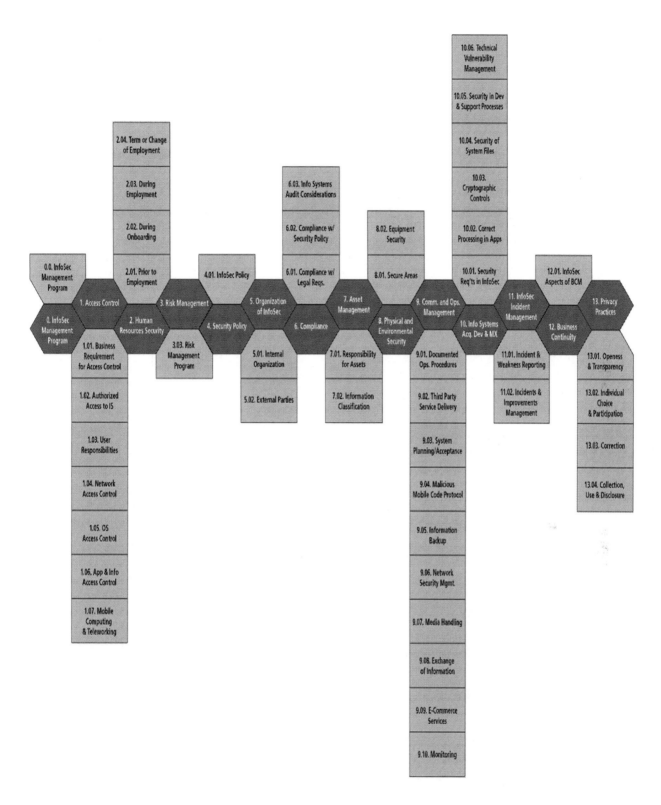

*Figure 1-4. HITRUST CSF (©HITRUST 2017 – HITRUST CSF diagram is proprietary to HITRUST and has been authorized for this publication. This is not to be reproduced, published, or disclosed further without the authorization of HITRUST.)*

My analysis of HITRUST CSF is drawn from my own experiences as well as from a review of the Introduction to the HITRUST CSF Version 8.1 Guide (HITRUST, 2017b).

### *Analysis*

- **Strengths:** If you want to reference ISO in your program, but do not want to pay or go through the hassle of requesting approval to use ISO, CSF solves that problem, as ISO is the basis for its framework, and the latest ISO versions (27001 and 27002) are already cross-mapped. HITRUST CSF's integration with NIST rates high marks from me in the comprehensiveness category. You should find no shortage of cybersecurity professionals who have experience in HITRUST CSF. NIST adopted HITRUST CSF for the NIST Healthcare Sector Cybersecurity Framework located at https://www.us-cert.gov/sites/default/files/c3vp/framework_guidance/HPH_Framework_Implementation_Guidance.pdf. HITRUST CSF is also a certifiable standard meaning you can have your organization become HITRUST CSF certified to demonstrate your compliance with the required safeguards in place to protect health information. CSF is frequently updated ensuring it stays fresh and current with its standards mapping efforts.

- **Weaknesses:** HITRUST CSF has come under criticism for its cost and complexity of achieving full certification. In reviewing HITRUST CSF, I would have to say that its robustness is a dual edge sword: on one side, it provides a comprehensive approach for large cybersecurity programs; on the other side, it may be too complex for small to midsize organizations. HITRUST however, recently announced a scaled-down version to address this concern (HITRUST, 2017a). One of HITRUST CSF's biggest detractors has published a series of open letters on LinkedIn pointing out various concerns that you may wish to review before making your decision. These concerns cover areas of complexity, cost, and approach (Govindaswamy, 2016).

- **Bottom line:** If you are a healthcare organization, HITRUST CSF is a no brainer. It is the de facto standard within the healthcare industry and already harmonizes virtually all major cybersecurity control frameworks. However, you must be fully committed to HITRUST CSF before you embark on the certification path because the process of achieving certification is not designed to be easy. If the cost is a concern, remember that HITRUST CSF's harmonization with other standards such as PCI DSS and HIPAA results in complying with many standards through HITRUST CSF. Despite HITRUST CSF's aim toward the healthcare industry, I personally have found its framework to be applicable to virtually any industry.

## 1.10.2 Information Security Forum (ISF) Framework

Founded in 1989, the UK-based Information Security Forum (ISF) is an independent, not-for-profit association of global organizations dedicated to investigating, clarifying, and resolving key issues in cybersecurity. In 1998, ISF developed a compendium of information security good practices named the Standard of Good Practice (SoGP). ISF subsequently developed an assessment to identify benchmark environments and measure compliance with the SoGP. ISF revises SoGP biannually and adds new sections according to ISF member requests and best-practices research. You can read all about ISF at their website https://www.securityforum.org/.

The ISF's SoGP for Information Security (the Standard) is one of the more comprehensive information security frameworks available. It provides complete coverage of the topics set out in ISO/IEC 27002, COBIT 5 for Information Security, NIST Cybersecurity Framework, CIS Top 20 Critical Security Controls for Effective Cyber Defense and Payment Card Industry Data Security Standard (PCI DSS).

Although the framework is based on research by ISF and published in the UK, many organizations around the world use it standalone or in conjunction with ISO or NIST. The ISF SoGP framework focuses on controls in the following security domains:
- Audit and risk management.
- Business continuity and availability.
- Change management.
- Operational monitoring.
- Trusted access.

ISF has updated the context of their approach to cybersecurity through the release of their ISF Protection Process. This approach is risk-based and focuses on protecting the most critical information and assets. Figure 1-5 shows the approach beginning with identifying critical assets and ending with protecting the information life cycle.

# THE ISF PROTECTION PROCESS

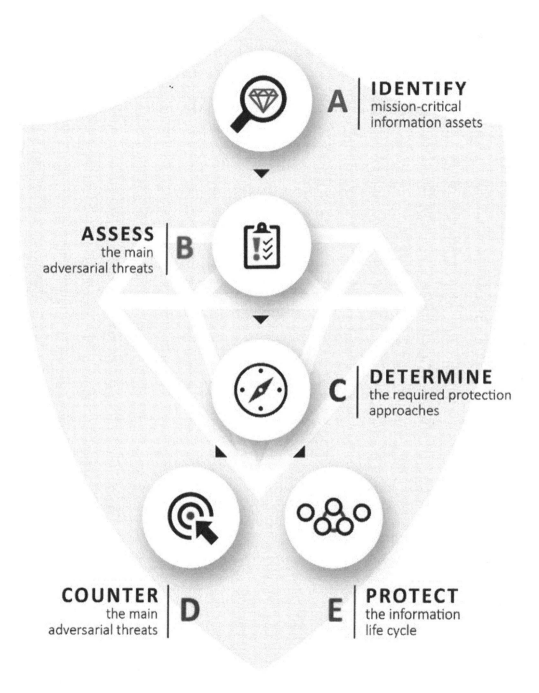

**A** | **IDENTIFY** mission-critical information assets

**ASSESS** the main adversarial threats | **B**

**DETERMINE** the required protection approaches | **C**

**COUNTER** the main adversarial threats | **D**

**E** | **PROTECT** the information life cycle

*Figure 1-5. ISF Protection Process. (Copyright ©2016 Information Security Forum Limited. Diagram has been authorized for use by ISF for this publication.)*

ISF recommends using its Protection Process along with the broader protection capability of an organization. This capability consists of a range of different supporting elements (Information Security Forum, 2016) as follows:

- Governance, risk management, and compliance (GRC): Set direction for security, promote ownership, and collaborate with stakeholders.
- People: Invest in skilled and experienced IT practitioners, security specialists, and risk experts.
- Technology: Automate protection of mission-critical information assets using security architecture, specialized technical security controls, and advanced security solutions.
- Security Assurance: Determine policy, statutory, and contract obligations.

### *Analysis*

- **Strengths:** ISF is both a framework and a standard with exposure to 10,000 members worldwide, many on the Fortune 500 and Forbes 2000 listings. For nearly 30 years, ISF has been evolving, adding a risk and maturity approach and many advances in its control library. In 2016, ISF launched a global ISF consultancy of services, focused on providing short-term, professional counsel to support the implementation of the non-profit's resources and products. ISF actively works to maintain compatibility with ISO through several publications, and to map various ISO standards to its framework and SoGP. In 2011, ISF joined other leading US security associations' in endorsing 12 information security principles for security practitioners.
- **Weaknesses:** Some view the UK-based association not relevant for the US market and something that European companies would reference in their cyber security program. US auditors are less familiar with ISF. ISF has chosen not to cover records management, operational transparency, and segregation of duties or operational controls within this framework.
- **Bottom line:** The SoGP comes as close to best practices as I have seen in a framework or standard. ISF addresses maturity through their Maturity Model Accelerator Tool, a high-level maturity model aligned with the ISF's SoGP. With this framework, you also get a risk assessment methodology and a supply chain assurance framework (SCAF). If an international organization is looking for an integrated approach in which risk maturity and GRC are covered within a single framework, ISF may be the answer.

## 1.10.3 ISO/IEC 27001/27002 Information Security Management System (ISMS)

International Organization of Standards (ISO) and International Electrotechnical Commission (IEC) standards 27001 and 27002 are widely seen as the international information security standards. This ISO standard has its origins going back to 1995, when it was known as the British Standard 7799 before it was adopted by ISO/IEC in 2000. Interestingly, while working on a security project for Dutch Royal Shell, I learned that the company wrote the standard and donated it to the UK government; so, it has been around for quite some time. Using an "all roads lead to Rome" analogy, think of ISO as Rome. ISO provides a link on its website to download an Excel file with ISO 27001 certification survey results located at https://www.iso.org/the-iso-survey.html. I downloaded the file, did a little analysis, and found that since 2006, over 39,500 ISO 27001 certifications have been granted. Japan leads all countries with 23% of the certifications; the US ranks fifth with 3.84%. The ISO 27001 standard is the one by which you can certify, not ISO 27002.

ISO 27001 and 27002 are complementary standards: ISO 27001 focused on creating an information security management system (ISMS) and ISO 27002 providing a code of practice for information security controls. Many organizations base their programs on ISMS.

ISO restricts how much anyone can say about an ISO standard without violating its copyright, even to mention the ISO framework and publications in the press. In stark contrast, NIST's position is to make its standards freely available without charge or restriction. The strict guidelines placed on the ISO standards, in my opinion, have backfired, as evidenced by the 500,000+ results one would get by Googling ISO 27001 on any given day. I would estimate 80% of these documents are recreations of the original, which means that they violate ISO copyright and contain many inaccuracies. If the ISO standards were more economically priced and you did not have to apply for a ruling on how much of the standard could be used in your cybersecurity program based on the number of words... Well, you get my point. In Table 1-3, I have summarized, from my own experience, the 14 clauses from ISO 27001 and 27002.

**Table 1-3. ISO 27001 and 27002 Coverage Areas**

| Area of Coverage | Focus |
|---|---|
| Policy | Publishing security policies. |
| Organization | Roles and responsibilities of personnel. |
| Personnel | Controls over hiring and firing personnel. |
| Assets | Classifying and inventorying assets. |
| Access control | Restricting access to information and assets. |
| Encryption | Encrypting information. |
| Physical security | Physical security of facilities and assets. |
| Operational security | ITIL like controls for change, configuration, backups, and security basic functions like malware protection. |
| Communications security | Secure network design and messaging. |
| System development life cycle (SDLC) | Secure development practices. |
| Third-parties | Controlling and monitoring partners. |
| Incident management | Incident response and reporting. |
| Business continuity management (BCM) | Security interface aspect of BCM. |
| Compliance | Identification and compliance with regulations and laws. |

If you wish to see the exact names and text of the clauses go to the preview of ISO 27001:2013 standard at the ISO website https://www.iso.org/obp/ui/#iso:std:54534:en. The 27002 standard is available for viewing at https://www.iso.org/obp/ui/#iso:std:iso-iec:27002:ed-2:v1:en. ISO 27001 contains Annex A, containing clauses or categories of security controls, which are explored in more depth in ISO 27002.

In April of 2017, the British Standards Institution (BSI) released a corrigendum to the 27001:2013. A corrigendum is simply an amendment to an existing standard to correct minor inaccuracies and add usability recommendations. Previous corrigenda were issued in 2014 and 2015. The 2017 is a minimal update incorporating previous updates, declares it's a European standard, considers information an asset and emphasizes a Statement of Applicability through bullet points versus the previous paragraph of text.

## *Analysis*

- **Strengths:** ISO 27001/27002 is an internationally adopted standard that is also considered a framework with wide acceptance from many industries and company sizes. It is also a certifiable standard with no shortage of assessors who understand how to guide organizations toward certification. You can also declare a specific aspect of your organization for certification and have just that aspect certified. Hiring ISO-knowledgeable personnel is also not an issue. The ISO security standard is one of the easier and more cost-effective standards or frameworks upon which to become certified.
- **Weaknesses:** ISO is the most difficult standard to use because it is almost entirely text-based without graphical representations and use of the text is highly restricted. For example, if you want to include the text of the controls in your program, you must ask for permission, and based on how much text pay a license fee. Updates are not frequent and when the standard is updated, the changes are minimal. For example, ISO removed 26 controls and added 12 in the 2013 version compared to the 2005 version. The last major release was dated 2013 with 2005 being the previous release. In the past 17 years, there have only been three releases. ISO published an update in 2017; however, the changes were nothing more than minor text changes of a few controls. ISO is also deemphasizing certain clauses, such as disaster recovery, and moving them into their own standards, which require additional permissions and cost.
- **Bottom line:** The ISO standard has lots of international support, momentum. You really cannot go wrong using it, provided your organization could afford the cost and you receive approval for your request regarding how you wish to use the standard in your own organization. ISO dominates the international standards with literally no competition. To use portions of ISO in your program, you are required to ask permission and provide an estimate of the percentage of text you will use directly in your program. ISO will quote you a price to grant your request. It is also my experience that ISO is one of the easiest frameworks you can use to receive certification.

**Note:** No graphic is available to explain the ISO materials, since they exist solely in text format. ISO standards are reviewed every five years making changes to the standard a very slow process.

## 1.10.4 NIST Cybersecurity Framework

The National Institute of Standards and Technology (NIST) Cybersecurity Framework (CSF) originates from Presidential Executive Order 13636, "Improving Critical Infrastructure Cybersecurity," issued February 12, 2013 (Executive Order, 2013). Within this order was the call for developing a cybersecurity framework. Check out the full text if CSF at https://www.nist.gov/sites/default/files/documents/cyberframework/cybersecurity-framework-021214.pdf.

The CSF, published February 12, 2014, builds on and does not replace security standards like NIST SP 800-53 or ISO 27001. It is a great starting point for organizations looking to improve their cybersecurity. NIST SP 800-53 is a regulatory document, encompassing the processes and controls needed for a government-affiliated entity to comply with the Federal Information Processing Standards Publication 200 – Minimum Security Requirements for Federal Information and Information Systems (FIPS PUB 200) certification. Read the full text of FIPS PUB 200 at http://nvlpubs.nist.gov/nistpubs/FIPS/NIST.FIPS.200.pdf. In contrast, the CSF is voluntary for organizations and therefore allows more flexibility in its implementation. The fact that the framework is written for government agencies should not be reason not to use it. Your information and assets do not know if they are owned by a bank or government agency. My point is NIST is applicable to any organization from any industry. Figure 1-6 is a representation of the NIST Cybersecurity Framework.

The CSF specifies that business drives an organization's cybersecurity activities and that cybersecurity risks should be part of an organization's risk management processes. CSF is comprised of three parts (NIST, 2014):
- *Framework core:* This part is a set of cybersecurity activities, desired outcomes, and applicable references that are common across critical infrastructure sectors. The core presents industry standards, guidelines, and practices in a manner that allows for communication of cybersecurity activities and outcomes across the organization from the executive level to the implementation/operations level. The framework core consists of five concurrent and continuous functions – identify, protect, detect, respond, and recover.
- *Framework profile:* This part represents the outcomes based on business needs that an organization has selected from the framework categories and subcategories. The profile is the alignment of standards, guidelines, and practices to the framework core in a particular implementation scenario. Profiles can be used to identify opportunities for improving cybersecurity posture by comparing a "current" profile (the "as is" state) with a "target" profile (the "to be" state).
- *Framework implementation tiers:* This part provides context on how an organization views cybersecurity risk and the processes in place to manage that risk. Tiers describe the degree to which an organization's risk management practices exhibit the characteristics defined in the framework (e.g., risk and threat aware, repeatable, and adaptive). The tiers characterize an organization's practices over a range, from partial (tier 1) to adaptive (tier

4). These tiers reflect a progression from informal, reactive responses to approaches that are agile and risk informed.

## NIST Cybersecurity Framework

### Framework Functions

| Identify – ID | Protect – PR | Detect – DE | Respond – RS | Recover – RC |
|---|---|---|---|---|
| **Categories** | | | | |
| Asset Management | Identity Management and Access Control | Anomalies & Events | Response Planning | Recovery Planning |
| Business Environment | Awareness & Training | Security Continuous Monitoring | Communications | Improvements |
| Governance | Data Security | Detection Processes | Analysis | Communications |
| Risk Assessment | Information Protection Processes & Procedure | | Mitigation | |
| Risk Management Strategy | Maintenance | | Improvements | |
| Supply Chain Risk Management | Protective Technology | | | |

*Figure 1-6. NIST Cybersecurity Framework 1.1. (Diagram has been provided by NIST without restriction of use.)*

## *Analysis*

- **Strengths:** NIST CSF is a risk-based approach to cybersecurity. It provides a platform for communication among firm leadership across an enterprise around cybersecurity posture, issues, and challenges. The outlined implementation tiers function as a method to determine how well organizations have incorporated cybersecurity risk management into culture and practices throughout the organization. NIST has achieved a level of importance to the point that most all other frameworks maintain alignment. NIST does not place any restrictions on using its materials or adapting it for specific purposes. It provides mappings to other standards and frameworks and provides an Excel version of its controls for quick integration with existing programs.

- **Weaknesses:** NIST is still viewed by many organizations as applicable only to US government agencies or critical infrastructure industries. The shear amount of information and supporting documents can be overwhelming to many who first attempt to use the framework. The CSF provides an outline of the implementation process; however, there is little guidance beyond the high-level concepts which are: Prioritize and Scope;

Orient; Create a Current Profile; Conduct a Risk Assessment; Create a Target Profile; Determine, Analyze, and Prioritize Gaps; and Implement Action Plan.

- **Bottom line:** NIST CSF is most effective when used in conjunction with NIST Special Publication 800-53A Revision 5 – Security and Privacy Controls for Information Systems and Organizations. Between these two documents, you have the perfect baseline for a cybersecurity program, framework, and accompanying control schema. One of the most attractive features is that NIST is free of charge and without restriction. Many view NIST as a US standard. Most other countries have a mistrust in adopting a US-centric security standard. NIST can also be a little overwhelming; however, when you realize that it is scalable and you can use just parts that make sense for your organization, it begins to look more manageable. the latest version of NIST CSF (1.1) was published April 16, 2018.

**TIP:** NIST has stated they will release revision 5 of NIST SP 800-53 by the end of 2019. This version will align CSF 1.1. Validate you are referencing the most current revision in your cybersecurity program.

## 1.11 Cybersecurity Program Technologies

I have found that the level of technical expertise of cybersecurity personnel varies widely; regardless of your own level of technical understanding you will require an understanding of the cybersecurity technologies available to protect information and assets. To help you in the design of your cybersecurity program I have outlined the available key categories and types of technology. However, I do not wish to rehash what many IT Security books have already covered. To that end, I have chosen to focus on leading cybersecurity technologies that, in my opinion have the greatest chance of detecting and preventing a cyberattack. In my role as an instructor for a Chief Information Security Officer (CISO) certification course, I have met literally hundreds of CISOs over the past several years. This contact affords me with the ability to learn what cybersecurity technologies work and conversely, which one's really don't work.

As you design your cybersecurity program, I strongly recommend you evaluate the feasibility of deploying some or all of the technologies described next to protect your organization's attack surface. The technologies are presented alphabetically as not to give one category credence over another. Cybersecurity programs should be risk-based as one organization may find more value in one technology versus another based on their risk profile. You can learn about risk profiles in Chapter 4.

The following are my top picks for categories of cybersecurity technologies that should be considered in every cybersecurity program and would in combination with other recommendation within this book prove instrumental in thwarting most cybersecurity attacks. I have addressed each category to a lessor or greater extent based on my opinion of assumed knowledge by the reader.

> **TIP:** To locate other companies that provide cybersecurity products and services check out Cybersecurity Ventures' Cybersecurity 500 List. This list provides detailed information on the world's most successful providers of tools and services to protection assets and information.

## 1.11.1 Application security

One of the most pervasive threat vectors in an organization's attack surface is their application portfolio. With millions of lines of code, it is virtually impossible for organizations to test every line for vulnerabilities. You will need to invest in application and software security whether it's common off-the-shelf (COT) or custom applications. To help you identify the correct types of application security products, I have outlined the main categories of products used in today's cybersecurity programs. This category focuses on how to identify vulnerable code whereas other categories can assist in surrounding the code with safeguards.

- **Application Security Testing (AST)** products are used by application development teams to validate that security has been designed and implemented into applications prior to deployment. AST products can be viewed as white box or black box testing, each taking a decidedly different approach to application security testing. The following outline these areas:
  - **Static Application Security Testing (SAST)** – Referred to as white-box testing because testers have full disclosure of the application design and coding. SAST tools provide a comprehensive review of application source code, which allow developers to catch vulnerabilities in their applications early in the development cycle. SAST include code scanning, vulnerability scanning and assessment, and subroutine analysis.
    **Example providers:** AppScan, Checkmarx Ltd., Fortify Static Code Analyzer, Veracode.
  - **Dynamic Application Security Testing (DAST)** – Referred to as black-box testing because applications are tested from a hacker's point of view where they would have little inside knowledge of the code. SAST products work by looking for vulnerabilities in web applications while running, providing an assessment from the hacker's perspective. DAST techniques include forms of

penetration testing, fuzz testing, web app security scanning, and proxy scanning tools. A DAST approach is designed to look for a broad range of vulnerabilities, including input/output validation issues that could leave an application vulnerable to cross-site scripting or SQL injection.

DAST is effective at identifying configuration mistakes and errors as well as identifying other specific problems with applications. While DAST is an essential part of application security testing, it cannot provide a complete picture of the vulnerabilities in an application.
**Example providers:** Acunetix, Veracode.

DAST and SAST testing should be combined as no one approach can detect all application vulnerabilities.

- o **Interactive Application Security Testing (IAST)** – DAST and SAST have been application testing staples for over 20 years, but they are not without their detractors. Application developers with whom I have worked were of the opinion DAST and SAST were ill equipped to identify vulnerabilities in application program interfaces (APIs), web services or Representational State Transfer (REST) endpoints, today's modern application landscape. If you're not a programmer, don't worry – I will explain the jargon. An API defines how software components should interact without the need to continually create code to do so. This code can be used over and over by all programmers that require the application to interact in a similar manner. and resides in a library to be used by all programmers. REST determines how an API looks serving as a set of rules on how to retrieve data. You can imagine that having a coding flaw in an API or REST would propagate to all the code used by all the programmers who used the REST or API modules.

  These products are designed to locate vulnerabilities in web applications, web APIs, and source code before hackers can exploit these application vulnerabilities. IAST products use embedded application agents to collect data in real time so they are always on.
  **Example providers:** Hdiv Detector, Seeker.

- o **Run-time Application Security Protection (RASP)** – Similar to ISAT, RASP products run inside an application. Runtime tools are designed to protect applications running in their operational environments. They detect intrusions while running inside an application, or inside a security perimeter. RASP products run continuous security checks on an application, responding to live attacks by terminating an attacker's session and raising alerts in the SOC.
  **Example providers:** Application Defender, Contrast Protect, Prevoty.

o **Web Application Firewall (WAF)** – WAFs can be an appliance, a cloud-based service or run directly within web services or application code. WAFs analyze and inspect incoming application requests looking for threats. WAFs use a fail open architecture to ensure application vulnerabilities detected and blocked don't bring down a production application. By design, WAFs block Open Web Application Security Project (OWASP) top attacks, account takeovers, bots, application denial of service attacks, etc.
**Example providers:** FortiWeb, Impervia, Signal Sciences.

## 1.11.2 Authentication

To ensure that only trusted individuals have access to your organization's information, you will need to have them prove their identity. The process of proving one's identity is called authentication or identity assurance. Authentication can be based on five factors consisting of knowledge, possession, inherence, time and location. The more factors that are combined to authenticate someone, the less likely someone will gain unauthorized access. Authentication can be configured as a cloud service or on premise.

The knowledge factor includes the information a user must know in order to access a system such as their user ID, password, passphrase or personal identification number (PIN). A possession factor requires a user have possession of a physical device that can generate a onetime use passcode (OTP). OTPs can be soft where an OTP is generated on a smartphone, or hard where a physical device is carried by the user that generates an OTP. Inherence or biometric factors consist of user human factors such as fingerprint scans, iris scans, and facial or voice recognition. The last two factors are time and location where a user is expected to access information at specific locations during certain times. Your access authentication plan will need to consider the right number of factors commensurate with the value of your information.
**Example products**: Authy, Okta, PingID, SecureID.

## 1.11.3 Cloud security

Organizations that have adopted cloud computing have come to realize that moving operations to the cloud does not absolve them of their responsibility to protect data. Data residing in the cloud presents a unique set of security challenges as not only must you be concerned with how you handle the secure data transfer on your end, you must also be concerned with how the cloud service provider protects your data. Cloud security covers policies, technologies, and controls used to protect data, applications, and their associated cloud infrastructure of cloud.

The primary technology used to protect information in the cloud is a Cloud Access Security Broker (CASB). CASBs defend against what the Cloud Security Association refers to as the "Treacherous 12." CASBs can be installed on premise at your location or reside in the cloud. They sit between your enterprise and the cloud service provider. CASBs enforce policies that you set for how data should be accessed, governed and protected. You may think of them as a unified threat management solution as they combine the capabilities of a firewall, access control, data loss prevention, intrusion prevention and malware prevention. CASBs are effective at enforcing the same security polices deployed at the enterprise-level to the cloud.

**Example providers:** Bitglass, Netskope, Proofpoint.

## 1.11.4 Container security

You may be asking yourself, what is a container? Think of a container as a subset of virtualization where you can launch an application without the need for a dedicated virtualized machine. Containers can work directly on hardware, cloud instances as well as virtual machines. They provide maximum flexibility to package and deploy applications.

Protecting and ensuring the integrity of these containers is critical as they extend the attack surface of your enterprise. Container providers such as Docker, Kubernetes, etc. do a fairly good job of building in security; however, more is required. Vulnerabilities can impact containers like any legacy environment. Container security has to support the entire container stack consisting of images, containers, hosts, registries, etc.

It is important that you create a view of your container environment as a subset of the enterprise attack surface. Once known, you can deploy an appropriate container security solution to protect where you're most vulnerable.

**Example providers:** Alert Logic, Aqua, Tenable.io, WhiteSource.

## 1.11.5 Data Loss Prevention (DLP)

DLP software monitors internal network traffic and outflow of information looking for indicators of data breaches. DLP software uses policies to compare documents and data to a baseline of sensitive data markers. Violations where structured or unstructured data containing private information is being sent outside the company, received internally or copied to endpoints can be detected and blocked. DLP products are designed to monitor data in-use (endpoint actions), in-motion (network traffic), and at-rest (data storage).

DLP solutions are used in conjunction with existing cybersecurity tools such as anti-malware, firewalls, Intrusion Prevent Systems (IPS) and Security Information and Event Management (SIEM) platforms. Firewalls can block access to systems storing protected information, IPS's can alert when hackers attempt to access private information, anti-malware can prevent bad actors from compromising information and SIEMs can alert to indicators of data compromise. DLP provides the next layer of defense.

DLPs can monitor traffic at the edge to detect sensitive data sent in violation of security policies, lockdown endpoints to prevent confidential information from being copied to USB devices in

violation of polices, monitor the internal network to monitor how sensitive data is used; DLP solutions can even detect policy violations in PDF and encrypted documents.
**Example providers:** Digital Guardian, Forcepoint, McAfee, Symantec.

## 1.11.6 Digital forensics

Whether an organization decides to pursue legal means of redress for a cyberattack or simply wishes to know what happened, there is a need for an organization to have digital forensics capability. Additionally, you may have to prove that your organization was properly protecting its information and assets in the event of a regulatory investigation; in these cases, digital forensics will be critical.

At the core of your organization's ability to conduct forensics investigations is a sophisticated forensic platform that provides the ability to organize case data, investigate browser files, identify metadata as well as other digital artifacts. These solutions use scientifically proven methods to identify, collect, validate and preserve evidence.
**Example products:** EnCase, Forensic Toolkit (FTK), NetAnalysis®.

## 1.11.7 Distributed Denial of Service (DDoS) Mitigation

One of the most disruptive types of attacks is a DDoS attack where an army of compromised computers are used to flood a legitimate server or website with incoming messages or transactions. Although DDoS attacks cannot be stopped, the effects can be reduced through the application of DDoS mitigation technologies. Most leading-edge DDoS attack mitigation solutions are appliance and cloud based. These solutions identify good vs. evil incoming traffic using behavioral attack detection. The bad traffic is blocked before it even reaches the firewall. The solutions are also intelligence based with the ability to block outbound traffic where DDoS botnets attempt to communicate with command and control (C2) sites.
**Example products**: Akamai, F5 Herculon DDoS Hybrid Defender, Netscout

## 1.11.8 Deception technology

One of the newer cybersecurity defenses is deception technology. For organizations who operate under the assumption of breach, deception technology can be effective at reducing the damage hackers can do once they're in your network. These products work by strategically deploying decoys throughout an enterprise. They contain bait such as faux accounts where hackers believe they're stealing real account credentials and escalating their privileges. Each time a trap has been sprung; alerts are sent to a command station to record the activity. SOC personal can respond to the attack and close off the attack vectors used by the hackers.

Deception technology emerged from the use of honeypots where fake enterprise servers with faux data was exposed to the Internet in hopes of attracting hackers to a seemingly easy target.

As hackers learned how to recognize honeypots, a new approach was needed. Deception technology continuously maps an enterprise's network assets, cloud services and end points to automatically learn how to create realistic layers of deception. Deception technology is an advanced cybersecurity strategy used by mature organizations.

**Example providers:** Attivo Networks, Cymmetria MazeRunner, Illusive Networks, Smokescreen.

## 1.11.9 Domain Name Services (DNS) Attack Security

> ### Did You Know?
>
> In January 2019, New West Health Services of Helena, Montana reported that a laptop containing unencrypted Personal Health Information (PHI) as well as financial information of 25,000 patients was stolen from an employee. This event violated Montana's Privacy Protection Act, HIPPA and PCI-DSS.
>
> *Is all your company's confidential and personal data encrypted?*
>
> **Source:**
>
> https://www.mtpr.org/post/data-breach-affects-25000-new-west-health-services-customers

A DNS attack takes advantage of vulnerabilities in DNS where hackers can launch a zero-day attack, denial of service attack, replace legitimate IP addresses with rogue addresses, etc. Hackers are attracted to DNS as almost all web traffic requires a DNS query. Once a hacker controls the DNS, they can redirect inbound traffic to malicious sites and collect a tremendous amount of confidential information. DNS was designed for speed and efficiency of IP address processing, not security. To make up for the lack of security in DNS the originators of DNS created DNS Security Extensions (DNSSEC). DNSSEC addresses the lack of security by providing DNS authentication using digital signatures to protect DNS queries and responses from being hijacked.

To improve upon DNSSEC, a niche of security category emerged to provide additional layers of security. These products as well as their service versions redirect your DNS traffic to a secure infrastructure that will enforce security policies. DNS security services block malicious or unauthorized sites used by the majority of phishing, ransomware and botnets to connect with command and control sites. DNS firewalls can block hackers from overwhelming DNS infrastructure as well as block connections to sites known to distribute malware, SPAM and botnets.

**Example products**: Cloudflare, Cyren, Infoblox.

## 1.11.10 Encryption

The process of transforming plaintext to ciphertext using an algorithm and an encryption key is encryption. Returning ciphertext to plaintext is referred to as decryption. What makes the transformation of plain to cyphertext possible is an encryption key that unlocks the deciphered text making it readable again. Keys can either be private or shared. These processes fall under the broader category of cryptography. You don't have to become a cryptography expert to make decisions regarding the protection of data, but you should understand where and how encryption is required to protect critical and sensitive information. Today's data privacy laws uniformly require organizations to protect personally identifiable and private health information. Encryption is the most effective way to protect information whether the data is in-flight, at-rest or in-use. Encryption is typically applied to email, messaging, file transfers, data, documents and disks.

There are several encryption algorithms used in enterprises today, each with varying complexities and cost. When selecting an encryption solution for your organization you will need to consider how keys are generated, revoked and managed overall. You will also need to consider the strength of the encryption algorithm: the more bits, the higher degree of difficulty required to break the encryption code.

- Triple DES (3DES, TDES) is still the workhorse of enterprise encryption with a useful life estimated to 2030. This is when it is projected that hackers will have the technology to break Triple DES. Triple DES uses three individual keys of 56 bits each allowing up to 168-bits.
- Blowfish is an algorithm favored by ecommerce and payment sites because of its speed and flexibility. This algorithm parses data into blocks of 64 bits and encrypts them individually. The fact that that it's free gains it much popularity.
- RSA, named for the authors (Rivest, Shamir, Adleman) is a public key encryption algorithm popular for protecting information sent over the Internet. RSA uses a private and public key and supports up to 4095-bit keys.
- Advanced Encryption Standard (AES) is considered the uber encryption standard, used by the U.S. Government and virtually all defense and security agencies. AES can scale to 256-bits and is considered impossible to break at present. AES is gaining more traction in the private sector as more encryption products emerge with solutions based on the algorithm.

All of the aspects of encryption are beyond the scope of this book; however, if you want to learn more, I highly recommend checking out An Overview of Cryptography written by Gary C. Kessler (Kessler, 2019). This paper is regularly updated online and serves as a valuable resource on all thing's encryption.

**Example products:** IBM Guardium Data Encryption , McAfee Complete Data Protection, SafeNet.

## 1.11.11 Endpoint Protection Platform (EPP)

Next-generation EPP platforms are designed to provide an all-encompassing protective approach for desktops, laptops, smartphones, tablets, servers, etc. They combine the protection of anti-malware, data loss prevention, encryption, intrusion prevention, firewalls, network access control (NAC), web filtering and whitelisting. These hybrid security platforms monitor, detect and prevent attacks likely to occur at the endpoint. Endpoints are also typically used outside the corporate network void of enterprise cybersecurity safeguards. EPPs compensate for this by essentially extending the same protection afforded a corporate enterprise to the endpoint.

**Example providers:** Absolute, Carbon Black, CrowdStrike, Cylance, Symantec.

## 1.11.12 Firewalls (FW)

Firewalls are an undisputed method of protecting a network that has been in use for decades. What is relatively new are the next generation of firewalls (NGFW), which provide advanced capabilities far beyond a traditional firewall. NGFWs incorporate application inspection, network device filtering, DNS security, intrusion prevention and whitelisting. They also include VPN support to ensure connections between the Internet, network and firewall are secure. If your organization chooses to move toward NGFWs, it is a great time to evaluate all your network protection approaches for overlapping technologies.
**Example providers:** Cisco, Fortinet, Juniper Networks, Palo Alto Networks.

## 1.11.13 Identity and Access Management (IDAM)

IDAM is a framework of policies, services and technologies to manage user access rights, ensuring the correct users have the correct access to authorized information. Users and resources managed by the IDAM can be within your own organization or others in a federated model. The objective of IDAMs is to have one unified digital identity for each user throughout the entire lifecyle. IDAMs can provision user identities and their associated resources automatically based on their roles and attributes of access. IDAMs provide comprehensive functions to track user roles and activities as well as produce compliance reports on user access and associated rights.

IDAM products can include a suite of access control tools consisting of password management, user provisioning and single sign-on (SSO). IDAMs can be installed on premises or offered as a cloud-based service.
**Example products:** ForgeRock Identity Management, IDMWORKS, Layer7® Identity & Access

## 1.11.14 Internet of Things (IoT) Security

In the expanding IP universe, the growth of internet connected devices is explosive. The adoption of these devices is spreading into our daily lives, from consumer to industrial applications. Like any Internet connected device, they contain vulnerabilities and are desired by hackers as a means to launch botnet attacks or to serve as a hacker entry point to industrial or corporate networks. The rapid development of IoT devices and rush to market has left little time for original equipment manufacturers to design proper security into the IoT devices. Additionally, most IoT devices have a small form factor with sufficient compute power to support advanced security features.

Numerous security vendors have created security products and services for IoT devices, many of which mimic standard security offerings. For example, anti-malware, device authentication, encryption, API security, security analytics, etc. are available to protect IoT devices. It is important to create a security architecture specifically for IoT devices; however, it should also integrate with your existing cybersecurity program.

**Example products**: Forescout Unified IoT Security, Nanolock, SecureRF

## 1.11.15 Intrusion Protection Systems (IPS)

Intrusion prevention systems have been monitoring networks for anomalous activity for nearly as long as firewalls. IPS's have evolved from hybrid network scanners to Next-Generation Intrusion Prevention System (NGIPS) offering sophisticated intelligence-based threat prevention. However, unlike NGFWs, which include IPS capabilities, NGIPS's do not include firewall capabilities. Today's IPS's focus on network behavior analysis, user identity tracking and integration with threat intelligence for real-time threat blocking. You will need to decide if a standalone IPS versus an IPS integrated into a next-generation firewall is appropriate for your enterprise.

**Example providers:** Cisco, F5 Networks, TippingPoint.

## 1.11.16 Network Access Control (NAC)

The proliferation of bring-your-own-device (BYOD) and mobile workers has created an environment where users rarely connect to the corporate network. This lack of connection to the enterprise network prevents these devices from being adequately protected by enterprise security policies and practices. To correct this situation and resolve the risk introduced to a network from devices whose security state is often unknown, NAC was created.

Using NAC, when a device first connects to a network its hygiene and security state are validated compared to existing policies. The device's patch level, anti-malware engine currency and identity, etc. are checked before access is allowed. This preadmission health check is crucial to eliminating the introduction of threats to an enterprise network. Devices that don't pass are quarantined until they're remediated.

**Example products:** Aruba ClearPass, Forescout, Portnox.

## 1.11.17 Privileged Account Management (PAM)

The most important accounts to protect are your organization's privileged accounts because they have the ability to perform elevated functions such as installing software, changing user or system accounts and accessing secure data. Elevated privileges, otherwise known as root access, should be restricted to trusted employees, but not without oversight. However, trust should never be absolute and privileged accounts should always be monitored and managed.

PAM solutions offer a way to authorize, monitor and revoke privileged users on a need-to-have basis. This eliminates the need to grant certain users unfettered enterprise access to the organization's most sensitive systems. PAM allows organizations to tightly manage privileged accounts where privilege is granted for access only when required or revoked when the user requirement or time expires.

**Example providers**: BeyondTrust, Layer7, Wallix Bastion.

## 1.11.18 Security Information and Event Management (SIEM)

Organizations are deluged with device, account and system information that requires analysis to uncover indicators of compromise. However, substantial compute power is required to aggregate and correlate this enormous and disparate information. SIEMs provide real-time analysis of the security alerts generated by application, network and system log data. SIEMs are the workhorse of the security operations center feeding analyst workstations with actionable security information. SIEMs also provide compliance reporting and aid in the incident investigation process.

Today's SIEMs include big data repositories and sophisticated data analytics to collect, normalize and search log data for anomalous or malicious events and activity. Next generation SIEMs have moved passed standard rules and correlations to artificial intelligence and deep

pattern learning to detect insider threats and targeted attacks. SIEMs also integrate with security orchestration and automation solutions to streamline security operations and incident response. This capability can be harnessed to detect threats and automate responses to contain the threat.
**Example products:** McAfee SIEM, QRadar, Splunk.

## 1.11.19 Security Orchestration, Automation and Response (SOAR)

Cyber threats happen at the speed of light and ripple throughout the Internet in a matter of minutes. Cybersecurity teams find it increasingly difficult to keep pace with bad actors and the attacks they perpetrate. Even the most experienced and knowledgeable security operations personal cannot operate at machine speed. Many organizations find correlation between various SecOps tools slow and cumbersome. This time lag to understand threats prevents SecOps personnel from investigating indicators of compromise and launching their responses against attacks. To keep up with attacks, SecOps teams are turning toward methods to automate workflows to handle threat analysis and incident response.

This is accomplished through the introduction of automation and orchestration solutions. Automation platforms process rote manual tasks at machine speed. Orchestration solutions focus on integrating SecOps tools to pass information at machine speed. The combination of automation and orchestration solutions defines a security stake coined by Gartner as SOAR (Englebrecht, 2018). SOAR differs from SIEM as SIEM is one of the tools that SOAR integrates. The SIEM identifies the suspicious behavior and alerts SecOps personnel. What comes next is the response to the alerts. SOAR solutions take action on the alerts generated by the SIEM reducing the manual intervention required of SOC operators.
**Example products:** LogRhythm, Splunk, Swimlane.

## 1.11.20 Threat Intelligence Platform (TIP)

TIPs are a technology designed to aggregate, correlate, and analyze threat information from inhouse, subscription, government and public sources. TIPs analyze relevant threat data to produce a threat profile that supports manual or automated means of an organization to adjust their cybersecurity defenses. TIPs are highly customizable leveraging application program interfaces (APIs) to facilitate configuration and data feed integration from many sources including Whois information, reverse IP lookups, website analysis, domain name servers, SSL certificates and many other threat source information.

TIPs make extensive use of machine learning and artificial intelligence to reduce false positives to ensure threat analysts only spend their time on actionable threats. Some TIPs even offer an app store where specialized threat feeds can be added as required. TIPs can be deployed on premises, in the cloud or hosted in your own organization.
**Example providers:** Anomali ThreatStream, FireEye iSIGHT Threat Intelligence, LookingGlass Cyber Solutions.

## 1.11.21 User and Entity Behavior Analysis (UEBA)

Knowing how users will behave while accessing a network is never certain– trusted users can compromise data while other users can simply make mistakes that expose personal information. Each user community, motivation triggers and networks are different. This is why it's important to understand the behavior of users in an organization's network. Insiders and bad actors are always coming up with innovative ways to compromise information, making it increasingly difficult to identify their actions. The way to leverage user behavior is to deploy a solution that collects information and produces analysis of network events that users generate every day. UEBAs produce analytics to facilitate the detection of compromised credentials, lateral movements, and other malicious behavior by analyzing how accounts are used.

User and entity behavior analytics (UEBA) focus on the behavior of systems and the user accounts on them. User behavior analytics enables the determination whether a potential threat is an outside party pretending to be an employee or an insider who presents some kind of risk. UEBAs monitor and correlate network activity of user accounts vs. IP address and assets. With this insight, users who misbehave or indicate unusual or unlikely activities will be flagged for investigation long before traditional security monitoring solutions.
**Example providers**: Digital Guardian, Forcepoint, FortiInsight, Rapid7.

## 1.11.22 Virtualization security

Protecting many operating systems and applications running on a single host can prove challenging. Not only must the host machine be protected to prevent the virtualized machines from inheriting its threats, but the inherent vulnerabilities of virtualization must be addressed. Virtualization security is designed to address issues on the host as well as the virtualized environment. Virtual security is a collection of safeguards, procedures, processes, and tools that secure a virtualized infrastructure.

The primary risks to a virtualized environment begin with the fact that virtualization adds additional layers of complexity. For example, virtual machines (VMs) that are dynamically deployed without oversight creates a phenomenon called virtual sprawl. This is where organizations lose track of their VMs, what is and is not patched creating a situation where the integrity of the security of a virtualized environment can no longer be assured. Protecting a virtualized environment requires a separate but integrated approach to information security. Security solutions that track virtualized assets, encrypted data within virtual machines, protect offline VMs, control access to the hypervisor that control VMs, etc., provide protection over the vulnerabilities of operating a virtualized environment.
**Example providers:** DataGravity for Virtualization (DGfV), Sophos Virtualization Security, TrendMicro.

## 1.11.23 Vulnerability management

An organization will never be able to eliminate all vulnerabilities, subsequently they need to be managed. A balance is needed between which vulnerabilities can be mitigated and which ones must be carefully watched until they can be mitigated. Vulnerability management is a lifecycle where weaknesses are identified, classified, prioritized and remediated. An organization's enterprise is continuously scanned with results bifurcated to a vulnerability management platform and the security operations center. Threat and risk analysts use the vulnerability management platform to strategize on vulnerability remediation based on the threat posed to the enterprise. Vulnerability management platforms can be deployed as a cloud-based service, appliance or on-premise deployment.

**Example products:** Skybox Security, Tenable SecurityCenter, Tripwire IP360.

## 1.11.24 Web filtering

This technology is effective at stopping users from accessing restricted websites or URLs by blocking browsers from loading web pages. Web filters block content by comparing URLs to a library of restricted sites. Restricted sites are rated based on their reputation rating of hosting botnets, malware or other malicious tools. Web filters prevent users from accessing sites that can introduce harm to an organization.

Web filters can use a blacklist or whitelist to restrict or allow website access. Another approach is where web filters restrict access based on keywords or content. Web filtering is effective for stopping phishing attacks, accessing to social media messaging accounts and inspecting HTTPS that may have fraudulently obtained Secure Sockets Layer (SSL) certificates. Web filter solutions can be appliance or cloud based.

**Example products:** Cyren, Forcepoint, TitanHQ

## 1.11.25 Whitelisting

One of the most effective ways to ensure only authorized applications are allowed access to an enterprise is to create a list of the applications necessary to the business. All other applications will be denied access. With whitelisting it is possible to stop virtually all malicious applications. Whitelisting is considered more secure than blacklisting where an organization must continually add applications to a blacklist. This method is far more cumbersome and more error prone then simply whitelisting authorized programs. Whitelisting can be applied to the enterprise as well as endpoints.

**Example providers:** Airlock Digital, Carbon Black, Digital Guardian, Ivanti.

# 1.12 Security Training Program

Every cybersecurity program requires a robust security awareness training program that should contain on-line tutorials, classroom instruction and digital simulations. Regardless of the size of an organization, training is a cornerstone of information and asset protection. Cybersecurity training can be an in house or outsourced discipline depending of the size of an organization and budget. I have broken out a training program into three disciplines.

## 1.12.1 Awareness Training

Employees are the first line of defense in preventing cyberattacks. Building a culture of security is enforced through security awareness training. Organizations should build a customized approach to security awareness making it as relevant and realistic as possible in order to gain the widest possible acceptance. Security awareness training is based on scenarios covering a broad spectrum of cyber threats including such topics as email security, avoiding social engineering, identifying insider fraud, and dozens of other scenarios. Table 1-4 provides sources of some top providers security awareness training programs.

**Table 1-4. Security Awareness Training Programs**

| Product | Company | Website |
|---|---|---|
| Security Awareness Training | Proofpoint | https://go.proofpoint.com/ |
| Cybersecurity Quotient (CyQ) | Inspired eLearning LLC | http://www.ivtnetwork.com/article/cybersecurity-and-cyq |
| Security Awareness Training | Curricula | https://www.getcurricula.com/ |
| End-User Training | SANS™ Institute | https://www.sans.org/security-awareness-training |
| KnowBe4 | Security Awareness Training | https://www.knowbe4.com/products/kevin-mitnick-security-awareness-training/ |

*Note: Links contained in the table are current as of September 22, 2019.*

## 1.12.2 Phishing Attack Training

A phishing attack delivered through an email is often the first phase of a larger attack. Training employees not to fall victim to phishing attacks is most effectively accomplished through repetitive training. Training employees how to spot phishing emails using mock malicious emails can substantially reduce the potential of employees falling victim to a phishing campaign. Table 1-5 lists several of the leading providers of phishing attack simulation products you can deploy immediately to begin testing and training employees.

**Table 1-5. Phishing Attack Simulation Products**

| Product | Company | Website |
|---------|---------|---------|
| PhishSim | SecurityIQ | https://securityiq.infosecinstitute.com/ |
| Gophish | Jordan Wright (Open-Source Framework) | https://getgophish.com/ |
| LUCY | Lucy Security USA | https://lucysecurity.com/ |
| PhishMe | SANS™ Institute | https://cofense.com/product-services/phishme/ |

*Note: Links contained in the table are current as of September 22, 2019.*

## 1.12.3 Ransomware Attack Simulations

Ransomware is one of the most egregious attacks an organization can experience causing rapid widespread impact on critical systems. Training employees to avoid falling victim to a ransomware attack as well as testing your organization's preparedness should be a top priority. One of the best ways to train employees to avoid being an unwitting accomplice or test if you have weak defenses to repel a ransomware attack is to put your employees through ransomware threat simulation.

Ransomware attack simulation software mimics how an attack would unfold from infiltration to safely encrypting test files. Table 1-6 provides a listing of several of the top products you may enlist to test your cybersecurity staff and processes to defend against ransomware.

**Table 1-6. Ransomware Simulation Products**

| Product | Company | Website |
|---|---|---|
| RanSim | KnowBe4 | https://info.knowbe4.com/ransomware-simulator-tool |
| PowerShell Encrypter/Decrypter | WatchPoint | https://www.watchpointdata.com/ransomware-simulator/ |
| Ransomware Simulation Tool | Smartfense | https://www.smartfense.com/en-us/products/ransomware/ |
| WannaCry ransomware simulation | Threatcare | https://www.threatcare.com/ransomware-simulation/ |

*Note: Links contained in the table are current as of September 22, 2019.*

# 1.13 Maturing Cybersecurity Programs

Have you ever been called immature? Stings a bit, right? Well, having your cybersecurity program called immature will do more than just sting; it could cost you a poor audit report, a loss of a security certification, a breach of security, or even a loss of your job. Cybersecurity program maturity is directly related to how prepared you are to fend off a cyberattack. The lower your program's maturity the higher your susceptibility to attack. To keep your program from being called immature, I am going to cover what a maturity model is and the types available. Your cybersecurity program will need a roadmap for continuous improvement. Some of the improvements will come from changes in regulations and technology. Other improvements will come from raising the level of maturity of your program.

## Did You Know?

A study conducted by Norway's SecureLink company found the average maturity rating of people, process and technology, across all verticals was 1.6 on a five-point scale. Three is considered a good practice. The survey results are drawn from European cybersecurity executives.

*What is the maturity of your cybersecurity program?*

**Source:** https://securelink.net/nb-nb/campaign/sma/security-maturity-report-2019/

A *maturity model* is a measure of the completeness of an organization's cybersecurity program. I carefully avoided the word *effectiveness* because that implies significant testing. Completeness is determined by reviewing your program's use of good practices. Maturity scales begin at zero, meaning you are doing nothing, to a five, which indicates you are a rock star. You can almost think in terms of stand, crawl, walk, jog, and run. Despite the fact there are over 20 maturity models to choose from, they are all about 80% the same. Many of their differences are in terminology, but their levels of maturity offer very similar definitions. A cybersecurity maturity model will allow you to baseline your program from day one and track its improvement over time according to some accepted standard of maturity. This will help you answer the $64,000 question, "Are we getting better?"

Once you select and begin to define your cybersecurity program framework you will need to begin thinking about the level of maturity you desire your program to achieve. Remember that not every aspect of your cybersecurity program requires the same level of maturity. I mentioned previously that cybersecurity programs should be risk-based; this is one of the reasons. Those components of your program that contribute the most to defending against attacks should have the highest level of maturity. Table 1-7 is a generic maturity model to provide you with a basis for how cybersecurity programs are measured.

**Table 1-7. Generic Maturity Model**

| Level | Description |
|---|---|
| 5: Optimized | Service-operation focused; good practices moving to best practices; countermeasure innovation demonstrated. |
| 4: Managed | Metrics used to improve processes; less dependence on key personnel; beginning or predictable repeatable results. |
| 3: Defined | Competency being demonstrated, but not always consistent; standards published and generally followed. |
| 2: Repeatable | Some processes are repeatable; reliance on key individuals is required; results not always predictable. |
| 1: Ad hoc | Undocumented efforts; reactive to cyber events; generally chaotic. |
| 0: No activity | No demonstrable capability. |

Figure 1-7 shows how to use the color-coding on the maturity model above to overlay maturity levels within your cybersecurity program blueprint to quickly show and track the maturity of your program according to the model used.

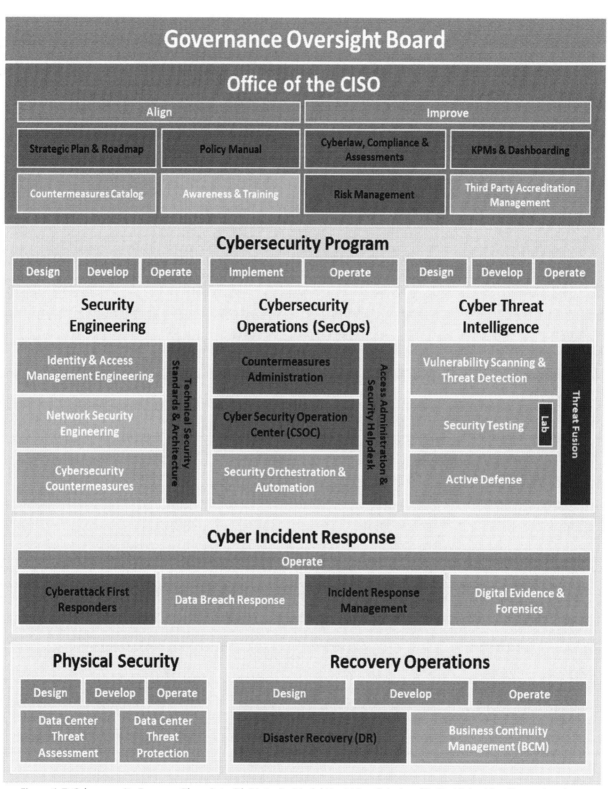

Figure 1-7. Cybersecurity Program Blueprint with Maturity Model Heat Map Coloring. (By Tari Schreider, licensed under a Creative Commons Attribution-NonCommercial-NoDerivatives 4.0 International License)

Maturity models address virtually every aspect of cybersecurity programs:

- **Cybersecurity controls:** How mature and well-functioning are your controls used to protect information and assets?
- **Information assurance:** How complete is the information life cycle beginning with data creation to data disposal in your program?
- **Personnel competency:** What is the level of cybersecurity competency of the personnel running your cybersecurity program?
- **Program capability:** What is the overall maturity of your cybersecurity program?
- **Program governance:** How well governed is your cybersecurity program?
- **Risk management:** How well does your organization assess and manage risk?

> **TIP**: Maturity models may be mixed for different components of the cybersecurity program. For example, you may wish to use a maturity model for application development security that is different from the model used for the whole of your program.

Table 1-8 provides you with an overview of my top five maturity models that I have referenced most in my program designs.

**Table 1-8. Top Five Maturity Models**

| Maturity Model | Purpose | Source |
|---|---|---|
| Cybersecurity Competency Model | Improve competency of workers in the field of cybersecurity. | US Department of Labor Employment and Training Administration (ETA) |
| NIST Program Review for Information Security Assistance (PRISMA) Maturity Model | Information security program maturity approach aligned to NIST SP 800-53. | National Institute of Standards and Technology (NIST) |
| RIMS Risk Maturity Model (RMM) | Improved risk management practices. | Risk Management Society (RIMS) |
| Open Information Security Management Maturity Model (O-ISM3) | Technology-neutral model focused on common information security processes. | The Open Group |
| Software Assurance Maturity Model (SAMM) | Application development security process improvement model. | Open Web Application Security Project (OWASP) |

*Note: Links contained in the table are current as of September 22, 2019.*

A comprehensive listing of maturity models is in Appendix A. Start with one or more with which you are most comfortable. I would suggest selecting no more than two initially.

### 1.13.1 Security Ratings

Another way to gauge the maturity of your organization's cybersecurity program is to subscribe to a security ratings service. These types of services grade how well an organization protects their information. An organization's score is determined like how a credit rating agency determines a consumer credit rating. Ratings are derived by a rating service scanning your network looking for risk factors as well as looking at cyber intelligence to detect if you have been or are targeted for attack. Based on these factors a letter grade of A though F or numeric score is assigned.

Risk factors included DNS health, patching currency, password strength, firewall rules, hacker chatter, posted compromised credentials, social engineering attempts, etc. organizations use this service to validate the security and reputation of their cloud service providers. An advantage of this service is increased transparency of cybersecurity programs. If you do decide to move forward with this type of service, make sure they offer a dispute and appeal process where you can correct inaccuracies. According to BitSight's research of 27,000 companies, companies who score 550 or below on their scale are five times more likely to experience a data breach (BitSight, 2019).

**Example providers:** BitSight, FICO® Cyber Risk Score

## 1.14 Cybersecurity Program Design Checklist

The best way I know to accomplish all my tasks in a project is to follow a checklist. To help ensure you cover all the important bases of designing your cybersecurity program, I have provided a checklist for you to follow in Table 1-9.

**Table 1-9. Cybersecurity Program Design Checklist**

| Step | Activity |
|------|----------|
| 1 | Select design methodology – adopt the design methodology in Section 1.1.2 or a similar format to guide the development of the cybersecurity program. |
| 2 | Publish design principles – adopt and publish design principles listed in Section 1.2.1 that will guide the development of the cybersecurity program. |
| 3 | Select good practices source – select a source of good practice to use within the cybersecurity program. |
| 4 | Define detail for architectural views – define attributes of the four architectural views outlined in Section 1.6. |
| 5 | Create the cybersecurity program blueprint – create a cybersecurity program architectural blueprint like the example provided in Section 1.7. |

| Step | Activity |
|------|----------|
| 6 | Align and define program structure – use the program structure guidance in Section 1.8 to articulate program structure definitions. |
| 7 | Select a guiding cybersecurity program framework or model – select at least one framework or model listed in Section 1.9 to define cybersecurity controls and countermeasure requirements. |
| 8 | Establish a baseline maturity level – select a maturity model from the list in Table 1-5 to establish a maturity baseline for your cybersecurity program. |

## Summary

At this point, you could call yourself a junior architect with your understanding of architectural techniques required to build a cybersecurity program.

- Your architect apprenticeship has begun with understanding that you must adopt a program design methodology.
- You recognize the difference between architectures, frameworks, and models and see the importance of creating a good blueprint to follow.
- You should be confident in knowing what types of detail your program design requires and which frameworks you can leverage to provide you with more knowledge and direction. You can apply this knowledge regardless of the level of involvement you may have with your organization's cybersecurity program.

# References

BitSight Technologies. (2019). *BitSight Security Ratings Correlate to Breaches.* Retrieved from https://www.bitsight.io/hubfs/Datasheets/BitSight_Security_Ratings_Correlate_to_Breac hes.pdf

Engelbrecht, S. (2019, July 27). *The Evolution of SOAR Platforms.* SecurityWeek. Retrieved from https://www.securityweek.com/evolution-soar-platforms

*Executive Order 13636 – Improving critical infrastructure cybersecurity*, 78 Fed. Reg. 11739 (2013, February 19). pts. III. Retrieved from https://www.gpo.gov/fdsys/pkg/FR-2013-02-19/pdf/2013-03915.pdf

Forest, E. (2014, January 29). *ADDIE model: Instructional design.* Retrieved from http://educationaltechnology.net/the-addie-model-instructional-design/

Govindaswamy, K. (2016, February 25). *An open letter to the HITRUST Alliance* (Part III). [LinkedIn post]. Retrieved from https://www.linkedin.com/pulse/open-letter-hitrust-alliance-part-iii-kamal

HITRUST Alliance. (2017a). *HITRUST announces HITRUST CSF roadmap including a new simplified program for small healthcare organizations and NIST cybersecurity framework certification* [Press release]. Retrieved from https://hitrustalliance.net/hitrust-csf-roadmap-including-new-simplified-program-small-healthcare-organizations-nist-cybersecurity-framework-certification/

HITRUST Alliance. (2010, July 22). *HITRUST CSF now most widely adopted security control framework.* [Press release]. Retrieved from https://hitrustalliance.net/hitrust-csf-now-widely-adopted-security-control-framework/

HITRUST Alliance. (2017b, February). *Introduction to the HITRUST CSF*. Retrieved from
https://hitrustalliance.net/documents/csf_rmf_related/v8/CSFv8_1Introduction.pdf

Information Security Forum (ISF). (2016, February 8). *Protecting the crown jewels*. Retrieved
from https://www.securityforum.org/uploads/2016/09/ISF_Protecting-the-Crown-Jewels-
Executive-Summary-final.pdf

Kessler, G. (2019, June 13). *An Overview of Cryptography*. (Online). Retrieved from
https://www.garykessler.net/library/crypto.html

National Institute of Standards and Technology (NIST). (2014, February 12). *Framework for
improving critical infrastructure cybersecurity*. Retrieved from
https://www.nist.gov/sites/default/files/documents/cyberframework/cybersecurity-
framework-021214.pdf

# Self-Study Questions

The following questions will help you build your expertise in designing a cybersecurity program.

1. What is the most important activity within the Align phase of the ADDIOI Model?
    Alignment with business goals.

2. Why are there no industry standard definitions for cybersecurity architecture, frameworks or models?
    The lack of a uniform definitions of architectures, frameworks and models allowed standards bodies and associations to use whichever term they deem appropriate.

3. What is the difference between a good and best practice?
    A good practice is an activity specified by an authoritative standards body. A best practice is an activity where its use is subject to assessment and peer review with noted improvements published.

4. What is the purpose of defining a technical view within an architectural schema?
    The technical view answers the question of how something will be done by declaring a solution; however, not a specific technology.

5. Which activities is security engineering principally involved?
    Security engineering is involved in the design of the network and operating environment's security safeguards and construction. It is also concerned with the technical integration and automation of security technologies.

6. What is active defense?

    Active defense carries the mission of actively seeking out or hunting bad actors, abnormal behaviors, and malicious activities within a network. It is the next level down from scanning and reporting.

7. What is a Recovery Time Objective (RTO)?

    The period within which critical business functions must be restored before unacceptable or intolerable business impacts are incurred. Generally expressed in hours or days.

8. What two ISO standards are used to create an Information Security Management Systems (ISMS)?

    ISO 27001 and ISO 27002

9. Which framework is generally accepted as best practices-based?

    The Information Security Forum (ISF) Framework.

10. What behaviors would you expect to see in an organization operating a defined level of maturity?

    Standards and policies have been published, are generally followed with cybersecurity personnel performing predictable following standard operating procedures. Less reliance on key performers.

# Chapter 2

# Establishing a Foundation of Governance

Now that you are designing your cybersecurity program like an architect, it is time for you to think about how you will administer your program or, in other word s, apply some governance. It makes no sense to create a great program and then let it go to seed. Governance ensures your program performs as intended. So, what is governance? If you ask ten people, you will get ten different answers. Dictionary definitions will only leave you puzzled. Simply put, governance is managing your program ethically and responsibly according to a set of principles and policies. Think in terms of doing the right things for the right reasons to allow the right things to happen.

Since the acronym GRC (governance, risk, and compliance) popped up in early 2000, a great deal of confusion on what constitutes governance ensued. GRC is only a vendor acronym serving as nothing more than a marketing umbrella for three separate functions or products. The use of the acronym allows anyone with a standard or solution aligning to any one of the letters of GRC to claim the governance moniker. In my experience, I have found that few true governance models, standards, or frameworks exist. In this chapter, I will focus on the "G" of GRC and decipher what governance *is* and *is not* as well as provide you with overviews of what I believe are credible frameworks or models to serve as your cybersecurity program governance foundation. I cover the "R" in Chapter 4 and the "C" in Chapter 5. My goal in this chapter is for you to learn what governance really is, what authoritative governance reference materials to rely on, and how to apply the right measure of oversight to your cybersecurity program.

*This chapter will help you to:*
- Understand what should be included in your governance foundation.
- Define an effective cybersecurity governance foundation.
- Familiarize yourself with the top governance frameworks and models.
- Recognize ways to automate your governance program.

## Chapter 2 Roadmap

The outcome of this chapter is that you will have established your foundation of governance for your cybersecurity program. Governance is essential to directing users, clients and service providers to behave in a manner that ensures the protection and privacy of information. Governance also ensure the cybersecurity program is professionally managed.

Figure 2.0 shows a reference architecture of how the cybersecurity program would look when you follow the direction provided within this chapter as well as the design checklist at the end of the chapter. The reference architecture is an abstraction view of your governance program. Your governance foundation, like all aspects of your program, will grow stronger as you add layers of maturity. All the components of the governance foundation exist within the governance playbook. In the reference architecture, components in gray are outcome-based or, in other words, they yield some form of program deliverable.

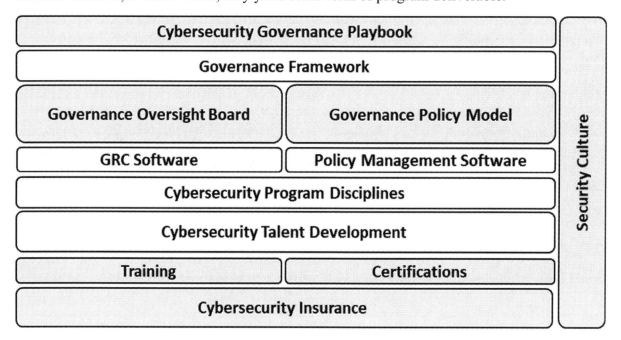

*Figure 2.0. Governance Foundation Reference Architecture*

Each component and subcomponent of the reference architecture is covered in more detail later in the chapter.

On this, the second stop of your journey you will need to establish a sound governance foundation, which ensures your cybersecurity program is managed responsibly and ethically. To help direct your energies toward the establishment of the governance foundation I have laid out the required outcome-based steps. The other content presented in the chapter is more reference, foundational or background oriented.

- **Step 1: Create Governance Playbook** – The playbook is where you will house all the components of the governance framework. Your organizations security principles, policies, training plans and insurance policies are stored here.
- **Step 2: Appoint Governance Oversight Board** – An oversight board, otherwise referred as a steering committee, has the critical job of ensuring your cybersecurity program is operated efficiently. The board validates business alignment, policy enforcement, budget allocation, and many more governance activities.
- **Step 3: Create Governance Policy Manual** – Identify the necessary policies aligned to their respective target audiences to provide clear direction on the responsibilities of protecting information and assets.
- **Step 4: Develop Cybersecurity Talent** – The growing shortage of IT talent in general, let alone cybersecurity talent, requires a concerted effort in talent retainment and motivation to reduce turnover. Talent development requires an investment in training and certifications to groom your cybersecurity staff to be the best they can be.
- **Step 5: Acquire Cybersecurity Insurance** – Understanding which policies provide which coverage is essential to applying a risk transfer or risk treatment. Cyberattack cost can be covered by general liability, data breach or cybersecurity insurance policies.
- **Step 6: Establish a Culture of Security** – If users, customers and partners don't care about protecting information and assets, even the best cybersecurity program will be hard-pressed to be effective. Investing in security training and user awareness pays off handsomely when people know *the right thing to do* to prevent a cyberattack or thwart an insider from causing harm to the organization.

When your back is up against the wall with limited resources, these are the mission critical governance activities you should address first:

- **Create Your Cybersecurity Policy Manual** – Follow the SANS Policy Project to create effective security policies to define the acceptable use of information and assets. Locate cybersecurity policy templates at https://www.sans.org/security-resources/policies.
- **Invest in Training and Certifications** – Even the most innovative cybersecurity technologies won't work effectively if cybersecurity personnel are not properly trained and certified. Trained personnel can make up for the shortcomings of a cybersecurity program by applying their tradecraft based on leading industry certifications.

- **Acquire Cybersecurity Insurance** – One of the fastest growing cybersecurity categories is data breach and cybersecurity policies. This type of insurance can serve as an effective stopgap for cybersecurity programs under development. It is important to note however, that just because you have one of these types of insurance policies doesn't mean you're off the hook from properly protecting your information and assets.

The advice from the previous chapter holds true for this chapter: you cannot consider this portion of your program complete by finishing just these three activities. As with the previous chapter, go back through the balance of the material covered in the chapter to finish the buildout of the governance framework.


## 2.1 Governance Overview

I once thought it was safe to assume everyone understood what governance was; that, however, turned out to be a rather fanciful notion. It is not that most people cannot cite some definition of *governance*; it is they cannot provide practical working examples. Seems odd, right? Try it yourself; in the context of cybersecurity, quickly try to come up with a definition of *governance*. See what I mean? To some, governance includes all the letters of GRC (governance, risk, and compliance); to others it includes just two of the letters of GRC, and so on. At this point in the process, I want you to think only of the "G" in GRC.

So, what exactly is *governance*? For that answer, let us start with the Merriam-Webster dictionary definition: "the way that a city, company, etc., is controlled by the people who run it" (Governance, 2017). In our context, it is how your organization's management controls its cybersecurity program. Note the emphasis on controlling the program, not defending against threats and vulnerabilities through the use of controls. Extending your governance program beyond the outer boundaries of governance will only cause confusion and complicate your efforts to build an appropriate governance foundation.

In my way of thinking, governance refers to independently guided direction of an organization according to its principles and policies. Governance is all about independent oversight of a cybersecurity program to ensure it is performing to your design and fulfilling the requirements of your organization's cybersecurity principles and policies. In my dealings with organizations, I consistently found that the primary missing element in understanding governance was always that of independence. My customers easily understood the rational of independent board members on their board of directors and the need for auditors to be independent, but when it came to independent governance in their cybersecurity programs, it was greeted with skepticism.

> **TIP:** Ensure that separation of duties in your cybersecurity program's oversight policy excludes those involved in the program's daily activities from monitoring and reporting on the program's effectiveness.

I concede that separating those involved in your cybersecurity program's operations from governance roles will not be a popular position for several reasons, not the least of which is the practical limitations of staff size and loss of span of control. I have seen and analyzed many governance programs, and one common observation is lack of proper governance oversight. For example, if the chief information security officer (CISO) of your organization is the one reporting on the integrity, ethics, and overall performance of your organization's cybersecurity program, that practice needs to cease. The CISO, of course, can provide a state of the union overview, but when it comes to providing an independent analysis to the board, it is a poor practice. Unfortunately, this practice is repeated thousands of times annually by CISOs the world over.

I often shudder when I begin a cybersecurity program assessment and see the program's organization chart with a box labeled "governance." Just because it is part of GRC, that does not mean it belongs in the cybersecurity program. I will agree that there are certain supporting activities of governance that belong to the office of the CISO, but those activities need to be appropriate and to align with daily activities. In my last book, _The Manager's Guide to Cybersecurity Law_, I discussed the use of an accountability matrix or RACI (responsible, accountable, consulted, and informed) diagram. The governance activity is perfectly suited for a RACI exercise in assigning legal, human resources, finance, and senior management oversight roles.

> **TIP:** Challenge yourself to go a step further adding an outside party to your cybersecurity program's governance oversite board or committee. This individual should serve as an independent advisor with no stake in your program. Populating your cybersecurity program oversight board with internal staff only goes against the very nature of independent oversight.

## 2.2 Cybersecurity Governance Playbook

I believe that we should keep the definition of governance to its purest form and eliminate many of the remora-like attachments that have latched on to governance programs over the years. For example, I do not define security controls as part of governance; rather, they are part of a control library aligned to a program's countermeasures. It is these attachments that contribute to the many and varied definitions of cybersecurity governance offered today. Developing a governance program is much like a bill going through a congress. To pass a bill, sponsors often add earmarks (pork barrel spending) to the bill in return for votes. Once the bill makes it through committee, however, it has lost its original form and substance. This often happens to a governance program – everyone wants to add his or her something to the program. This goes to the heart of governance program sprawl. A playbook explains a program clearly and succinctly in layman's terms. Once reading the playbook, the reader will have a working understanding of how governance is organization and administered.

Not every cybersecurity program activity requires incorporation within your governance program. Take for instance the activity of risk management. Governance per se has nothing to do with risk management, yet there it is included in many governance programs. You may think this is a fine line, but in the context of pure governance, the line is clear. Your governance program oversees the risk management program, but it stops short of actively participating. Governance requires independence and subsequently can only provide oversight and not be actively involved. I know that I am not alone in this view as evidenced by bill H.R. 5069 – Cybersecurity Systems and Risks Reporting Act that is currently in the House Committee on Financial Services. This bill, an amendment to the Sarbanes-Oxley Act of 2002, if passed, will require companies to have independent cybersecurity systems officers just as they do financial officers (H.R. 5069, 2016). The bill is still alive as of 2019; however, I don't see any movement until after the 2020 elections.

This stop on your journey of creating a cybersecurity program requires you to define a governance foundation. The following is what I consider to be the primary components of cybersecurity program governance:

- **Business Case.** An understanding of the organization's business proposition. Specifying the business case helps ensure that governance aligns with your organization's goals.
- **Stakeholders.** Internal or external groups or individuals whose interests in the organization or cybersecurity program are either direct or indirect. Aligning stakeholders by program outcomes will determine which category your stakeholders align with. You need to know your stakeholders and know them well.
- **Principles.** The foundational rules or values of your cybersecurity program. Policies align to principles. An example of a well-defined principle is "Foster a risk aware and security positive culture." The governance oversight committee is focused on whether you meet that objective, not necessarily how you met that objective.
- **Ethics.** Statements of ethical values required to set the tone and standard of behavior of the cybersecurity program. An example of a well-defined statement of ethics is "We will hold ourselves accountable to comply with applicable laws and regulations."
- **Scope of Governance.** An understanding of who and where to govern is critical; you should have clearly defined boundaries of the organization, constituents, operations, and parties to which the cybersecurity program applies. For example, if the cybersecurity program excludes joint ventures or recovery of data, state it.
- **Oversight.** The heart of governance is oversight, in fact, independent oversight to be exact. The people charged with oversight should not be involved in the daily execution of the activities to protect information and assets.
- **Accountability Model.** The most effective cybersecurity programs involve organizations that hold their employees accountable for their actions. Employees must carry out the mandate of the program's principles and policies ethically and professionally.
- **Decision Rights.** It is critical in a cybersecurity program that the right people make the right decisions. To ensure this occurs, those involved in the program must have the authorization, time, and knowledge to make decisions. The RACI previously discussed can also serve as the basis for a decision model.

- **Ownership Model.** It is difficult to hold someone ultimately accountable for something not owned by them personally. All assets and data should have clearly defined owners.
- **Policies.** Statements describing the rules or practices of behavior, actions, or desired state of the cybersecurity program. An example of a well-defined policy statement would be: "Only recognized and authorized computing equipment will have access to the organization's network and resources."
- **Investment.** Funding of the cybersecurity program which should be commensurate with the value of the organization's assets at risk. Governance is not involved with daily budget management, but rather with the goals of investment.
- **Monitoring.** The continuous monitoring of the program through the systematic collection of key performance measures (KPM) is required to provide the oversight board with insight into compliance with the program principles and policies. KPMs are a set of coherent data measures that are indicative of your organization's cybersecurity program's ability to accomplish its stated goals.

- **Measurement.** Governing effectively requires measuring the effectiveness of the cybersecurity program through KPMs. These need to be easy to understand, meaningful, and actionable. If you cannot take a KPM result and act on it to make a program improvement, it is of little to no value.
- **Reporting.** Effective governance requires transparency through reporting. Governance reporting is different from daily cybersecurity program reporting. Reporting on the cybersecurity program's governance state entails a vastly different audience than daily operational reports.
- **Enforcement.** Consequences are required for violations of the governance program's principles and policies. Organizations cannot govern effectively if there are no consequences (warnings, suspensions, dismissals, etc.) to violations of the organization's principles, ethics, or policies.

> **TIP:** You should document each of the elements mentioned above within a governance playbook. The playbook would describe each activity in terms of inputs, outcomes, and processes to complete, and include the assignment of personnel to the governance program.

The governance oversight board presented in the cybersecurity blueprint uses the governance playbook. Members of the board are responsible for the playbook's upkeep. The data from the playbook will provide valuable input to sections of the cybersecurity program design guide introduced in Chapter 1.

## 2.3 Selecting a Governance Framework

Just as a house requires a sturdy framework to support its walls and roof, a governance program requires a framework to serve as the support structure for building your cybersecurity program. Which framework you choose is just as important as the tools and methods you will use to defend your company against cyberattacks. I have found it best to think about a framework as a conceptual structure that serves as a representation of your cybersecurity program. I want to emphasize the conceptual aspect because at this level you should not be thinking about which security tools, processes, or methods you will use. Doing so places the cart before the horse, and I want you to focus on the bigger governance picture at this point.

Your first important decision before building your cybersecurity program will be to decide which governance framework or model to select. Several good ones are available to choose from, and each is comprehensive and suitable for use as your cybersecurity program governance framework. The following top five most widely used governance frameworks and models are discussed in this chapter:
1. COBIT® 5: Control Objectives for Information and Related Technologies Framework.
2. COSO: Committee of Sponsoring Organizations of the Treadway Commission Internal Control – Integrated Framework.
3. IGRM: Duke University Information Governance Reference Model.
4. ARMA IC-IGM: Information Coalition – Information Governance Model.
5. OCEG: Open Compliance and Ethics Group GRC Capability Model™ 3.0 (Red Book).

As I mentioned earlier, do not become too caught up in whether the term *model* or *framework* is used. Focus on selecting one that makes the most sense to your organization. Table 2-1 provides a high-level side-by-side comparison of these five governance frameworks and models.

**Table 2-1. Governance Framework Comparison**

| Criteria | COBIT® | COSO | IGRM | ARMA IC-IGM | OCEG |
|---|---|---|---|---|---|
| **Membership cost** | Yes | No | No | Yes | Yes |
| **Professional certifications** | Yes | Yes | No | No | Yes |
| **Version** | 5 | 2013 | 3.0 | 3.1 | 3.0 |
| **Members** | 115,000 | 90% of SEC annual filings | 300 | 400 | 60,000 |
| **Format** | Framework | Framework | Model | Model | Model |

| Criteria | COBIT® | COSO | IGRM | ARMA IC-IGM | OCEG |
|---|---|---|---|---|---|
| Circa | 1996 | 1992 | 2014 | 2016 | 2002 |
| Focus | Enterprise IT | Financial controls | Information governance | Information governance | GRC |
| Maturity model | Yes – Process capability model | Yes – ERM maturity model | No | Yes – EIM[3] | Yes – Maturity model for integrated GRC |

My selection and presentation of governance frameworks and models does not constitute an endorsement for anyone. To provide equal billing to each of the frameworks and models I list them in alphabetical order providing an overview of the sponsoring organization, links to learn more, and an analysis where I discuss their strengths, weaknesses, and my bottom-line opinion.

## 2.3.1 COBIT® 5: Framework for Information Technology Governance and Control

The Control Objectives for Information and Related Technologies (COBIT) framework, advertised as a good practices-based framework, is available through the Information Systems Audit and Control Association (ISACA). ISACA, established in 1969, asserts in its literature and website that COBIT is the leading framework for governance and management of enterprise information technology (IT) with 115,000 constituents in 180 countries. You can read all about COBIT 5 at the ISACA website at http://www.isaca.org/cobit/pages/default.aspx.

I first became acquainted with COBIT in 1996 with the introduction of version 1. At that time, COBIT was primarily oriented toward audit controls; however, over 20 years later it has evolved into one of the most robust governance frameworks available. What I particularly like about COBIT is that it is not prescriptive, but it is rather descriptive in that it advocates that companies implement governance and management processes that overarch an entire cybersecurity program. While I will not be able to cover the entirety of COBIT 5 due to its depth and breadth, I will focus on the portions of COBIT 5 that address security directly. COBIT addresses governance holistically, emphasizing program management, managing the change of the program, and continuously improving the program.

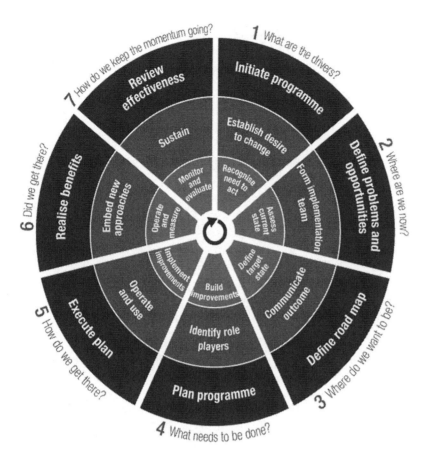

● **Programme management**
(outer ring)

● **Change enablement**
(middle ring)

● **Continual improvement life cycle**
(inner ring)

*Figure 2-1. ISACA COBIT 5 Implementation Sphere. (Diagram has been provided with authorization of ISACA.)*

Although not originally written for cybersecurity, many of COBIT's principles, enablers, and practices are wholly applicable to building a cybersecurity program. To bridge the gap in addressing cybersecurity, COBIT released a professional guide in 2012 called *COBIT 5 for Information Security*. In previous years, it offered the COBIT Security Baseline, security survival kits, and mapping to security standards such as ISO 27001. COBIT 5 for Information Security builds on the COBIT 5 framework to provide practical advice and guidance on implementing information security within an organization. This professional guide provides the same basic guidance as the COBIT 5 framework with the main difference being its view through the lens of information security. The following will provide you with an understanding of the primary COBIT 5 framework components covered in the information security professional guide:

- Principles: Guidance of the type of conduct your cybersecurity program should adhere to and exhibit. COBIT defines five minimum principles to form the foundation of your governance program (ISACA, 2012).
    1. Meeting Stakeholder Needs: This principle is all about aligning the governance program with the needs and goals of the organization.

2.  Covering the Enterprise End-to-End: This principle emphasizes that governance is not a one off, but rather applies to the whole of the organization. Governance should not stop at security technology but include all business functions.
3.  Applying a Single Integrated Framework: In this principle, COBIT recognizes that it must interact with cybersecurity frameworks and subsequently, advises that COBIT serve as the overarching governance framework.
4.  Enabling a Holistic Approach: The focus of this principle is the promotion of efficient and effective governance with interdependent enablers.
5.  Separating Governance from Management: The last principle makes the strong case for separating management from governance; it is all about independent oversight.

- Enablers: COBIT 5 provides guidance on the factors that will influence whether your cybersecurity program will be successful or not. To accomplish this, COBIT 5 defines seven interconnected enablers (ISACA, 2012):
  1.  Principles, Policies, and Frameworks: Governance strategy to drive a desired behavior for managing risk and security.
  2.  Processes: An organized set of practices and activates to achieve a set of outcomes of information and asset protection.
  3.  Organizational Structures: Key risk and security decision making entities within the organization.
  4.  Culture, Ethics, and Behavior: Individual and organizational adoption of ethics, correct behaviors, and a culture of security.
  5.  Information: Protection, and Recoverability of Organizational Information.
  6.  Services, Infrastructure, and Applications: Security services and products used to protect information and assets.
  7.  People, Skills and Competencies: Competency training, certifications, and roles and responsibilities to correctly complete security processes and activities.

What I like about the COBIT 5 for Information Security guide is that it builds on these enablers with direction in:

- Initiative Alignment: Considerations on implementing information security as a life cycle considering the security context of the organization beginning with addressing the organization's existing information and asset protection pain points.
- Connection to other Frameworks, Models and Standards: Designed as an umbrella framework, COBIT 5 aligns to virtually any cybersecurity standard that would address the specifics of your organization's industry, technology and risk profile.
- Detailed Guidance: Advice on deploying enablers within the organization organized and numbered as governance controls.

Table 2-2 presents the sections of COBIT 5 that provide the most direct guidance to cybersecurity. This guidance is located in four control areas located within the COBIT 5 process reference model.

**Table 2-2. COBIT 5 Security Practices**

| ID | Process Enabler | Area | Domain | Practices | Goals | Metrics | Activities |
|---|---|---|---|---|---|---|---|
| AP012 | Manage risk | Management | Align, plan, and organize | 6 | 2 | 2 | 6 |
| AP013 | Manage security | Management | Align, plan, and organize | 3 | 3 | 8 | 19 |
| DSS04 | Manage continuity | Management | Deliver, service, and support | 8 | 1 | 3 | 8 |
| DSS05 | Manager security services | Management | Deliver, service, and support | 7 | 5 | 11 | 49 |
| 4 | | | | 24 | 11 | 24 | 82 |

## *Analysis*

- **Strengths:** COBIT is an excellent governance framework for cybersecurity programs when coupled with ISO or NIST standards. It provides a comprehensive structure and includes a rich set of tools for implementing metrics, defining roles and responsibilities, and establishing maturity tiers and risk management. There is no shortage of security practitioners with COBIT experience.
- **Weaknesses:** COBIT requires a substantial investment in time to become proficient with the materials as well as to understand the framework. COBIT's complexity is exemplified in its dozens of IT processes, hundreds of control objectives, and many detailed metrics. I find that much of the guidance provided by COBIT is generic, requiring customization to suit the needs of each organization.
- **Bottom line:** COBIT can easily serve as a comprehensive foundation for your cybersecurity governance program. You will still need to connect COBIT to a security-specific framework to achieve its full value in the context of cybersecurity. COBIT should be part of any organization's evaluation of a governance framework. Access to COBIT does come with a cost; however, the cost is minimal and well worth the investment. A wealth of materials is available from ISACA, keeping you from reinventing the wheel and allowing you to streamline your approach to governance. You must commit the time and effort to COBIT to extract all its benefits. For more information go to: https://www.isaca.org/COBIT/Pages/info-sec.aspx.

## 2.3.2 COSO 2013 Internal Control – Integrated Framework

The Committee of Sponsoring Organizations of the Treadway Commission (COSO) is a joint initiative of five private sector organizations consisting of:

- Institute of Management Accountants (IMA)
- American Accounting Association (AAA)
- American Institute of Certified Public Accountants (AICPA)
- Institute of Internal Auditors (IIA)
- Financial Executives International (FEI)

Formed in 1985, COSO emerged to support the findings of the National Commission on Fraudulent Financial Reporting, also known as the Treadway Commission (IMA, 2017). The commission was established to create a standardized way to protect financial records through a set of uniform controls. In 1992, COSO released a four-volume report entitled *Internal Control – Integrated Framework*. As a cybersecurity professional, you need to understand the concept of controls as a process originated from COSO. (The 1992 version was retired in 2014; the 2013 version is the most current release of the framework.) More information is available at the COSO website, https://www.coso.org/Pages/default.aspx

COSO has been widely adopted as a framework for internal controls; in fact, in 2015 the consulting firm Protiviti reported that 95% of US Securities and Exchange Commission (SEC) filings they analyzed used some version of COSO as their control framework (DeLoach, 2015). The majority of companies use the 2013 COSO internal control framework, although a good number still use the 1992 version owing to its resiliency as a control framework (Whitehouse, 2015).

COSO represents its Internal Control – Integrated Framework by means of a three-sided interconnected cube, the "COSO Cube." (See Figure 2-2.). The top of the cube presents three *objectives*: operations, reporting, and compliance. The front face of the cube presents five framework *components*: control environment, risk assessment, control activities, information and communication, and monitoring activities. The right-facing side of the cube presents four *subjects* of control applicability: entity level, division, operating unit, and function.

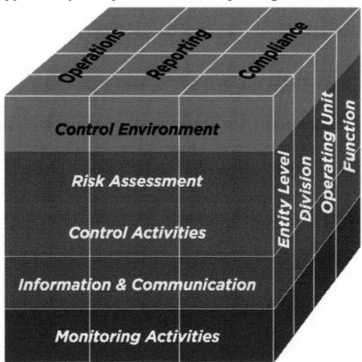

*Figure 2-2. COSO Cube. (Copyright ©2013, Committee of Sponsoring Organizations of the Treadway Commission (COSO). Used by permission.)*

The top of the cube represents an organization's objectives consisting of:

- Operations: Supporting operational processes and activities to ensure accomplishment of objectives.
- Reporting: Inclusive and transparent reporting of control effectiveness based on a need to know basis.
- Compliance: Assurance of adherence to legal and regulatory statutes.

The COSO objectives ensure a disciplined approach to evaluate and improve the effectiveness of an organization's governance, risk and compliance activities.

The front of the cube defines the essential components of control focus, supported by defining principles, and a robust number of points of focus consisting of:

- Control Environment: This component is where the theme or tone of the organization's control environment is set. The environment by which controls exist must be above reproach and operate with complete integrity void of influence. The component specifies the organization's values, ethics, and authority from the board of directors, to management, to employees. This component's principles consist of the following:
  - Adopt ethical values.
  - Prescribe an independent board of directors.
  - Ensure appropriate authorities and responsibilities.
  - Commit to attract competent personnel.
  - Instill individual accountability.
- Risk Assessment: This component addresses assessing and managing internal and external risk. Clearly, defining risk treatment objectives and focusing on relevant risks is an emphasis. This component's principles consist of the following:
  - Publish clarity of objectives.
  - Analyze risks as a basis for determining risks relating to objectives.
  - Consider the potential for fraud.
  - Identify and asses change.
- Control Activities: This component contains the policies and procedures that direct the activities of controls. Controls at all levels of the organization must be in pursuit of risk reduction and management. Controls are processes consisting of definitions, approvals, performance monitoring, and protection of assets. This component's principles consist of the following:
  - Select controls that contribute to risk mitigation.
  - Develop control activities over technology.
  - Adopt policies that establish what is expected.
- Information and Communication: This component addresses the creation and dissemination of information pertaining to operational, financial, and compliance aspects of a program. The flow of information at all levels of the organization is what drives a business and provides a basis to make informed management decisions. Information must flow to applicable internal and external entities. This component's principles consist of the following:
  - Obtain and disseminate relevant information.

- o Communicate information necessary to support controls.
- o Communicate with external parties.
- Monitoring Activities: This component defines the monitoring of internal controls to assess their effectiveness, performance, and quality. Internal control deficiencies detected are to be reported and corrective actions taken. This component's principles consist of the following:
  - o Use separate and ongoing evaluations of controls.
  - o Evaluate and communicate control deficiencies.

On the right side of the cube are subjects that accommodate an organization's structural breakdown in which to apply controls:
- Entity Level: The organization as a whole – generally a company, educational institution, government agency, etc.
- Division: The first level of organizational division – generally a subsidiary, school, business unit, etc.
- Operating Unit: A standalone unit that provides a specific operation such as sales, marketing, or manufacturing.
- Function: A discrete activity or function that provides a work product. For example, telemarketing would be a function within the sales operating unit.

Using General Motors Corporation (GM) as an example of this subject hierarchy, GM would be the entity, Cadillac would be the division, manufacturing would be the operating unit, and body painting would be the function. As you can see, controls would exist at each subject level; this separation allows you to focus on defining controls at a level that is not so overwhelming.

In case you are wondering why I have not touched on the COSO Enterprise Risk Management (ERM) Framework, I cover that in Chapter 4.

## *Analysis*
- **Strengths:** COSO provides a basis to implement controls within any type of business within any type of industry at any level of granularity. Controls are risk-based allowing layering of controls within an organization to address the greatest risk. COSO is the framework of choice of many auditors and boards of directors and can serve as an excellent platform of governance when combined with ISO or NIST. COSO provides guidance on how to deploy controls regardless of origin; this guidance is universally missing in many frameworks.
- **Weaknesses:** COSO is widely used as a framework for governance of financial systems and controls; however, it is not widely adopted within the context of cybersecurity. The issue with adoption within cybersecurity practices is due in part to the "not invented here" mentality, meaning that if it was not written for security, then it could not be very good for security. I have also seen that cybersecurity practitioners do not have much respect for the financial controls side of their organizations and look down on its efforts. You also have a situation where the finance side of the organization grew up on COSO

and the IT side of the organization grew up on ISO and NIST, making it hard for either party to move to something else.

- **Bottom line:** I suggest that you strip away any blinders you may have and take a fresh look at COSO. Using COSO as a governance framework does not mean you walk away from your conventional cybersecurity control approach, only that you consider using the COSO framework to organize your controls. Using an integrated approach reduces the time required to map the security controls used to protect financial systems with the monitoring and reporting requirements of COSO. I wish to bring your attention to an excellent research report commissioned by COSO in 2015 titled *COSO in the Cyber Age*. In this report, the authors Galligan and Rau (2015) do a great job in connecting the dots of using COSO in the context of cybersecurity. Read the full report at: https://www.coso.org/documents/COSO%20in%20the%20Cyber%20Age_FULL_r11.pdf.

> **TIP:** Leverage COSO's 1st (Risk Owners), 2nd (Risk, Control and Compliance), and 3rd (Internal Auditing) Lines of Defense approach with your own defense-in-depth approach. COSO's defensive lines will provide organization structure when defining a defense-in-depth model for your cybersecurity program.

## 2.3.3 Information Governance Reference Model (IGRM)

The Information Governance Reference Model (IGRM), launched in 2014 as an extension of Duke University's Electronic Discovery Reference Model (EDRM) (Colgan, 2014) is not as widely known as the other governance frameworks I cover; however, it does show promise. Its genesis results from many of the over 300 users of Duke's EDRM model who wanted to extend the model to include security and privacy. The university, not wanting to distract from the EDRM, created the IGRM. Although in name and appearance IGRM seems focused on information governance, I do believe its structure is applicable to the whole of a cybersecurity program. I found recently an increase in my university clients wanting to evaluate IGRM. Also, the IGRM is beginning to gain some traction outside of academia. I have heard colleagues mention they are now looking at Duke's model in comparison to other well-known models. (See Figure 2-3.) Learn more about IGRM at Duke's EDRM website at http://www.edrm.net/frameworks-and-standards/information-governance-reference-model/.

Reasons for preferring this model range from its clean simplistic design to its melding of information governance with corporate governance. The model presents as a sphere with stakeholders establishing an outer marker, an outer ring of interoperating processes, and a core comprised of an information life cycle (EDRM, 2017).

- The stakeholders: The model seeks to overcome a major challenge of information management, namely, that most information management efforts are crippled by insufficient collaboration among key stakeholders. The model groups stakeholders into three categories:

- o Business – users who need information to operate the organization.
- o IT departments – people who must implement the mechanics of information management.
- o Legal, risk, and regulatory departments – people who understand the organization's duty to preserve information beyond its immediate business value.

This top-level view describes the stakeholder's role in information management with an emphasis on true information management achieved through collaboration with other groups across the enterprise. Duke provides subsidiary diagrams for additional granularity and perspective.

- The outer ring: Starting from the outside of the diagram, successful information management is about conceiving a complex set of interoperable processes and implementing the procedures and structural elements to put them into practice. It requires:
  - o An understanding of the business imperatives of the enterprise.
  - o Knowledge of the appropriate tools and infrastructure for managing information.
  - o Sensitivity to the legal and regulatory obligations with which the enterprise must comply.
- The center: In the center of the model is a workflow, or life cycle diagram, to illustrate the fact that information management is important at all stages of the information life cycle – from its creation through its ultimate disposition.

# Information Governance Reference Model (IGRM)

Linking duty + value to information asset = efficient, effective management

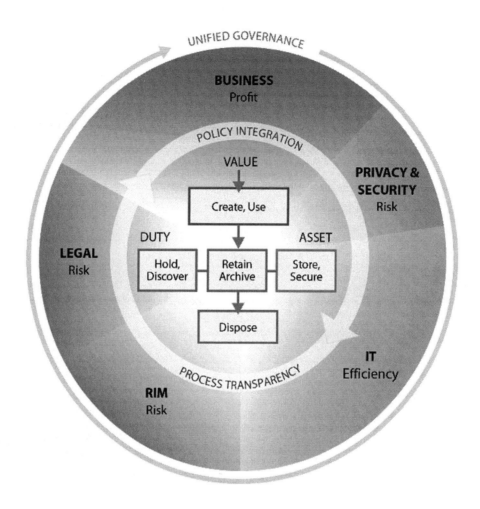

Figure 2-3. Information Governance Reference Model, © 2012, v3.0. EDRM (edrm.net), Used by permission.

**Duty:** Legal obligation for specific information

**Value:** Utility or business purpose of specific information

**Asset:** Specific container of information

## *Analysis*

- **Strengths:** The IGRM is available as a tool for structuring a governance program using information governance as the focal point. This may be ideal for those organizations that lean toward structuring their cybersecurity program around information assurance or protection. What I particularly like about the framework is its promotion of a cross-functional dialog with executives of an organization. The model's focus on stakeholders ensures a unified governance approach. This model is a favorite with legal and record management departments because of its origin in the e-discovery domain as well as alignment to the Association of Records Managers and Archivers (ARMA) International's Generally Accepted Recordkeeping Principles (GARP®). GARP is a common set of principles that describe the conditions under which business records and related information should be maintained.

- **Weaknesses:** IGRM is not widely known outside of academia and has a small user community. Finding security practitioners familiar with the model may prove challenging. Little material exists to provide detail or implementation guidance about the model.
- **Bottom line:** IGRM offers a nice governance model alternative for small to medium size companies that are looking for sound guidance without too much detail. Although the model lacks detail, its structure and naming conventions allow you to match content from ISO or NIST to fill the void. The emphasis on legal and information life cycle management makes the model a great fit for data breach programs.

## 2.3.4 ARMA – Information Coalition – Information Governance Model

The Information Coalition (IC) is a community-oriented organization chartered to drive best practices of enterprise information. The coalition seeks to differentiate itself from other governance organizations stipulating it is neither a consulting company nor an association, but a coalition of the collective knowledge of its community of members. Founded in 2016, IC is one of the newer entries in the governance framework/model arena with an estimated 400 members. Although its focus presents as solely information governance, I feel its model is applicable to several applications – cybersecurity governance to name one. On October 9, 2018, Association of Records Managers and Administrators International (ARMA) merged with the Information Coalition (2018, ARMA). You can learn more about IC at its website, https://infocoalition.com/.

The IC refers to its Information Governance Model (IGM) as a framework from which to build a comprehensive information governance program. Although the drift between model and framework wording can be a little confusing, their model does nonetheless provide a nice framework and organizational construct to ensure that your governance foundation is complete. It is my opinion that its model is a great example of an architectural blueprint with an embedded framework. The IC was formerly associated with the management consulting company Optismo with senior members of both companies working between both organizations.

The design of IC's model lends itself for use as an assessment and benchmarking tool. With this tool, organizations can assess and measure themselves over time against two categories of business and technology as well as six subcategories. Within each of the subcategories are entities, shown white in Figure 2-4 below.

- Business subcategories:
  - Authorities – Clearly defining the roles and stakeholders that should be a part of a governance program.
  - Supports – Supports defined to underlay governance efforts to ensure ongoing, sustainable success.
  - Processes – Processes to ensure that governance efforts are actionable.
- Technology subcategories:
  - Capabilities – Information life cycle beginning with creation through to disposal.
  - Structures – Definition of technology structures to taxonomic structures to create a governance architecture.
  - Infrastructure – Technology alignment.

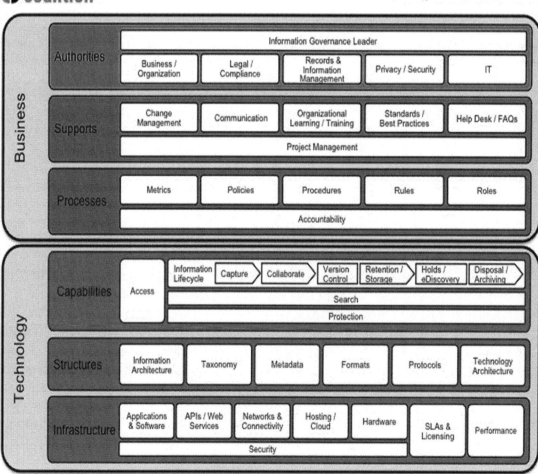

*Figure 2-4. Information Governance Model. (By Information Coalition, licensed under CC BY 4.0)*

The IC has done a great job in creating a governance architectural blueprint with an embedded framework. The blueprint portion includes the categories and subcategories (colored areas), whereas the entities (in white) serve as the governance framework. In 2016, when members voted on topical areas for growth, information security drew the second highest votes at 79%.

### Analysis

- **Strengths:** The Information Governance Model in Figure 2-4 is a well-articulated blueprint with an embedded framework that by design aligns business with technology. I believe the maturity of the model reflects the real-world perspective that the Optismo partnership brings to the organization. A rich set of documentation is available to members to assist in their implementation. The Creative Commons Attribution-NonCommercial-NoDerivitives 4.0 licensing of the model makes adopting it within an organization straightforward.

- **Weaknesses:** The current model does not cover information security to a point where it could be considered for both cybersecurity and governance. However, I expect that to change to reflect the consensus of its members. Some of the references to the model as a framework can be a little confusing. As with other governance models, you can easily map ISO or NIST to the model.

- **Bottom line:** The depiction of governance in this model comes closest to what I believe is a proper blueprint and framework of governance. The structure and licensing make it easily extensible to accommodate a complete cybersecurity program. The IC does offer a nice set of high-level documents as a free member, although there is a cost to access the rich content. However, if the free content is a harbinger of the paid content, you should not be disappointed.

## 2.3.5 OCEG GRC Capability Model™ 3.0 (Red Book)

The Open Compliance and Ethics Group (OCEG), founded in 2002, is a nonprofit think tank with 60,000 members. Its focus is to inform, empower, and certify its members in the disciplines of governance, risk, and compliance. Michael Rasmussen, one of the founders of OCEG, is widely acknowledged as the one who coined the term *GRC* while he was an analyst with Forrester (Marks, 2015). The OCEG publishes the *Red Book* to help organizations plan, assess, and improve their GRC capabilities. The *Red Book* approaches GRC in a mature manner, changing old or wrong behaviors of governance. After reviewing the *Red Book* and understanding that it evolved through the help of over 100 experts, I find its approach to be pragmatic and effective. You can read more about the OCEG and its GRC Capability Model at the OCEG website at http://www.oceg.org/about/.

The *Red Book* has four main components that outline an iterative improvement process to achieve principled performance. Principled performance is OCEG's point of view and approach to business to help achieve governance objectives. While a sequence is implied, components operate concurrently (OCEG, 2015).

- Learn: Examine and analyze context, culture, and stakeholders to learn what the organization needs to know to establish and support objectives and strategies.
  - L1 External Context: Consider the external business context in which the organization operates.
  - L2 Internal Context: Consider the internal business context in which the organization operates.
  - L3 Culture: Understand existing culture, organizational climate, and individual mindsets concerning governance, assurance, compliance, and risk.
  - L4 Stakeholders: Ensure stakeholders understand expectations and requirements that may affect the organization.
- Align: Align performance, risk and compliance objectives, strategies, decision-making criteria, actions, and controls with the context, culture, and stakeholder requirements.
  - A1 Direction: Provide clear mission, vision, and value statements.
  - A2 Objectives: Establish a set of measurable objectives that are consistent with decision-making criteria.
  - A3 Identification: Identify forces that may cause opportunities or threats to achievement of objectives.
  - A4 Assessment: Analyze approach to address opportunities and threats.
  - A5 Design: Develop strategic and tactical plans to achieve the objectives.
- Perform: Address threats, opportunities, and requirements by encouraging desired conduct and events, and preventing what is undesired, through the application of proactive, detective, and responsive actions and controls.
  - P1 Controls: Establish a mix of management, process, human capital, technology, information, and physical actions and controls that serve governance, management, and assurance needs.
  - P2 Policies: Implement policies and associated procedures to address opportunities, threats, and requirements and set clear expectations of conduct for the governing authority, management, the workforce, and the extended enterprise.
  - P3 Communication: Deliver and receive relevant, reliable, and timely information to the right audiences.
  - P4 Education: Educate the governing authority, management, and the workforce.
  - P5 Incentives: Implement incentives that motivate desired conduct and recognize those who contribute.
  - P6 Notification: Report progress toward objectives, and the actual or potential occurrence of undesirable and desirable conduct, conditions, and events.
  - P7 Inquiry: Analyze data and seek input about progress towards objectives, and the existence of undesirable conduct, conditions and events.
  - P8 Response: Execute responses to identified or suspected undesirable conduct, conditions, events, or weaknesses in capabilities.
- Review: Conduct activities to monitor and improve design and operating effectiveness of all actions and controls, including their continued alignment to objectives and strategies.
  - R1 Monitoring: Motivate desired conduct and recognize those who contribute.

- R2 Assurance: Report progress toward objectives, and the actual or potential occurrence of undesirable and desirable conduct, conditions, and events.
- R3 Improvement: Review information from periodic evaluations, detective and responsive actions and controls, monitoring, and assurance, to identify opportunities for capability.

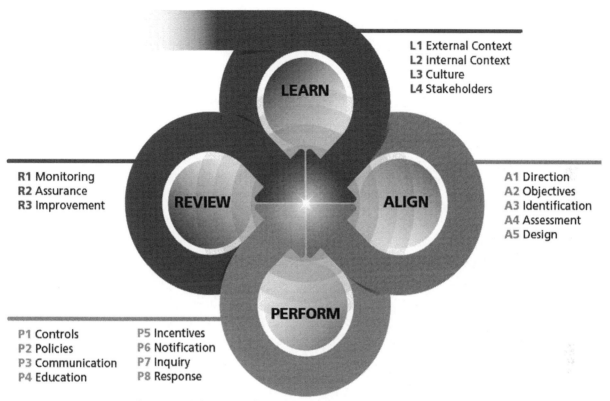

L1 External Context
L2 Internal Context
L3 Culture
L4 Stakeholders

A1 Direction
A2 Objectives
A3 Identification
A4 Assessment
A5 Design

R1 Monitoring
R2 Assurance
R3 Improvement

P1 Controls    P5 Incentives
P2 Policies    P6 Notification
P3 Communication    P7 Inquiry
P4 Education    P8 Response

*Figure 2-5. OCEG GRC Capability Model. (Copyright ©2015, OCEG. Permission by OCEG is required for reproduction and/or use of material.)*

## *Analysis*

- **Strengths:** OCEG licenses the *Red Book* under Creative Commons Attribution, which makes it easier to use than some other approaches as it is open source and subsequently free from licensing costs. Anyone may use and build upon the Red Book with open source expansions. The *Red Book* is also comprehensive and should suit any governance program need. Its extensibility in the areas of risk and compliance allows growth in other parts of a cybersecurity program.
- **Weaknesses:** The *Red Book* is not presently included in the Unified Compliance Framework (UCF), which since 2004 has served as the control mapping framework of record for the cybersecurity industry. Virtually all other security standards and regulations you could ever require are included in the UCF. A spreadsheet of controls is

available for purchase online and you may use a CSV (Comma Separated Value) import into an existing program control database or the UCF. To learn more about UCF go to: https://www.unifiedcompliance.com/. I am hard pressed to find weaknesses in the Red Book.

- **Bottom line:** The OCEG offers a companion book called the *Burgundy Book*, which contains GRC assessment tools. These tools provide the most comprehensive set of objectives and controls that I have seen associated with a GRC model. Basic membership is free and does afford you a decent amount of access to OCEG resources. An all access pass provides access to a wealth of information including guides, eBooks, standards, illustrations, training, and more. If you are serious about governance and seek an enterprise class approach, you need to consider the *Red Book*.

**TIP:** If you are not able to find one of the frameworks or models that meets your needs, I suggest creating a hybrid framework comprised of the best of the ones previously presented.

## 2.4    Governance Oversight Board

The governance oversight board is responsible to oversee the cybersecurity program in areas such as business alignment, risk strategy, program structure, positioning within the organization, financial practices, and regulatory compliance. Members of the board should define the following:

- An understandable governance structure.
- The process of oversight necessary to ensure transparency of cybersecurity operations.
- The operating budget the cybersecurity program requires to operate effectively.
- The level of enforcement the cybersecurity program should pursue.
- The roles and responsibility of the CISO.
- Incentives to cybersecurity program staff.
- Performance objectives of the cybersecurity program.
- Clear decision rights of cybersecurity program personnel.
- Risk tolerances of the organization.
- Legal and regulatory requirements.
- Ethical boundaries and principles of program personnel.
- Board reporting cadence and detail.

## 2.5  Cybersecurity Policy Model

Your cybersecurity program will require a set of policies that define what it means to your organization to achieve a state of security. Policies direct the behavior of users toward assets and information outlining the boundaries of their responsibility in protecting information. Policies can only be expected to be followed if they are enforced for everyone equally. Policies are important because they drive investments in cybersecurity technology. For example, if a policy is not enforceable, then it would not make sense to invest hundreds of thousands of dollars on enforcement technology.

In my own practice, I limit policies to concise and descriptive policy statements. The more text you use in writing a policy, the more policies may be left open to interpretations that you did not intend. I have reviewed hundreds of cybersecurity policy manuals, and it never ceases to amaze me when I see a 100-page plus policy manual. Such behemoths are virtually impossible to enforce and create a maintenance nightmare.

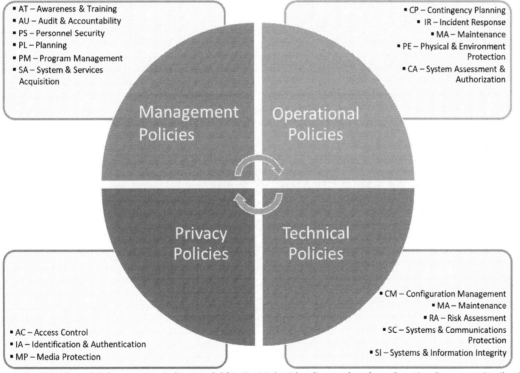

*Figure 2-6. NIST Aligned Cybersecurity Policy Model (By Tari Schreider, licensed under a Creative Commons Attribution-NonCommercial-NoDerivatives 4.0 International License)*

Policies for the most part should be static requiring little change even if your environment or technology changes. Figure 2-6 shows an organizational model of aligning cybersecurity policies to NIST SP 800-53 control families.

- **Management policies:** These policies define the structure of the cybersecurity program, direct and train personnel covered by the program, provide for the planning of organizational cybersecurity, acquisition of technology and development of applications, and ensure the program adheres to audit guidelines.
- **Operational policies:** These policies require an operation or service to protect assets and information including responding to cyberattacks and IT disruptions and securing the data center from damage or interruptions. They also cover the certification and accreditation of the cybersecurity program and third-party providers.
- **Technical policies:** These policies apply technical practices to secure assets and information, identify and address risk, provide boundary protection, encrypt information, and secure all aspects networking.
- **Privacy polices:** These policies ensure the privacy of information through access control and authentication and security of media throughout its life cycle.

Using the above cybersecurity policy model as your guide, you can restrict your policies to less than 20 policy categories. Avoid using NIST or ISO and creating a policy for every single control.

TIP: Organize policies by audience (management, user, cybersecurity personnel, contractors, etc.) on a need-to-know basis to reduce policy maintenance, training, and distribution efforts.

> **Did You Know?**
>
> According to a survey by ClubCISO of 56 CISOs, 53% of reported that their security policies don't exist or are ineffective. ClubCISO is a private members' forum for European information security leaders working in public and private sector organizations.
>
> *When was the last time you stress tested your InfoSec policies?*
>
> **Source:**
> http://www2.company85.com/clubciso-report-2019

## 2.5.1 Cybersecurity Policy Management

Policies become one of the more critical aspects of a governance program. Policies ensure that everyone in the organization, including all those accessing organization information and assets, abide by a set of rules and practices. Having strong, effective policies is the first layer of defense in a cybersecurity program. Many excellent books and programs have been written on cybersecurity policies; thus, I do not intend to cover what so many others have already covered. My focus is on policy management. If you need actual policies, I suggest you check out the SANS Information Security Policy Templates at https://www.sans.org/security-resources/policies/. Here you can access a robust set of cybersecurity policies on which to model your own. If that is not enough, Google cybersecurity policies and hundreds of policy manuals will appear from many organizations.

Managing the lifecycle of cybersecurity policies is what ensures you have the most current, most effective policy in place always. In addition, it ensures that you have the right policy directed at the right audience. You can manage your policies manually with spreadsheets or use an automated policy management solution. Effectively managing your policies can help avoid poor audit and assessment scores, missed opportunities to close a security gap, or the inability to take an enforcement action. The following are some of the moving parts of policy management:

- **Policy writing:** Make sure that policies have a uniform look and feel, are not too specific, and comply with generally accepted policy frameworks and standards. Details of safeguards should reside in procedures and processes, not in policies, in order to reduce the potential for policy revisions.

- **Change management:** As your environment changes, so will policies. Tracking the "adds, moves, deletes, and changes" of text is critical to ensure the most current policy is in force.

- **Acceptance and training tracking:** Tracking policy training and acknowledgements of reading and accepting the policy are essential to the integrity of cybersecurity policies. This is where automation excels.

- **Policy repository:** Most people consider their policy manual table of contents as their policy inventory and repository. However, that approach leaves little room to assign attributes on policy categories, audience, control mapping, and other important associations to a policy.

- **Control mapping:** Policies require enforcement mechanisms and unless they are mapped to specific controls, it is difficult to identify what those mechanisms entail.

- **Compliance mapping:** Some policies are in support of, or are required specifically for, certain laws and regulations. Identifying which policies apply to which statutes is critical.

- **Reporting:** Reporting is a key aspect of policy mapping. Many times, you will need to report on policies through various optics that without a reporting mechanism you will be unable to fulfill.

- **Policy review and approval tracking:** Policies require a lot of review and more importantly, a lot of signoff. Automating this process will save you many hours of effort and time.

> **TIP**: First, try to manage your policies using Microsoft's SharePoint or another form of content management software already in place. Any solution for product workflow automation, content inventory, scheduling, and security will suffice. It is always better to use something you have before purchasing another product.

If this leads you toward finding an automated solution, I have covered it in the next section.

### 2.5.2 Cybersecurity Policy Management Software

The time and effort involved in manually managing cybersecurity policies makes implementing an automated solution attractive. Whether you are a small, medium, or large organization there is a solution tailored just for you. Automation tools have many different features. They range from simply providing boilerplate policies you may customize, to integrating policies on network devices, to monitoring and reporting on violations. It is important to note the more feature-rich the product, the more difficult it will be to implement. Also, remember, we are talking about governance and not network security or defense-in-depth technology; so, the level of policy software we are focused on is the development and management of the policy itself and not applying policies to firewalls, intrusion detection systems, etc. A comprehensive list of policy management software is in Appendix A.

## 2.6   Governance, Risk, and Compliance (GRC) Software

By now, you should have reached the conclusion that building a governance program involves many moving parts and juggling all of them could prove to be overwhelming. Others have come to that same realization and sought out ways to automate their GRC program. Enough others, in fact, that an entire industry was born. This industry, known as eGRC (electronic GRC) had an estimated market size of $19.42 billion in 2016 and is expected to grow to $38 billion by 2021, at a compound annual growth rate (CAGR) of 14.4% (MarketsandMarkets, 2016). I mentioned at the beginning that I was going to focus on the "G" of GRC in this chapter; however, I am not aware of any G-rated (only) software. You will have to accept that the solution you acquire will likely also include modules for risk management and compliance. You will need these for the other capabilities of your cybersecurity program.

I wanted to see just how many eGRC products were available, so I went to my go-to website http://www.capterra.com. Capterra is a popular free service which allows you to search over 400 categories of software. Using this service, I searched on GRC-related terms and found nearly 175 products to choose in the following categories:
* Compliance – 51.
* Governance – 8.
* GRC products – 22.
* Policy – 40.
* Risk – 52.

This site should certainly be in your browser bookmarks, as you will find use for it in searching many other cybersecurity software categories such as network security and incident management.

The GRC software market is like an arms race, with feature advantage changing almost daily. I suggest that you view a list of current versions of a Gartner Magic Quadrants (Gartner, 2017) for the security category you are seeking, after which you can search for the products listed in

Capterra, at no charge. Many of the vendors of favorably positioned GRC products that you are looking for will provide a free copy of the Magic Quadrant on their website.

For help in selecting the best GRC product for your purposes, I recommend the article "Criteria and Methodology for GRC Platform Selection" (Singh & Lija, 2010). Although written a few years ago, it is as valid and comprehensive today as it was when it first appeared in the *ISACA Journal*. A comprehensive list of GRC management software is in Appendix A.

## 2.7   Key Cybersecurity Program Management Disciplines

There are certain key cybersecurity program management disciplines that I commonly find missing during my assessment engagements. Each of these disciplines directly relates to governance, that without which your program may not reach its full potential or operate as intended. Ignoring these disciplines can lead to financial mismanagement, poorly managed projects, and inappropriate audit follow up.

- **Budget management:** Cybersecurity programs require investment, and management expects those investments will be properly managed. You must manage the budget of your cybersecurity program correctly if you expect to receive future funding. You will need to demonstrate that you are fiscally responsible for capital (CapEx) and operational (OpEx) expenses. CapEx is the monies you receive to make large onetime purchases of cybersecurity technologies, and OpEx is monies used for ongoing costs of operating the program. I have found that it is effective to show investments in cybersecurity from a seat perspective. For example, the cost of anti-malware is $2.49 per month per seat. A seat equates to a computing device whether fixed or stationary. I like this approach because it is easy to for management to calculate and understand.

- **Procurement:** One of the areas of greatest waste I have seen in cybersecurity programs is in organizations paying too much for cybersecurity technologies and services. Vendors typically have the upper hand in negotiations because they do this for a living. If you ask the people around you on an airplane what they paid for their plane ticket, you will hear many different prices. Cybersecurity technology is no different. I have

> **Did You Know?**
>
> The fastest growing IT security budgets are from Asia-Pacific with 15% dominated by India and China. On average, the United States is rising by 5.1%. Over the last 5 years, there has been an incredible rise in the security budget makes it very clear that the larger the organization, the greater the spending on security. Businesses are now spending a higher percentage of their IT budgets on security. An average of 11% is being spent by larger organizations of their IT budget on security, whereas the smaller businesses spend nearly 15% on security.
>
> *What are you spending on your cybersecurity program?*
>
> **Source:**
> https://wesecureapp.com/2019/03/13/planning-your-2019-cyber-security-budget-a-how-to-guide/

negotiated hundreds of contracts and have identified the following key negotiation points to save money:

- **Reference discount:** Ask for financial consideration if you agree to become a reference or appear in a product testimonial. The vendor's marketing department often has a budget for subsidizing new customers who agree to be references. If you are converting from another product and are willing to openly discuss the reasons, you have hit the jackpot in discounts.
- **Pilot customer discount:** The largest discounts can be had if you agree to become a pilot customer of an emerging cybersecurity technology. While there is certain downside to this approach, particularly in product stability, the reward could be substantial.
- **Purchasing timing:** Knowing when to purchase is critical; the best time is at the end of the vendor's fiscal year, followed by their halfway point, and then at the end of a quarter.
- **Ask for free floor mats:** Many technologies and services have multiple chargeable options that cost the vendor next to nothing to include in a deal. Know what these options are and ask for them.
- **Best and finale:** If you go the route of a request for proposal (RFP) and have already evaluated responses, issue a best and final price request to the technology or service finalists.
- **Hold your cards close to your vest:** Do not appear to be in a hurry, and do not share your budget or when you intend to make a purchase. Also, subtly let the vendor know that its product does not meet all your needs.
- **Know the numbers:** You should be intimate with the CapEx and OpEx of the technology you are evaluating, the cost of providing or developing the service in house, and what the return on investment would be over three years. You will not be able to effectively negotiate without a firm command of the numbers.

Following these negotiating points has saved my customers up to 60% on the list cost of cybersecurity technologies. On average, you should expect 20-30% for the most part.

- **Project management:** A little-known fact I have come to realize during my tenure as a cybersecurity expert, is that general project managers fail miserably when assigned to cybersecurity projects. The technology, methods, and practices are so different from what they are used to that they are unable to understand the nuances of a cybersecurity project. Project managers are also heavily involved in quality assurance and placing someone without cybersecurity experience in that role is ineffective. These reasons alone are why you will see in specifications that project managers assigned to cybersecurity projects need to have cybersecurity experience. The Project Management Institute – as well as other certification bodies – has created specialized security project manager certifications tailored to the unique requirements of managing security projects. I strongly advise using an experienced cybersecurity project manager for the establishment of your cybersecurity program.

- **Audit findings and recommendations management:** Addressing audit findings is a fundamental part of cybersecurity program governance. Your program will likely be one of the most audited programs in your organization. You will need to respond to internal or external audit findings and recommendations. But exactly what are they? A finding is where an auditor notes a condition that is out of the normal boundaries of a standard. For example, a standard may state that you must have an encryption policy, and you do not. A recommendation would be that you must have one is place. Auditors also have degrees of findings ranging from serious infractions to simple recommendations. The auditor will also typically cite a specific standard clause, estimate the impact if you do not comply, and cite a cause for the deficiency.

  As a rule, you will have ten business days to respond, during which you can fully, partially, or not concur with the findings. In each case, you will need to provide a detailed response outlining your approach and timeframe to remediate the audit deficiency.

# 2.8 Security Talent Development

With the growing shortage of cybersecurity talent, estimated by some to be over one million, its critical to treat cybersecurity staff as talent versus employees. In my experience employees don't quit companies; they quit poor managers. To have an effective cybersecurity program you must invest equally in technologies and personnel. The stress of always being on, the threat of cyberattacks and keeping up with rapidly evolving technology can create a stressful work environment. I have seen toxic employees or contractors wreak havoc on an organization. Cybersecurity managers need to be sensitive to their personnel's needs and create a harmonious working environment. I strongly believe that even a world-class cybersecurity program is ineffective without strongly motivated talent. Reducing personnel turnover and retaining key talent is crucial to a program's success. You must find the right balance of training and motivation.

## 2.8.1 Training

Organizations need to invest in training cybersecurity personnel to show they are invested in their career. The amount of time allocated to training should be calculated in weeks, not hours. I have seen a significant difference in personnel who receive three to four weeks of training vs. a single week. The complexity of cybersecurity and myriad of technologies does not allow personnel to keep pace with a single week of training. The amount of training required by cybersecurity personnel should be commensurate with their roles and responsibilities. For example, security administrators who work directly with security products would receive more training than a security risk analyst.

## 2.8.2 Certifications

In my capacity of as an instructor for CISOs I have heard many stories of companies that won't pay for cybersecurity certifications. The reasons range from "you already have a certification" to "you'll just get it and leave." It is shortsighted for companies to restrict the attainment of certifications for their employees. Organizations should view certifications as an instrumental component of the overall program much the same as paying maintenance on cybersecurity technologies. In Chapter 6, Cybersecurity Roles and Responsibilities, I highlight a number of leading cybersecurity certifications by position.

# 2.9 Creating a Culture of Cybersecurity

Even the best made governance programs cannot predict every situation that should be guided by a principle or policy. At some point, you will have to rely on the employees of your organization to do the right thing. How do you train every employee to do the right thing every time? The answer is you cannot; no amount of training will accomplish this. What you must do is change the culture over time where doing the right thing becomes intuitive. Training will help but is not the sole answer. Culture begins at the top. If the management of the organization does not play by the same rules or actively participate in in your organization's cybersecurity program, the culture will not change. I have found the best way to change the culture is to identify respected change agents and disburse them throughout the organization, having them lead by example, subsequently changing the culture. Change agents include:

- **Senior management.** Senior leadership from the chief executive officer to the chief financial officer must actively and visibly support cybersecurity with more than the occasional obligatory email. They need to be seen in awareness training, oversee data breaches, and speak with members of the cybersecurity team.
- **Business line management.** If the business leaders with budget authority do not believe in the value of cybersecurity – and fail to invest in their own people and projects without waiting for corporate funding – the culture will never change.

> **Did You Know?**
>
> The Centre for the Protection of National Infrastructure (CPNI) has made available a comprehensive Security Awareness Campaign site without cost. The site has series of security awareness campaigns, designed to provide organizations with a complete range of materials they need.
>
> Each campaign set has full guidance on how to run the campaign, and materials such as downloadable posters that can be customized to the organization, wallet cards, flyers, videos and checklists.
>
> *What are you spending on your cybersecurity program?*
>
> **Source:**
> https://www.cpni.gov.uk/security-awareness-campaigns

- **Cybersecurity champions.** Champions are strategically named and placed throughout the organization from the boardroom to the shop floor. They constantly pose the questions, "Are we secure?" and "Is this the right thing to do?"
- **Employees.** Employees are the human firewalls, the line of defense. They should have the "if you see something, say something" attitude.
- **Contractors.** Contractors need to be viewed as partners or employee extensions. They play an integral role in reinforcing the culture of cybersecurity.

## 2.10 Cybersecurity Insurance

Cyber liability insurance policies evolved from errors and omissions (E&O) insurance policies. Twenty years ago, companies could purchase policy riders for software failures, unauthorized access to systems, destruction of data, and computer viruses. Early policies were referred to as network security or Internet liability policies. At the beginning of 2005, policies emerged to provide coverage for data breach incidents. These policies were particularly popular with retailers who held a significant amount of exposure from the credit card data they held and processed. Based on customer demand, insurance companies launched cybersecurity and privacy liability policies. It is estimated that one in three companies now has some form of data breach insurance policy (DiCanio, 2015). According to AIG, insurance underwriters collected $1.6 billion in premium income in 2015. Allianz projects premium income to grow to $20 billion by 2025 (Ramsinghani, 2016). In my experience with customers, premiums can range from $15,000 to $50,000 for one million dollars in coverage depending on risk. Cyber liability policies can include the following components:

> **Did You Know?**
>
> In June of 2019, Lake City, Fl's insurance company paid a ransomware payment of $460,000 to recover 16 terabytes of encrypted files as well as restore their email system. One hundred years of municipal records were held hostage for nearly one month. The attackers provided the decryption key after the ransom was paid, but not all files were able to be recovered. The attack began as a spearfishing email that deposited a triple-threat Ryuk payload.
>
> *Would your insurance policy cover a similar event?*
>
> **Source:** https://www.infosecurity-magazine.com/news/it-director-fired-lake-city-1-1/

- **Errors and Omissions:** This type of insurance covers non-fraudulent causes of failures or errors occurring in the performance of computer services. Technology companies offering cloud, software, or consulting services typically acquire this type of insurance.
- **Media Liability:** This type of insurance covers customer injury claims resulting from intellectual property infringement, copyright or trademark infringement, libel, and slander. Coverage could also be extended to patents or trade secret violations. This coverage is important to organizations with sizable online presences.
- **Network Security:** This type of insurance covers network equipment failures or external attacks against your network including denial of service attacks. Network outages or

breaches covered can include data breaches of consumer information, cyber extortion, data alteration or destruction, or malware infestations.

- **Privacy:** This type of insurance covers breach of physical records caused by theft, loss, or accidental disclosure. Other incidents that may be covered include improper disposal of equipment containing sensitive data and inadvertently collecting confidential information.
- **Network Security and Privacy Liability:** This type of insurance is a hybrid policy that also provides coverage for both the insured company and their third-party service providers. It covers the costs for responding to and recovering from data breaches, including penalties assessed from a lawsuit.

For more detailed information on cybersecurity insurance check out The Manager's Guide to Cybersecurity Law (Schreider, 2019).

## 2.11 Governance Foundation Checklist

To help you focus on the important steps of this chapter, I have provided an eight-step plan, shown in Table 2-3, that you should follow to achieve the creation of your cybersecurity program's governance foundation.

**Table 2-3. Governance Foundation Checklist**

| Step | Activity |
|------|----------|
| 1 | Create a governance playbook – use the outline in Section 2.2 to draft your playbook. Complete the sections as you progress through the chapter. |
| 2 | Declare your governance framework – select one of the frameworks in Section 2.3 that you are most certain will meet the needs of your organization. |
| 3 | Create governance oversight board – nominate members to populate the oversight board and create the charter outlined in Section 2.4. |
| 4 | Define cybersecurity policies – create a cybersecurity policies manual prescribed in Section 2.5. |
| 5 | Implement a policy management system – adopt the recommendations for managing cybersecurity policies listed in Section 2.5.2. |
| 6 | Consider acquiring GRC software – select a GRC product suggested in Section 2.6 if the effort of manually managing policies becomes unwieldy. (See Appendix A for products to evaluate.) |
| 7 | Implement key program management disciplines – ensure the key differences in Section 2.7 are implemented. |
| 8 | Adopt a culture of security – begin moving toward a culture of security following the suggestions in Section 2.8. |

## Summary

Creating the proper governance foundation for your cybersecurity program is essential to the effectiveness of all cybersecurity program components. Your principles and policies are the cornerstone of the integrity of your program as well as establishes your enforcement baseline. When developing your governance foundation, you need to ensure your focus remains on the "G" of GRC and resist the temptation to address risk ("R") and compliance ("C") until later in the evolution of your cybersecurity program. Automation can help the process of managing governance activities, but they cannot replace sound governance decisions. Select a governance framework or model that best suits your needs regardless of its title.

# References

ARMA (2018, October 9). *ARMA International Merges With Information Coalition*. [Press Release]. Retrieved from https://www.arma.org/news/421835/ARMA-International-Merges-With-Information-Coalition.htm

Colgan, J. (2014, May 22). *What's in a name? Information governance finds a home on the EDRM*. Retrieved from https://www.nuix.com/2014/05/22/whats-in-a-name-information-governance-finds-a-home-on-the-edrm

*Cybersecurity systems and risks reporting act of 2016, H.R. 5069*. (2016). Retrieved from https://www.congress.gov/bill/114th-congress/house-bill/5069/text

DeLoach, J. (2015, March 26). COSO 2013 Framework adoption – strong so far ... *The Protivi View*. Retrieved from https://blog.protiviti.com/tag/coso-internal-control-framework/

EDRM. (2017). *IGRM information governance reference model*. Retrieved from http://www.edrm.net/frameworks-and-standards/information-governance-reference-model/ [Summary only.]

Galligan, M. & Rau, K. (2015, January). *COSO in the cyber age*. Retrieved from https://www.coso.org/documents/COSO%20in%20the%20Cyber%20Age_FULL_r11.pdf

Gartner. (2017). Gartner magic quadrant. Research Methodologies. Retrieved from http://www.gartner.com/technology/research/methodologies/research_mq.jsp

Governance. (2017). [Definition.]. Retrieved from https://www.merriam-webster.com/dictionary/governance

IMA. *Committee of Sponsoring Organizations of the Treadway Commission [COSO].* (2017, March 12). Retrieved from https://www.imanet.org/about-ima/advocacy/committee-of-sponsoring-organizations-of-the-treadway-commission-coso?ssopc=1

ISACA. (2012). *COBIT 5 for information security.* Retrieved from https://isaca.org/COBIT/pages/info-sec.aspx [for purchase or preview]

MarketsandMarkets. (2016, July). *Enterprise governance, risk, and compliance (egrc) market by component (software (type & usage), service), deployment model (cloud & on-premise), organization size, business function (finance, it, legal, & operations), & vertical - Global forecast to 2021.* Retrieved from http://www.marketsandmarkets.com/Market-Reports/enterprise-governance-risk-compliance-market-1310.html#utm_source=whatech&utm_content=whatech.com/191891

Marks, N. (2015, May 4). Reviewing the state of GRC. *Internal Auditor Online.* Retrieved from https://iaonline.theiia.org/blogs/marks/2015/reviewing-the-state-of-grc

OCEG. (2015). *GRC capability model 3.0 (Red Book).* Retrieved from https://www.oceg.org/resources/red-book-3/ [Summary only. Full report downloadable by members.]

Singh, A. & Lija, D. (2010). Criteria and methodology for GRC platform selection. *ISACA Journal.* Retrieved from https://www.isaca.org/Journal/archives/2010/Volume-1/Documents/1001-criteria-and-methodology.pdf

Whitehouse, T. (2015, April 13). Report: Majority adopt new COSO framework. *Compliance Week.* Retrieved from https://www.complianceweek.com/report-majority-adopt-new-coso-framework/12381.article

# Self-Study Questions

The following questions will help you build your expertise in establishing a foundation of governance.

1. What does the acronym GRC stand for?
   Governance within the Governance, Risk and Compliance model.

2. What is a playbook?
   A playbook explains a program clearly and succinctly in layman's terms. Once reading the playbook, the reader will have a working understanding of how a program is organization and administered.

3. Why would COBIT be used as a cybersecurity governance framework?
   Organizations that have already adopted COBIT for their corporate and financial controls framework find it easier to extend the framework to cybersecurity.

4. What is the main objective of a cybersecurity policy?
   To clearly identify the company's position on the acceptable use of information and assets.

5. What are some examples of NIST security program management policies?
   Awareness and training, audit, personnel security, planning, program management and service acquisition.

6. What is the purpose of requesting a best and final price in the RFP process?
   The term best and final inform the bidding suppliers to extend their very best price as there will be no further price negotiations.

7. Who in the organization is best suited to lead the change toward a culture of security?

    Senior management consisting of the CEO, COO and CFO.

8. Investing in certifications for cybersecurity staff is often a waste of money as they soon leave upon receiving their certification, true or false?

    False.

9. What is the difference between capital expenses (CapEx) and operating expenses (OpEx)?

    CapEx is the monies you receive to make large onetime purchases of cybersecurity technologies, and OpEx is monies used for ongoing costs of operating the program.

10. What type of coverage does errors and omissions policies provide?

    Non-fraudulent causes of failures or errors occurring in the performance of computer services.

# Chapter 3

# Building a Cyber Threat, Vulnerability Detection, and Intelligence Capability

Congratulations, you have made it to the third stop of your journey toward building a cybersecurity program. At this point you have learned how to create the initial design of your program as well as formulate a governance foundation. Now it is time to build in the capability to identify and manage the threats and vulnerabilities that could besiege your organization. I would be underestimating the importance of this step if I did not tell you that it is crucial to the rest of your journey. The prime reason for having a cybersecurity program in the first place is to protect your information and assets against threats and vulnerabilities. However, knowing which threats to protect against requires you to undertake a process of discovery to uncover the threats that hold the greatest potential to impact your organization. Having a list of threats is one thing but knowing how each threat could exploit vulnerabilities within your information technology (IT) infrastructure is another. Finding the soft chewy side of your organization where you are most vulnerable will require you to look at your organization as a hacker would. To do this, you will need to know how to view your organization as an attack surface. Essentially the sum of all your vulnerabilities constitutes your *attack surface*. To help you with identifying threats and locating vulnerabilities, I will show you how to develop a cyber threat intelligence capability.

***This chapter will help you to:***

- Understand the relationship between threats and vulnerabilities.
- Understand how to identify and categorize threats.
- Know how to detect vulnerabilities within your organization.
- View your organization as an attack surface.

## Chapter 3 Roadmap

The outcome for this chapter is that you will have created a real time cyber threat, vulnerability detection, and intelligence capability. This capability is essential to proactively address threats and then comparing those threats to the vulnerabilities of your assets and information through a well-thought-out intelligence capability.

Figure 3.0 shows a reference architecture for how the cyber threat, vulnerability detection, and intelligence capability would operate. The reference architecture is an abstraction view showing the primary components supported by a host of subcomponents. Security testing is a primary component of the architecture where defenses for managing or mitigating threats are validated and attack surface vulnerabilities have been remediated. Cybersecurity staff are actively engaged in security testing through several processes ranging from penetration testing to war gaming. Primary architecture components are depicted in gray.

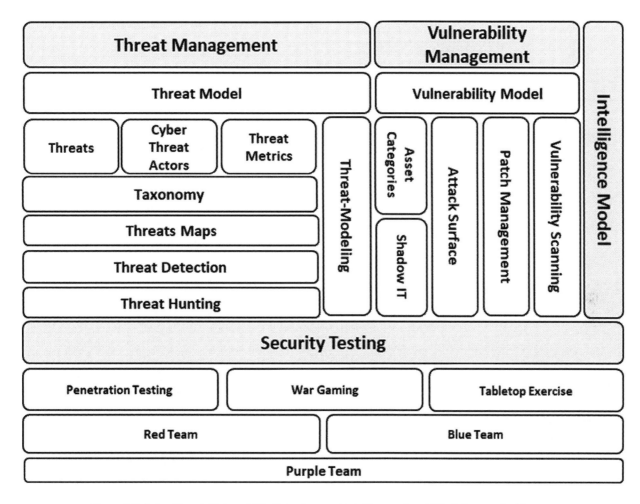

*Figure 3.0. Cyber Threat, Vulnerability Detection, and Intelligence Capability Reference Architecture*

Each main component (gray) and sub-component of the reference architecture is covered in more detail later in the chapter.

On this third stop of your journey you will focus on deploying the capability to identify, articulate and assess the most likely threats to your organization. Once the threats are registered in a taxonomy, you will assess the vulnerability of your enterprise to those threats exploiting an asset or information weakness. Confirmed vulnerabilities will be addressed through vulnerability management. Your enterprise will undergo continuous security testing to locate and remediate vulnerabilities.

To help direct your energies toward the creation of this capability, I have outlined the outcome-based steps required. The other content presented in the chapter is more reference, foundational or background-oriented, which will help you place detail into the noted outcomes.

- **Step 1: Create Threat Management Program** – Identifying the threats most likely to affect your organization is essential to your risk management program. Here you will need the ability to identify and determine the likelihood of various threats to your organization. Threats are identified, assessed and registered in a threat taxonomy. You will also need the ability to hunt for threats within your enterprise.
- **Step 2: Create Vulnerability Management Program** – Continuously scanning or evaluating your attack surface for weaknesses is what vulnerability management is all about. Determining if any threats previously identified can exploit a vulnerability in your enterprise drives the process of continuous remediation.
- **Step 3: Define Intelligence Gathering Capability** – Threats and vulnerabilities can already exist in your enterprise or emerge as zero-day exploits where no known remediation exists. You will need to maintain a pulse on the threat and vulnerability landscape to stay one step ahead of the bad actors who seek to harm your organization.
- **Step 4: Implement Security Testing Program** – Police SWAT teams are successful because they practice and test their special weapons and tactics. Security testing is where your organization tests its ability to defend against an attack through war gaming or tabletop exercises. Here is where you also think like a hacker and attempt to infiltrate your enterprise using the tactics, techniques and procedures (TPP) of hackers.

If you find yourself requiring only the minimum daily protection requirements of threat and vulnerability management that will yield the greatest result with the least effort, focus on these activities:

- **Identify Top-5 Threats** – Examine the top threats present in Table A.17 of the appendix and ensure that you are protecting your organization against the historically worst of the worst cyber threats.
- **Identify Attack Surface** – You can't protect what you can't see. Make sure you have an accurate inventory of the hardware, software, suppliers and personnel who make up your attack surface.
- **Perform Vulnerability Scanning** – Scan your environment to identify devices or applications with vulnerabilities that could be exploited.
- **Patch Highest Risk Vulnerabilities** – Remediate high-risk vulnerabilities through patching to reduce the exploit potential of your attack surface.
- **Deploy Virtual Patching** – For areas that cannot be easily patched, deploy virtual patching to stop exploits before they reach an unpatched asset. This would include intrusion prevention, web application firewalls, etc.
- **Penetration Test High Value Assets** – Perform penetration testing on the most critical web-facing applications and infrastructure. This ensures the front door is metaphorically locked to keep hackers out.

The advice from the previous chapter holds true for this chapter: you cannot consider this portion of your program sufficient by only completing the activities immediately above. As with the previous chapter, go back through the balance of the material covered in the chapter to finish the buildout of your threat and vulnerability management capabilities.

## 3.1 Cyber Threats and Vulnerabilities

In Chapter 1, I discussed the importance of business alignment to drive the scope and tenor of your cybersecurity program. This ensures that your program supports the needs of the organization, elastically expanding and contracting to accommodate new business opportunities and keeping pace with the changing regulatory landscape. Each move your business makes to gain market share or improve profits potentially introduces new threats and vulnerabilities that must be evaluated and addressed. In addition, upgrades in computing hardware, software, and networking can change your organization's attack surface. As a manager working with your organization's cybersecurity program, you will need an inventory of likely threats and a way of identifying vulnerabilities and threats that may be exploitive causing an impact to your business. Matching threats to vulnerabilities are something that must be carefully orchestrated so the right emphasis is placed on the threats that pose the greatest potential harm to your information and assets. Later in the book I address how to handle threats through the application of countermeasures.

Risk management is inexorably linked to threats and vulnerabilities, but I will cover that topic in its own chapter (Chapter 4) owing to the size of the subject. In this chapter, I will focus on threats, vulnerabilities, and the production of intelligence to gather information on both. I also cover how to look at your organization with the same eyes as a hacker. I want you to know how to visualize your organization as an attack surface, understanding where the barbarians can come through your firewalls so to speak. Think of this chapter as a three-legged stool. The legs are represented by threats, vulnerabilities, and intelligence, but the seat is the attack surface. The stool is of no value if it is missing any one of its parts. The same is true of incorporating the capability to leverage *intelligence* to identify *threats* that can exploit *vulnerabilities* within your organization's *attack surface*.

### 3.1.1 Threats, Vulnerability, and Intelligence Model

Three things must come together to tell the story of who wants to harm your organization. First, you will need to gather intelligence from various sources on the bad actors out there who would want to cause harm to your organization. Next, you will need to uncover known and potential vulnerabilities that may lurk within your organization. Last, you will need to make sense of the first two to determine if the threat is real or perceived. You can go about performing these tasks in one of two ways. You can use in-house resources or outsource to organizations that will perform the tasks at your behest. The difference is the quality of information and of course cost. You will need to balance the cost of gathering threat and vulnerability information with the effort and cost to produce the information.

I have seen my fair share of organizations which produce volumes of threat and vulnerability data only to become paranoid and overwhelmed. Threat information must be actionable to be of value. It might be nice to know every threat reported since the dawn of time, but why would you want or need that information? Focus is the name of the game here – only deal with threats that would keep you up at night. Only exploitable threats that have a high likelihood of causing an impact deserve attention. Figure 3-1 shows the relationship of intelligence gathering, vulnerability detection, and threat analysis.

*Figure 3-1. Intelligence Interaction Model*

116

In this model, the actions of intelligence gathering, vulnerability detection, and threat analysis are continuous. Threats never sleep and neither should your efforts of detection. Here are the roles each gear of the model plays:

- **Intelligence gathering:** Intelligence gathering can include anything from reading threat reports in cybersecurity magazines and blogs to contracting for cyber intelligence services and everything in between. If your organization represents a likely target (financial, retail, critical infrastructure, etc.) for hackers then knowing in advance who may be targeting your systems and by what techniques is extremely valuable. Actionable information will give you enough time to prepare a proper cyber defense. If you have watched a spy movie or a US Senate Intelligence Committee meeting on CSPAN, you have heard people testify to the importance of good, actionable intelligence. This is what you want to strive for in your cybersecurity program.

- **Vulnerability detection:** Vulnerability detection involves the analysis of your intelligence data and comparing it to observable conditions. Now that you understand there are specific bad actors and what the likely tools in their possession are, you want to know if you are vulnerable. For example, intelligence lets you know a known robber or break-in artist is working your neighborhood, successfully gaining entrance to those homes with weak home security. However, you are not vulnerable because you have a home security monitoring service, warning signs posted, security cameras on the outlook, deadbolt locks, a dog, and your lights on a timer. Vulnerability detection tells you where you are vulnerable and which pieces of security you are missing considering the threat.

- **Threat analysis:** Putting it all together is what threat analysis is all about. It is where you take your intelligence, compare it to your vulnerabilities, and determine if a threat exists. Making the connection between threats and vulnerabilities is key to making investment decisions in your cybersecurity program. Evaluating the threats in context of vulnerabilities provides you with the ability to score threats by criticality. Threat analysts are expert at making decisions such as: Is the threat only a threat for a specific window of time? Can the threat exploit a vulnerability in your IT enterprise? Alternatively, are there enough hackers with the technical knowledge to execute the threat against specific vulnerabilities to cause harm? Threat analysis is the key to answering these questions.

## 3.2 Cyber Threats

A cyber threat is a threat that leverages or affects your cyber assets and requires the use of the Internet or wireless-based network to disrupt or cause harm to your organization's information and assets. Threats can be manmade or natural events but nonetheless have the potential to affect your organization's business. I want you to keep in mind that even though a threat exists, it may not actually happen. Threats require a trigger for them to become a concern. Take for example, the known threat of unpatched servers. The threat exists but requires missing patches to trigger an impact. A threat also requires something to exploit such as a vulnerability or weakness in a system. Threats also need something to attack; in our example here, it is servers. Now think of all your servers, applications, databases, and everything else as one big something to attack or an attack surface. Understanding the relationship between threats, triggers, and vulnerabilities is an important concept of threat management. A vulnerability in of itself is not a threat absent of a trigger. For example, a match requires someone to strike it (trigger) before it represents a threat. The flame from the match must touch something flammable (vulnerability) before it causes that item to burn (impact).

**TIP:** Do not fall into the dilemma I have seen many companies succumb to, an inability to separate real from perceived threats. There are enough real risks out there to cause you real concern; so be pragmatic about which threats are worth caring about.

### 3.2.1 Lesson from the Honeybees

If you are still grappling with the concept of threat, think about the lesson honeybees can teach us. Yes, honeybees. My wife (attack surface) is highly allergic to bees, her greatest threat. Not only is it her greatest threat, almost 8% of the US population (expanded attack surface) is equally allergic. Therefore, if we have an outdoor party with 30 guests, two will be allergic to bee stings. What is the likelihood of bees stinging only people allergic to stings? Let us assume a likelihood, as a reasonable estimate for planning purposes, of approximately 3%. Is there a higher likelihood of one person being stung over another? Yes, there is. People with a fragrance attract bees (trigger). However, we never know if a bee will sting if it lands on someone. We must assume it will; so, a defensive action is necessary – we swat it away (countermeasure). If a bee does sting someone, what can we do? In my wife's case, we carry an EpiPen so we can mitigate the impact of the sting.

Bees typically do not go around just stinging people at random; they need to be provoked or triggered. The threat triggers in this example would be someone disturbing a beehive or swatting at a bee passing by. If we tell our guests to refrain from doing this, we can lower the threat. We can also avoid areas where bees are known to congregate, but bees have minds of their own and go wherever they wish. We do have a reprieve in the winter months because bees hibernate in their hive; so, there is a window of time that the threats exist. Given that data or intelligence, we could estimate the risk of a bee sting remains with us 60% of the time when we are outside. If we are inside, the threat may exist only 1% of the time. We say 1% because no threat is zero, and a bee could possibly sneak inside our house.

This type of thought process is required to evaluate threats. In our bee example, people are targets, and those allergic to stings are vulnerable. The bee still generally requires a trigger (disturbed beehive) to sting an allergic person (attack surface) to exploit the vulnerability (allergy) causing an impact. If you think about the threats in the context of bees, it makes the process of threat management just a bit easier. The lesson here is: If you get bogged down by threat management (or by explaining the concept to management), think like a bee.

## 3.2.2 Cyber Threat Categories

Cyber threats can take many shapes and forms from insider attacks to sophisticated nation-state attacks. It is important for you to understand the differences to plan your countermeasures accordingly. Selecting the wrong threats to focus on can be costly in terms of investing too much in countermeasures. Chasing the wrong threats also takes your eye off the ball, diverting attention to areas of little consequence. Let me give you an example. Not long ago I was asked to review the threat inventory of a Fortune 500 company. I quickly noticed it was focusing on a disproportionate number of threats oriented toward mainframe applications that could only be accessed internally – no web-facing components. Yet, the sales force had insecure mobile devices permitting access to far more sensitive information, allowing them to freely download customer privacy information. The potential for harm from mobile threats was far greater than that from mainframe threats. Management's perception was that the mainframe applications were the "bread and butter" of the company's operations and, consequently, efforts should be focused on protecting this platform. In reality, there was a much higher risk of a data privacy breach resulting from a lost or stolen mobile device.

Categorizing threats is the first step to creating a threat inventory or taxonomy. I am not going to cover threats that align to the category of natural disasters as there are many sources and books already available on this subject and our focus is cybersecurity. Table 3-1 provides an overview of the most common categories of cyber threats that you are likely to face including identifying their respective threat levels.

**Table 3-1. Common Cyber Threat Categories**

| Category | Description | Threat Level |
|---|---|---|
| 1. Cyber terrorists. | Cyber terrorists launch politically motivated attacks against networks and computers. Preferred tactics include distributed denial of service (DDoS) or targeted attacks against critical infrastructure. Cyber terrorism commonly accompanies physical terrorist campaigns. | Guarded |
| 2. Foreign intelligence services. | Formally, sanctioned spy organizations of foreign governments that engage in espionage (E-espionage) to gain intelligence or disrupt a sovereign nation's critical infrastructure. Various reports have placed the number of nations with sophisticated E-espionage capabilities at over 100. | High |
| 3. Hackers. | Hackers pursuing thrills or profits hack into companies to gain trophies or illicit gain. Hackers operate individually or in small groups. An industry has grown from the hacker community which markets hacker's tools and sales of ex-filtrated information such as credit card information. | High |
| 4. Hacktivists. | Politically motivated hackers who band together to raise awareness to their cause. These groups target companies or countries with unpopular positions or controversial products. Their impacts are generally isolated and short-lived. | Elevated |

| Category | Description | Threat Level |
|---|---|---|
| 5. Industrial spies. | State-sponsored or rouge companies that seek to ex-filtrate intellectual property, trade secrets, bid responses, design documentation or other information that would provide a decided economic advantage. Blackmail is a commonly used tactic. | High |
| 6. Insiders. | One or more disgruntled employees or contractors with access to information and assets who seek revenge through stealing confidential information or sabotaging systems in retribution to a perceived wrong. Insider threats can also be accidental where a user succumbs to a phishing attack. | High |
| 7. Internet scammers. | Quick-hit criminals who almost exclusively use email to launch large-scale spam or phishing attacks against individuals to acquire identity information. Scammers seek credit card or financial information. | Severe |
| 8. Nation-state attackers. | Countries with cyberwar capabilities that launch attacks against other countries where disputes exist. Some attacks have been crippling to infrastructure while others seek to disrupt visible national companies, banks, or government institutions. | Elevated |
| 9. Organized cybercrime rings. | Organized and well-funded criminal gangs or organizations that launch malware attacks, spam campaigns, and phishing attacks to lure individuals into revealing their identities or their system access credentials, to facilitate theft of information. | High |

The threat levels listed in Table 3-1 provide a broad indication of the likelihood of an attack and serve to alert employees to the seriousness that each category presents. To aid you in assigning threat levels, Table 3-2 outlines the model provided by the Center for Internet Security that I recommend to my clients (Center for Internet Security, 2017).

**Table 3-2. Threat Level Categories**

| Threat Level | Condition |
|---|---|
| Severe | Indicates a severe risk of hacking, virus, or other malicious activity resulting in widespread outages and/or significantly destructive compromises to systems with no known remedy or debilitates one or more critical infrastructure sectors. |
| High | Indicates a high risk of increased hacking, virus, or other malicious cyber activity that targets or compromises core infrastructure, causes multiple service outages, causes multiple system compromises, or compromises critical infrastructure. |
| Elevated | Indicates a significant risk due to increased hacking, virus, or other malicious activity that compromises systems or diminishes service. Known vulnerabilities are being exploited with a moderate level of damage or disruption. |
| Guarded | Indicates a general risk of increased hacking, virus, or other malicious activity. The potential exists for malicious cyber activities, but no known exploits have been identified, or known exploits have been identified but no significant impact has occurred. |
| Low | Indicates a low risk. No unusual activity exists beyond the normal concern for known hacking activities, known viruses, or other malicious activity. |

**TIP:** Exercise caution in changing your threat levels. Changing levels too often can cause warning fatigue. A justification should be used when raising or lowering threat levels, so users understand the rational for the change. You can also vary threat levels by attack surface.

## 3.2.3 Threat Taxonomies

With your understanding of threats and the categories they align with, you will want to inventory threats so you can give them the attention deserving of their individual level of seriousness. This will require something referred to as a *threat taxonomy*. A *taxonomy* is the process of naming, describing, and classifying something. In our case, it is a threat taxonomy. Some security practitioners refer to this as a *threat inventory*. I prefer *threat taxonomy* as it is more descriptive of the effort of inventorying and cataloging threats. The taxonomy is where you will review and update the threats to your organization at least semiannually. I suggest you begin with a spreadsheet to create your taxonomy. Table 3-3 provides an organizational construct that I use in my own threat taxonomies.

**Table 3-3. Threat Taxonomy Structure**

| Threat Category | Threat ID | Threat Name | Threat Rating | Threat Group | Threat Description | Threat Target | Threat Vector | Threat Impact | Threat Actor |
|---|---|---|---|---|---|---|---|---|---|
| Internet Scammer | CYU-010 | Spear-Phishing Attack | 5.0 | (CY) Cyber | Deception to lure users to perform dangerous actions via email enticement. | (US) User | Email | Luring a user to perform acts that lead to a system compromise. | APT 10 |

Depending on the sophistication of the threat program, there could be other threat attributes tracked in the taxonomy. I have created taxonomies for large global organizations that had over 25 threat attributes. However, what I have provided below, in the way of instructions for each of the attributes in Table 3-3, should get you started:

- **Threat category:** Align the threat to one of the nine threat categories described in Table 3-1.
- **Threat ID:** Assign a unique identification number to threats. The identification should have some meaning. For example, the number used in the table uses an abbreviation for the threat group (CY), an abbreviation for the threat target (US) and a sequentially assigned number of the order the threat was entered in the taxonomy.
- **Threat name:** Use standard industry names for threats or what they are commonly referred to in your organization.
- **Threat rating:** Use a rating scale, recommended one to five, to assign a raw threat score. Zero represents the lowest and five the highest threat score. Scores are referred to as raw before adjustments to reflect compensating controls. The following scale can be used to rate threats in the taxonomy:
  - **1** = Low – unlikely to occur.
  - **2** = Moderate – possible, but unlikely.

o  **3** = Substantial – strong possibility of occurring.
o  **4** = Severe – highly likely of occurring.
o  **5** = Critical – imminently expected to occur.
Threats with the highest score require immediate attention. Threat ratings differ from threat categories. Threat ratings apply to a specific threat whereas threat categories relate to the general threat condition.

- **Threat group:** Categorize threats by group to facilitate their management. Typically, group type consists of:
  o  Cloud – threats unique to cloud applications and services.
  o  Cyber – cybercrimes and cyber-related threats.
  o  Disaster – naturally occurring threats including tornadoes, earthquakes, etc.
  o  Personnel – insider threats or fraudulent activities.
  o  Physical – theft or destruction of information and assets.
  o  Technical – hardware, network, or software malfunctions or maintenance errors.
- **Threat description:** Summarize the threat. Leverage the threat taxonomies mentioned below to gather the information for your threat description.
  o  **Threat target:** List the most direct target of the threat. In some cases, the threat may have multiple targets. Begin with focusing on the primary target. You may add attributes for secondary targets. Align to your attack surface as much as possible.
  o  **Threat vector:** Provide the path or tool used by a bad actor to attack a target. Vectors can include unpatched vulnerabilities in operating systems or an email containing malicious links.
  o  **Threat impact:** Provide a brief description of the threat's impact.
  o  **Threat actor:** Provide the name or designation of known threat actor.

> **TIP:** Resist the temptation to load your taxonomy with every known threat to life and limb. Focus on real threats that could have real impacts to your organization. For example, if your organization does not use software as a service (SaaS), do not include SaaS threats in your cloud category.

### 3.2.3.1 Threat Taxonomy Sources

To keep you from having to reinvent the wheel, I have located several open source threat taxonomies you may access to populate your threat taxonomy.

- A Taxonomy of Threats for Complex Risk Management – A detailed report outlining the content of a comprehensive threat taxonomy. It covers a broad range of threats organizations face. Released in 2014, this taxonomy provides substantial detail on threat definitions and descriptions. Read more at: https://www.jbs.cam.ac.uk/faculty-research/centres/risk/publications/multi-threat/a-taxonomy-of-threats-for-complex-risk-management/.

- ENISA Threat Taxonomy – Tool for structuring threat information produced by the European Union Agency for Network and Information Security (ENISA). This taxonomy released in 2016 provides a spreadsheet of threats along with a comprehensive guide. Read more at: https://www.jbs.cam.ac.uk/faculty-research/centres/risk/publications/multi-threat/a-taxonomy-of-threats-for-complex-risk-management/.

- HITRUST Threat Catalogue – A threat catalog mapped to the controls available in HITRUST's Cybersecurity Framework. Cataloged threats are aligned to cyber threats, risk factors and controls. Read more at: https://hitrustalliance.net/hitrust-threat-catalogue-advances-healthcare-industry-cyber-risk-management-improves-effectiveness-organizational-risk-analyses/.
- Threat Agent Risk Assessment (TARA) – A methodology created by Intel that identifies which threats pose the greatest risk, what they want to accomplish and the likely methods they will use. The methods are cross-referenced with existing vulnerabilities and controls to determine which areas are most exposed. Read more at: https://www.sbs.ox.ac.uk/cybersecurity-capacity/system/files/Intel%20-%20Threat%20Agent%20Library%20Helps%20Identify%20Information%20Security%20Risks.pdf.
- The Open Threat Taxonomy – A free, community-driven, open source taxonomy of potential threats to information systems, first available in 2008. Although not nearly so comprehensive as the ENISA taxonomy, it is a great start offering a simple and straightforward approach. Read more at: https://www.auditscripts.com/free-resources/open-threat-taxonomy/.

## 3.2.4 Cyber Threat Actors

Shakespeare said, "All the world's a stage." In the cyber world, Shakespeare's quote is as apropos today as it ever was. Only in our case, the stage is the Internet with threat actors serving as performers. Threat actors are the ones who commit the crimes against our organizations. Each has their own motivation and techniques. Cyber threat actors should not be confused with threat categories even though category names often sound like the name of a threat actor. Cyber threat actors operate within threat categories. Tracking the actors allows us to determine who is out to get us, how they intend to do it, and what damage they could cause. It is not good enough to know the category; we also need to know who is operating within a category. Threat actors can be around for a very long time; some have been operating for over ten years and there is no sign of their stopping. Table 3-4 shows the attributes of a threat actor profile populated with sample information derived from the <u>Munk School of Global Affairs</u> at the University of Toronto (Scott-Railton, Marquis-Boire, Guarnieri, & Marschalek, 2015).

**Table 3-4. Threat Actor Profile**

| Threat Category | Threat Actor Name | First Seen | Targets | Region of Operation | Technique | Tools | Sophistication |
|---|---|---|---|---|---|---|---|
| Hacktivists | Packrat | 2008 | High profile political figures and journalists. | Venezuela, Ecuador, Argentina, and Brazil | Retention of compromised domains and servers over many years acquired through malware and phishing attacks. | COTS Remote Access Trojans (RATs) | Medium |

Threat actor profiles can be as complex as you have the time and resources to dedicate. Adding a threat actor profile capability to your threat management approach will benefit you in many ways. First, it will allow you to simulate attacks by known and likely aggressors; second, it will provide your incident response personnel with vital background information on evaluating an attack and responding to the techniques used. Last, profiles allow you to align countermeasures in anticipation of expected attacks. You will find that knowing the plausible *tactics*, *techniques*, and *procedures* (TTP) of aggressors is tantamount to defining an effective countermeasures strategy.

If you find you do not have the resources to produce your own threat actor profiles or reports, you can contract the effort out to a cybersecurity firm. Table 3-5 lists the threat actor reporting services I have used in the past.

**Table 3-5. Threat Actor Profile Reporting Services**

| Provider | Service | Format | URL |
|---|---|---|---|
| CrowdStrike | Falcon Threat Intelligence | Service | https://go.crowdstrike.com/ThreatIntelligence |
| Flashpoint | Adversary Services | Service | https://www.flashpoint-intel.com/solutions/#advisory_services |
| Intel 471 Inc. | Actor-Centric Intelligence Collection | Product | http://intel471.com/ |
| NSFOCUS | Threat Intelligence Subscription Service | Report | https://nsfocusglobal.com/products/threat-intelligence-ti/ |
| Pricewaterhouse Coopers | Threat Actor Profile Report (TAPR) | Report | http://www.pwc.com/us/en/forensic-services/publications/assets/threat-actor-profile-report.pdf |
| Symantec Corporation | DeepSight™ Managed Adversary and Threat Intelligence | Service | https://www.symantec.com/services/cyber-security-services/deepsight-intelligence |

*Note: Links are current as of September 22, 2019.*

## 3.2.5 Cyber Threat-Hunting

If you are tired of the suspense of waiting for the bad actors to come to you, consider going to them. A rapidly emerging practice is cyber threat-hunting. As the name implies, some organizations have gone on the offensive and have begun to hunt down bad actors, seeking evidence of their malicious activity within their network. Threat-hunting leverages cyber intelligence, threat analytics, and security information and event management solutions to hunt advisories. Cyber threat-hunting is "what's next" for your security operations (SecOps).

A 2016 SANS Institute survey of nearly 500 participants on threat-hunting revealed that nearly 86% of organizations are involved in some form of threat-hunting today, albeit informally. According to the survey author, Dr. Eric Cole, respondents are still figuring out exactly what a threat-hunting program should look like, how to attract the right skills, and how to automate their hunting processes. You can read all about threat-hunting and the survey in the SANS Institute white paper, Threat Hunting: Open Season on the Adversary. Read the full white paper at: https://www.sans.org/reading-room/whitepapers/analyst/threat-hunting-open-season-adversary-36882.

> **Did You Know?**
>
> In June of 2019, NASA's Jet Propulsion Laboratory (JPL) was cited by the Inspector General for not implementing a threat hunting program recommended by IT security experts to aggressively pursue abnormal activity on its systems for signs of compromise, and instead rely on an ad hoc process to search for intruders.
>
> **Have you investigated deploying threat hunting?**
>
> **Source:**
> https://oig.nasa.gov/docs/IG-19-022.pdf

Rather than focusing on the noise of attacks crashing the gates of your firewall, hunting focuses on what may already be happening inside your network. Identifying lateral or east-west movement of attackers searching your devices to gain access privileges is where the big game is now. Lateral attacks occur behind the firewall where attackers move sideways going from application to server looking for something to compromise that will grant them elevated privileges. Many prominent attacks have occurred when attackers have been inside the network for months if not years. You must face a reality of life today – hackers or insiders with ill intent may already live behind your firewall, searching your network for vulnerabilities to exploit.

Cyber threat-hunting efforts range from informal manual efforts to sophisticated big data-driven approaches. However, all share a common goal – stay one-step ahead of the hackers to be there waiting when they arrive. Hunting has been around in various incarnations for ten years and has matured from advanced intrusion detection systems (IDS) signatures to automated solutions that actively and aggressively seek out and destroy malware left by attackers.

**TIP**: To get up to speed quickly on threat hunting, download a copy of Threat Hunting for Dummies produced by Carbon Black. Get your copy here: https://dbac8a2e962120c65098-4d6abce208e5e17c2085b466b98c2083.ssl.cf1.rackcdn.com/threat-hunting-for-dummies-ebook-pdf-5-w-3239.pdf.

### 3.2.5.1 Cyber Threat-Hunting Tools

Taking the right guns and ammo with you on a hunt is tantamount to the hunt's success. You will need weapons that can detect stealth attacks that move slowly and laterally through your network. These tools use different techniques to bag their quarry. For example, a product called Sqrrl relies on security information and event management (SIEM) data, endpoint devices, and outside threat feeds to detect network behaviors missed by conventional security dashboards. Another product, Infocyte HUNT, on the other hand, dispatches dissolving agents to all endpoints on the network to report suspicious activity. Then there are products like Endgame, which deploy permanent agents with the power to destroy threats. Table 3-6 presents the leading threat-hunting tools available.

---

**Did You Know?**

According to CrowdStrike, the window of time from when an adversary first compromises an endpoint machine, to when they begin moving laterally across your network is less than two hours.

*Do you have threat detection services to detect lateral movement in your network?*

**Source:**
https://www.crowdstrike.com/resources/reports/2018-crowdstrike-global-threat-report-blurring-the-lines-between-statecraft-and-tradecraft/

---

**Table 3-6. Cyber Threat-Hunting Tools**

| Company | Product | URL |
|---|---|---|
| Carbon Black | CB Response | https://www.carbonblack.com/products/cb- |
| Endgame | Endgame | https://www.endgame.com/platform |
| Infocyte, Inc. | Infocyte HUNT | https://www.infocyte.com/products |
| Sqrrl Data Inc. (Amazon) | Sqrrl Enterprise | https://cybersecurity-excellence-awards.com/candidates/sqrrl-enterprise |

*Note: Links are current as of September 22, 2019.*

## 3.2.6 Cyber Threat-Modeling

Cyber threat-modeling is a process used by security practitioners to identify potential threats to their IT enterprise. Most organizations do what amounts to stacking furniture at the front door to block intruders from entering, not really thinking about all the other ways they can gain access. What I want you to do is what I did when I first became a father. I got down on my hands and knees and crawled around the house to see the world as a toddler. I wanted to see the world from that perspective to see what I needed to do to keep my child safe. In effect, what I was doing was threat-modeling. Metaphorically speaking, you will need to crawl around your IT enterprise looking at it from the perspective of an aggressor.

There are three approaches when it comes to threat-modeling:

1. **Asset-centric:** This approach is where assets are identified and classified according to data sensitivity and their potential value to an attacker. Once identified, you can produce threat or attack trees or other visualizations to present your most vulnerable assets.
   o Attack tree – a form of independent modeling where the focus is on the attack itself. Attack trees depict an attack as a hierarchical event using graphical diagrams that show how low-level hostile activities interact and combine to achieve an adversary's objectives – usually with negative consequences for the victim of the attack.
   o Threat tree – a form of independent modeling where the focus is on the threat that could lead to an attack. Threat trees enumerate the potential threats to a system or application to understanding the overall inherent risk.
2. **Attacker-centric:** This approach requires profiling an attacker's characteristics, skillset, and motivation to exploit vulnerabilities; using those profiles to understand the type of attacker who would be most likely to execute specific types of exploits; and implementing a mitigation strategy accordingly.
3. **Software-centric:** This approach involves the design of the system and can be illustrated using software architecture diagrams such as data-flow diagrams, use case diagrams, or component diagrams. This method is often used to model threats to networks and systems and has been adopted as the de-facto standard for threat-modeling.

Threat-modeling requires a paradigm shift in thinking where you go from focusing on building to breaking. However, the shift is necessary, as it is a fundamental aspect of threat management. I have used several threat-modeling approaches, each having their own application. Table 3-7 presents the threat-modeling solutions available.

**Table 3-7. Threat-Modeling Solutions**

| System | Source | Overview | Approach | URL |
|---|---|---|---|---|
| Application Threat-modeling | OWASP | A structured approach to analyzing the security of an application to identify, quantify, and address security risks. | Software-centric | https://www.owasp.org/index.php/Application_Threat_Modeling |
| AttackTree | Isograph | A software tool that allows users to define indicators that quantify the cost of an attack, the operational difficulty in mounting the attack, and any other relevant quantifiable measure that may be of interest. | Attack-centric | https://www.isograph.com/software/attacktree/ |
| DREAD | Microsoft Corporation | A classification scheme for quantifying, comparing, and prioritizing the amount of risk presented by each evaluated threat consisting of damage, reproducibility, exploitability, affected users, and discoverability. | Asset-centric | https://en.wikipedia.org/wiki/DREAD_(risk_assessment_model) |
| Persona Non-Grata | DePaul University | An approach focused on attackers, their motivations, and abilities. Developers brainstorm about targets and likely attack mechanisms attackers would deploy. | Attacker-centric | https://www.computer.org/csdl/mags/so/2014/04/mso2014040028.pdf |
| Secur/Tree® | Amenaza® Technologies Limited | A software tool that was created expressly for analyzing hostile threats using attack tree analysis. | Attacker-centric | https://www.amenaza.com/ |

| System | Source | Overview | Approach | URL |
|---|---|---|---|---|
| Security Threat Discovery Cards | University of Washington | A flash card-based approach to identify unusual or more sophisticated attacks. Cards facilitate brainstorming about potential cyber threats. | Attacker-centric | http://securitycards.cs.washington.edu/ |
| STRIDE | Microsoft Corporation | A method to evaluate systems according to six threat categories: spoofing, tampering with data, repudiation, nonrepudiation, information disclosure, denial of service, and elevation of privilege. | Attacker-centric | https://msdn.microsoft.com/en-us/library/ee823878(v=cs.20).aspx |

*Note: Links are current as of September 22, 2019.*

### 3.2.6.1 Cyber Threat Analysis and Modeling (TAM) Products

There are a few tools available to assist in somewhat automating your approach to threat-modeling, but you may find that creating your own hybrid version of threat-modeling using spreadsheets will be just as effective. Table 3-8 provides an overview of the TAM products available.

**Table 3-8. Threat Analysis and Modeling Tools (TAM)**

| Product | Source | Overview | URL |
|---|---|---|---|
| Microsoft Threat Modeling Tool 2016 | Microsoft Corporation | Free product that assists in locating threats in the design phase of software projects. | https://www.microsoft.com/en-us/download/details.aspx?id=49168 |
| Practical Threat Analysis | PTA Technologies | Quantitative risk analysis technology to assist in | http://www.ptatechnologies.com/default.htm |

132

| Product | Source | Overview | URL |
|---------|--------|----------|-----|
|  |  | building practical threat models. |  |
| ThreatModeler™ | MyAppSecurity | Automated threat-modeling solution that enables an automated, repeatable, and scalable modeling process enterprise-wide. | http://threatmodeler.com/ |
| Trike | Open source | Spreadsheet-based open source threat-modeling methodology and tool. | https://www.helpnetsecurity.com/2005/07/26/trike-a-conceptual-framework-for-threat-modeling/ |

*Note: Links are current as of September 22, 2019.*

### 3.2.7 Cyber Threat Detection Solutions

**Did You Know?**

Ponemon Institute LLC. published a 2018 report sponsored by IBM that stated the mean-time-to-identify (MTTI) a breach is 197 days, and the mean-time-to-contain (MTTC) a breach is 69 days.

*How long would it take your company to detect and contain a breach?*

**Source:**
https://www.forbes.com/sites/louiscolumbus/2018/07/27/ibms-2018-data-breach-study-shows-why-were-in-a-zero-trust-world-now/#582c8d9868ed

Now that you have a way to identify cyber threats, you will need methods to detect them. There is a wide array of products and services that detect cyber threats and either alert, or act to block or eliminate, the threat. In fact, the selection of threat detection solutions is so vast that it can be downright confusing. To help you decide which solutions fit your threat management program, I have categorized and commented on the solutions that I believe will address the top cyber threats of 2017 to 2018 in Table 3-9. I emphasize solutions as generally no single solution can detect a single threat.

**Table 3-9. Cyber Threat Detection Solutions**

| Threat | Detection Approach | Detection Solutions |
|---|---|---|
| **Advanced persistent threats (APT):** Sophisticated network attacks executed over long periods of time. | Monitor networks to identify signs of APT breaches, examine network behavior to distinguish subtle, covert patterns that characterize an APT attack. | • APT products (e.g. Cyberreason).<br>• Managed APT services (e.g., SecureWorks, Inc.). |
| **Botnets:** Remote controlled compromised computers. | Detect and remove bots that compromise computers so they cannot be remotely controlled by a command and control (C2) server to perform nefarious acts. | • Anti-malware products (e.g., Malwarebytes).<br>• Firewalls (e.g., FortiGate NextGen Firewall).<br>• Honeypots and honeynets (e.g., Canary).<br>• Host and network-based botnet detection tools (behavioral and signature-based) (e.g., Core Security.<br>• Next generation intrusion prevention system – NGIPS (e.g., Palo Alto Networks, Inc. NGIP).<br>• Network traffic analyzer (e.g., SolarWinds NetFlow Traffic Analyzer).<br>• Security information and event management platforms (e.g., AlienVault). |
| **Data loss or theft:** Accidental or intention loss and theft of sensitive information. | Monitor networks to detect unauthorized transmission of sensitive information. Privacy policies are enforced where violations can result in alerts, document transmission suspension, etc. | • Enterprise DLP products – full enterprise DLP solution (e.g., Digital Guardian).<br>• Integrated DLP solutions – DLP capabilities included in an existing product (e.g., Zecurion). |

| Threat | Detection Approach | Detection Solutions |
|---|---|---|
| **Distributed denial of service (DDoS) attacks:** Act of intentionally interfering with ecommerce. | Prevent or lesson impact of hackers flooding your website with malicious traffic to overwhelm your servers to shut your site down. | • Cloud-based DDoS prevention (e.g., Kona Site Defender).<br>• DDoS protection services (e.g., AT&T DDoS Protection Service).<br>• DDoS attack mitigation solutions (e.g., Radware). |
| **Domain name service (DNS)-based attacks:** Bot, DDoS, and phishing attacks. | Monitor and inspect DNS traffic to detect botnets in a network, unauthorized DNS requests, and DDoS attacks. | • DNS security solutions (e.g., Cisco Umbrella).<br>• Next generation firewalls.<br>• Next generation intrusion prevention system – NGIPS.<br>• Network traffic analyzers |
| **Inside threat actor:** Trusted individual who steals or destroys information and assets. | Identify employees, contractors, or business partners authorized to use the organization's information technology systems who commit cybercrime. | • User activity monitoring (e.g., Teramind Insider Threat Detection).<br>• Data loss prevention (DLP).<br>• Security information and event management (SIEM).<br>• Digital forensics data analytics (e.g., Congruity360). |
| **Malware and viruses:** Malware detection. | Scan network traffic to detect exploits, malicious files, and network attacks, and to identify actively infected endpoints for advanced threats and zero-day exploits. | • Anti-malware products (behavioral and signature-based) (e.g., Trend Micro Anti-malware and Advanced Threat Protection).<br>• Endpoint protection solutions (e.g., Symantec Advanced Threat Protection).<br>• IDS. |
| **Password hygiene:** Poor password quality that contributes to access compromises. | Enforce strong passwords and usage as well as encrypted passwords to eliminate applications and systems compromise. | • Two-factor authentication (e.g., SecurAccess).<br>• Password managers (e.g. Keeper). |

135

| Threat | Detection Approach | Detection Solutions |
|---|---|---|
| **Phishing and spear-phishing attacks:** Cyber criminals attempting to obtain sensitive information with malicious emails with compromising URLs. | Detect malware associated with phishing attacks and prevent users from clicking infected URLs. | • Anti-malware products.<br>• Next generation firewalls.<br>• DNS security solutions (e.g., Cisco Umbrella).<br>• Email security products (e.g., SECURE Email Gateway).<br>• Security awareness training.<br>• URL blocking and filtering.<br>• Web security gateways (e.g., Barracuda WSG). |
| **Ransomware:** Cyber criminals holding data for ransom under threat of data deletion. | Detect and deactivate known ransomware, isolate infected files and, prevent data from becoming encrypted. | • Endpoint security products (e.g., Trend Micro Apex One).<br>• Ransomware prevention products (e.g., WatchGuard Host Ransomware Prevention).<br>• Security awareness training. |
| **Social engineering:** Attackers using advanced social deception skills to obtain sensitive information. | Train users to identify social engineering ploys prevent sending of executive personation emails. | • Security awareness training (e.g., KnowBe4).<br>• Impersonation fraud prevention products (e.g., Mimecast). |
| **System file integrity compromise:** Changes in security state of applications and operating systems. | Identify changes to IT systems where configurations may have been altered by hackers or malware to install rootkits, botnets, or alert to an exploit in process. | • File integrity monitoring (FIM) (e.g., Tripwire). |

*Note: Links are current as of September 22, 2019.*

## 3.2.8 Cyber Threat Metrics

Most organizations can list their threats, and most can arrive at some working description, but few can define a working set of threat metrics. We first must define what a *threat metric* is before going forward. A metric is a standard of measurement for how something is performing. For example, one metric could be how many attempted DDoS attacks were experienced in the last 30 days. A corresponding metric could be how many of the DDoS attacks degraded customer web traffic by more than 35%? The first metric measures quantity; the second metric measures quality. Metrics allow us to improve our cyber threat protection capability by understanding how it is performing.

Metrics can be difficult to define. What makes a good metric? First, it must be clear and unambiguous. Second, it must be easy to track, and last, you must be able to make decisions on the results of the metric. Ask yourself, "Is the data actionable?" and "What will I use the data for?" I prefer metrics that are objective and not subjective, and I like numeric results. In the example above we could see a result of 20 DDoS attacks in the last 30 days and that 10 DDoS, which is 50% of the attacks, degraded customer web traffic by 35% or more. We also do not want to create our metrics in a vacuum. Staying with our same example, we know from working with the marketing department that a 35% degradation in traffic equates to a 60% drop in online purchases and 40% increase in abandoned shopping carts. Remember how I have mentioned business alignment previously? Well, here is a perfect example.

I encourage you to create a manageable set of threat metrics for your program. Begin with no more than ten, and only when you can demonstrate you can consistently and accurately report out on these metrics add others that you feel are important. Metrics must represent things in your cybersecurity program worth being counted or evaluated, and which can be influenced by an action, or directly managed against.

### 3.2.8.1 Example Cyber Threat Metrics

To get you started in the right direction setting of threat metric, I have provided you with several examples in Table 3-10. I encourage you to access the NIST Special Publication 800-55 Revision 1 Performance Measurement Guide for Information Security to assist you in defining your threat metrics. See the full publication at: http://csrc.nist.gov/publications/nistpubs/800-55-Rev1/SP800-55-rev1.pdf.

**Table 3-10. Sample Threat Metrics**

| ID | Title | Measure | Period | Metric | Data Source |
|----|-------|---------|--------|--------|-------------|
| MA010 | Undetected Malware Incidents | Number of undetected malware infestations. | Monthly | 0.00% | Symantec Advanced Threat Protection |
| EM005 | Successful Spear-Phishing Attacks | Number of spear-phishing click-throughs. | Weekly | 0.00% | Barracuda Web Security Gateway |
| IN030 | Undetected File Changes | Number of undented file state changes in tier 1 servers. | Weekly | <1.0% | Tripwire File Integrity Monitoring |

## 3.2.9 Cybersecurity Threat Maps

Cybersecurity threat maps are an effective way to visualize where external threats emanate and what types of threats are emerging as having the greatest potential to cause harm. These maps can be used as part of a cybersecurity awareness program or as threat tracking displayed on screens within your cybersecurity operations center (C-SOC). C-SOCs are discussed in Chapter 6. Table 3-11 provides a listing of cybersecurity threat maps I have used in various projects.

**Table 3-11. Threat Source Provider Table**

| Threat Map | Source | Overview | URL |
|---|---|---|---|
| Chubb Cyber Index℠ | Chubb Insurance Company | Interactive tool providing insight into Chubb's cyber claims over the past 20 years. | https://chubbcyberindex.com/#/dashboard |
| Cyberthreat Real-Time Map | Kaspersky Labs | Worldwide malware infections reported by eight of Kaspersky's malware and Internet threat detection solutions. | https://cybermap.kaspersky.com/ |
| Cyber Threat Map | Blueliv Threat Exchange Network | Tracking of active crime servers throughout the world. | https://community.blueliv.com/map/ |
| Digital Attack Map | Arbor Networks, Inc. | Top daily DDoS attacks worldwide. Sliding scale to select view by day, month, and year. | http://www.digitalattackmap.com/#anim=1&color=0&country=ALL&list=2&time=17284&view=map |
| DNS Attack Map | OpenDNS Security Labs (Cisco) | OpenDNS queries for botnet, phishing, and malware requests. Views can be requested by country. | https://umbrella.cisco.com/blog/global-network/ |
| FireEye Cyber Threat Map | FireEye, Inc. | Who's attacking whom global map. | https://www.fireeye.com/cyber-map/threat-map.html |
| Fortiguard Attack Detection Map | Fortinet, Inc. | Live streaming of attacks defended by Fortinet products. | https://threatmap.fortiguard.com/ |

| Threat Map | Source | Overview | URL |
|---|---|---|---|
| Internet Malicious Activity Maps | Team Cymru | Activity intensity maps presenting malicious activity on the Internet. | http://www.team-cymru.org/malicious-activity-maps.html |
| Spam and Malware Map | Talos (Cisco) | Top spam and malware senders include top 10 cyberattack sender lists by country. | https://talosintelligence.com/ |
| Threatbutt Internet Hacking Attack Attribution Map | Threatbutt | Digital attack maps with a wide range of information about each attack, including origin country, IP address and destination. | https://threatbutt.com/map/ |
| ThreatCloud | Check Point Software Technologies, Inc. | Live global view of attacks, attacking countries, and target country. | https://threatmap.checkpoint.com/ThreatPortal/livemap.html |

*Note: Links are current as of September 22, 2019.*

# 3.3 Adversary Profile

Advanced threat intelligence involves moving closer to the bad actors to understand their TTP. Accomplishing this requires an understanding of the bad actors most likely to target your organization. Many of the threat intelligence platforms provide this information; however, there are other sources of bad actor profiles. Table 3-12 provides sources to obtain profiles of adversaries you can incorporate into a threat intelligence capability.

**Table 3-12 Adversary Profile Sources**

| Threat Map | Source | Overview | URL |
|---|---|---|---|
| Adversary Simulation Service | Accenture and iDefense | A realistic adversary and accompanying objective to simulate attacks. | https://www.accenture.com/us-en/services/security/cyber-defense |
| ATT&CK™ | MITRE | Knowledge base of adversary tactics and techniques based on real-world observations. The knowledge base is used as a foundation for the development of specific threat models and methodologies. | https://attack.mitre.org/ |
| Automated Adversary Emulation System | Caldera (MITRE) | Automated adversary emulation system that performs post-compromise adversarial behavior within Windows Enterprise networks. | https://github.com/clong/caldera |
| Diamond Dashboard | ThreatConnect | SIEM inject for adversaries to guide threat hunting activities. | https://threatconnect.com/blog/diamond-dashboard-hunting-your-adversaries/ |

*Note: Links are current as of September 22, 2019.*

# 3.4 Vulnerability Management

Vulnerability management is a continuous process of assessing the areas of your organization's attack surface that could be exploited by a threat. You can also look at this as strengthening the weaknesses in your IT infrastructure. Vulnerabilities range from missing patches on servers and workstations to improperly coded applications. It is not unusual for a midsize organization to have hundreds of unresolved vulnerabilities. Thinking about this number alone makes the process of addressing all those vulnerabilities a daunting task. However, you must remember that not all vulnerabilities are created equally. You will need to prioritize addressing the vulnerabilities by order of greatest potential impact. This is what vulnerability management is all about – assessing, prioritizing, and remediating. Vulnerability management entails the following:

- **Vulnerability scanning:** Scanning your attack surface to identify weaknesses that must be remediated to reduce the potential for a threat exploiting a vulnerability.
- **Risk scoring:** An evaluation of vulnerabilities in comparison to known threats and the abilities of the threat actors to launch the threat against your vulnerabilities. Vulnerabilities are assigned a risk score. The higher the score, the more immediate the vulnerabilities should be remediated.
- **Risk acceptance:** This is the process where management determines that the effort and expense to remediate a vulnerability is not worth the investment. In these cases, management accepts the risk and does nothing. Risk acceptance decisions are formally documented and become part of your organization's overall risk statement.
- **Vulnerability remediation:** Identified vulnerabilities will need to be remediated at some point based on their risk score. In some cases, you may decide to wait to apply a missing patch because you are close to the regular patching cycle and the vulnerability pose only a medium risk. Most remediation will need to go through change management. You may also consider creating a corrective action plan for more complex remediation.
- **Remediation validation (rescan):** Once an asset has been remediated, it is customary to rescan the asset to ensure the remediation was either done correctly or addressed the vulnerability completely.
- **Compliance reporting:** Scanning solutions provide a rich array of compliance reports that can be submitted for audit purposes to verify due diligence at the time a security breach occurred.

> **Did You Know?**
>
> In their 2019 web Application Vulnerability Report, Acunetix reported that 46% of websites have high security vulnerabilities.
>
> *How many high security vulnerabilities are in your web applications?*
>
> **Source:**
> https://cdn2.hubspot.net/hubfs/4595665/Acunetix_web_application_vulnerability_report_2019.pdf

Vulnerability management is a requirement by every security standard and regulation that I have read, and I have read a lot. It is one of those fundamental aspects of cybersecurity that you must get right to have a chance at keeping your information and assets protected.

## 3.4.1 Vulnerability Scanning

Assessing is performed by scanning your IT enterprise with sophisticated commercial or open source scanning technology. Scanners evaluate IT assets against databases of known vulnerabilities and produce criticality reports and recommendations for remediation. Scanning your environment can be accomplished using an in-house solution, a managed security service provider (MSSP) or SECaaS (Security as a Service). You will need to acquire a scanning solution that will recognize assets regardless of whether they are virtual, mobile, or cloud assets. Scanning your assets is not for the weak of heart. Until your scanning solution of choice is properly tuned you will be inundated with thousands of vulnerability alerts. Not to worry though, as most of these will be false positives. A false positive is an oxymoron, meaning that a security condition met all the criteria of a vulnerability, but when placed in context it turned out to be false.

Knowing when and how often to scan your environment requires a strategy. Some organizations scan their environment nightly, some quarterly, and others rotate through critical systems. The time between your scans is known as your vulnerability exposure window. The best scanning strategy is to have a process of continuous scanning. New systems should be scanned prior to their promotion to production. Application code should be scanned. Scanning should be integrated with change control to ensure major changes in systems or applications are scanned to look for the introduction of new vulnerabilities. Scans can be performed in several ways:

- **Good – external scan:** This scan looks at your enterprise from the outside as a hacker would. This type of scan is focused on vulnerabilities visible from the outside and evaluates the various layers of network security between the external scanner and internal systems.
- **Better – internal scan:** This scan looks at vulnerabilities from the point of someone located behind your firewall. This scan evaluates host-based security controls.

- **Best – with credentials:** Scanning with credentials allows the scanner to authenticate itself to the attack surface asset to extract more detailed information such as patch levels and security configurations.

> **TIP:** Keep your scans manageable and start off small focusing on your most critical systems first. Remember that scans quickly age, so only scan assets that you have time to remediate. Inform the network and security operations centers that scanning will occur so they do not think your organization is under attack.

Scans work on Internet protocol (IP) address ranges. The more addresses you scan, the longer the scan will take. Also, the number of checks you initiate in a scan affects the amount of time a scan can take. You can be checking for patch levels, firmware levels, ports, etc. There are dozens of checks that can be performed during a scan. Initial scans are important as they establish a baseline. Future scans will be compared to this baseline.

A comprehensive list of vulnerability scanning solutions is included in Appendix A.

## 3.4.2 Patch Management

### Did You Know?

According to BulletProof's 2019 cyber security report, 22% of the high and critical-risk issues reported consisted of missing patches, out-of-date or no longer supported software.

*How current are your patches?*

**Source:**
https://www.bulletproof.co.uk/industry-reports/Bulletproof%20-%20Annual%20Cyber%20Security%20Report%202019.pdf

Patch management is an integral component of vulnerability management for many organizations. Evidence of this is the fact that 43% of companies will make timely patching and remediation a higher priority in 2017 (Moreno, 2017). The clear majority of attacks target known vulnerabilities that can be easily patched. Effective patch management goes a long way in reducing your organization's attack surface. However, to be truly effective, patch management requires intelligent prioritization reflecting vulnerability risk scores. There are many patch management solutions available, which can make deciding on which one to use confusing. To help you with this decision, check out NIST's SP 800-40 Rev 3 publication, Guide to Enterprise Patch Management Technologies. You can read the entire publication at: http://nvlpubs.nist.gov/nistpubs/SpecialPublications/NIST.SP.800-40r3.pdf.

### 3.4.2.1 Virtual Patch Management

Organizations disenchanted with conventional patch management have turned to virtual patching. The theory behind this is that applying vendor security patches is a losing proposition with a low or no cost benefit. A typical IT organization can expect to apply thousands of patches annually with no guarantee that all devices are properly patched or that the patch will address the known vulnerability.

Virtual patch management works by enveloping assets in layers of protection such as firewalls, intrusion protection, etc., that will stop an attack before it reaches the asset. The layers of defense protecting assets look for the behavior of the very same attack that a patch is supposedly designed to protect against. The virtual patch environment intercepts attacks in transit; so malicious traffic never reaches the target. The resulting impact of virtual patch is that, while the actual source code of the application itself has not been modified, the exploitation attempt fails.

A comprehensive list of security patch management and virtual patching solutions is included in Appendix A.

> **TIP**: Perform a cost benefit analysis of conventional patching versus virtual patching to determine that if identified savings were applied elsewhere in your cybersecurity program, your program could benefit from funding more advanced information protection strategies.

## 3.5 Security Testing

Once the cybersecurity program is built, the work is just beginning, every aspect of the program requires testing to ensure compliance and validation that safeguards are fit for purpose. There are many forms of testing with varying levels of complexity and cost. Choosing the right methods of testing is essential as testing is a continuing process requiring involvement of all cybersecurity personnel and a commitment for investment. The primary goals of testing are to uncover weaknesses in the attack surface and cybersecurity personnel's ability to respond to cyberattacks.

Each cybersecurity program requires a progressive testing plan that is based on an iterative process of testing based on risk. A risk-based approach that testing efforts are oriented toward areas of greatest vulnerability and threat. Testing can include automated or manual methods. Figures 3.2 presents the most common types of security testing.

| Black Box Testing | White Box Testing |
|---|---|
| • Testers have little to no prior knowledge of the systems or environment before performing testing.<br>• Testers must use the same techniques as hackers.<br>• Most rigorous of all penetration testing techniques | • Testers have substantial knowledge of the systems and environment before performing testing.<br>• Potentially more vulnerabilities are exposed due to the methodical nature of the test.<br>• No inhibitors to performing detailed system analysis of target applications. |
| Gray Box Testing | Crowdsourced Testing |
| ▪ Testers have limited knowledge of some or all of the systems and environment before performing test.<br>▪ Combination of black and white testing techniques used | • Testers are professional hackers with substantial experience penetrating systems.<br>• Testers can be selected based on expertise in compromising specific systems and environments. |

*Figure 3-2. Security Testing Options*

## 3.5.1 Penetration Testing

A penetration test can be conducted internally or externally to uncover weaknesses to an attack surface. These types of tests are software-based and use the same tactics, techniques and procedures (TTP) as hackers to infiltrate an enterprise. Figure 3-3 presents the five phases of penetration testing. Phase one involves the gathering of information about the potential target. In Phase two, hackers scan a network looking for weaknesses to exploit. Using the identified weaknesses, hackers gain access in Phase 3. In Phase 4 hackers leverage the access and move laterally looking for credentials to exploit in order to increase privileges. In Phase five, hackers cover their tracks to avoid detection.

**Did You Know?**

A healthcare industry survey of 166 US-based healthcare information security professionals reported that 75% of organizations regularly conduct penetration testing.

*Does your organization conduct regular penetration testing?*

**Source:**
https://www.himss.org/valuesuite/5-takeaways-2017-himss-cybersecurity-survey

146

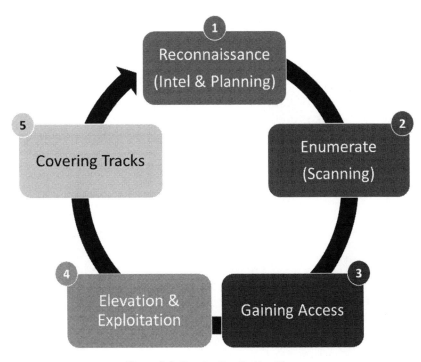

*Figure 3-3. Penetration Testing Phases*

## 3.5.2 Red Teams

Red teaming is an organized method of professional penetration testers acting as hackers to gain access to an enterprise and exploit its weaknesses. Red teaming is all about knowing how bad actors view an organization as well as how they can exploit vulnerabilities to gain access. Red teams can take on the persona of internal or external hackers to focus on attack scenarios. The results of the vulnerabilities identified by the red team are provided to another team, a blue team to guide remediation efforts.

## 3.5.3 Blue Teams

Blue teams defend against red team attacks to test the detection and prevention controls and safeguards deployed throughout the enterprise. Be teams are adept at detecting intrusions and blocking privilege escalations. Blue teams leverage layered defenses to verify how attacks can be detected, deterred and prevented. Blue teams can also be responsible for performing the actual remediation of weaknesses.

### 3.5.4 Purple Teams

In situations where blue teams do not have the time to remediate vulnerabilities, a separate team, a purple team is used. Purple teams are popular with organizations that desire an independent team remediate vulnerabilities. The purple teams specialize in integrating layered defensives and tactics identified to ward off future attacks.

### 3.5.5 Bug Bounties

Bug bounty programs are a reward-based program where hackers are incentivized to find application flaws. They can best be characterized as a crowdsourcing activity. Bounty programs pay cash for results. Bounty hunters submit proof of a detected vulnerabilities which the sponsoring company validates, and payment is made. Companies large and small rely on bounty programs to find bugs in their applications. This strategy is effective for companies that either cannot afford their own security testing teams or want an independent test performed.

With a bounty program, hackers are invited to attempt to penetrate an organization's network, web sites, etc. If a vulnerability is found, it is documented, verified and submitted for payment. Two of the most reputable bug bounty program managers are Bugcrowd Security and HackerOne. Using either platform, you can professionally manage your organization's vulnerability disclosures and payments.

> **Did You Know?**
>
> In April of 2018, Uber Technologies agreed to a 20-year settlement with the Federal Trade Commission (FTC) for deceiving consumers about its privacy and data security practices and for violating a previous FTC settlement agreement. One of the charges proven by the FTC was that Uber used it's bug bounty program to pay a ransom of sorts to hackers who stole 25 million customer records
>
> *Does your bug bounty program include an ethics policy?*
>
> **Source:** https://www.ftc.gov/news-events/press-releases/2018/04/uber-agrees-expanded-settlement-ftc-related-privacy-security

### 3.5.6 War Gaming

One of the most effective ways to prepare for a cyberattack is to perform war game exercises. These can be done using red and blue teams organized around a specific attack scenario. War games are cross-functional exercises where many parts of an organization are used to test their ability to work cohesively to respond to an attack. The focus of war gaming is to determine how long it would take notice a breach and stop the attack.

War games can be conducted with minimal impact on an organization and varying degrees of complexity. Wargames are effective at testing an organization's incident response plan. Wargames can be live or mock events and ultimately prove effective in raising an organization's overall security awareness posture.

### 3.5.7 Tabletop Exercises (TTX)

A form of war gaming is a tabletop exercise, an activity I consider to be the minimal amount of data breach testing an organization should conduct. As the name implies, TTXs are performed at a table with participants following a script led by a facilitator. The script is based on an attack scenario with various injects or complications that participants must work through. Participants are encouraged to work as a team to resolve the complications introduced by the injects. Team responses should draw on existing incident response plans to make the activity as realistic as possible.

When organizations get more adept at wargaming, the scenarios and injects can become more advanced. The purpose is to stress test the organization's response to a cyberattack before one occurs.

## 3.6 Attack Surface

Hackers look at your organization not as a building with offices where people arrive each morning to work, but as something they can exploit – an *attack surface*. Your attack surface is comprised of assets. Assets can be tangible or intangible. Tangible assets are your servers, network devices, mobility devices, etc. Intangible assets would be your information, intellectual property, trade secrets, etc. If you think about an asset as anything that has value, then you have the correct mindset. Hackers dissect your organization into an attack surface, which is the sum of all your assets. Getting at those assets is where hackers accel, searching for vulnerable points of entry or attack vectors. Just as your building has many entry points such as doors, windows, conduits, roof vents, etc., so does your infrastructure. Think about your technology not as doors and windows but as ports and code that serve as digital gates hackers can enter. Left unprotected by your cybersecurity program, hackers can enter, steal, and remove sensitive information. If you do not think like a hacker and likewise think of your organization as an attack surface, you place your abilities to protect your organization at a significant disadvantage. Attack surfaces have moved way beyond open ports and unpatched systems, and you need a way to visualize the vulnerabilities within your organization susceptible to compromise by threats. The object is to reduce the size of your attack surface by locking down or eliminating potential breach points and assets.

Attack surface diagrams can take many forms and shapes. Some organizations choose to represent their attack surface as a series of spreadsheets while others try a graphical depiction. Personally, I like the graphic representation because I can visualize what I must protect. Figure 3-3 shows one example of how I have represented an attack surface.

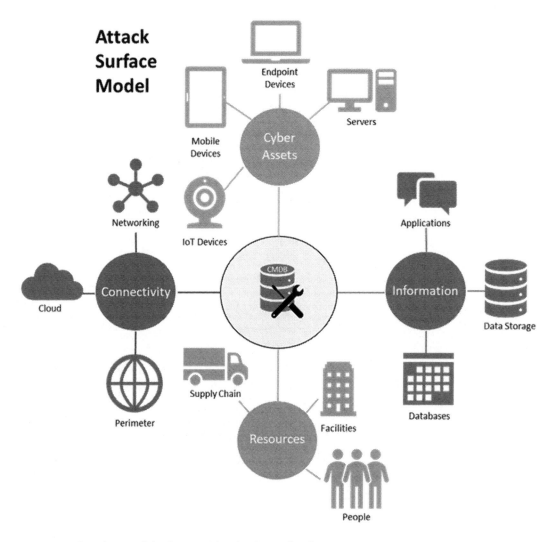

*Figure 3-3. Attack Surface Model™. (By Tari Schreider, licensed under a Creative Commons Attribution-NonCommercial-NoDerivatives 4.0 International License)*

150

This is a simplified version of an attack surface for illustrative purposes. Here is what I do to take it to the next level. For each of the small bubbles (subcomponents) I have an inventory of what is contained. For example, in the desktop bubble I will have a detailed inventory of all the organization's desktops including operating system level, owners, memory, attached devices, USB ports, software, etc. – essentially anything that could prove to be an attack vector.

Creating an attack surface can be rather complex when you categorize your organization's IT enterprise into hardware, software, and your network – all prime targets of hackers. This is where you quickly realize that if your IT assets are not properly inventoried with assigned owners, the job of creating an attack surface becomes nearly impossible. If you have not already done so, complete an inventory of your hardware, software, and network assets. Moreover, when I say software, I am including applications and databases. Third-parties are inching their way to the top of the list as point for hackers find their way into organizations; so, you must include them as well in your inventory.

**TIP:** Defining an attack surface is a fundamental activity of designing a cybersecurity program. It should never be an option to have a complete and accurate inventory of all hardware, software, network components, and service providers.

Now that you have your asset inventory at the ready, it is time to construct your attack surface. I suggest you begin with vectors or digital gates that provide the closest entry to your most critical assets. You will find these include anything connected to the Internet, and access control and authentication systems. Hackers generally come in through the Internet directly or indirectly via the Internet access of a third-party that you conduct business with. Once in, they look to compromise access and authentication controls, elevating their privileges so they can go anywhere. At this point, we are looking further downstream or to the nearest entry points, and not upstream at all the ways they could fool people through social engineering to obtain access privileges. The key to remember is entry points, and they could number in the thousands if you are a large enterprise, and certainly in the hundreds for smaller organizations. Table 3-13 provides you with an example of an attack surface itemization for application entry points.

**Table 3-13. Attack Surface Threat Itemization – Software: Applications**

| Component | Subcomponent | Threat Vector | Threat Rating |
|-----------|--------------|---------------|---------------|
| Software | Applications | Admin interface | Low |
| | | Application programming interfaces (API) | Moderate |
| | | Cookies | Low |
| | | Database access | Critical |
| | | HTTP headers | Substantial |
| | | Local storage access | Low |
| | | Login and authentication | Moderate |
| | | Messaging interfaces | Critical |
| | | Monitoring interfaces | Moderate |
| | | Run-time arguments | Low |
| | | Service accounts | Low |
| | | User interface – forms and fields | Severe |

Using the format above, you will need to create threat itemizations for hardware, software (non-applications), and networks. The reports produced by the IT asset management solution will aid in the completion of these inventories.

152

Nearly every cybersecurity standard places asset inventory and management within its top 10 cybersecurity controls. This is fundamental blocking and tackling that unfortunately many organizations only partially complete. You should complete this activity before attempting to map out your attack surface.

## 3.6.1 Attack Surface Mapping

It is imperative that you know as much about your attack surface as potential aggressors know. Any forgotten servers, web applications, or other network endpoints within your attack surface serve as a digital gateway of potential attack. Defining your attack surface will require some discovery tools as manually maintaining an attack surface is time consuming and error prone. To aid you in defining your attack surface I suggest you use a solution that automatically collects all relevant data on all your network devices including detailed operating system and device statistics. The solution you select should provide the following inventories:

- **Application Inventory**: All applications deployed throughout the enterprise.
- **Hardware Inventory**: All network attached assets consisting of make and model including CPU, memory, peripherals, etc.
- **Network Inventory**: All devices connected to the network, tracking adds, moves, changes, and removals.
- **Software Asset Inventory**: All software consisting of licenses, version numbers, owners, etc.
- **Third Party Inventory**: All IT and cloud services providers, including a description of the exact interaction with your organization's data,

You will find these solutions provide much more capability than simply inventorying IT assets. Many integrate service desk functionality, device scanning for patch level management, and configuration management. You will need to investigate what tools or solutions are available within your IT enterprise for use in creating and maintaining an attack surface. Once you have verified the right solutions exist or you have acquired them, create a set of reports that present the most comprehensive view of the IT enterprise. The attack surface data will be used later to produce attack trees. An attack tree is a conceptual diagram showing how an asset, or target, may be attacked.

## 3.6.2 Shadow IT Attack Surface

Shadow IT are applications, computers, cloud services, and other technology services not supported by an organization's IT department. Shadow IT has grown out of frustrated users who cannot achieve their business needs through standard IT services. A Logicalis Global CIO Survey found that 90% of lines of business are going around IT departments and using cloud services to get their jobs done. You can read the entire white paper at http://www.us.logicalis.com/globalassets/united-states/whitepapers/CIO-Survey-2015-Shadow-IT-Phenomenon.pdf. If this is not already happening within your own organization, be prepared because chances are it will to a lesser or greater degree. It could be as simple as a user saving information to a cloud storage service or an entire department that acquired its own business application.

Shadow IT represents a blind spot in your organization's attack surface. Unauthorized IT services introduce risk into your organization through software and services that may not comply with your security policies and required controls to protect assets and information. You will need to find a way to identify the shadow IT in your organization to understand the threat vectors requiring protection.

You can locate shadow IT using some of your existing IT tools:

- **Bandwidth analysis:** Baseline your bandwidth utilization and alarm on unexplained increases.
- **Cloud billing alerts:** Set billing alerts such as Amazon Web Services (AWS) CloudWatch to notify of cloud service overspending.
- **Flow analysis:** Review network traffic to identify changes in flow or file sharing patterns or unexpected network protocols.
- **Network discovery:** Use network auto-discovery to identify new devices attached to the network immediately.
- **Web proxy log:** Review logs to identify websites your organization connects to; flag and investigate unauthorized sites.

The last option is to invest in an application designed to identify and control shadow IT. The biggest area of growth in shadow IT is in the cloud. I am suggesting looking at acquiring a cloud access service broker (CASB). Not only can you manage your current cloud service providers and implement security policies, but you can also identify unauthorized IT sprawl.

A comprehensive list of CASB products is available in Appendix A.

## 3.6.3 Attack Surface Classification

One of the most effective ways to determine which components of your attack surface are the most critical is to conduct an asset classification project. Classifying assets removes ambiguity as to which assets should be protected first and to what extent should investment be made in treating risk to those assets. Asset classifications provide an expectation to the degree of countermeasures and integrity controls that should apply. For example, if mobile devices for financial analysts were given an asset classification of restricted, then they would receive countermeasures and controls matched to restricted devices. I have used as a rule of thumb that the asset classification of a cyber asset is paired to the highest data classification to which the asset has access. Table 3-14 presents the cyber access classifications I use in my own projects.

**Table 3-14. Cyber Assets Classification Schema**

| Level | Designation | Description | Examples |
|-------|-------------|-------------|----------|
| 1 | Public | Information should be classified as public when the unauthorized disclosure, alteration, or destruction of that data would result in little or no risk to the organization and its partners. Minimal or no controls are required to protect the confidentiality of public data; however, some level of control is required to prevent unauthorized modification or destruction of public information. | • Annual reports.<br>• Brochures.<br>• Press releases.<br>• Publicly released information. |
| 2 | Internal | Information should be classified as internal when not approved for general circulation outside the organization where its loss would inconvenience the organization or its partners but where disclosure is unlikely to result in financial loss or serious damage to credibility. A reasonable level of security controls should be applied to internal information. | • Job descriptions.<br>• Internal phone numbers.<br>• Non-sensitive meetings minutes.<br>• Organization charts. |

| Level | Designation | Description | Examples |
|-------|-------------|-------------|----------|
| 3 | Confidential | Information should be classified as confidential when the unauthorized disclosure, alteration, or destruction of that information could result in a moderate level of risk to the organization and its partners. A high level of security controls should be applied to confidential information. | • Customer information.<br>• Financial budgets.<br>• Future product plans.<br>• Sensitive meeting notes. |
| 4 | Restricted | Information should be classified as restricted when the unauthorized disclosure, alteration, or destruction of that information could cause a significant level of risk to the organization or partners. The highest level of security controls must be applied to restricted information. | • Board meeting notes.<br>• Business plans.<br>• Cybersecurity program documentation.<br>• IP addresses.<br>• Personally identifiable information (PII). |

### 3.6.4 Attack Surface Management (ASM)

Attack surfaces are ever changing and require oversight and management. One way to accomplish this is through the deployment of an attack surface management product. ASM products continuously discovery assets on the network and identity threat vectors or attacker pathways. ASM products are a subset of asset management tools. Asset management tools can also be used to identity and quantify threat vectors. Table 3-15 presents providers of attack surface management.

**Table 3-15. Attack Surface Management Software**

| Product | Source | Overview | |
|---|---|---|---|
| Attack Surface Manager | Illusive Networks | Provides perpetual discovery and selective automation needed to find and remove high-risk pathways, easily and at scale. | https://www.illusivenetworks.com/technology/platform/attack-surface-manager |
| Digital Attack Surface Management | RiskIQ | Tracking of active crime servers throughout the world. | https://www.riskiq.com/attack-surface-management/ |
| Attack Surface Visibility | Skybox Security | Attack surface modeling, to display the complex interaction of security controls, network topology, vulnerabilities and threats in the context of a business. | https://www.skyboxsecurity.com/solutions/attack-surface-visibility |

*Note*: Links are current as of September 22, 2019.

# 3.7 Cyber Threat Intelligence

Organizations ready to move to the next level of threat management can turn to external intelligence services to aid in their threat decision-making process. Actionable intelligence is key to guiding threat management investments. Dedicating personnel to scour the Internet looking for threat intelligence or gleaning threat data from information sharing and analysis center (ISAC) alerts has proven ineffective. Check out the National Council of ISACS at: https://www.nationalisacs.org/. The alternative is to outsource threat intelligence gathering to companies specializing in sourcing threat information.

For over twenty years, companies have offered threat intelligence services to help organizations stay ahead of the threat curve. Early services relied on manually sifting through vendor vulnerability reports. Now, intelligence services are faster, more in-depth, and highly targeted toward advanced persistent threats. Today's services have solved the relevance problem that plagued this industry for some time. Now, only threat information aligned to an organization's attack surface or industry makes it to the chief information security officer's desk.

In the past, companies found themselves with multiple threat feeds or services that resulted in various levels of redundancy. Redundancies caused multiple alerts for the same threat costing valuable research time to sort out the overlap. As a user of several of these services over the years, I was disappointed with how many low-value alerts where rated as high. I also found much of the reporting run-of-the-mill already known threats.

Requirements guide the gathering of threat intelligence and its analysis to make it actionable. Documenting a proper set of requirements will help you:

- Track bad actors targeting your organization.
- Acquire threat information aligned to your attack surface.
- Know which hacktivist organization targets your industry.
- Understand the types of techniques adversaries use to exploit vulnerabilities in your enterprise.

### 3.7.1 Cyber Threat Intelligence Services

According to Research Report, the threat intelligence market is growing at 18.4% compound annual growth rate (CAGR) and should reach $8.94 billion in 2022. Read the entire report at: https://markets.businessinsider.com/news/stocks/threat-intelligence-market-growing-at-a-cagr-of-18-4-during-2017-to-2022-says-a-new-research-at-reportsnreports-1002223536. Presently, there are nearly 30 providers of cybersecurity intelligence services of various flavors. Some services focus on providing intelligence on professional hackers and hacktivists, while others focus reporting on emerging threats and vulnerabilities based on your attack surface. Approaches vary widely from those firms that provide human intelligence harvested from the deep web to others who provide sophisticated platforms that integrate threat intelligence directly as a feed to your security information and event management (SIEM) solution.

A comprehensive list of threat intelligence service providers is available in Appendix A.

### 3.7.2 Cyber Threat Intelligence Program Use Cases

If you are still wondering how an intelligence capability would benefit your organization, I have highlighted several tactical use cases.

- **Countermeasures alignment:** Countermeasures rely on rules, filters, and signatures to be effective. Intelligence provides advanced warning of specific threats that countermeasures can address if properly configured. Using high quality intelligence reduces false positives.

- **Incident response (IR):** The IR team can use threat intelligence to validate indicators that triggered alarms accelerating response time. The intelligence can provide valuable data about a threat's origin, behavior, and associated adversaries.
- **SecOps:** Threat intelligence can assist SecOps personnel to triage SIEM alerts through the attachment of risk score tags. Threat intelligence systems can interface directly with the SIEM to automate alert prioritization.
- **System hygiene:** Patching systems is a significant effort for any organization and knowing what and when to patch can save precious resources, time, and budget. Most organizations operate on a patching backlog and prioritizing patching efforts allows you to focus on your most at-risk systems.

## 3.8 Cyber Kill Chain

Created by defense giant Lockheed Martin, the term *Cyber Kill Chain*® has been widely used by the security community to describe the different stages of cyberattacks. Shown in Figure 3-5, it's a compelling model, easy to understand, and, let's face it, the name sounds really cool. In military parlance, a "kill chain" is a phase-based model to describe the stages of an attack, which also helps inform ways to prevent such attacks. You can read more at: http://www.lockheedmartin.com/us/what-we-do/aerospace-defense/cyber/cyber-kill-chain.html.

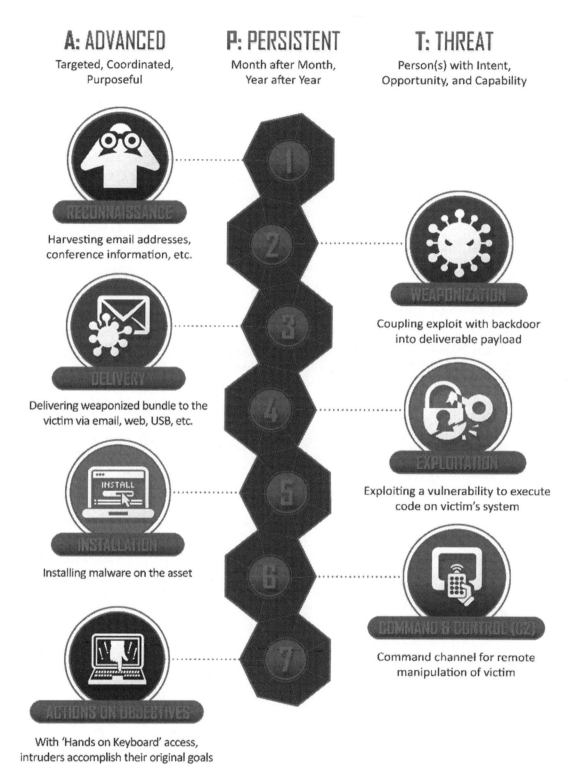

*Figure 3-5. Cyber Kill Chain®. (Registered by Lockheed Martin. Diagram has been authorized for use by Lockheed Martin for this publication.)*

160

The stages of an attack are referred to as:

1. **Reconnaissance** – The employee identifies data he or she wishes to steal and tests the criminal or competitor market to determine worth. The malicious employee will also find ways to escalate privileges and accesses to view sensitive information.
2. **Weaponization** – This may take the form of preparing encrypted flash drives or hidden partitions on removable media for the storage of stolen data. In the event of sabotage, the malicious insider may insert malware to disrupt or cripple organization operations.
3. **Delivery** – This may represent the actual copying of data or theft of physical devices from the employer. More sophisticated delivery techniques include the deployment of a remote access Trojan, allowing direct access from an external entity.
4. **Exploitation** – This involves the manipulation of a system weakness or vulnerability compromise of a target application or system.
5. **Installation** – In some circumstances, this may take the form of backdoors or logic bombs installed on company systems to give the employee remote access after his or her departure. In addition, this may take the form of wiping of systems to cover the employee's tracks.
6. **Command and control** – If backdoors are installed by the employee, this step would enable a rogue employee to maintain access to corporate proprietary data, and to potentially manipulate company data after his or her departure.
7. **Action on objectives** – This would include the sale of the stolen data, posting the data to the Internet, or providing the data to a competitor company for enabling the competitor an unfair advantage. Continued theft of corporate proprietary data and data manipulation also may occur in this phase.

Ideally, the further towards the beginning of the Cyber Kill Chain an attack can be stopped, the better. The less information an attacker has, for instance, the less likely someone else can use that information to complete the attack later. The Cyber Kill Chain model provides security professionals a general roadmap for the lifecycle of a compromise, whether that be an internal or external compromise. Additionally, the Cyber Kill Chain model allows for the mapping of a complex compromise in terms and phases that can be understood without diving "into the weeds" in technical details. The use of the Cyber Kill Chain model is optimized when in competent hands, and used with coherent incident response procedures, a healthy infrastructure, and organizational support.

## 3.9 Threat Frameworks

Collecting, processing and analyzing threat information requires a lot of processing horsepower and a normalization framework for organizations to make the most of threat intelligence. Frameworks allow companies to make the most threat data by turning the ingested raw data into actionable information. Threat frameworks provide automated information sharing for cybersecurity situational awareness, real-time network defense, and complex threat analysis.

Table 3-16 lists the most widely used threat frameworks used and integrated into threat management platforms.

**Table 3-16. Threat Frameworks**

| Framework | Summary | URL |
|---|---|---|
| Cyber Threat Framework (CTF) | The Cyber Threat Framework was developed by the US Government to enable consistent characterization and categorization of cyber threat events, and to identify trends or changes in the activities of cyber adversaries. | https://www.dni.gov/index.php/cyber-threat-framework |
| Open-Source Intelligence Gathering Training (OSINT) | A cybersecurity framework, a collection of OSINT tools to make intel and data collection tasks easier. Used by security researchers and penetration testers for digital footprinting, threat research, intelligence gathering, and reconnaissance. | https://www.sans.org/course/open-source-intelligence-gathering |
| Structured Language for Cyber Threat Intelligence (STIX) | A language and serialization format used to exchange cyber threat intelligence (CTI). STIX is open source and free allowing those interested to contribute and ask questions freely. | https://oasis-open.github.io/cti-documentation/stix/intro |
| Trusted Automated eXchange of Indicator Information (TAXII™) | An application protocol for exchanging CTI over HTTPS. TAXII defines a RESTful API (a set of services and message exchanges) and a set of requirements for TAXII Clients and Servers. | https://taxiiproject.github.io/ |

*Note: Links are current as of September 22, 2019.*

## 3.10 Assumption of Breach

The assumption of breach model was first coined by Kirk Baily, former CISO of the City of Seattle (Guy, 2012). The concept is that breaches have already or will soon occur within your enterprise and you should refocus your energies from preventing breaches from occurring to responding to breaches. Some security technology companies such as CrowdStrike have built their business model around the assumption of breach. CrowdStrike is so confident of their approach that they began offering a $1 million warranty for customers who become compromised (Jackson, 2018).

The assumption of breach model is a perfect scenario for red team exercises where faux attackers (red team) are defended by a blue team. It can also serve as the new bar for investing in protecting assets and information. If you assume breach it changes the perspective of how you design and invest in security processes.

Organizations that assume breach should focus on:

- Detection of attacks.
- Detection of penetrations.
- Response to attacks.
- Response to penetrations.
- Recovery from data attacks.
- Halting data exfiltration.

## 3.11 Cyber Threat, Vulnerability Detection, and Intelligence Checklist

Creating a cyber threat, vulnerability detection, and intelligence capability will be one of the more important, yet complex undertakings in your journey of building a cybersecurity program. There are many options that should be considered before finalizing your approach. You should recognize that some of the topics discussed in this chapter, such as threat-modeling, may be too advanced to address initially. This is perfectly normal, and you should only tackle those portions of this chapter you are comfortable with. To help guide you in the process, I have provided a checklist in Table 3-17.

**Table 3-17. Cyber Threat, Vulnerability Detection, and Intelligence Checklist**

| Step | Activity |
|------|----------|
| 1 | Define threat, vulnerability, and intelligence model – use the example model in Section 3.1.1 to create a visual of the model your organization will follow for identifying threats, vulnerabilities, and intelligence. |
| 2 | Select cyber threat categories – select the categories of cyber threats identified in Table 3-1 that your organization is most likely to face. |
| 3 | Adopt threat category levels – create a threat category matrix based on the example in Table 3-2. |
| 4 | Create a threat taxonomy – create a threat taxonomy in Excel using the attributes listed in Table 3-3. Leverage the threat taxonomy sources listed in Section 3.2.2.1. |
| 5 | Create threat actor profiles – identify and document the threat actors most likely to target your organization. Leverage threat actors profile reporting services listed in Table 3-5. |
| 6 | Define a cyber threat-hunting strategy – define the policy and strategy that your organization adopts to perform threat-hunting. Leverage a threat-hunting tool listed in Table 3-6. |
| 7 | Perform threat-modeling – adopt a threat-modeling approach and begin the process on the most damaging impacts such as a data breach. Leverage solutions listed in Table 3-7. |
| 8 | Select threat detection solutions – select cyber threat detection solutions to address the top threats identified in your threat taxonomy. Use Table 3-9. |
| 9 | Define cyber threat metrics – define and implement a manageable set of cyber threat metrics. Reference sample metrics in Table 3-10. |
| 10 | Display cyber threat maps in C-SOC – select most effective threat maps to display on a C-SOC screen. |

| Step | Activity |
|------|----------|
| 11 | Deploy vulnerability scanning solution – select and deploy a vulnerability scanning solution to scan the attack surface components. |
| 12 | Deploy patch management solution – leverage a patch management solution to remediate detected vulnerabilities. |
| 13 | Inventory your attack surface – inventory organization cyber assets and organization into an attack surface representation. |
| 14 | Identify shadow IT – account for and assess the threats and vulnerabilities associated with shadow IT. |
| 15 | Adopt cyber asset classification schema – Leverage Table 3-12 to create a cyber classifications schema. |
| 16 | Select cybersecurity intelligence sources – identify and implement feeds or sources of cyber threat or threat actor intelligence. Adjust threat detection solution appropriately. |

## *Summary*

Understanding the threats your organization is most vulnerable to is arguably one of the most important roles you will play in your organization's cybersecurity program. Selecting the right threats to focus on drives your investments in countermeasures and ensures that you have the proper safeguards in place to defend your information and assets from harm. Identifying as well as detecting cyber threats and determining attack surface vulnerabilities require a delicate balance of human assets and technology. A scenario of too much technology and too little human interaction or just the reverse leaves gaps. Learning to leverage actionable intelligence helps close that gap. In Chapter 4, your next stop on your journey will take what you have learned about threats and vulnerabilities and show you how to create a risk profile of your organization.

# References

Center for Internet Security. (2017). *Alert level information: What do the different alert level colors indicate?* Retrieved from https://www.cisecurity.org/cybersecurity-threats/alert-level/

Moreno, H. (2017, January 20). Rewriting cybersecurity playbooks. *Forbes.* Retrieved from https://www.forbes.com/sites/forbesinsights/2017/01/20/rewriting-cybersecurity-playbooks/#63464cd31d16

Scott-Railton, J., Marquis-Boire, M., Guarnieri, C., & Marschalek, M. (2015, December 8). *Packrat: Seven years of a South American threat actor.* (Munk School of Business Affairs, University of Toronto.) Retrieved from https://citizenlab.ca/2015/12/packrat-report/

Guy, J. (2012, May 11). *Who coined "assumption of breach?* Armatum Networks. Retrieved from http://armatum.com/blog/2012/who-coined-assumption-of-breach/

Jackson, K. (2018, June 5). *CrowdStrike Launches $1 Million Security Breach Warranty.* DarkReading. Retrieved from https://www.darkreading.com/cloud/crowdstrike-launches-$1-million-security-breach-warranty/d/d-id/1331972

# Self-Study Questions

The following questions will help you build your expertise in establishing a foundation of governance.

1. What three things must come together to create an intelligence model?
   Intelligence gathering, vulnerability discovery, and threat determination.

2. What is the motivation of a hacktivist?
   Politically motivated and cause-based to right a perceived wrong.

3. What are the five standard threat levels?
   Low, guarded, elevated, high and severe.

4. What is threat hunting?
   Offensive means of targeting hackers who may already be in a network using similar tactics, techniques and procedures (TTP).

5. What is the primary purpose of vulnerability scanning?
   To uncover weakness in a network.

6. What are the three types of threat modeling?
    Asset, attacker and software-centric.


7. What is virtual patching?
    The surrounding of an asset that cannot be practically patched with security safeguards that will defend against the vulnerability that a patch is designed to accomplish.


8. What is an attack surface?
    The assets or anything of value that a hacker can potentially exploit.


9. What is shadow IT?
    Applications, technology or cloud services deployed by end users that are not officially supported by the organization. Represents unknown risk to an organization.


10. What is the Cyber Kill Chain?
    A model developed by Lockheed Martin that describes the stages of a cyberattack. Knowing each stage enables an organization to prepare to stop an attack in that stage.

# Chapter 4

# Building a Cyber Risk Management Capability

Knowing the threats and vulnerabilities that could impact your organization is one thing, doing something about it is something else. Building a cyber risk capability will be your chance to address the threats and vulnerabilities identified in Chapter 3. In this chapter, you will learn how to take what you learned about threats and vulnerabilities and convert that knowledge into creating a risk profile of your organization. Understanding risk is fundamental to protecting your organization's assets and information. Risk is what you will balance countermeasures against to reduce the impact of threats exploiting vulnerabilities on your organization. Not only will you have to worry about your organization's risk, but you will also have to be concerned with the risk profile of the organizations you conduct business with.

In this chapter, I will also address third-party risk management. Risk management is part art and part science. The science part I will show you in this chapter; the art part is up to you, or rather I should say your intuition. Sometimes you just need to trust your instincts on which risk is greater than another. You will need to apply critical thinking and take a pragmatic approach to managing risk, recognizing that you must find an approach to risk management that balances the need to protect assets and information with sound business judgement.

*This chapter will help you to:*

- Understand the fundamental concepts of risk management.
- Estimate your organization's appetite for risk.
- Determine the right amount to spend on reducing risk.
- Learn how to track and manage risk effectively.

## Chapter 4 Roadmap

Building a cyber risk management capability upon which you can reliably base your cybersecurity program, knowing it has been designed to address the greatest risk to your organization, is the outcome of this portion of your journey.

Figure 4.0 presents a reference architecture of how risk is identified, evaluated and treated in your organization. There are many nuances to risk management, not the least of which is identifying just how much risk your organization is willing to accept. You will also need to draw that line in the sand that sets the threshold of risk your organization will never cross.

The cyber risk capability provides ways for you to calculate risk so that you can rank risk from high to low in order to focus your energies and investments on those risks that could cause the greatest harm, by treating the highest risk through avenues of mitigation, insurance, etc. Risk is managed from your enterprise assets to your supply chain or third parties.

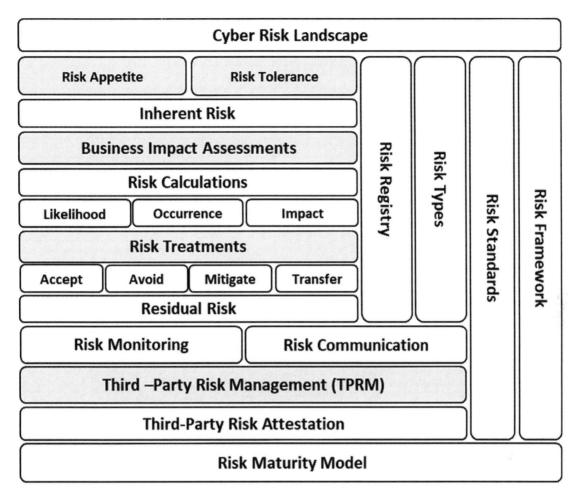

*Figure 4.0. Cyber Risk Management Capability Reference Architecture*

Each main component (gray) and sub-component of the reference architecture is covered in more detail later in the chapter.

This fourth stop of your journey is arguably one of the most important stops as you will determine the risk profile for your organization. Cybersecurity programs are best deployed when they are risk-based – virtually every security standard emphasizes that protecting information and assets needs to be based on a risk profile. The following outlines where to focus your initial energies:

- **Step 1: Determine Risk Appetite** – The amount of risk your organization is willing to accept in return for pursuing a benefit is your appetite. You will need to understand how much or how little of an appetite your organization has for retaining risk.
- **Step 2: Establish Risk Tolerance** – Establishing a maximum amount of risk your organization is willing to tolerate in numerical terms drives risk acceptance, risk

insurance and investments in risk treatments. Tolerance is expressed as a percentage – you will need to know your organization's risk maximum level of tolerance.

- **Step 3: Conduct Business Impact Assessments (BIA)** – Understanding how your organization is disrupted during a cyber or disaster event is critical to knowing how much energy and investment to apply to mitigating or managing the impacts. BIAs should be required for all critical components of your attack surface. If your organization has separate BIA functions within the disaster recovery or business continuity group, leverage those.
- **Step 4: Apply Risk Treatments** – Once risks are known they will require treatment. Treating risk can involve simply accepting the risk, avoiding the activity that causes the risk, mitigating the condition that causes the risk in order to lower the risk score, or transferring the risk to an insurance policy. Regardless of the treatment, your organization still owns the risk.
- **Step 5: Define Third-Party Risk Management Program** – Your organization's supply chain or third-party risk could account for your greatest threat. Here you will need to apply your risk management processes to organizations with whom you have a contractual relationship. Third-parties are part of your attack surface.

As with other chapters, if you have limited resources to analyze and treat risk, here are the minimum risk management activities you should engage:

- **Define Risk Tolerance** – Meet with your organization financial management and have them specify an exact dollar amount of risk your organization cannot exceed. This number is a blend of self-insurance, risk management, and insurance coverage. Ensure this risk reflects impacts occurring from cyber threats.
- **Acquire BIA Assumptions** – Performing individual BIAs can be time-consuming. Go to application or critical business process owners and have them provide an impact estimate based on their best guess. Borrow BIAs from other parts of the organization if possible. Work with them to provide a realistic number. Rank the assets by their loss potential.
- **Treat Highest Rated Risks** – Approach your highest rated risks in manageable batches and apply risk treatments. Apply multiple layers of controls at the higher end of the ranking. Once you have completed one batch, move to the next. Addressing manageable numbers makes the task less overwhelming.
- **Identify and Treat Third-Parties Risk** – Focus your risk treatment efforts on suppliers that have access to your network and/or information; require they provide evidence of information protection and treat the gaps.

Risk management generally has the most moving parts in a cybersecurity program. Risk changes dynamically and requires constant attention. You must have a continuously improving program to manage and treat risk before their score changes, even when you're not looking. Don't assume by addressing the quick hits mentioned above that your program is complete. You will need to buttress your program through the application of all components of the reference architecture.

## 4.1 Cyber Risk

In the previous chapter, you learned about threats and their relationship to vulnerabilities, which when combined can cause an impact to your business. In this chapter, we explore the concept of risk. Risk is the possibility of a threat exploiting a vulnerability, as well as the cost associated with the loss of use or value of your assets and information. You learned in Chapter 3 that assets and information represent your attack surface. In the context of cyber risk exposure, you need to consider impacts resulting from financial loss, regulatory fines, operational disruption, and reputational damage. Figure 4-1 shows the relationship between threats, vulnerabilities, and risk using a Venn diagram.

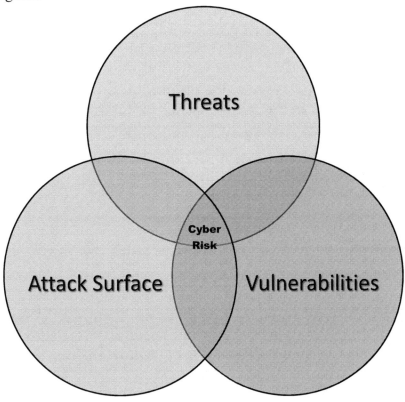

*Figure 4-1. Threats, Vulnerabilities, and Risk Relationship Model*

In the model in Figure 4-1, we can see that the intersection of threats, vulnerabilities, and your attack surface is where risk exists. Managing the risk created from threats and vulnerabilities is the capability of your cybersecurity program that we will now focus on. It is important that you do not repeat a common mistake by confusing threats and risks. Always remember that risk represents both the potential that a threat will exploit a vulnerability, plus the impact to

173

information and assets should that exploitation occur. For example, a distributed denial of service (DDoS) attack is a threat that could exploit a vulnerability in an organization where no Internet load balancing exists. The risk is the likelihood of a DDoS attack occurring and the impact that could be caused.

## 4.1.1 Cyber Risk Landscape

The risk landscape that you need to beware of includes the risk to your organization and the risk to your cyber assets. Think of your organization in terms of a topographical map. By looking at the map you can see the rugged terrain as well as the smooth plains. Your risk landscape is very much like this map. There are areas of your organization that will have greater or lesser risk based on the threats and vulnerabilities that exist within their respective areas. Always remember that your risk landscape is forever changing. According to a recent report sponsored by Aon, organizations now value cyber assets 14% more than property, plant, and equipment assets (Aon & Ponemon, 2017). You will need to keep an eye on your risk landscape to observe any changes and what value your organization places on the assets and information protected. I have found that when management feels cyber assets are less important, it becomes difficult to gain cybersecurity program funding. To help you keep watch over your risk landscape, here is a list of common landscape components:

- Cyber assets.
- Equipment that is not related to information technology (IT).
- Plants.
- People.
- Property.
- Supply chain.
- Third-party providers.

Risk management is all about reducing financial losses, avoiding regulatory fines, and mitigating damage to your organization's reputation. Quantifying the value of your organization's reputation and estimating a diminished reputation resulting from a cyberattack are not easy tasks. If you are a public corporation, you can use the goodwill stated in your financial statement as a guide to figuring out the cost of diminished reputation. Estimating the cost of incurring regulatory fines is straightforward, since the regulations by which your organization abides state the consequences of non-compliance.

Fortunately, estimating the financial losses from a cyberattack is much easier. Many reports on cybersecurity impacts are published annually. Just do a quick Google search and they will come flying at you right and left. One study I like is produced by Cybersecurity Ventures. Its Cybersecurity Almanac provided these sobering statistics about the impacts of a security breach (Morgan, 2019):

- Cybercrime damages will cost $6 trillion annually by 2021.
- Global ransomware costs are predicted to hit $20 billion in 2021.
- 90% of successful hacks and data breaches stem from phishing scams.

## 4.1.2 Risk Types

At the highest level of risk management, risk is grouped into four categories: compliance, financial, operational, and strategic. Examples of each type of risk are included in Table 4-1.

**Table 4-1. Risk Types**

| Risk Type | Overview |
|---|---|
| Compliance | <ul><li>Contractual agreements.</li><li>Global data protection requirements.</li><li>Violation of laws or regulations:<ul><li>Cybersecurity.</li><li>Data breach.</li><li>Data privacy.</li></ul></li></ul> |
| Financial | <ul><li>Currency exchange, funding and cash flow, credit risk.</li><li>Fraud or embezzlement.</li><li>Financial misstatements (e.g., Sarbanes-Oxley Act).</li></ul> |
| Operational | <ul><li>Cyberattack.</li><li>Data theft.</li><li>Disruption to supply chain.</li><li>Disruption to utilities.</li><li>Inefficient use of resources, increasing business costs.</li><li>Loss of key personnel.</li><li>Physical property damage or disruption.</li><li>Product counterfeiting.</li></ul> |
| Strategic | <ul><li>Competition for skilled talent.</li><li>Loss of intellectual property and trade secrets.</li><li>Loss of trust.</li><li>Negative impact to reputation.</li><li>Poor business decisions or mismanagement.</li></ul> |

You should be most concerned with operational risk within the context of building your cybersecurity program. However, you should be aware of other areas of risk as most organizations now look at risk from an enterprise or company-wide perspective. Specifically, ask yourself how your risk management program can aid in any other areas of organizational risk management. Each area you find an intersection point will increase the value of your cybersecurity program. For example, a lower operational risk score could lower insurance premiums, reduce capital reserve requirements, and increase sales by raising the confidence level of potential customers.

## 4.1.3 Cyber Risk Appetite

The first place we want to start is determining your organization's appetite for risk. If you have ever invested in the stock market using a financial advisor, you were asked to complete a questionnaire so the advisor could determine your appetite for risk in investing. This is very similar. Knowing your organization's appetite for risk drives the entire program. For example, if your organization has a high tolerance for risk, a sort of a throw-caution-to-the-winds attitude, then your job will be easy. On the other hand, if the appetite is low, you have your work cut out for you. The trick is to find your organization's sweet spot.

Risk appetite is the predilection an organization has toward pursuing business understanding that one is aggressive, there will always be risk. It is the age-old axiom of risk versus reward. An example of a risk appetite in a cybersecurity context would be an organization that decided to release a revenue generating application before completing all the necessary security testing. This organization weighed the cost of lost new revenue and market position by delaying the application against the probability and cost of a data breach. To this organization, its appetite of risk was defined as acceptable losses. Documenting your organization's risk appetite will require something called a risk appetite statement.

### 4.1.3.1 Risk Appetite Statement

You will need to create and publish a set of cyber risk appetite statements to articulate the level and type of risk your organization is willing to accept while pursuing its business model. Five types of risk appetite statements can be produced. The totality of these five statements is what produces your organization's overall risk appetite score. Risk appetites can vary by category. You may have a large appetite for risk within the category of regulatory risk, but a very low one in the category of financial risk. Table 4-2 provides you with an example set of risk appetite statements.

**Table 4-2. Risk Appetite Statements**

| Category | Statement (Sample) | Risk Tolerance Level |
|---|---|---|
| Financial Risk | The organization's approach to investments in cybersecurity countermeasures is commensurate with the organization's value of assets and information at risk. The organization will not expend without considered justification more than 8% of the overall IT budget on cybersecurity countermeasures. This amount is based on the estimated cost of a serious data breach, the coverage provided by the organization's cybersecurity policy, and an amount of self-insurance allocated in the general fund. | Moderate (2) |
| Operational Risk | The organization's appetite for operational risk is limited to investing in people, procedures, and processes that enable a minimum uptime of critical business functions of 99.999%. Uptime target extends to contracted third-parties. | Low (1) |
| Regulatory Risk | The organization's regulatory compliance risk appetite is based on a policy of following a unified compliance framework that when asked by a regulatory agency would demonstrate compliance with the subject regulation. The organization believes the cost and resources of complying individually with over fifty separate legal and regulatory compliance statutes is not feasible economically or resource allocation wise. | Moderate (2) |
| Technology Risk | The organization's appetite for technology risk is based on using information technology that has passed Common Criteria for Information Technology Security Evaluation (CC). Only products with valid certificates issued from CC Certificate Authorizing Members will be connected to the network. | High (3) |
| Third-Party Risk | The organization's risk appetite for using third-party service providers is limited to contracting with third-parties who can provide a current accredited cybersecurity certification. Acceptable certifications include CSA Security, Trust & Assurance Registry (STAR), HITRUST Third-party Assurance Program, ISO 27001 Certification and AICPA SOC 2®. | Low (1) |
| **Overall Score** | | **9** |

| Scale | | |
|---|---|---|
| Low (1 to 5) | Moderate (6 to 10) | High (11 to 15) |
| Authorized and Approved by | Date | |
| _____ | _____ | |
| Jane Doe | | |
| CEO | | |

*Note: Links are current as of July 7, 2019.*

Depending on your need, you can add statements for reputation, human capital, etc. You will need to incorporate senior management signatures to formally acknowledge the acceptance of risk. The next section will show you how to arrive at assigning risk tolerance levels of each statement (as shown in the third column of Table 4-2). It is the total of the assigned risk appetite levels in all categories that yields your organization's overall risk appetite score.

## 4.1.4 Risk Tolerance

Risk tolerance is a quantification of the maximum amount of risk an organization is willing to assume. Let's use our previous example (from section 4.1.3). In this case, the organization quantified the cost of a data breach from performing a business impact assessment (BIA). (BIAs will be discussed later in the chapter.) The analysis showed a worst-case example of a potential loss of $1 million, consisting of regulatory fines, data breach remediation, and customer goodwill gestures. This would be offset by $100 million in new revenue. The organization determined that its loss reserve pool of $1 million could easily handle the financial consequences of a data breach without the need to access other areas of liquidity.

Several factors need to be considered when defining risk tolerance levels, including impeding operational readiness, financial loss, etc. Table 4-3 provides sample definitions of risk tolerance levels:

**Table 4-3. Risk Tolerance Definitions**

| Level | Definition |
|---|---|
| 1 - Low | The risk results in less than $50,000 in financial losses, does not substantially impact operations, and any loss of customer goodwill will return within 30 days. |
| 2 - Moderate | The risk results in less than $250,000 in financial losses, impacts delivery of core services but does not halt services, and organizational impact is limited to a small set of customers. |
| 3 - High | The risk results in more than $500,000 in financial losses, organizational reputation is impacted by negative national press, and customer losses could exceed 20%. |

You can define whatever definition you feel best captures the level of risk tolerance your organization is willing to accept.

> **TIP:** Remember that although the terms *risk appetite* and *risk tolerance* are similar, they mean very different things. Appetite is a broad characterization of a company's attitude toward risk, while risk tolerance is more specific about an exact tolerance level.

## 4.1.5 Risk Threshold

As if risk appetite and risk tolerance were not confusing enough, I need to throw another term your way, *risk threshold*. Risk threshold is a specific level of a risk category that an organization does not wish to cross. You can refer to this as the risk "over and under." Using what was previously defined I will craft an example. If your organization has a low tolerance for financial loss, the threshold is set at $50,000. Anything below that threshold is accepted, anything over is not tolerated. When risk crosses a threshold, decisive action must be taken to bring the risk back below the threshold. I suggest that you put metrics in place to track the degree to which your organization goes over or stays under established risk thresholds.

To help keep risk appetite, risk tolerance, and risk threshold straight, Figure 4-2 shows how each interacts with one another using a specific example. Here we can see the appetite for risk in a category is low or $100,000. The organization has set a risk tolerance of plus or minus 5%, allowing for the fluidity of risk and application of countermeasures. However, an absolute ceiling or threshold has been set at $5,000 that your organization cannot pass.

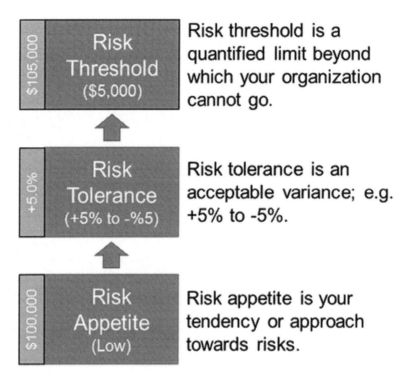

Figure 4-2. Risk Terms Relation

## 4.1.6 Risk Acceptance

Risk acceptance is the concept of accepting risk. You would arrive at this point once you have determined that you either do not want to take any actions to address a specific risk because the likelihood and impact are too low to be concerned about, or you determine that the cost of addressing or controlling the risk prevents you from acting. In any event, you cannot take any further action; you have done all that you can. Just because you accept a risk does not mean you can ignore it. You must carefully document the risk and all the reasons why you could not lower the current risk level. This means that if you have a risk that scored high after a risk assessment, it remains high because you have accepted that score. Your documenting the reason why you accepted the risk will be critical when you have a breach of security and questions are raised on why a high risk was left untreated. The process of documenting your organization's risk acceptance is accomplished using a risk acceptance statement.

### 4.1.6.1 Risk Acceptance Statement

A risk acceptance statement, also referred to a risk acceptance letter or memo, is the instrument used to document your organization's acceptance of one or more risks. A risk acceptance statement has several objectives. The first one is to document to auditors and regulators why your organization chose not to address certain risks. The second is to be a method of disclosure to the other parties you have a business relationship with that could be impacted by your organization not addressing these risks. Lastly, it serves as notice of accountability through which senior management of your organization must formally acknowledge the acceptance of risk. The acknowledgement of acceptance of risk will be logged within your organization's risk registry. I will cover a risk registry later in the chapter.

## 4.1.7 Inherent Risk

Inherent risk is the probability of loss occurring from a threat exploiting a vulnerability absent of any countermeasures or controls to protect against the threat. What this means is that you need to know what the risk is to your information and assets before you start piling on countermeasures and controls. In many cases, you will be involved in a cybersecurity program where countermeasures and controls have already been applied to reduce risk. In this event, it is not so easy to unwind the safeguards to determine inherent risk. You can make some general assumptions; however, do not spend too much time attempting to define inherent risk as the rewards of doing it are limited. Focus your time ensuring the current safeguards are known and well documented.

## 4.1.8 Residual Risk

Residual risk is what you are left with after you have applied countermeasures and controls. Another way you can look at inherent and residual risk is gross and net risk. All cybersecurity programs will retain some level of residual risk regardless of the maturity of the program. It is important for you to understand that in most cases risk can never be set to zero; some level of risk is always retained. There are several reasons why risk must be retained. One is that there are obvious cost constraints to reducing risk. Think of your house – you can add alarms and deadbolts, but you likely stop short of putting bars on your windows. The lack of bars means that someone can still break in, but you are willing to accept that risk.

Organizations can only practically invest in protecting assets and information commensurate to either their value or estimated impact loss. Plus, there is no crystal ball on when a threat will exploit a vulnerability causing a loss. This means that it is not necessarily practical to protect a risk as if it were at risk 100% of the time. In risk management, we refer to this as "building a church for Easter." This is where I introduce you to the concept of annualized loss expectancy (ALE) which is how we properly plan for risk events. Figure 4-3 will help you understand inherent and residual risk.

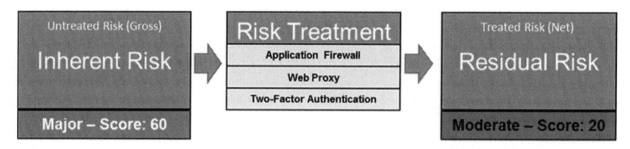

Figure 4-3. Inherent Versus Residual Risk

## 4.1.9 Annualized Loss Expectancy (ALE)

If we were to build a church for Easter, the busiest day of the year where the full congregation shows up for church, it could increase the construction budget by nearly 50% – not something churches can afford. Rather, we would want to know the average number of parishioners sitting in the pews for each Sunday service and work around that average to build to that specification. If we consistently exceed capacity, we can add extra services, etc. Estimating the number of times, a threat occurs requires the same type of thinking only we have a formula called annualized loss expectancy (ALE) to help us. The ALE is the expected monetary loss that can be expected for an asset annually. In risk management, we typically use a ten-year period. ALE includes the following components:

- **Asset value (AV):** The value you have determined an asset to be worth. Assets can be information, cyber assets, or even intangible things of value such as reputation or goodwill. For example, you may have arrived at a customer record value of $7 each; if you had one million records, the asset value would be $7 million.
- **Exposure factor (EF):** The estimated percentage of damage or impact that a realized threat would have on the asset. The range is zero to 100%. The concept is that exploited threats generally do not result in 100% loss during a cyberattack. This would be more of a cyber black swan event that I discuss later.
- **Single loss expectancy (SLE):** Here we take the asset value multiplied by the exposure factor to determine what the expected loss would be for a single event. If we were to estimate that we expected only 25% of our records to be compromised, the SLE would be $1.75 million of our $7 million asset value.

- **Annual rate of occurrence (ARO):** The last number we need to determine for our formula is how many times over a ten-year period we expect the threat event to occur. To arrive at this, we would either use our own organization's experience or do some research on reported averages. ARO ranges from 0.0 (never) to 1.0 (always). If you were to select 1.0, you are stating the event happens once a year; if you specify 0.30, you are stating that it will happen three times over ten years.
- **Annualized loss expectancy (ALE):** Arriving at our final calculation we take the SLE multiplied by the ARO to arrive at what our estimated annual loss could be. The ALE spreads out the expected loss over ten years. Figure 4-4 presents the formula for determining ALE.

| ALE Calculator | | | | |
|---|---|---|---|---|
| Asset Value (AV) | Exposure Factor (EF) | Single Loss Expectancy (SLE) | Annual Rate of Occurrence (ARO) | Annualized Loss Expectancy (ALE) |
| $7,000,000 | .25 | $1,750,000 | 0.1 | $175,000 |
| **(AV x EF = SLE) x (ARO) = ALE** | | | | |

Figure 4-4. Annualized Loss Expectancy Calculator

The main value of an ALE formula is that it provides guidance on how much you should invest in reducing risk. Using our records compromise example, it would not be necessary to invest $1,750,000 to protect against a data compromise of $7,000,000 worth of customer records because we have estimated a data breach event would only impact us once over a ten-year period making an annual investment of $175,000 in data breach prevention technology appropriate. Arriving at a number helps you determine whether you want to self-insure or acquire cyber breach insurance for example.

## 4.1.10 Return on Investment (ROI)

One of the traits you will require as a manager involved with your organization's cybersecurity program is the ability to discuss your program in monetary terms. You will need to present financial justifications for investments in your organization's program to your senior management. Even if your management is very keen on investing in cybersecurity, at some point, you will be asked, "Are we spending the right amount to protect our assets and information?" Would you be able to answer that question? The ALE gives us an amount that is reasonable considering the damage that could occur from a cyberattack, but how do we use that number to prove we can achieve a return on investment?

There are different criteria by which to measure ROI, and there are many ways to quantify it. You will need to check with your organization's chief financial officer (CFO) on the best way to calculate ROI. In its simplest form, though, ROI is the ratio of present value of expected benefits over the present value of expected costs. For our purposes, present value of expected benefit is not experiencing an ALE of $175,000 from our previous data breach example, and the present value of expected costs is the investment we will need to make in countermeasures to prevent the loss. I do wish to provide you with fair warning that not all senior management will buy in to the approach that $175,000 is an actual annual savings. They will argue that it does not show up on the bottom line each year. I have countered these arguments in the past by stating that cyber breaches are too numerous and frequent to ignore and that losses are indeed real.

Beginning with our ALE number in the previous section of $175,000 we will calculate an ROI. The first thing we must do is estimate the cost of treating the data breach risk. For purposes of illustration I will determine that we invested in data encryption and data loss prevention (DLP) software. The capital expense to purchase both products is $155,000. I need to also include the cost of maintenance and updates, which is customarily 20% annually or $31,000 for both products. I will also assume my organization requires an ROI to be achieved within three-years; so, I will add up the cost of acquiring my countermeasures over three years. This brings my total to $246,000. So far, so good. Now let's put it all together. I bring forward my ALE from the previous section of $175,000 and multiple that by three years to arrive at $525,000. I then divide by the cost of my countermeasures over three years, $246,000. This gives a result of 2.13. Now convert that to a percentage, and you will show a 213.41% ROI. Not bad. Figure 4-5 presents the formula for determining this ROI.

| 3-Year Countermeasures Cost | | | | | | |
|---|---|---|---|---|---|---|
| Countermeasures | CapEx | OpEx | Year 1 | Year 2 | Year 3 | Total |
| Data Encryption Software | $75,000 | $15,000 | $90,000 | $14,000 | $14,000 | $118,000 |
| Data Loss Prevention (DLP) | $85,000 | $16,000 | $96,000 | $16,000 | $16,000 | $128,000 |
| Totals | $155,000 | $31,000 | $186,000 | $30,000 | $30,000 | $246,000 |

| 3-Year ALE | Countermeasures Cost | ROI | Project Payback (Years) |
|---|---|---|---|
| $525,000 | $246,000 | 213.41% | 0.47 |

Figure 4-5. ROI Calculation

What should you target for an ROI? It has been my experience that unless you can show an ROI of at least 100% you really don't stand a shot of getting your project approved. Anything over 100% has a better chance of passing the CFO's scrutiny.

Also, an important point to consider is the project's expected payback – when the expected benefit exceeds expected costs, and when that benefit is expected to be realized. If you can achieve ROI within the first year of the project implementation, the more likely the project is to proceed. In our example, the payback is expected in 1.41 years. You will notice that our example does not meet the 100% ROI. If this happens you will need to revisit your investment looking for less expensive alternatives to reach the 100% threshold.

## 4.2 Cyber Risk Assessments

Cyber risk assessments are required to determine the greatest risks to your organization and business and should also assess the adequacy of cyber security controls against a recognized standard or framework. As part of the process, threats and vulnerabilities to an organization will be documented including any insufficient or ineffective controls to mitigate assessed risks. Control gaps will be discussed in Chapter 5. Figure 4-6 presents a risk assessment process I have used over the years. This approach gets you to a risk score before you apply risk treatments.

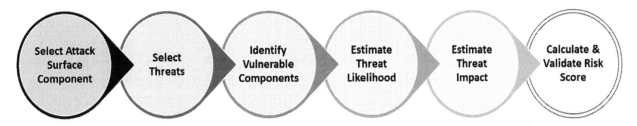

*Figure 4-6. Risk Assessment Process. (By Tari Schreider, licensed under a Creative Commons Attribution-NonCommercial-NoDerivatives 4.0 International License)*

Each phase of the process is carefully constructed to provide the risk score of any component of an attack service. The following describes each one of the phases:

1. **Select attack surface component:** Risk assessments are meant to be formed on discrete components of the attack surface. A component can range from a third-party service provider to a new Internet facing application. Ultimately all components of the attack surface should have a risk assessment on file. You only need one of each component if they are similarly configured and placed within the attack surface. For example, if there are 100 Hewlett Packard (HP) Windows 10 desktop computers, you only need to perform one risk assessment. The same cannot be said of your third-party service providers where each one will require a risk assessment on file. Don't be surprised by the fact that you potentially may require hundreds of risk assessments on file to cover your entire attack surface.
2. **Select threats:** The threat component of the risk assessment process begins with selecting threats from the threat taxonomy, ascertaining if they can exploit known vulnerabilities within the component of the attack surface selected. You may select as many threats as you

wish; however, a word of caution from experience is to begin with a small set of related threats. Because threats and vulnerabilities are so closely linked, you can take some shortcuts that will not diminish the value of the risk assessment. Whenever I perform a risk assessment on applications, I simply select the threat actor profile for a hacker and then match the vulnerabilities known for the application. Staying with my application example, I would leverage the OWASP Top Ten Project application vulnerabilities and assess whether a hacker could exploit any of those vulnerabilities. An example of this is provided in the risk calculator example.

3. **Identify vulnerable components:** For each attack surface component, you will need to locate a list of vulnerabilities. Vulnerabilities can be identified from your vulnerability scans or from authoritative sources such as the OWASP example. Another great source is the National Vulnerability Database (NVD) maintained by the National Institute of Standards and Technology (NIST). In the last chapter, I discussed intelligence sources as a great way to build a list of vulnerabilities that you can match to your attack surface.

4. **Estimate threat likelihood:** Estimating the likelihood of something happening can be very subjective as there are few sources that estimate cybersecurity events with any level of accuracy. Unfortunately, this is where you will need to invest a bit of legwork in researching historical data to identify how often a cyberattack or event happens and over what period. Previously, I presented the framework you will use, annual rate of occurrence (ARO), but you still need to answer the question of how often. Based on my experience and the ponderous amount of cyberattack information published, I can tell you that it is a near statistical certainty your organization will be compromised in one form or another at some time. History also works against us in that the longer your organization exists, the more times you will be attacked. I have started to see many companies that experienced a major breach several years ago circle back around to announce they have been breached yet again.

I can point you in the right direction of how to gather likelihood information through an example. Consider the fact that according to the Experian 2018 Data Breach Industry Forecast 91% of all healthcare organizations reported at least one data breach over a two-year period. The full Experian report can be accessed here: http://www.experian.com/assets/data-breach/white-papers/2018-experian-data-breach-industry-forecast.pdf. Here is how I would use that information if my organization were a hospital. First, I would determine how many hospitals existed in the US; there are 5,564 (American Hospital Association, 2017). Using the Experian number, I now know that 5,063 were compromised over a two-year period. Here I will assume that the number of compromises occurred half in each year, or 2,531 annually. This tells me that I would have had a better than 45% chance of being compromised. Now that I know the percentage of likelihood, I can match that to the likelihood scale and see that 45.5% equates to the "possible" category. The following shows all the likelihood categories:

- **Certain:** 90% to 100%.
- **Likely:** 50% to 89.99%.
- **Possible:** 11% to 49.99%.
- **Unlikely:** 3% to 10.99%.

- **Rare:** 0% to 2.99%.

5. **Estimate threat impact:** Determining threat impacts is like a business impact assessment (BIA) exercise. You can include as many variables as you wish to arrive at a BIA score. However, not all organizations have the time to perform a BIA on all their attack surface components. You will learn more about performing a BIA later in the chapter should you decide to go in that direction.

Estimating threat impacts is generally subjective as no one really knows what is going to happen. What is important, however, is that you have degrees of impacts so that everyone in your organization know a score of five is significantly worse than a one, but they really do not need to know by specifically how much. This is called an ordinal scale. An ordinal scale simply shows, in order of magnitude, how numbers compare with no measurement of differences. The scale I like to use when I do not have a more sophisticated BIA to draw from is the following:

- **Significant – 20.00:** Threat is expected to cause catastrophic damage or loss of information and assets or essential third-party providers. Core business operations will be halted for more than one business day.
- **Major – 15.00:** Threat will degrade core business operations for at least one business day; some damage or loss will occur to assets and information.
- **Moderate – 10.00:** Threat will cause intermittent disruptions to core operations degrading service levels. Damage to assets and information will be localized.
- **Minor – 5.00:** Threat will cause limited disruptions to localized operations; however, core business functions will continue. No loss of assets or information is expected.
- **Insignificant – 1.00:** Threat is considered a nuisance and no impact to operations, assets, or information is expected.

6. **Calculate and validate risk score:** The last phase requires calculating and validating the risk score. This is accomplished using a risk calculator that you can easily create in a Microsoft Excel spreadsheet. Figure 4-7 shows a sample risk score calculation where the likelihood of a threat occurring is multiplied by the impact the threat could have to arrive at a risk score. In this example, I focused on web applications with the threat of a hacker. I chose the OWASP Top Ten vulnerabilities and assigned scores for likelihood and impact.

| Risk Assessment Score | | | | | | | | |
|---|---|---|---|---|---|---|---|---|
| **Attack Surface Component** | **Threat** | **Component Vulnerabilities** | **Likelihood** | | **Impact** | | **Risk Score** |
| Web Application | Hacker | A1 – Injection | Rare | 1.00 | Insignificant | 1.00 | 1.00 |
| Web Application | Hacker | A2 – Broken Authentication and Session Management | Unlikely | 2.00 | Minor | 5.00 | 10.00 |
| Web Application | Hacker | A3 – Cross-Site Scripting (XSS) | Possible | 3.00 | Moderate | 10.00 | 30.00 |
| Web Application | Hacker | A4 – Broken Access Control | Likely | 4.00 | Major | 15.00 | 60.00 |
| Web Application | Hacker | A5 – Security Misconfiguration | Certain | 5.00 | Significant | 20.00 | 100.00 |
| Web Application | Hacker | A6 – Sensitive Data Exposure | Rare | 1.00 | Minor | 5.00 | 5.00 |
| Web Application | Hacker | A7 – Insufficient Attack Protection | Unlikely | 2.00 | Moderate | 10.00 | 20.00 |
| Web Application | Hacker | A8 – Cross-Site Request Forgery (CSRF) | Certain | 5.00 | Moderate | 10.00 | 50.00 |
| Web Application | Hacker | A9 – Using Components with Known Vulnerabilities | Unlikely | 2.00 | Insignificant | 1.00 | 2.00 |
| Web Application | Hacker | A10 – Underprotected APIs | Certain | 5.00 | Significant | 20.00 | 100.00 |
| | | 10 | | | | | 37.80 |

*Figure 4-7. Risk Assessment Score Example*

The benefit of calculating and tracking risk scores in this manner is that you not only have the insight into individual risks, but you also have a composite score of risk of a portfolio such as web applications shown above.

> **TIP:** Begin with a simple-to-use calculator like the one above. Try to avoid creating overly complex risk scoring approaches as you will find the results will not vary significantly.

## 4.2.1 Business Impact Assessment (BIA)

Business impact analysis (BIA) is a systematic process to determine and evaluate the potential effects of an interruption to critical business operations. BIAs are typically a part of business continuity programs; however, their use in cybersecurity programs is growing. A BIA is a formalized assessment of the impacts that could occur from a disruption in business operations. With cyberattacks increasing as a prime cause of business operations it is no wonder BIAs are now being considered a component of cybersecurity. I have seen many organizations keep the performance of BIAs separated between business continuity planning and cybersecurity only to result in duplication of efforts. I encourage you to cease that practice if you currently separate these activities.

Although the primary purpose of the BIA is to prioritize the order of business operations for restoration following a disaster, the result can be closely aligned to the effects of a cyberattack. This will help with your impact rating when calculating your risk scores. Even if your organization does not combine the efforts, consider using the same impact scale. Typical impacts to consider in a BIA include the following:

- Contract performance implications.
- Customer dissatisfaction.
- Financial losses.
- Loss of market share.
- Regulatory fines.
- Remediation expenses.
- Reputation loss.

## 4.2.2 Calculating Risk

Calculating risk is part art and part science, or rather an inexact science. There are several models available to help you in calculating risk, but at the end of the day there are only two factors that matter: the likelihood of the event occurring, and the impact it could cause to your organization. Figure 4-8 is a model that I have honed over the years to help identify risk dimensions for my clients. You can easily recreate this model in a Microsoft Excel spreadsheet. The model works by multiplying impact by likelihood to arrive at a risk score. What I like about this model is that you only need to ask two questions: "What is the likelihood of the threat occurring?" and "What could the impact be if the threat occurred?" I also make a very important assumption, which is that the threat can exploit a vulnerability.

| | Category | Score | Threat Impact | | | | |
| | | | Insignificant | Minor | Moderate | Major | Significant |
| | | | 1.00 | 5.00 | 10.00 | 15.00 | 20.00 |
| Likelihood of Occurrence | Certain 90% to 100% | 5.00 | 5.00 | 25.00 | 50.00 | 75.00 | 100.00 |
| | Likely 50% - 89.99% | 4.00 | 4.00 | 20.00 | 40.00 | 60.00 | 80.00 |
| | Possible 11% to 49.99% | 3.00 | 3.00 | 15.00 | 30.00 | 45.00 | 60.00 |
| | Unlikely 3% to 10.99% | 2.00 | 2.00 | 10.00 | 20.00 | 30.00 | 40.00 |
| | Rare 0% to 2.99% | 1.00 | 1.00 | 5.00 | 10.00 | 15.00 | 20.00 |

Figure 4-8. Cyber Risk Calculator

189

I have also created far more complex models for clients that wanted up to six different impact categories such as reputation, financial, or operational impacts. These more complex risk calculations also had an exploitation difficultly attribute to formulate. The exploitation attribute considered the degree of difficulty in exploiting a vulnerability. For example, if a vulnerability required a difficult-to-build exploit code to cause an impact, that factor would be considered and could lower the risk rating. Working as a Microsoft business partner in 2008 I was introduced to the Microsoft Exploitability Index. This index is a rating system that identifies the likelihood that a specific vulnerability could be exploited 30 days after the release of a vulnerability bulletin. Since that time many companies and security research organizations have released their own versions of an exploitability index, and most of the commercial vulnerability scanning products have implemented some form of exploitability index. The gold standard in exploitability scoring is provided by the NIST Computer Resource Center – National Vulnerability Database. You can check out their Common Vulnerability Scoring System Calculator at https://nvd.nist.gov/vuln-metrics/cvss/v2-calculator?calculator&version=2.

Do not try to make your risk calculator more science than art or strive for multi-decimal-point accuracy. You could spend a tremendous amount of time over-complicating something that will end up taking you further away from your goal of assessing risk. Your goal is to rank all your risks by a priority that your organization can remediate. How you arrive at the ranking is less important than the fact that you know which risks you feel must be dealt with first.

### 4.2.2.1 Risk Calculation Software

To help you with calculating risk, there are products available with varying degrees of sophistication. Table 4.4 provides a list of the ones my clients have used successfully.

**Table 4-4. Risk Calculation Software**

| Product | Provider | Summary | URL |
|---|---|---|---|
| @RISK® | Palisade Corporation | Performs risk analysis using Monte Carlo simulation to show multiple possible risk outcomes. | http://www.palisade.com/risk/ |
| Aon Cyber Risk Diagnostic Tool | Aon plc | Online risk analysis and diagnostics tool. | https://www.aon.com.au/australia/risk-solutions/cyber-risk/aon-cyber-diagnostic-tool.jsp |

| | | | |
|---|---|---|---|
| Cyber Risk Modelling and Prediction Platform | Corax Cyber Security Inc | Cyber risk analytics platform for security, compliance, and insurance. | https://www.risklens.com/platform/ |
| RiskLens® | RiskLens (Based on Factor Analysis of Information Risk (FAIR) model | Software as a Service (SaaS) platform that enables Security and Risk teams to quantify and manage cyber risk from the business perspective. | https://www.risklens.com/platform/ |
| Cyber Risk Analytics (CRA) | Risk Based Security | Pre-breach ratings calculations for third-party service providers and organizations. | https://www.cyberriskanalytics.com/ |

*Note: Links are current as of September 22, 2019.*

## 4.2.3 Risk Registry

The hub of your risk management program will be your risk registry. Sometimes referred to as a risk log or risk register, the risk registry is a repository, typically a Microsoft Excel spreadsheet or Access database, in which all identified risks are stored, tracked, and managed. It is undeniably the most important moving piece of your risk management capability. Risk never leaves you. It requires long-term management. Having a central location to manage your risk allows you to identify top risks, align countermeasures, and manage risk treatment plans. Registering your risk also allows you to access an inventory of risk that can be assigned to various components of your attack surface. For example, if you have a set of risks associated with C++ applications you only need to select risk associated with C++ from the registry each time a new C++ application is developed. This significantly reduces duplication of effort in the risk assessment process. Table 4-5 provides you with a format of a risk registry.

**Table 4-5. Risk Registry**

| Risk Summary | | | | | |
|---|---|---|---|---|---|
| Risk number | Unique identification number assigned to the risk when first entered in the registry. | | | | |
| Risk name | Short title name of risk that easily identifies the risk. | | | | |
| Risk overview | Brief description of the risk, cause (threats and vulnerabilities), and impacts. Links to the threat inventory are appropriate. | | | | |
| Threats and vulnerabilities associated with risk | Provide the scenario of the threats that could exploit the vulnerability to create the risk condition. | | | | |
| Risk score | The score for the risk that is a product of likelihood and impact. Scores are produced using a risk calculator. | | | | |
| | Likelihood rating | 1.00 – 5.00 | Impact rating | 1.00 – 20.00 | Score | X |
| Risk ranking | Overall ranking of the risk in comparison to other risks in the registry. | | | | |
| Risk trigger | Listing of risk triggers. Risks can be dormant until a trigger is initiated. For example, a business may have a product defect that injures customers, which could trigger hacktivists to launch a DDoS attack. | | | | |
| Attack surface alignment | Designate which portion or portions of the attack surface the risk applies to. | | | | |
| Risk Treatment | | | | | |
| Inherent risk score | Score of the risk without the application of cybersecurity countermeasures or controls. | | | | |
| Countermeasures & cost | Itemization of the cybersecurity technologies, services, or solutions implemented to address this risk. | Cost: $0 | | | |
| Controls & cost | Itemization of specific controls used to address | Cost: $0 | | | |

| | |
|---|---|
| | this risk. A link to the cybersecurity controls catalog is appropriate. |
| Residual risk score | Score of the risk after the application of cybersecurity countermeasures and controls. |
| Risk treatment owner | Owner of the risk treatment plan. |
| **Risk Management** | |
| Risk owner | Owner of risk. All risk must have an owner responsible for the management or mitigation of the risk. |
| Business alignment | Portion or portions of the business the risk applies to. |
| Date | Date the risk entered the registry. |
| Review date | Data the risk was last reviewed for applicability and appropriateness. |
| Risk status | Enter a status for the risk: active, inactive, or under review. Some risks maybe be retired once the threat vulnerabilities and triggers no longer exist. |

### 4.2.3.1 Risk Registry Products

Managing all the various attributes of risk can be time consuming with many opportunities for error. Fortunately, risk registry tools are available to make this process easier to manage. Most of these tools were originally developed for project management; however, their applicability to cybersecurity is perfect. They provide risk dashboards, risk heatmaps, and advanced attribute mapping. Table 4-6 provides a list of some risk registry tools.

**Table 4-6. Risk Registry Tools**

| Product | Company | URL |
|---------|---------|-----|
| EtQ Risk Register | EtQ, Inc. | https://www.etq.com/solutions/qms/ |
| IT Risk Register | EDUCAUSE | https://library.educause.edu/resources/2015/10/it-risk-register |
| Risk Register Tool | Info-Tech Research Group | https://www.infotech.com/research/risk-register-tool |
| Risk Register+ | i2e Consulting LLC | http://riskregistersharepointapp.i2econsulting.com/ |
| Verse Risk Assessment – Risk Register Module | Verse Solutions | http://www.versesolutions.com/risk-management-software/ |

*Note: Links are current as of September 22, 2019.*

## 4.3 Cyber Risk Standards

Several standards bodies have published guidelines, good practices, or frameworks on how to structure a risk management program. Table 4-7 provides a list of the current, most widely adopted, cybersecurity risk standards that you may wish to reference when completing your cyber risk management program.

**Table 4-7. Cyber Risk Standards**

| Standard | Summary | URL |
|---|---|---|
| AICPA Risk Assessment Standards (SAS Nos. 104 - 111) | A series of standards offered to auditors to aid their them in performing assessments of risk management programs. | https://www.aicpa.org/forthepublic/auditcommitteeeffectiveness/auditcommitteebrief/downloadabledocuments/the_risk_assessment_standards.pdf |
| ISO 31010:2019, Risk Management – Risk Assessment Techniques | Guidance on the selection and application of techniques for assessing risk in a wide range of situations. | https://www.iso.org/iso-31000-risk-management.html |
| ISO Guide 73:2009, Risk Management --- Vocabulary | Provides the definitions of terms related to risk management. Encourages mutual consistent understanding of, and a coherent approach to, the description of activities relating to the management of risk. | https://www.iso.org/standard/44651.html |
| NIST SP 800-37 – Guide for Applying the Risk Management Framework to Federal Information Systems: A Security Life Cycle Approach | Provides guidelines for applying the Risk Management Framework to federal information systems to include conducting the activities of security categorization, security control selection and implementation, security control assessment, information system authorization, and security control monitoring. | https://nvlpubs.nist.gov/nistpubs/SpecialPublications/NIST.SP.800-37r2.pdf |
| NIST SP 800-39 – Managing Information Security Risk: Organization, Mission, and Information System View | Provides guidance for an integrated, organization-wide program for managing information security risk to organizational operations (i.e., mission, functions, image, and reputation), organizational assets, individuals, and other organizations. | http://nvlpubs.nist.gov/nistpubs/Legacy/SP/nistspecialpublication800-39.pdf |

> **TIP:** Ensure you locate the cyber risk management standards applicable to your industry before embarking on the development of your risk management capability. Many regulatory agencies have published their own risk management standards to which you may need to adhere.

## 4.4 Cyber Risk Management Lifecycle

An effective risk management program includes an articulated lifecycle ensuring that risk is managed in a continuous and methodical manner. Figure 4-9 shows the lifecycle of your cyber risk management lifecycle.

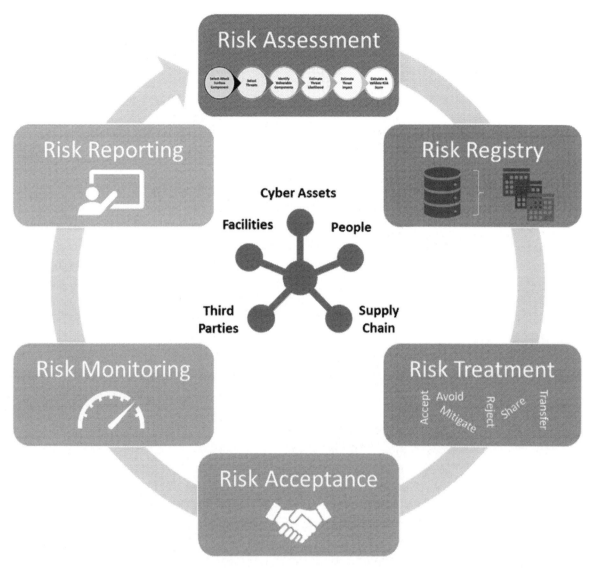

*Figure 4-9. Risk Management Lifecycle. (By Tari Schreider, licensed under a Creative Commons Attribution-NonCommercial-NoDerivatives 4.0 International License)*

The following describes each component of the model:

- **Risk assessment:** The lifecycle begins with performing risk assessments that will determine quantitatively or qualitatively the risk that exists between a relationship of threats, vulnerabilities, and attack surface components. The determination of risk is a product of the likelihood a threat can exploit a vulnerability and the ensuing degree of compromise. Risk assessments should have a defined shelf-life because the attack surface changes, threat profiles change, and the exploit tools used by threat actors change. Your higher risk-rated applications, for example, should be reviewed annually, whereas lower

197

risk computing equipment would be risk reviewed every 24 to 36 months depending on the complexity of your attack surface components. There are three primary categories of risk assessments:

- **Quantitative assessments** – This approach uses numbers to identify the degree of risk an organization would face. These risk assessment results are based on facts and figures.
- **Qualitative assessments** – This approach uses interpretive and observations to dimension the risk an organization would face. These risk assessments results are descriptive and subjective.
- **Hybrid assessments** – This approach uses both qualitative and quantitative methods to present the state of risk of an organization.

- **Risk registry:** Once assessments are completed, they will need to be stored in a central repository for continuous management. Each risk registered adds to the inventory of risks that may be assigned to other applications, software, hardware, or networking devices. The registry is the hub of the risk management workflow where risks and risk treatments are regularly reviewed. Change control is an integral aspect of the registry with each action related to managing risk well documented.

- **Risk treatment:** Risks entered in the registry are considered untreated until they are assigned a risk treatment plan. The treatment plan can range from simply accepting the risk to applying layers of sophisticated countermeasures. Your highest rated risks must be addressed first regardless of how complicated the treatment plan. The treatment plan is what elevates the inherent risk score to a treated risk score. What is left is residual risk. Treatment plans may require improvement based on audits, advances in regulatory controls, or changes in the threat landscape.

- **Risk acceptance:** Accepting risk is much more than saying you accept it. Acceptance requires a formal written declaration by senior management that your organization understands the consequences and a conscious decision was made that no further risk treatment can be made. Risk acceptance must also be communicated to any entity that could be impacted by the decision to accept this risk. You may have to issue a risk waiver when a risk owner cannot comply with the risk treatment plan. This is considered risk acceptance.

- **Risk monitoring:** Risk management must be transparent consisting of tracking and reporting of risk to stakeholders. Monitoring is a closed-loop approach where risks are tracked from identification through the implementation of their treatment plans. An important aspect of monitoring is tracking risks that have occurred. Risk treatment plans do not guarantee that a risk will never occur. Each time a risk event occurs, a postmortem of the treatment plan is required.

- **Risk reporting:** Timely and accurate risk reporting is an integral part of your risk management capability. Communicating the risk profile of your organization to the right audience raises risk awareness and moves you toward a risk aware culture. Risk reporting can range from self-serve dashboarding to publishing risk reports. Utilizing a set of well thought out cyber risk metrics will increase the effectiveness of your risk reporting.

# 4.5 Cyber Risk Treatment

Risk treatment is the process of managing or mitigating risk to lower its score. The objective is to invest in reducing a risk score to an acceptable level. Table 4-8 shows the various options in which risk can be treated.

**Table 4-8. Risk Treatment Options**

| Option | Summary |
|--------|---------|
| Accept risk | Acceptance of the risk in its inherent or treated state with no further efforts to reduce the risk level. |
| Avoid risk | A conscious decision not to undertake or avoid a certain project or activity should potential risk exceed the potential benefits. |
| Mitigate risk | A systematic reduction of the exposure to risk by applying countermeasures or controls commensurate with the value of the assets at risk to mitigate the impacts. |
| Reject risk | Rejecting the premise by which the risk was determined. Generally, management has found fault with the correlation of threats and vulnerabilities and their ability to cause an impact. |
| Share risk | A self-insurance method of managing or reducing exposure to cyber risk by spreading (sharing) the burden of loss among several units of an enterprise or business syndicate. |
| Transfer risk | A method of transferring or shifting risk in whole or part to other entities. This would include spreading risk among contracts (indemnification clauses, warrantees, or cyber insurance policies). |

# 4.6 Risk Monitoring

Monitoring your organization's risk profile is essential to managing risk. You cannot manage what you cannot see. Monitoring ensures that risk treatment plans are properly executed, risk assessments are completed in a timely manner, countermeasures perform effectively to reduce risk, and risk scores do not fall outside of acceptable boundaries. The following minimum risk conditions should be monitored:

- Expiring risk assessments.
- Risk trigger occurrences.
- Risk score changes.
- Risk treatment plan completion progress.
- Attack surface changes that would prompt new risk assessments.
- Service provider additions that would trigger new risk assessments.
- Countermeasure cost changes that affect ROI calculations.

Critical to your risk management program is a review and reporting process to ensure risks are effectively assessed, and that appropriate risk responses and controls are in place. Monitoring through the processes of testing, auditing, and assessments should be performed by independent, objective personnel. This process provides assurance that risk responses are consistently implemented, procedures are understood and followed, and appropriate controls are in place.

Risk management functional leadership and business unit management should be tasked with monitoring the effectiveness of your organization's risk mitigation activities as well as the overall risk capability through review of metrics and dashboards on a periodic basis. Additionally, these measures should be reviewed with your organization's compliance committee or other enterprise governance teams, the executive committee, and the board of directors.

As a manager involved in your organization's risk management capability, you should analyze metrics, incidents, trends in auditing, testing and assessment results, and other risk-related information to identify emerging risks. In addition, you will identify ways to improve the risk management program including new risk mitigating controls, new or revised standards, or other initiatives.

## 4.7 Risk Reporting

One of the most effective ways to gain support for the risk management capability of your cybersecurity program is through transparent, consistent, and accurate reporting on the state of risk in your organization. Reporting should be in several formats and consistent with how your organization already ingests and consumes information. If your organization has a monthly newsletter, blog, or webcasts, seek to integrate your communications approach within them. Reporting should also be suited for the intended audience; the level of risk reporting you provide to technical personnel should be vastly different than senior management. I have found that leveraging the security awareness program can be an effective way of getting the message out.

One of the primary goals of risk reporting is to build a risk aware culture within the organization. The intent is not to be alarmist, but informative. You will need to tailor content to the audience for maximum impact. Providing too much detail to certain audiences or providing provocative information could leave the audience with the wrong opinion on your organization's risk preparedness.

> **TIP:** Keep in mind that information regarding the state of risk within your organization can be open for discovery in the event your organization is ever sued over a breach of security. Any statements of risk readiness can be especially damning in a court of law.

## 4.8 Risk Management Frameworks

If you wish to review the body of knowledge around the practice of cyber risk management, there are several excellent sources. Table 4-9 provides an overview of the risk management frameworks I reference in my own consulting practice.

**Table 4-9. Risk Management Frameworks**

| Framework | Source | Summary |
|---|---|---|
| COSO Enterprise Risk Management Framework | Committee of Sponsoring Organizations of the Treadway Commission (COSO) | Comprehensive enterprise risk management framework aligned with business risk requirements. |
| Factor Analysis of Information Risk (FAIR) | FAIR Institute | A practical framework for understanding, measuring and analyzing information risk, and ultimately, for enabling well-informed decision making. |
| Information Security Forum (ISF) – Information Risk | Information Security Forum Ltd | A methodology that provides risk practitioners with a complete end-to-end |

| Framework | Source | Summary |
|---|---|---|
| Assessment Methodology 2 (IRAM2) | | approach to performing business-focused information risk assessments. |
| IRGC Risk Governance Framework | International Risk Governance Council | Framework which includes a risk pre-assessment – early warning and framing of the risk in order to provide a structured definition of risk. |
| NIST Risk Management Framework (RMF) | NIST | A process that integrates security and risk management activities into the system development life cycle. |
| Operationally Critical Threat, Asset, and Vulnerability Evaluation (OCTAVE) Allegro | Carnegie Mellon University | An approach used to assess an organization's risk based on asset importance. |
| Operational Risk Management Framework | Risk Management Association (RMA) | Risk framework designed to be scalable regardless of the size, scale, or complexity of the institution. |
| Risk Management Framework (RMF) for DoD Information Technology (IT) | US Department of Defense (DoD) | Comprehensive cybersecurity purpose-built risk management framework. |
| The Risk IT Framework | ISACA | End-to-end, comprehensive view of all risks related to the use of IT and a similarly thorough treatment of risk management, from the tone and culture at the top, to operational issues. |

*Note*: *Links are current as of September 22, 2019.*

## 4.9 Risk Maturity Models

Once you have reached a point where you feel you have created a fully functioning risk management capability within your cybersecurity program, you may wish to turn your attention toward maturing your capability. Table 4-10 provides a list of the risk maturity models I have referenced in risk assessment projects.

**Table 4-10. Risk Management Maturity Models**

| Risk Maturity Model | Source | Summary | URL |
|---|---|---|---|
| Aon Risk Maturity Index | Aon plc | Free tool that is designed to capture and assess an organization's risk management practices and provide participants with immediate feedback in the form of a risk maturity rating, along with comments for improvement. | http://www.aon.com/rmi/default.jsp |
| Cyber Insider Risk Mitigation Maturity Matrix | Institute for Security and Resilience Studies at University College London (UCL) | Qualitative ten-attribute maturity assessment matrix oriented to the chief information security officer (CISO). | http://www.cybersecurity-review.com/wp-content/uploads/2016/11/Chris-Hurran-article-CSR-Autumn-2016.pdf |
| RiskCenter KYBP | Dow Jones | Dow Jones provides solutions to coordinate all aspects of third-party risk management, including screening data, due diligence services and scalable technology for implementing compliance-led workflows. | https://visit.dowjones.com/lp/third-party-risk-management/ |
| ERM Assessment Tool | Chartered Global Management Accountant | Free enterprise risk maturity (ERM) assessment tool. | http://www.cgma.org/resources/tools/evaluate-enterprise-risk-management.html |
| RIMS Risk Maturity Model | Risk and Insurance Management Society, Inc. (RIMS) | Free online risk program maturity assessment covering 25 competency drivers. | https://www.rims.org/resources/ERM/Pages/RiskMaturityModel.aspx |

*Note: Links are current as of September 22, 2019.*

# 4.10 Third-Party Risk Management (TPRM)

Third-parties account for an alarming number of cybersecurity incidents annually. Take for example the huge Target Corporation data breach in 2013 where third-party service provider Fazio Mechanical, who provided HVAC services, was compromised with a phishing attack. Hackers gained access to Target's internal systems for billing, contract management, and contract submission via a vendor portal called Ariba (Krebs, 2014). This event raised the red flag on the organizations efforts to assess their exposure to third-party risk. A survey by Soha Systems places the percentage of all data breaches linked directly or indirectly to third-party access at 63 percent. (Sher-Jan, M, 2017).

To address the risk introduced to your organization through third-parties you will need a third-party risk management (TPRM) program. TPRM is the process of analyzing and controlling the risks your organization faces through the connectivity or access to data by third parties. This can be a daunting task as many companies interact with dozens, if not hundreds, of third-parties. I recently completed a project to design a TPRM for an organization that had over 5,000 third-parties that required risk assessments. When you think of third-parties, think of these:

- Counterparties.
- Cloud service providers.
- Customers.
- Fourth-parties.
- Joint ventures.
- Vendors.

Fourth-parties will prove particularly challenging as they serve as silent support providers to your third-party providers. I have found that a single cloud service provider, for example, can have several partners providing services ranging from hardware, software, to infrastructure, making them all fourth-parties. The same risk assessment you conduct on your internal systems should be the same used to assess the risk of your third-party providers.

## 4.10.1 TPRM Program Structure

I have found it best to have a sound plan for assessing the risk of third-parties beginning with contractually requiring them to comply with your organization's cybersecurity policies and practices and as well as implementing some form of continuous compliance monitoring. Figure 4-10 is a model that I use when designing TPRM programs.

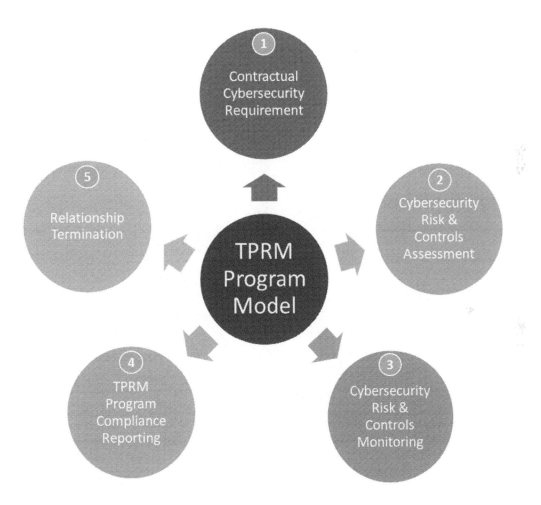

*Figure 4-10. TPRM Program Model. (By Tari Schreider, licensed under a Creative Commons Attribution-NonCommercial-NoDerivatives 4.0 International License)*

The following describes each component of the model:

- **Contractual cybersecurity requirement:** Contractual agreements and terms of services that require third-parties to comply with your organization's cybersecurity policies and practices.

- **Cybersecurity risk and controls assessment:** A hybrid assessment that looks at the potential risk introduced by the third-party as well as the controls they have deployed to reduce identified risk. Third-parties should be rated by their potential to cause harm to your organization. For example, if they are provided network access, they introduce more risk than a service provider that is only provided guest WiFi access. Third-party assessments should include at least the following:
  - Certifications and attestation reports.
  - Cybersecurity architecture review.
  - Cybersecurity or privacy breach history.
  - Cybersecurity policies and practices.
  - Disaster recovery plans.
  - Disclosure of fourth parties.
  - Financial stability verification.
  - Incident response plans.
  - Onsite reviews of key staff and tour of operations.
  - Program documentation.
  - Reputation verification.
  - Risk assessment reports.

  To assist you in performing third-party assessments, download a free third-party risk program maturity assessment tool including cybersecurity, IT, privacy, data security, and business resiliency controls from Shared Assessment available at https://sharedassessments.org/.

- **Cybersecurity risk and controls monitoring:** Continuous monitoring through automated or manual means to ensure that any changes in risk and controls are identified. Monitoring can include onsite audits, independent reviews, questionnaires (self-attestation), security scanning, etc. The higher the risk of the third-party, the more in-depth the monitoring.
- **TPRM program compliance reporting:** The third-parties should be contractually committed to report on any deviations in security controls or risk profile status. Reports should be timely and comprehensive.
- **Relationship termination:** Each third-party contract should be terminated methodically when expired. This includes disposal or return of assets and information. You should be thinking of your exit strategy when signing the original agreement. The reserved right to audit a third-party's environment should be incorporated in all third-party agreements.

## 4.10.2 Third-Party Attestation Services

The time and effort required for organizations to manage their own TPRM programs has given birth to an industry of service providers who independently assess and report on a third-party's cybersecurity and regulatory status. Table 4-11 provides a list of the more well-known third-party attestation services.

**Table 4-11. Third-Party Attestation Services**

| Service | Source | Summary | URL |
|---------|--------|---------|-----|
| AICPA SOC 2® | American Institute of CPAs | Internal control reports on the services provided by a service organization providing valuable information that users need to assess and address the risks associated with an outsourced service. | https://www.aicpa.org/InterestAreas/FRC/AssuranceAdvisoryServices/Pages/SORHome.aspx |
| BSI Kitemark™ for Products | The British Standards Institution | BSI Kitemark scheme involves an initial assessment of conformity to the relevant standard and an assessment of the quality management system operated by the supplier. | https://www.bsigroup.com/en-GB/kitemark/product-testing/ |
| CSA STAR Registry | Cloud Security Alliance (CSA) | Registry of over 100 cloud service providers who passed the CSA security assurance program. | https://cloudsecurityalliance.org/star/#_overview |
| CSTAR | UpGuard | Rates vendor security against 50+ criteria using the CSTAR score. Sends targeted security questionnaires to vendors reports results on a dashboard. | https://try.upguard.com/vendor-risk/ |
| HITRUST Third-party Assurance Program | HITRUST Alliance | Third-party assurance program for healthcare IT service providers. | https://hitrustalliance.net/thirdparty/ |

| Service | Source | Summary | URL |
|---------|--------|---------|-----|
| Continuous 360° | iTrust | Panoramic view of cyber risks – inside, outside, and independent ratings. | https://itrustinc.com/solutions/ |
| ISO 27001 Certification | The British Standards Institution | Companies that have been certified compliant with the ISO 27001 standard. | https://www.bsigroup.com/en-GB/our-services/certification/certificate-and-client-directory/ |
| Shared Assessments Program | Santa Fe Group | Collaborative, global, peer community of practitioners working to assess third-party provider risk. | http://sharedassessments.org/about/ |

*Note*: Links are current as of September 22, 2019.

## 4.11 Cyber Black Swans

An advanced form of risk management is to contemplate the effects of a cyber black swan event. A black swan is a designation for something so rare that we don't believe it can happen, like a giant asteroid striking Earth. An event so outside of the norm and beyond contemplation seems silly by most. Although it has happened, we still don't believe it could happen again. In cybersecurity terms, a black swan is a cyberattack or widespread event that even all your controls and countermeasures cannot counteract. Think Edward Snowden, where a single individual bypassed the most secure countermeasures and layers of defense money can buy, and caused an international intelligence failure storm through the release of stolen government documents. Until I read *The Black Swan: The Impact of the Highly Improbable* by Nassim Nicholas Taleb back in 2007, I frankly did not consider cyber black swans. Even considering 9/11, I, like most, never believed it could happen again. But I was wrong; history has proven that black swans happen and will happen in the future so we must allocate some planning to these types of events.

**Did You Know?**

In 2015 Google began reinforcing its undersea Internet cables with Kevlar-like matting when learned that sharks were biting down on Pacific ocean fibre optic cables.

*Have you thought of black swan events?*

**Source:**
https://www.theguardian.com/technology/2014/aug/14/google-undersea-fibre-optic-cables-shark-attacks

The following are a few black swan events I include in my more advanced risk assessment and threat gaming projects:

- 9+ level Silicon Valley or Seattle earthquake destroying 50% or more of the IT industry.
- Attack on the Internet DNS infrastructure causing the Internet to collapse.
- Repeat of the solar storm of 1859 (the Carrington Event) causing many parts of the US power grid to fail for an extended period.
- Sleeper terrorist infiltrating Amazon, Google, or Microsoft and coding a zero-day vulnerability in collusion with a nation-state to launch a world-wide simultaneous cyberattack against millions of computers.

Realistically, I would begin with localized black swan events that would essentially affect your immediate area or company. Start the process with a brainstorming session of various people in your organization and ask the question, "What is the worst that could happen?" You may be surprised at the response you receive.

## 4.12 Cyber Risk Cassandras

In Greek mythology, Cassandra was a princess of Troy and according to the myth was provided the gift of prophecy by the God Apollo. After she spurned Apollo's advances, he cursed her such that no one would ever believe her prophecies. In one of her most famous visions, she predicted the Greeks would destroy Troy. In an often-used cybersecurity analogy, the Greeks parked a large wooden horse (Trojan horse) outside the gates as a form of tribute. Cassandra warned of Greeks bearing gifts but was ignored and the Trojan horse was brought into the city. The rest is history. But are there Cassandras today that we should be listening to?

History generally is the only way to prove those that fit the definition of a Cassandra, yet there are plenty. Take for example, Michael Burry, the founder of Scion Capital, who predicted in 2006 the crash of the housing market. No one would believe him, not even government regulators although he provided proof. Now, Burry is back predicting a water crisis (Flavio, 2016). I started wondering, from a risk perspective, how that might affect some of my largest customers that have massive data center footprints. Data centers consume large amounts of water to provide the electricity they require as well as to supply their cooling systems. According to a US Department of Energy study, combined US data centers consumed 626 billion liters of water in 2014, and it is estimated that consumption will increase to 660 billion liters in 2020 (Sverdlik, 2016). You can learn more at: https://www.datacenterknowledge.com/archives/2016/07/12/heres-how-much-water-all-us-data-centers-consume. After reading this report I found no mention of future estimates considering a water shortage or its impact, something I find shortsighted. My point here is you need to find your Cassandras who think outside of the risk box.

## 4.13 Cyber Risk Management Checklist

Building your risk management capability is what will drive your program. The risk scores you calculate must be offset by the countermeasures present in Chapter 5. To help you walk through the process of building your risk program I offer a checklist in Table 4-12.

**Table 4-12. Cyber Risk Management Checklist**

| Step | Activity |
|------|----------|
| 1 | Define your cyber risk landscape – identify all the components of your cyber risk landscape and understand how management feels toward each. Match to your attack surface to identify any missing components. |
| 2 | Identify your risk types – use Table 4-1 to identity all the risk types you should plan for. |
| 3 | Estimate risk appetite – estimate your organization's appetite for risk using the risk appetite state in Table 4-2. |
| 4 | Estimate risk tolerance – estimate the level of tolerance your organization has toward risk using the guidance in Table 4-3. |
| 5 | Determine risk threshold – determine the threshold of risk your organization will not cross. |
| 6 | Create policy on risk acceptance – define a policy on your organization's position on accepting risk. |
| 7 | Calculate ALE – calculate the ALE for risks in the risk registry. |
| 8 | Produce an ROI form – create an ROI form to use with all new cybersecurity program investments. |
| 9 | Document risk assessment process – use Figure 4-6 as a baseline to document your risk assessment process. Reference standards in Table 4-6. |

| Step | Activity |
|------|----------|
| 10 | Integrated BIAs – integrate BIA process from disaster recovery and business continuity management efforts. |
| 11 | Create risk registry – create a risk registry to house all noted risk and risk assessments. |
| 12 | Adopt policy on cyber risk treatments – create policy that describes the parameters of when risk treatment will be applied. |
| 13 | Implement risk monitoring – implement practices and solutions to monitor risk. |
| 14 | Implement risk reporting – implement practices for reporting the state of risk management. |
| 15 | Adopt a risk maturity model – create a maturity baseline and roadmap for a future state. |
| 16 | Create third-party risk assessment process – align risk management and assessment practices to use with third-party service providers. |

## Summary

Addressing the risk within your organization requires critical thinking and sound planning. If this chapter has taught you anything, it is that developing a risk management capability can be quite complex. The number one rule to remember however is: Keep it simple. Before going off and developing the next-generation risk assessment tool, start off simple and use the risk calculator approach I outlined in this chapter. Prove that you can have a fully functioning risk management capability before getting too fancy. You will also need to remember that risk lurks everywhere, and that every aspect of your attack surface should be evaluated for risk. The next chapter is where you will learn how to define and apply countermeasures and controls to reduce or mitigate the risk identified in this chapter.

# References

American Hospital Association (AHA). (2017). *Fast facts on US hospitals.* Retrieved from http://www.aha.org/research/rc/stat-studies/fast-facts.shtml

Aon & Ponemon Systems. (2017). *2017 global cyber risk transfer comparison report.* Retrieved from http://www.aon.com/risk-services/thought-leadership/2017-global-cyber-risk-transfer-comparison-report.jsp [Summary only. Report available for download.]

Flavio, A. (2016, May 12). *The man who predicted the housing crash in America now predicts a looming water crisis.* Retrieved from http://anonhq.com/man-predicted-housing-crash-america-now-predicting-looming-water-crisis-video/

Krebs, B. (2014, February 14). *Email attack on vendor set up breach at Target.* Retrieved from https://krebsonsecurity.com/2014/02/email-attack-on-vendor-set-up-breach-at-target/

Morgan, S. (2019, February 6). *2019 Cybersecurity Almanac: 100 Facts, Figures, Predictions and Statistics.* Retrieved from https://cybersecurityventures.com/cybersecurity-almanac-2019/.

Ser-Jan, M. (2017). *Surprising stats on third-party vendor risk and breach likelihood.* The privacy Advisor. Retrieved from https://iapp.org/news/a/surprising-stats-on-third-party-vendor-risk-and-breach-likelihood/

Sverdlik, Y. (2016, July 12). Here's how much water all US data centers consume. *Data Center Knowledge.* Retrieved from http://www.datacenterknowledge.com/archives/2016/07/12/heres-how-much-water-all-us-data-centers-consume/

# Self-Study Questions

The following questions will help you build your expertise in establishing a foundation of governance.

1. What three components equal cyber risk?
    The convergence of threats, attack surface and vulnerabilities equal cyber risk.

2. What are the four types of cyber risk?
    Compliance, financial, operational and strategic.

3. What is risk appetite?
    The amount of risk an organization is willing to accept in generalized terms.

4. What is risk tolerance?
    The maximum amount of risk an organization is willing to accept in specific quantifiable terms.

5. What is risk acceptance?
   An amount of risk that cannot be treated for reasons of cost or technical complexity that an organization accepts to carry.

6. What is residual risk?
   The amount of risk that remains after risk treatment is residual risk.

7. What is a business impact statement?
   An assessment to determine and evaluate the impact to an asset in the event of a disruption or damage.

8. What is risk treatment?
   The processing of addressing identified risk to lower its overall risk score.

9. What is a TPRM program?
   Third-Party Risk Management.

10. What is a cyber black swan?
    A threat event that by most standards and opinions no one believes would happen; however, evidence exists that it could.

# Chapter 5

# Implementing a Defense-in-Depth Strategy

At this point in the journey it is time for you to define the methods by which you will defend your organization's assets and information against cyber adversaries and insiders with malicious intent. The previous chapters have guided you to this point. You have learned how to design your cybersecurity program, define a governance foundation, create an ability to identify threats and vulnerabilities, and assess the risk to your organization. Now it is time for you to do something about it. In this chapter, you will learn how to structure a series of barriers to thwart the advance of bad actors and halt or deter their sophisticated, persistent threat methods. The barriers you select will be based on your organization's risk profile commensurate with the value of your organization's assets and information.

*This chapter will help you to:*

- Understand the fundamental concepts of defense-in-depth.
- Define defense-in-depth strategies to support your cybersecurity program.
- Look at defense-in-depth as a multi-dimensional strategy.
- Understand available countermeasures to protect assets and information.

# Chapter 5 Roadmap

On the second to the last stop of your cybersecurity journey you will leverage the lessons of risk management to apply controls and countermeasures to protect your organization's information and assets. In a world where we should be operating under an assumption of a breach and zero trust, layers of defenses ensure we don't place all our eggs in one basket by using a single control or countermeasure to protect all of our assets and information.

Figure 5.0 shows the high-level categories of the defensive layers that you can deploy to protect your organization. Countermeasures and controls should be aligned to the OSI model where threats manifest and exploits occur. Each domain discussed in this chapter includes a comprehensive model that guides you in selecting safeguards fit for purpose to protecting your organization.

*Figure 5.0. Service Management Reference Architecture*

Each main component (gray) and sub-component of the reference architecture is covered in more detail later in the chapter.

This stop will require you to make quite a few decisions in the face of the substantial number of safeguards you will need to select. I will try to make this decision process a little easier by walking you through the primary purpose of each domain:

- **Step 1: Select GRC Controls** – How effectively your cybersecurity program is managed is based in great part to the management controls used to perform strategic planning, governance, compliance, risk management, and business continuity. This layer is best viewed as a long-term plan owing much to the complexity of organizational research and planning. Here as with the other domains you will need to prioritize which controls are most important and execute on a critical path.

- **Step 2: Select TVM Controls** – The controls provided in this layer generally represent a higher level of maturity due to their sophistication and technical requirements. There is also a higher level of knowledge and experience required of program personnel to deploy and operate these controls.

- **Step 3: Select ADS Controls** – Protecting applications and software used within the enterprise is a combination of secure development practices and applying software and application security controls. The secure coding practices provides the basic blocking and tackling necessary to nip security flaws in the bud before they're deployed into the enterprise. To validate the secure coding works, applications and software would go through levels of security testing. The extra layer of protection would come from the deployment of security technologies such as web application firewalls, etc.

- **Step 4: Select SecOps Controls** – Security operations is considered the factory of the cybersecurity program. Most would agree the heavy lifting required to protect information and assets occurs here. The security operations center, security technologies administration, engineering, and incident response all take place here. Careful orchestration of safeguards bolstered by automation improves the operational efficiency of this domain.

- **Step 5: Select DDP Controls** – Applying controls that are uniquely designed to ensure the privacy of information in compliance with international data privacy laws is of utmost importance. Controls in this domain begin with data governance where you classify data and provide for their safekeeping throughout their data protection lifecycle. Encryption of data occurs within this domain regardless of whether the data-is-in-use, at-rest or in-transit.

- **Step 6: Select CIP Controls** – Your organization as well as most organizations today utilize various forms of cloud infrastructure. You may have a private cloud or use services provided by a public cloud provider to process data and provide services. Safeguards in this domain can be offered by your organization or the cloud service provider. Here you will need to understand the protection a cloud provider includes in their service model and what complementary controls your organization is responsible for.

This domain is the most difficult in which to identify the minimum safeguards you can get by with as many are out of your direct control. However, there are several things that you can do in the face of limited resources and investment:

- **Select Countermeasures Based on Highest Threat** – Select the top threats and match those to countermeasures identified within this chapter.

- **Ensure Countermeasures Address Each Layer of the OSI Model** – Select and deploy at least two to three countermeasures from Table 5-3 within each layer of the OSI Security Model.
- **Ensure Each Countermeasure Achieves a Minimum of 3.0 Maturity** – To except each countermeasure to perform as designed, it should be deployed at a minimum of a 3.0 level of maturity on a 5.0 scale. A 3.0 maturity level will ensure countermeasures are deployed according to standards and are competently implemented.

Defense-in-depth cannot be achieved overnight or simply by buying a boatload of cybersecurity technologies. It can only be achieved through a proper balance of blocking and tackling and application of complementary countermeasures. Once you have deployed the minimum number of controls required to provide an adequate level of security, you must go back through this chapter and pragmatically select the additional countermeasures to raise the level of maturity of your entire program.

## 5.1 Defense-in-Depth

### Did You Know?

In February of 2018, hackers from a Chinese intelligence agency stole 614 GBs of classified data from a Rhode Island-based Navy subcontractor on a secret submarine communications project known as Sea Dragon.

*Do your IT service providers follow defense-in-depth practices?*

**Source:**
https://www.cyberscoop.com/submarine-contractor-hacked-china-us-navy/

*Defense-in-depth* is a concept coined by the US military to describe the placement of defensive barriers to impede the advancement of combatants from overtaking a held position. This military strategy included monitoring the combatants' progress and responding to their advances with equal or greater force. Applying this same concept to the cybersecurity world where threat actors are the combatants and countermeasures are the defensive barriers is perfectly suited to protecting your organization's assets and information. The use of barriers or layers is the foundation of defense-in-depth. Each layer is designed to thwart a type of attack and leverage one another so that if one layer fails to stop an attack, another layer takes over. This strategy is ideal to combat hydra attacks where multiple attack methods are launched against an organization to compromise multiple attack-surface vulnerabilities.

You may have heard defense-in-depth referred to as the *castle* or *onion* approach. Castle analogies are not bad because you can visualize walls, motes, drawbridges, etc. – all varying levels of attack deterrence. The onion analogy is apropos as well as it represents the peeling back of layers of protection before reaching the bulb, the prized asset. Regardless of the analogy, the concept remains the same – place as many barriers between you and the bad guy. I first started using defense-in-depth strategies in the early 1990s to protect client-server environments, and although the options for layers were limited, they nonetheless worked well because attacks were simpler back then.

Today, cyberattacks are more sophisticated and threat vectors more numerous. Defense-in-depth approaches have also become more sophisticated but are still limited by their one-dimensional approach. Stacking layer upon layer like a wedding cake hoping that a cyberattack would pass neatly and sequentially through each layer did not always provide the level of protection necessary. I believe that defense-in-depth is as applicable today as it was when I first included the strategy in my early security designs. However, some fundamental changes in the strategy are required. This chapter is based on my work to develop defense-in-depth, moving it from a one-dimensional to a three-dimensional model. The first dimension has always been represented by the attack surface. The second dimension I defined based on the National Institute of Standards and Technology (NIST) cybersecurity framework (CSF) consisting of identify, protect, detect, respond, and recover categories. The third dimension is defined by my six cybersecurity architectural domains, discussed later. Figure 5-1 shows the three dimensions of my defense-in-depth model.

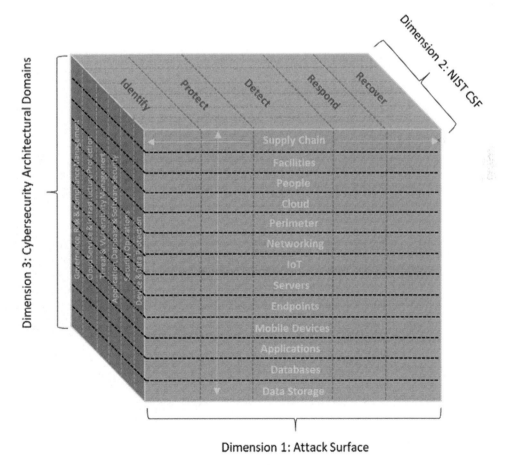

Figure 5-1. Three-Dimensional Defense-in-Depth Model. (By Tari Schreider, licensed under a Creative Commons Attribution-NonCommercial-NoDerivitives 4.0 International License)

I want you to look at your defense-in-depth from a three-dimensional perspective where you can visualize countermeasures wrapping around as well as cross-sectioning through your attack surface. Once you stop thinking about defense-in-depth as an onion or cake and visualize it as interconnected walls and cross-sections enveloping assets and information like a 360-degree shield of protection you will have taken an important step in outsmarting your adversaries.

> **TIP:** Defense-in-depth works best if all the layers integrate and harmonize as one. If you do not interconnect the layers through processes and automation you lessen the effectiveness of the strategy.

## 5.1.1 Industry Perception

In April of 2017, I was hosted by the EC-Council to give a speech on defense-in-depth to nearly 700 cybersecurity professionals from over 40 countries. During the session, I asked the audience, "What is your opinion of defense-in-depth?" Table 5-1 shows the results of the response to that question.

**Table 5-1. Defense-in-Depth Survey Question**

| Response | Percentage |
|---|---|
| It is as valuable now as it ever was. | 90.12% |
| Its relevancy is waning. | 6.17% |
| Its time has come and gone. | 3.70% |

The clear majority of those attending felt that defense-in-depth was as viable today as it ever was. During each of the CISO classes I teach, I continue to ask this same question and the results haven't changed. This is in stark contrast to a myriad of articles I have read over the past several years calling into question the continued usefulness of defense-in-depth. The dichotomy of defense-in-depth is that we as an industry apparently love it but lack proof that it works, so it takes a beating in the press. I was asked not long ago to evaluate a large big box retailer's defense-in-depth strategy. What I found were systemic problems experienced by many organizations' defense-in-depth approaches. First, my client's approach had aged and not kept up with the current threat landscape. Think about all your data residing inside your organization's castle walls. They're nice and safe, right? Now ask yourself, "Will those same walled defenses protect that data when it is moved to the cloud and resides outside the castle walls?"

Another mistake this client made was one I have seen repeated in many other defense-in-depth strategies. This mistake was not addressing the insider threat. Think of your defense-in-depth as a turtle – the outer shell is hard and virtually impenetrable but turn the turtle over and the soft underbelly is exposed. The threat and vulnerability assessment you learned about in Chapter 3 showed you how to find the soft underbelly of your attack surface. Insider attacks represent the soft underbelly of your organization. You need to act on that knowledge and apply the right countermeasures to protect this exposure point.

## 5.1.2 Defense-in-Depth Models

Over the years several types of defense-in-depth models have emerged, most assuming basic shapes consisting of circles, squares, pyramids, and even stairs. However, they all had one thing in common – a top down, layered approach to protecting data. Figure 5-2 shows the classic types of defense-in-depth models used today.

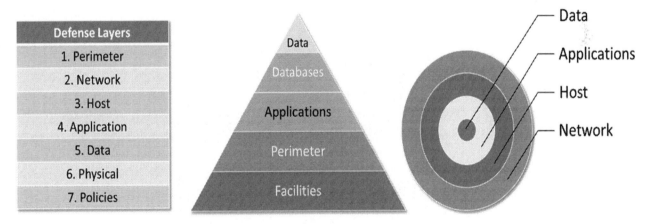

*Figure 5-2. Defense-in-Depth Models*

During that same EC-Council speech, I asked another question, "What model of defense-in-depth is in use?" In response, 57% of those who reported using a defense-in-depth model indicated they use a model based on concentric circles. Table 5-2 shows the results of that survey question.

**Table 5-2. Most Used Defense-in-Depth Models**

| Response | Percentage |
|----------|------------|
| Box | 10.10% |
| Concentric circles | 40.40% |
| None | 30.30% |
| Pyramid | 13.13% |
| Stairs | 06.06% |

The common denominator of these models is their seeming adoption of defined cybersecurity layers generally modeled after the OSI Model developed by the International Organization for Standardization (ISO). ISO is the very same organization that brought us many of the security standards we use today (e.g., 27001/27002). The Open System Interconnection (OSI) model is a networking framework with protocols defined in seven layers (applications, presentation, session, transport, network, data link, and physical) (Mitchell, 2016). These layers are used to define the layers of many variations of defense-in-depth. Another approach which, to this day, makes no sense to me is that some security practitioners used the standards of ISO 27001 or NIST 800-53 to define the layers of defense-in-depth. This was wasted effort, since all that is accomplished by this approach is simply to restate what was already defined by ISO or NIST.

Different models had different floors, ceilings, and number of layers, but many began with policies and ended with physical security. Layers ranged from 4 to 10 or more. Regardless of the shape, each model provided a way to visualize how cybersecurity countermeasures related to one another. My goal in this chapter is to show you a new visual approach to defense-in-depth that I believe includes the best of existing models without their shortcomings.

## 5.1.3 Origin of Contemporary Defense-in-Depth Models

In various models of defense-in-depth I have seen over the years it became clear to me that the majority were based in some part on ISO 7498-2:1989 Information processing systems – Open Systems Interconnection – Basic Reference Model – Part 2: Security Architecture. ISO 7498-2 was introduced by ISO to align their OSI model to mainstream thinking regarding the application of security from an architectural perspective. Even though the ISO 7498-2:1989 model provided little in the way of concrete recommendations, it did offer a formalization of defense-in-depth upon which many models and approaches were later based.

The most important aspect of the ISO security model is that the higher up you go in the security stack, the less you will need to rely on lower-level countermeasures. For years, many organizations have invested most of their efforts and investment in countermeasures in the network layer. The thought was to create a strong outer shell. However, as threat vectors changed and the perimeter of an organization became less defined with the advent of mobile computing, this approach proved fallible. A practical example of this would be email security. Email security lives in the application layer of the OSI security model. If you deploy a sound approach to email security in the application layer where email is encrypted and digitally signed, you can be less concerned with the security measures deployed within the network. If you were primarily focusing on protecting the network, your email remained vulnerable. By moving countermeasures close to the attack target, in this case email, you can receive email over an untrusted network and your mail will still be protected. Table 5-3 presents the ISO 7498:1989 security model aligned with the OSI layers with example countermeasures.

**Table 5-3. OSI Security Model with Countermeasures Examples**

| OSI Layer | | ISO 7498-2 Security Model | Example Countermeasures |
|---|---|---|---|
| 7. Application | Logical – Software Oriented | Authentication | • Directory security<br>• Email security<br>• Host firewall<br>• Privileged Account Management (PAM)<br>• Secure browser<br>• Secure coding<br>• Secure file transfer protocol (SFTP)<br>• Secure printing |
| 6. Presentation | | Access control | • Data encryption<br>• Identity and access management (IDAM)<br>• Message encryption<br>• Secure coding |
| 5. Session | | Non-repudiation | • Message non-repudiation<br>• Password encryption<br>• Remote login security<br>• Session expiration<br>• Token management |
| 4. Transport | | Data integrity | • Firewalls<br>• Port restriction<br>• Session security |
| 3. Network | Physical – Hardware Oriented | Confidentiality | • Access control list (ACL)<br>• Firewalls<br>• IPsec<br>• Network intrusion detection system (NIDS)<br>• Malicious packet inspection<br>• Network routing protection<br>• Secure domain name service (DNS) |
| 2. Data link | | Assurance/Availability | • Firewalls<br>• Media address control (MAC address) filtering<br>• Wireless security |
| 1. Physical | | Notarization/Signature | • Biometric authentication<br>• Data storage encryption<br>• Electromagnetic shielding |

## 5.1.4 Defense-in-Depth Layer Categorization

I am often asked which layer of defense-in-depth is the most important. There was a time that I could easily answer that question, but considering the diversity of cyberattacks, insider threat, and third-party originating compromises the answer has gotten complicated. To answer specifically for an organization, I would need to know its risk profile. However, there is no way I can know the risk profile of all my readers. Regardless, I feel you are owed an answer and I will share with you my thought process that hopefully provides you with the answer you seek.

**Did You Know?**

According to a report by Rapid7, a Financial Times Stock Exchange (FTSE) 250 company has up to 35 different avenues of attack.

*Do you know all your top attack vectors and have defenses in place to counter an attack?*

**Source:**
https://www.theguardian.com/technology/2019/jun/11/ftse-250-firms-exposed-to-possible-cyber-attacks-report-finds

I follow two general rules when designing a defense-in-depth strategy for my clients. First, the layers nearest to the data are the most important. For example, if you encrypt all your data and secure the encryption keys, several layers can fail, and the sensitive information remains secure. Second, not all layers should have the same goal. For example, I design layers to deceive attackers (such as deploying cyber deception), to meet hackers head-on using threat hunting, or to slow them down with firewalls. I have found using the NIST cybersecurity framework effective in defining the second dimension of my defense-in-depth model Table 5-4 explains the use of NIST CSF in dimension 2 of my defense-in-depth model.

In 1998, the National Security Agency (NSA) published an excellent guide that addresses defense-in-depth, the Information Assurance Technical Framework (IATF). The current unclassified version of the IATF is 3.1, published in 2002. Although dated, this framework stands the test of time in its articulation of the concepts of defense-in-depth. To review the entire framework go to: http://www.dtic.mil/dtic/tr/fulltext/u2/a606355.pdf.

In Chapter 2, I discussed the COSO control framework, which provides great direction and explanation on how to layer compensating controls. I encourage you to review this framework for ideas on structuring or refining your defense-in-depth approach.

**Table 5-4. NIST-Based Defensive Layer Strategy**

| Defense Strategy | Overview |
|---|---|
| Identify | Understand the risk of a cyberattack to personnel and assets. |
| Protect | Stop or contain the impact of a cyberattack through manual intervention or automated processes. |
| Detect | Detect attacks before they have an opportunity to achieve successful impact velocity. |
| Respond | Respond to cyberattacks with countermeasures that manage or mitigate their effects. |
| Recover | Stand up to cyberattacks and recover from their aftereffects. |

Next, align your layers to the types of attacks your organization is likely to experience. Which is to say all of them. No organization is immune to any type of attack, so you must assume they all can affect you. Table 5-5 is a model I use as a design guide in aligning countermeasures to attack classes. The countermeasures presented are a small sample of options to counteract the attack classes.

## Table 5-5. Attack Class Countermeasures Model

| Attack Class | Summary | Example Countermeasures |
|---|---|---|
| Active | An attacker attempting to break into a system by introducing or changing data. | • Distribute denial of service (DDoS) prevention<br>• Digital signatures<br>• Firewalls<br>• Intrusion prevention systems (IPS) |
| Close-in | An attack where the adversary has direct or near physical access to the target. | • Passwords, session timeouts<br>• Physical security<br>• Physical surveillance systems |
| Distribution | The utilization of a purposefully programmed hardware or software backdoor that attackers exploit. | • Application security scanning<br>• Default password prohibition<br>• Security testing<br>• Trusted hardware/software providers |
| Insider | A trusted insider with access stealing, altering, or damaging information. | • Access monitoring<br>• Data loss prevention (DLP)<br>• File auditing<br>• Privileged account monitoring |
| Passive | The secret monitoring or scanning of a network for open ports and vulnerabilities. | • Message cloaking<br>• Network layer encryption<br>• Patch management |
| Social | The use of deceptive social interaction to gain access to systems. | • Impersonation fraud detection<br>• Security awareness training<br>• Social engineering testing |

**TIP:** Deploy a minimum of three NIST CSF-based countermeasures between the adversary and your data for each attack class. At a minimum, these would include one for detection, one for protection, and one for response. Each countermeasure should present a unique strategy or obstacle to attackers.

Each year dozens of data breach reports are published. I have provided links to the ones I find the most interesting in Appendix A. The information published in these reports can provide valuable insight on how to structure your layers of defense-in-depth. Table 5-6 shows research from Gemalto's Breach Level Index from 2013 through 2019 that provides an example of how to align countermeasures based on the most common types of cyber incidents (Gemalto, 2018, p. 7).

**Table 5-6. Defense-in-Depth Layer Attack History**

| Incident Type | % | Countermeasures Strategy |
|---|---|---|
| Malicious outsider | 61.5% | Countermeasures around intrusion detection, advanced persistent threat (APT) detection, threat hunting, etc. |
| Accidental loss | 23.0% | Countermeasures that encrypt data, improve data handling security and disposal, track lost or stolen devices, and raise the awareness of users. |
| Malicious insider | 12.06% | Countermeasures involving access control monitoring and auditing as well as data loss prevention (DLP) and secure data enclaves. |
| Hacktivist | 1.65% | Countermeasures based on threat intelligence, web damage reversal, DDoS mitigation, and IP blocking. |
| State sponsored | 1.33% | Measures based on threat intelligence, intrusion detection, advance persistent threat (APT) detection, IP blocking, threat hunting, etc. |
| Unknown | 0.46% | Measures aligned from previously mentioned incident types. |

Knowing the percentage of attacks by incident type is important, but I caution you not to rely exclusively on this to drive your defense-in-depth approach. For example, if you place all your efforts in protecting against a malicious outsider and pay little attention to protecting the data you will leave large gaps in your strategy.

## 5.1.5 Defense-in-Depth Criticism

Defense-in-depth is not without its detractors. Some will argue that you need look no further than the rising success of cyberattacks as proof that defense-in-depth does not work. My take on this criticism is that defense-in-depth gets a bad rap mostly due to the strategy being misapplied. We need to consider that cyberattacks have become more sophisticated and that threat actors are now exploiting threat vectors that typically have never been part of defense-in-depth. These vectors include third-parties, social engineering, and mobile devices. I have also found in my own practice that few of my clients have documented their defense-in-depth strategy. They can certainly show me a picture of a circle, square, or pyramid but not a comprehensive diagram supported by countermeasures mapping. My hypothesis is that many organizations use defense-in-depth in name only. Without detailed analysis of which layer of defense-in-depth was compromised it is difficult to say with any certainty whether a defense-in-depth strategy is to blame. I believe defense-in-depth is not to blame.

There is only anecdotal research on the depth and breadth required for each layer of defense-in-depth. We as an industry lack actionable data on the percentage of attacks occurring at each layer. This data would be crucial in determining the appropriate level of investment for each layer, especially given that organizations with finite budgets and a shortage of cybersecurity staff face an adversary with seemingly unlimited resources and methods of attack. I am of the strong opinion that we have failed defense-in-depth rather than that defense-in-depth has failed us. This can all change, and you can reap the benefits of defense-in-depth as it was always intended if you apply defense-in-depth properly. This would include structuring your strategy around:

1. Attack surface layers.
2. Defensive layers.
3. NIST CSF layers.

## 5.1.6 Defensive Layers

In my three-dimensional defense-in-depth model I define six domains that serve as defensive layers. Each of these domains is discussed in detail later; however, as a precursor to how the defense-in-depth works, I have provided a schema in Figure 5-3 to show their relationship to the other dimensions.

| Defense-in-Depth Schema | | | NIST CSF (Dimension 2) | | | | |
|---|---|---|---|---|---|---|---|
| Attack Surface Layers (Dimension 1) | Defensive Layer (Domain) (Dimension 3) | | Identify | Protect | Detect | Respond | Recover |
| 01. Supply Chain | | Governance, Risk & Compliance (GRC) Management | ● | ● | ● | ● | ● |
| 02. Facilities | | Governance, Risk & Compliance (GRC) Management | ● | ● | ● | ● | ● |
| 03. People | | Governance, Risk & Compliance (GRC) Management | ● | ● | ● | ● | ● |
| 04. Cloud | Threat & Vulnerability Management (TVM) | Cloud Service & Infrastructure (CSP) Protection | ● | ● | ● | ● | ● |
| 05. Perimeter | | Security Operations (SecOps) Management | ● | ● | ● | ● | ● |
| 06. Networking | | | | | | | |
| 07. IoT Devices | | Device & Data Protection (DDP) | ● | ● | ● | ● | ● |
| 08. Servers | | | | | | | |
| 09. Endpoint Devices | | | | | | | |
| 10. Mobile Devices | | | | | | | |
| 11. Applications | | Application, Database & Software Protection (ADS) | ● | ● | ● | ● | ● |
| 12. Databases | | | | | | | |
| 13. Data Storage | | Device & Data Protection (DDP) | ● | ● | ● | ● | ● |

Figure 5-3. Three-Dimensional Defense-in-Depth Schema. (By Tari Schreider, licensed under a Creative Commons Attribution-NonCommercial-NoDerivitives 4.0 International License)

## 5.2 Improving the Effectiveness of Defense-in-Depth

Now that we have a sound structure for your defense-in-depth approach, a three-dimensional model, how can we make it more effective? I have learned that what is defined within the defense-in-depth model is as important as its skeletal structure. Improving the effectiveness of defense-in-depth comes from embedding countermeasures. Countermeasures, however, need to be properly aligned to each layer to maximize their ability to manage or mitigate the impact of a cyberattack. To accomplish this, you will need to stop viewing countermeasures as something that resides in a layer, but view countermeasures from a relationship perspective. You will need to answer the question, "What is the relationship of one countermeasure to another?" I have found that grouping countermeasures according to their ability to protect assets and information as well as considering the support they require to operate efficiently is the most effective approach. This may prove to be a difficult proposition to some organizations as they tend to align countermeasures by people. For example, firewalls are an integral part of the network, and with most of them taking the form of an appliance, they are not much different than a router or switch and should belong to the networking department.

To ensure I grouped countermeasures properly, I turned to something called entity relationship modeling. Entity relationship modeling was originally developed for database design by Peter Chen and published in *ACM Transactions on Database Systems (TODS)* (Chen, 1976). I found that entity relationship modeling worked perfectly to describe the inter-relations of countermeasures or controls within defense-in-depth layers. This relationship approach groups countermeasures and controls according to their ability to protect assets and information versus protecting them from specific threats or causes. This is the cause-and-effect notion where you focus on the effect, and not the cause. The old way of protecting against threats required that you layer your countermeasures and controls in anticipation of a cyberattack (cause) progressing through the various layers of defense. The relationship approach aligns countermeasures and controls according to their relationship with assets and information protecting the functions (effects) of the assets and information. There is no assumed primary attack vector for a cyberattack; the assumption is an attack can come from inside or out from any vector and will ultimately reach the intended target. Attacks tend to change the behavior of an asset or its functionality making it violate its own design principle or security policy. For example, a function of email is to allow files to be attached and sent with a message. Changing the email function of file attachments to allow malicious payload attachments is what certain malware accomplishes. So, if you worry less about how the attackers got to the email system and more on what they can change, you will have a higher degree of success in protecting your organization from cyberattacks.

Now what does all this mean? When a cyberattack occurs the objective is to change the behavior of a function of a target. Focusing on layering defenses to stop or slow down the cyberattack at the vector level has proven unsuccessful. The proof of this is offered each time you read about an organization that had a data breach yet complied with all security standards. The organization's failing was focusing exclusively on protecting the vectors and not the target. For example, there are many vectors that can be used to gain access to data, and history has proven attackers are like the Royal Canadian Mounties – they always get their data. If we assume this is correct, then why not protect the data? If we focused more on encrypting all the data, then protecting the vectors becomes less important. Also, from a cost perspective, I know as a cybersecurity architect that it is far more expensive trying to protect every vector than encrypting all my data.

This is not to say that we completely ignore protecting vectors; it is to say that we spend less on the vectors and more on the target. Another example is in securing the configuration of assets. Attackers want to change the configuration of an asset so they can control its functions. If we apply file integrity monitoring and automatically reverse any file changes any time malicious file changes are detected, we stop the attack.

Figure 5-3 presents the view of this new defense-in-depth model that I have been developing over the past 10 years. It is important to note that this is not an organizational construct for a cybersecurity program; rather, it is how you structure your defense-in-depth strategy. There may be some similarities in defense-in-depth layers and cybersecurity organization layers; however, that is only coincidence. Countermeasure modeling is based on the concept of entity relationship modeling. Figure 5-4 is a countermeasure relationship model I created following the entity relationship model.

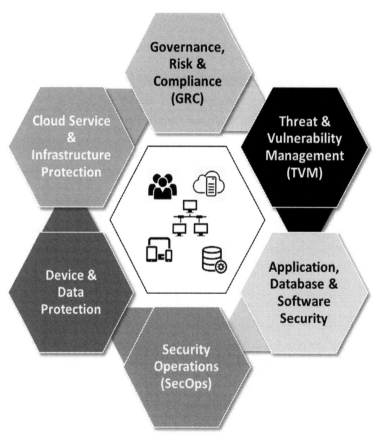

*Figure 5-4. Countermeasures Relationship Model. (By Tari Schreider, licensed under a Creative Commons Attribution-NonCommercial-NoDerivitives 4.0 International License)*

This view shows the six domains of the third dimension of the defense-in-depth model. Each domain has been further segmented into subdomains and primary components that were arrived at through the process of entity relationship modeling. The domains of this defense-in-depth strategy cover the full spectrum of a cybersecurity program.

## 5.2.1 Governance, Risk and, Compliance (GRC) Domain

This subdimension of the model is involved with the overall management of the cybersecurity program from ensuring the proper risk profile is used to base decisions of what countermeasures to use, to managing the budget and allocating the proper resources to staff the program. This subdimension covers many of the functions of the office of the chief information security officer (CISO). Figure 5-5 represents the structure of the GRC domain. Table 5-7 presents the subdomains and primary components.

*Figure 5-5. Governance, Risk, and Compliance Domain. (By Tari Schreider, licensed under a Creative Commons Attribution-NonCommercial-NoDerivitives 4.0 International License)*

235

**Table 5-7. Governance, Risk, and Compliance (GRC) Domain**

| Subdomain | Primary Components |
|---|---|
| **Strategic planning –** Direction and strategy of the cybersecurity program. | • **Body of knowledge (BOK)** – Central repository of all documentation, internal and external, used to design and operate the cybersecurity program.<br>• **Cybersecurity program playbook** – A quick guide or brochure that describes in layman's terms the scope, objectives, functions, and capabilities of the cybersecurity program.<br>• **Methods and practices** – Documentation of the procedures, processes, and practices used within the cybersecurity program.<br>• **Program maturity assessment and planning** – Baseline security assessment identifying the current maturity of the cybersecurity program. Includes a service improvement plan on how to improve the maturity of all or portions of the cybersecurity program.<br>• **Security architecture and design** – Compilation of all design documents used to develop the cybersecurity program. Includes frameworks, models, standards, blueprints, etc.<br>• **Security service catalog** – Catalog of each of the countermeasures deployed within the cybersecurity program. Describes countermeasures as a service including features, support, and cost.<br>• **Strategic roadmap** – A plan of how the cybersecurity program will evolve over time, reaching strategic objectives consisting of scope, capabilities, investment, reduction of risk profile, etc. |
| **Cybersecurity governance** – Overall management of the cybersecurity program and personnel. | • **Budget management** – Manage the capital expenditure (CapEx) and operating expense (OpEx) of the cybersecurity program finances. Justify that expenses are commensurate with value of assets at risk and annualized loss expectancy (ALE).<br>• **Cybersecurity metrics registry** – Repository of all cybersecurity program key performance measures and metrics with cross-mapping of metrics to provide an operational effectiveness view by program components.<br>• **Cybersecurity personnel management** – Ensure proper staffing and assignment of roles and responsibilities. Overview cybersecurity skills certifications and training.<br>• **Cybersecurity project management office** – Manage projects directly related to the cybersecurity program and monitor projects indirectly related to the program.<br>• **Cybersecurity policies** – Write and revise cybersecurity program policies, stipulating acceptable use of assets and information and articulating the principles of protecting the organization from cyberattack. |
| **Compliance –** Compliance with legal, regulatory, and contractual requirements. | • **Audit response** – Manage the internal and external cybersecurity or related regulatory audit process including remediation and tracking of audit citations. |

| Subdomain | Primary Components |
|---|---|
| | <ul><li>**Cybersecurity awareness and culture** – Maintain a cybersecurity aware culture through an awareness program consisting of training, reminders, and simulations.</li><li>**Cybersecurity law program** – Maintain a library of legal and regulatory statutes as well as requirements of compliance.</li><li>**Cybersecurity program performance dashboard** – Provide transparent reporting of the performance of the cybersecurity program leveraging the metrics registry.</li><li>**Regulatory compliance assessments and reporting** – Annually perform regulatory compliance assessments to determine degree of compliance with privacy and cybersecurity statutes.</li></ul> |
| **Risk management** – Determination and treatment of risk. | <ul><li>**Risk assessment program** – Perform risk assessments of projects, applications, or systems that could introduce risk to the organization.</li><li>**Risk treatment plans** – Create approaches to reduce or eliminate risk identified from risk assessments. Monitor and report on risk treatment progress.</li><li>**Cybersecurity controls catalog** – Maintain a catalog of compensating controls that are used to treat risk.</li><li>**Red teaming** – Perform independent cyberattack simulations against current countermeasures assuming the role of a threat actor.</li><li>**Risk monitoring** – Monitor the state of risk to the organization considering changes in asset and information state.</li><li>**Risk reporting** – Report on organization risk profile as well as the risk posture of applications, projects, and systems. Integrate Third-party risk reporting in overall risk profile.</li></ul> |
| **Third-party management** – Validation of cybersecurity policy compliance and risk monitoring. | <ul><li>**Compliance reporting** – Report on third-party supplier compliance with cybersecurity policies and risk profile.</li><li>**Continuity of supply chain** – Monitor state of supplier continuity and maintain continuity plans in the event of supplier failure.</li><li>**Risk management** – Perform periodic risk assessments of third-parties, assign risk scores, and monitor changes to risk scores.</li><li>**Security controls agreement** – Maintain current cybersecurity controls agreement with third-parties and monitor and act on compliance violations.</li></ul> |
| **Business continuity management (BCM)** – Resiliency and recovery of technology. | <ul><li>**Recovery of cybersecurity technology** – Make ready and test capability to recover cybersecurity countermeasures in the event of failure.</li><li>**Resiliency of cybersecurity technology** – Ensure the continued operations of cybersecurity countermeasures in the event of operational disruption.</li><li>**Recovery of cybersecurity program data** – Ensure the recoverability of security logs and security event data.</li><li>**Security of BCM operations** – Ensure the security of recovery operations and continuation of asset and information protection.</li></ul> |

## 5.2.2 Threat and Vulnerability Management (TVM) Domain

This domain is concerned with identification of the threats faced by the attack surface and the vulnerabilities that could be exploited by the threats. The attack surface is continuously monitored for vulnerabilities with noted vulnerabilities remediated to prevent exploitation. The threat landscape is assessed to identify current and emerging threats. Figure 5-6 represents the structure of the TVM domain. Table 5-8 presents the subdomains and primary components.

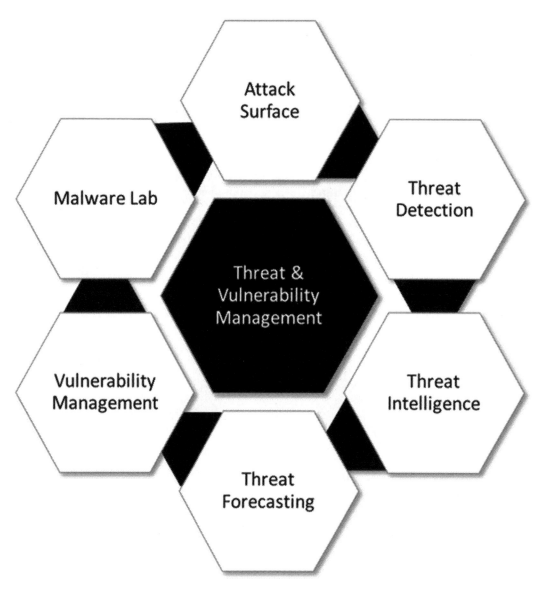

*Figure 5-6. Threat and Vulnerability Management Domain. (By Tari Schreider, licensed under a Creative Commons Attribution-NonCommercial-NoDerivitives 4.0 International License)*

**Table 5-8. Threat and Vulnerability Management Domain**

| Subdomain | Primary Components |
|---|---|
| **Attack surface** – Inventory and management of an organization's hardware and software assets. | • **Device and software inventory** – Detailed inventory of computing assets and software. Commonly contained in a configuration management database (CMDB). <br> • **IT asset discovery** – Automated network discovery and tagging of cyber assets connected to the network. <br> • **Shadow IT discovery** – Discovery of unauthorized cloud computing services. <br> • **Third-party service provider directory** – Directory of third-party service providers with detailed company and service descriptions. <br> • **User population management** – Identification and management of network user identities classified by threat class. |
| **Threat detection** – Detection of external and insider attacks. | • **Advanced persistent threat (APT) detection** – Series of countermeasures designed to detect the behaviors of an APT attack. <br> • **Data theft detection** – Data loss prevention to detect accidental or intentional data exfiltration. <br> • **Denial of service (DoS) attack prevention** – DoS prevention solution that detects degraded Internet service and counteracts attacks with load balancing and application acceleration. <br> • **DNS monitoring** – Secure DNS security and privilege access control and monitoring. <br> • **Malware detection and removal** – Detection, quarantine, and/or removal of malicious software on servers and endpoints. <br> • **Threat hunting** – Detection of lateral hacker movement inside the network. Techniques to halt hacker activity once detected. |
| **Threat intelligence** – Gathering, analysis, and dissemination of threat intelligence and attacker profiles. | • **Honeynets and honeypots** – Faux IT infrastructure with decoy information to attract hackers to waste their time on wrong targets. <br> • **Information sharing and analysis center (ISAC)** – Commercial critical infrastructure section threat intelligence shared by specific industries. <br> • **Open source intelligence feeds (OSINT)** – Intelligence collected from publicly available sources. <br> • **Security information and event management (SIEM)** – Security event log collection, aggregation, and analysis to detect malicious activity. <br> • **Threat intelligence subscriptions** – Commercial subscription to threat intelligence gathering and reporting service. |

| Subdomain | Primary Components |
|---|---|
| **Threat forecasting** – Forecast future and potential threats; issue threat advisories and warnings. | • **Cyber threat gaming** – Threat attack simulation exercises in the form of a game.<br>• **Threat actor profiles** – Profile of hackers, hacktivists, or other advisories. Includes overview of techniques, motivations, targets, etc.<br>• **Threat forecasting** – Leveraging threat intelligence to forecast likely attack targets of an organization.<br>• **Threat modeling** – Procedure identifying objectives and vulnerabilities, and then defining countermeasures to prevent attacks.<br>• **Threat registry** – Inventory of analyzed threats aligned to attack surface. |
| **Vulnerability management** – Scanning and remediation of attack surface vulnerabilities. | • **Patch management** – Remediation of hardware and software vulnerabilities through vendor patches and firmware updates.<br>• **Vulnerability remediation testing** – Testing of applied vulnerability remediation to verify mitigation of vulnerability.<br>• **Vulnerability scanning** – Automated scanning of internal and external networks to detect attack surface vulnerabilities. |
| **Malware lab** – Dedicated lab for reverse-engineering and study of malware. | • **Malware analysis service** – Malware analysis capability either in-house or as a service to evaluate new strains of malware to determine countermeasures.<br>• **Malware analysis system or sandbox** – Reverse-engineering of malware to determine how the malware would act when executed inside an isolated environment. |

## 5.2.3 Application, Database, and Software Protection (ADS) Domain

This domain ensures all new and legacy code is secure in its development, acquisition, and maintenance, meeting industry-accepted security standards. Countermeasures for in-house developed, common off the shelf (COTS), and database products meet secure coding standards; any exploitable code is identified and remediated prior to release to production. Figure 5-7 shows the structure of the ADS domain. Table 5-9 presents the subdomains and primary components.

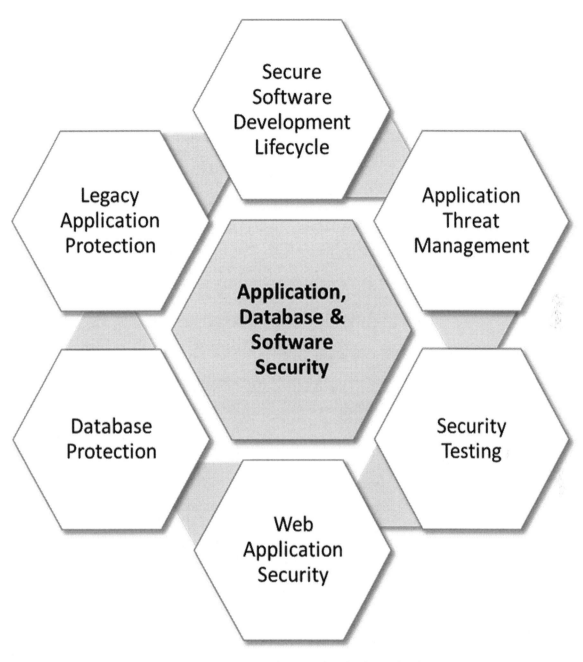

*Figure 5-7. Application, Database, and Software Domain. (By Tari Schreider, licensed under a Creative Commons Attribution-NonCommercial-NoDerivitives 4.0 International License)*

**Table 5-9. Application, Database, and Software Domain**

| Subdomain | Primary Components |
|---|---|
| **Secure software development lifecycle** – Methods and practices for secure coding standards. | • **Bug tracking** – Identifying and tracking application bugs and implementing remediation schedule and plans.<br><br>• **Development operations security integration** – Integration of security practices to reduce code vulnerabilities in application development.<br><br>• **Secure coding policies and practices** – Methods and practices of secure coding techniques.<br><br>• **Secure programing training** – Programmer training in secure coding techniques and good practices.<br><br>• **Software composition analysis** – Inventory of open source components to identify vulnerabilities, covering open source and commercial code.<br><br>• **Source code protection** – Secure access and monitoring of source code to prevent introduction of accidental or intentional adverse changes. |
| **Application threat management** – Detection of external and insider application threats. | • **Application patch management** – Patching of commercial application vulnerabilities.<br><br>• **Application risk profiles** – Profile of application's risk and control compliance score.<br><br>• **Application security monitoring** – Monitoring of application security event log for suspicious activity.<br><br>• **Application threat intelligence** – Threat intelligence and security vulnerability reporting specific to applications or application code. |

| Subdomain | Primary Components |
|---|---|
| **Security testing** – Scan applications for vulnerabilities and test for external and internal compromises. | • **Bug bounty program** – Program offered to hackers to receive recognition and compensation for reporting bugs, especially those pertaining to exploits and vulnerabilities.<br><br>• **Dynamic application security testing (DAST)** – The process of testing an application or software product in an operating state.<br><br>• **Manual code review** – Expert firsthand analysis of application code to detect vulnerabilities undetected by automated vulnerability scanning.<br><br>• **Penetration testing** – External or internal attempt to compromise a network or application using hacker techniques.<br><br>• **Static application security testing (SAST)** – Set of technologies designed to analyze application source code, byte code, and binaries for coding and design conditions that are indicative of security vulnerabilities. |
| **Web application security** – Protection of web applications. | • **Multi-factor authentication** – A method of access control in which a user is granted access only after presenting several separate pieces of evidence to an authentication mechanism.<br><br>• **Intrusion prevention system (IPS)** – Security device to monitor and log network or system activities for malicious activity and block or stop an attack.<br><br>• **Reputation filtering** – Mail flow policies based on sender reputation, which prevents malicious traffic from entering a network, allowing legitimate mail to flow unobstructed.<br><br>• **Web application firewall (WAF)** – Appliance, server plugin, or filter that applies a set of rules to a Hypertext Transfer Protocol (HTTP) conversation to prevent cross-site scripting (XSS) and Structured Query Language (SQL) injection attacks. |

| Subdomain | Primary Components |
|---|---|
| **Database protection –** Protection of databases and associated data. | • **Database access monitoring** – Privileged user and application access monitoring independent of native database logging and audit functions.<br><br>• **Database encryption** – Transformation of data stored in a database into cipher text that is incomprehensible without first being decrypted.<br><br>• **Database vulnerability scanning** – Scanning of databases for security vulnerabilities and configuration flaws, including patch levels. |
| **Legacy application protection** – Security and isolation of non-secure legacy applications. | • **COBOL and Fortran source code vulnerability scanning** – Legacy code scanning software to detect application vulnerabilities.<br><br>• **Mainframe access control** – Access control solutions such as Resource Access Control Facility (RACF) or Access Control Facility (ACF2).<br><br>• **Noncompliant application sandbox** – Segmenting or insulating applications with known security vulnerabilities that cannot be remediated into a secure zone.<br><br>• **Source code comprehension** – Application analysis tool that documents how an application functions when no documentation is available. Used for security analysis of legacy applications. |

## 5.2.4 Security Operations (SecOps) Domain

This domain handles the day-to-day operations of security countermeasures and controls to protect assets and information. Engineering of cybersecurity solutions to integrate into the organization IT infrastructure and the configuration and maintenance of cybersecurity technology and products occur within this component. The ongoing monitoring of cyberattacks and cyberattack response is driven from this component's big data analytics capability. Figure 5-8 represents the structure of the SecOps domain. Table 5-10 presents the subdomains and primary components.

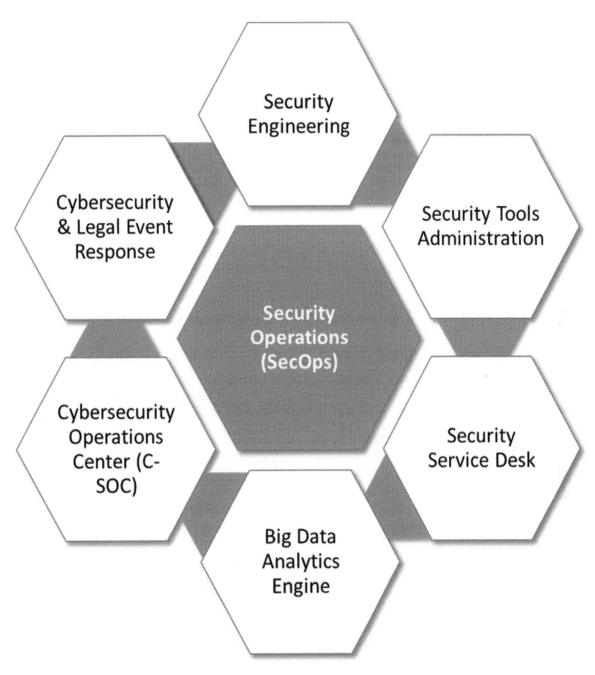

*Figure 5-8. Security Operations Domain. (By Tari Schreider, licensed under a Creative Commons Attribution-NonCommercial-NoDerivitives 4.0 International License)*

**Table 5-10. Security Operations Domain**

| Subdomain | Primary Components |
|---|---|
| **Security engineering –** Technology engineering consisting of script writing, connectors development, and engineering design. | • **Asset hardening** – Restricting open ports and enabled services as well as ensuring current patches are applied to cyber assets.<br><br>• **Countermeasures maintenance and testing** – Maintain current release and patch levels of cybersecurity technology and test functionality of new releases prior to deployment.<br><br>• **Identity and access management (IDAM) Engineering** – Write connectors to bridge IDAM technology with authoritative user and provisioning source applications.<br><br>• **Network security engineering** – Design secure network, establish secure networking practices, and harden network infrastructure devices (e.g., switches and routers).<br><br>• **Cybersecurity technology integration** – Test and evaluate new cybersecurity technologies to validate integration within current IT environment. |
| **Security tools administration –** Administration and maintenance of cybersecurity technology. | • **Countermeasure administration** – Daily operations support of cybersecurity technology and troubleshooting operational issues.<br><br>• **Cybersecurity technology updates and deployments** – User testing of cybersecurity product enhancements and deployment and training.<br><br>• **Firewall and IDS/IPS administration** – Application of firewall rules and IDS/IPS signatures following management of change procedures.<br><br>• **Proof of concepts** – Test new cybersecurity technologies against use cases.<br><br>• **Technology health checks** – Periodical assessment of the performance and effectiveness of cybersecurity countermeasures. |

| Subdomain | Primary Components |
|---|---|
| **Security service desk –** Provide user support for cybersecurity program technology, user device virus infections, and access administration. | • **Level 1 support countermeasures** – First-level support of cybersecurity countermeasures. Diagnose failed reporting, broken alert streams, etc.<br><br>• **Password resets** – Reset user passwords, issue initial passwords, and assist in user access issues.<br><br>• **Security incident reports** – Security incident and event reporting produced by various cybersecurity program products.<br><br>• **Security trouble ticketing** – Opening, processing, and closing of security-related user trouble tickets.<br><br>• **Token provisioning** – Provide or revoke new or replacement two-factor authentication software and hardware tokens.<br><br>• **User malware infection remediation** – Assist users in resolving localized malware infections. |
| **Big data analytics –** Perform advance data analytics using all available security event and intelligence feeds. | • **Big data analytics platform support** – Support of big data platform consisting of Hadoop, server clusters, analytic software, etc.<br><br>• **Data mining** – Advanced analytics using sophisticated threat analysis beyond SIEM analysis.<br><br>• **Facilities security feed integration** – Integration of closed-circuit television (CCTV), access control, life/safety, and other physical security controls into SIEM and big data analytic platforms.<br><br>• **Reporting and analysis** – Security event pattern analysis from big data sources.<br><br>• **Security feed administration** – Maintenance and support of internal, external, and open source data feeds. |

| Subdomain | Primary Components |
|---|---|
| **Cybersecurity operations center (C-SOC)** – Dedicated security event monitoring and response operation. | • **Alert triage** – Analysis and categorization of counsel alerts.<br><br>• **Incident response** – Response procedures to act on cyberattacks underway.<br><br>• **Log analysis** – Review and analysis of security event logs to detect suspicious activity.<br><br>• **Managed security service provider (MSSP) support** – Daily support and shift turnover of MSSP operations.<br><br>• **Network operations center (NOC) liaison** – Interface with NOC to coordinate NOC and C-SOC alerts.<br><br>• **Security event monitoring** – 24x7x365 live monitoring of security alerts and indicators of compromise.<br><br>• **Threat hunting** – Investigation and hunting of underway cyberattacks. |
| **Cybersecurity and legal event response** – Provide incident and legal event support. | • **Cybersecurity insurance** – Policy to cover costs associated with a data breach and related lawsuit.<br><br>• **Data breach response** – Response plan to handle specific data privacy breach regulatory violations.<br><br>• **Digital evidence gathering** – Procedures, practices, and products to gather legally admissible digital evidence.<br><br>• **Document discovery support** – Production and preservation of court ordered discovery documents.<br><br>• **Legal hold support** – Issuance and tracking of legal holds of documents requested under court order.<br><br>• **Security incident response support** – Operations support of incident response plans. |

## 5.2.5 Device and Data Protection (DDP) Domain

This domain focuses on device and data protection which are inexorably linked. Confidential and sensitive information is managed throughout its lifecycle to ensure the integrity of data creation, secure data movement, and finishing with secure data disposal. Countermeasures for protecting data share common and leveraged approaches, such as device and data encryption. Figure 5-9 shows the structure of the DDP domain. Table 5-11 presents subdomains and primary components.

*Figure 5-9. Device and Data Protection Domain. (By Tari Schreider, licensed under a Creative Commons Attribution-NonCommercial-NoDerivitives 4.0 International License)*

**Table 5-11. Device and Data Protection Domain**

| Subdomain | Primary Components |
|---|---|
| **Data governance** – Definition of data handling requirements and protection of data throughout its lifecycle. | • **Data archiving** – Retention of information for an extended period. Generally required by legal or regulatory statutes.<br><br>• **Data backup** – Duplication of data to allow retrieval of a backup set of data in the event of loss of original data.<br><br>• **Data classification** – Categorization of data into types or other distinct levels for data management and tracking.<br><br>• **Data integrity** – Assurance of the accuracy and consistency of data throughout its lifecycle.<br><br>• **Data retention** – Retaining of information for specific periods of time to meet business and legal requirements.<br><br>• **eDiscovery** – Electronic discovery of information during litigation investigations. |
| **Device protection** – Methods to prevent devices from compromise and malware infection. | • **Endpoint protection** – Integrated cybersecurity solution designed to protect user devices consisting of DLP, firewalls, IDS/IPS, anti-malware, etc.<br><br>• **Mobile device security** – Protection of smartphones, tablets, laptops, and other portable computing **devices** from wireless-related threats and vulnerabilities.<br><br>• **Server hardening** – Reduction of threat vectors through the disabling of services, closing of unnecessary ports, and application of security patches.<br><br>• **Server security solutions** – Server-specific security measures consisting of connection authentication, service restriction, firewalls, file integrity monitoring, and intrusion detection/prevention.<br><br>• **Virtualization security** – Protection of the hypervisor layer protecting all virtual machines on the host. Includes anti-virus, IDS/IPS, firewalls, etc.<br><br>• **Whitelisting/Blacklisting** – Restriction of applications that can and cannot run on cyber devices. |

| Subdomain | Primary Components |
|---|---|
| **Data protection** – Methods to maintain the privacy of data once stolen. | • **Data anonymization** – Removal or changing of record codes or keys to prevent the linking of sensitive data to actual data.<br><br>• **Data blurring** – Conversion of real data with rounded up data, average of all data, and other techniques to mislead viewer on exact data content.<br><br>• **Data camouflage** – Replacement of actual sensitive data with fictional data so that the information may be used without violating privacy protections.<br><br>• **Data de-identification** – Removal of personally identifiable information from datasets.<br><br>• **Data encryption** – Use of cryptographic techniques where data is rendered unreadable without the presence of a unique encryption key to decode the encrypted data.<br><br>• **Data masking** – Masking or concealing of sensitive data within a dataset so that the data can be used without revealing privacy-protected information.<br><br>• **Data obfuscation** – Scrambling of data to prevent unauthorized access to sensitive information.<br><br>• **Data perturbation** – Small changes to data to prevent identification of individuals from unique or rare data subsets of large populations.<br><br>• **Data redaction** – Expunging of sensitive information prior to disclosure. |

| Subdomain | Primary Components |
|---|---|
| **Messaging security –** Maintaining privacy and integrity of messages. | • **Content privacy monitoring** – Monitoring of content flow to determine violation of data privacy policies.<br><br>• **Data loss prevention (DLP)** – Monitoring of content flow within a network or egress points to identify accidental or unauthorized release of sensitive information.<br><br>• **Ephemeral messaging** – Messages that expire or disappear within a specified period.<br><br>• **Message compliance retention** – Retention of all forms of messaging that must be retained for legal or regulatory requirements.<br><br>• **Messaging encryption** – Sending and receiving messages through email, etc. where the recipients must have an encryption key to read and respond to the message.<br><br>• **Secure messaging** – Secure, private methods to facilitate sharing of sensitive information between parties. Messages can be configured to verify receipt, restrict printing or forwarding, etc. |
| **Content security –** Protection of content from alteration, theft, eavesdropping, and loss. | • **Piracy monitoring** – Internet scanning to locate and remove copyrighted material.<br><br>• **Content encryption** – Use of cryptographic techniques where content is rendered unreadable without the presence of a unique encryption key to decode the encrypted content.<br><br>• **Data alteration detection** – Method to detect the alteration or tampering of information from its original source.<br><br>• **Digital rights management (DRM)** – Control of the use of digital data restricting its storage, printing, forwarding, and modification.<br><br>• **Digital signatures** – Authenticated, non-repudiation signature that replaces a wet signature.<br><br>• **Email attachment security** – Configuration of email attachment functions to validate security policies. Includes attachment interrogation and remediation.<br><br>• **Screenshot detection and disablement** – Disabling of or detection of someone performing a screenshot within a web browser. |

| Subdomain | Primary Components |
|---|---|
| **Non-custodial data protection** – Protection of data held or processed by others. | • **Data controller privacy policies** – Privacy preserving and information handing policies that direct what a data custodian may or may not do with sensitive information.<br><br>• **Data fingerprinting** – Adding of unique identifiers to sensitive information to track movement.<br><br>• **Digital rights management** – Control the use of digital data restricting its storage, printing, forwarding, and modification.<br><br>• **Encryption key custody** – Retention of the second dual encryption key so that data custodians can comply with court orders without violating organization privacy agreements. |

## 5.2.6 Cloud Service and Infrastructure Protection (CIP) Domain

This domain addresses the protection of data stored in the cloud, and the security of the cloud services consisting of infrastructure as a service (IaaS), software as a service (SaaS), platform as a service (PaaS), etc. Figure 5-10 presents the structure of the CIP domain. Table 5-12 presents the subdomains and primary components.

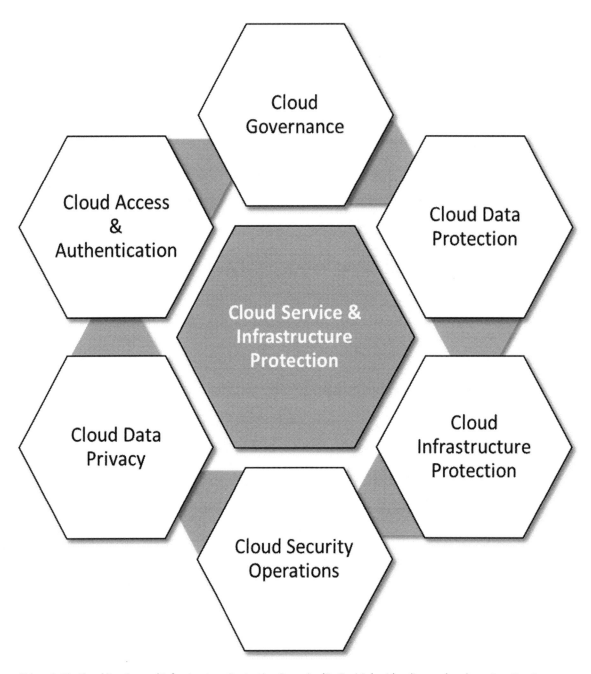

*Figure 5-10. Cloud Service and Infrastructure Protection Domain. (By Tari Schreider, licensed under a Creative Commons Attribution-NonCommercial-NoDerivitives 4.0 International License)*

**Table 5-12. Cloud Service and Infrastructure Protection Domain**

| Subdomain | Primary Components |
|---|---|
| **Cloud governance –** Oversight and control of cloud data and processing. | • **Amazon web service (AWS) control compliance monitoring** – Monitor control compliance state of AWS security settings.<br><br>• **Cloud access security broker (CASB)** – Cloud access security policy enforcement point for access, encryption, malware detection, etc.<br><br>• **Cloud security policy enforcement** – Monitoring, reporting, and enforcement of cloud security policies.<br><br>• **Shared responsibility security model** – Security model where both parties share in the responsibility to protect cloud assets and information. |
| **Cloud data protection –** Protection of data held or processed by cloud service providers. | • **Cloud collaboration software** – Secure cloud collaboration solution.<br><br>• **Cloud encryption gateways** – Cloud security proxy, which provides encryption, tokenization, or both.<br><br>• **Digital rights management** – Control the use of digital data shared in the cloud to restrict its storage, printing, forwarding, and modification.<br><br>• **Dual encryption key custody** – Two-key process to prevent the disclosure of information by cloud service provider. |
| **Cloud infrastructure protection** – Protection of hardware used to deliver cloud services, primarily private and hybrid cloud. | • **Cloud server intrusion detection system (IDS)** – IDS performed as software as a service (SaaS).<br><br>• **Cloud vulnerability assessment** – Scanning of cloud platform for vulnerabilities.<br><br>• **Configuration auditing** – Auditing of cloud service provider infrastructure security configurations.<br><br>• **High risk connection intelligence** – Monitoring of websites to determine if they have been compromised or hijacked. |

| Subdomain | Primary Components |
|---|---|
| | • **Virtualization security and virtual machine hardening** – Protection of the hypervisor layer protecting all virtual machines on the host. Includes anti-virus, IDS/IPS, firewalls, etc. |
| **Cloud security operations** – Ensuring the security of cloud operations and workload processes. | • **Cloud security monitoring** – Monitoring cloud service provider or cloud infrastructure security.<br><br>• **Cloud server configuration hardening** – Hardening of cloud infrastructure.<br><br>• **Cloud server misconfiguration detection** – Detection and alerting of cloud service provider server or service misconfigurations.<br><br>• **Cloud service provider certification validation** – Monitoring of cloud service provider security certification status including renewals and revocations.<br><br>• **Cloud topology visualization** – Cloud topographical diagram showing data path, attack surface, and data residency.<br><br>• **Cloud workload security** – Could workload visibility to identify security gaps created by unauthorized changes, suspicious behavior, unknown vulnerabilities, and zero-day threat hardening. |
| **Cloud data privacy** – Protection of data residing in or burst in the cloud. | • **Cloud data loss prevention (DLP)** – DLP policies extended to data residing in the cloud.<br><br>• **Cloud data privacy monitoring** – Monitoring of privacy violations of data residing or processed in the cloud.<br><br>• **Cloud-based email scanning** – Cloud-based email security scanning prior to delivery to enterprise email servers.<br><br>• **Data sovereignty policy** – Data privacy policies outlining privacy protections for individual countries where customers and/or data reside.<br><br>• **Security as a service (SECaaS)** – Contracted security services to replace or augment in-house security services. |

| Subdomain | Primary Components |
|---|---|
| **Cloud access and authentication** – Controlling the access to cloud data or resources. | • **Identity management as a service (IDaaS)** – Cloud-based centralized administration and provisioning of user accounts, applications, and devices.<br><br>• **Multitenant active directory (AD) hardening** – Hardening of AD used for cloud users, accounts, and applications.<br><br>• **Multitenant active directory (AD) monitoring** – Monitoring of AD for unauthorized or suspicious directory changes.<br><br>• **Privilege cloud account access monitoring** – Monitoring of administrator, service, and shared accounts for abnormal behavior.<br><br>• **Time-limited network port and out-of-band (OOB) access control** – Assignment of time-bound access to network ports or OOB maintenance and support ports. |

**TIP**: Check out the Cloud Security Alliance (CSA) Cloud Controls Matrix for additional insight into applicable countermeasures. The CSA website is: https://cloudsecurityalliance.org/download/cloud-controls-matrix-v3-0-1/.

It is important to allow countermeasures from one domain dimension to provide services to another domain dimension regardless. For example, vulnerability assessments may reside in the threat and vulnerability management domain of dimension-three, but those services can also be shared by other domains in dimension-three such as cloud service and infrastructure protection.

# 5.3 Zero Trust

A design concept that was first launched through the former Jericho Forum in 2004 (ATC, 2019) called Zero Trust was based on the premise that you should not trust any user or device connected to a network. The Jericho Forum, with a membership of leading European CISOs, recognized the need to change the way assets and users are authenticated to an enterprise network in light of rapidly developing cloud and mobile computing. The members of the Forum realized that the traditional network perimeter was quickly dissolving and being reimagined through mobile and cloud computing. Networks were becoming elastic where cloud and mobile endpoints dynamically defined the boundaries of a network. The Forum brought to light the problem but had not offered many solutions.

The concept of Zero Trust gained traction in 2010, when John Kindervag, a researcher at Forrester, coined the term "Zero Trust" or "Zero Trust Networks" to solve the de-perimeterization problem posed by the Jericho Forum (ATC, 2019). Zero Trust initially focused on network segmentation and challenging current trust assumptions of the day.

Today, Zero Trust proffers the following principles:

- Never trust users or assets, always verify.
- Continuously authorize all network and user access.
- The network is a hostile place and must be treated as such.
- External and internal threats already exist in the network, think assumption of breach.
- Security policies must be dynamic (software-defined) and leverage every available source of data for decision making.
- Isolate sensitive and confidential data.
- Accelerate threat and vulnerability detection.

Figure 5-11 presents an example of a Zero Trust model.

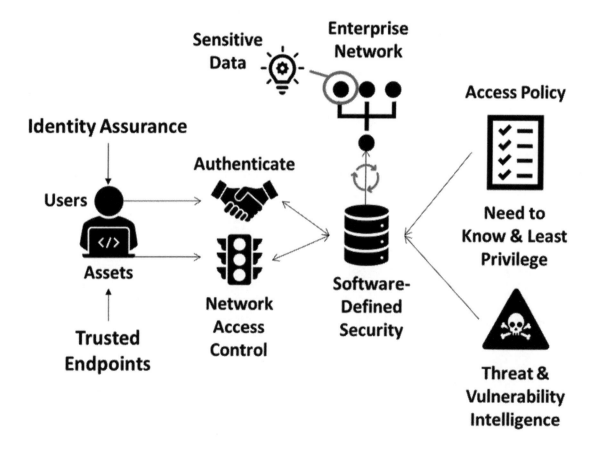

Figure 5-11. Zero Trust Model Example

Zero Trust has evolved over the years with numerous versions offered by various cybersecurity providers. Forester has even evolved their initial Zero Trust into what is now known as the Trust eXtended (ZTX) framework (Chase, 2019). The notion of trust but verify has evolved to Zero Trust models where all users and endpoints are trusted and authorized for access on a session by session basis.

Table 5-13 provides a list of Zero Trust model solution providers.

**Table 5-13. Zero Trust Providers**

| Company | Model | URL |
|---|---|---|
| Cisco Systems. Inc. | Cisco Trusted Access Portfolio | https://www.cisco.com/c/en_ca/solutions/security/trusted-access/index.html |
| Forcepoint | Dynamic Data Protection | https://www.forcepoint.com/solutions/need/dynamic-data-protection |
| Fortinet, Inc. | Fortinet Security Fabric | https://help.fortinet.com/fos60hlp/60/Content/FortiOS/fortigate-security-fabric/SF_Introduction.htm |
| Illumio | Illumio Adaptive Security Platform (ASP) | https://www.illumio.com/product-overview |
| Palo Alto Networks | PAN-OS 8.1 | https://www.paloaltonetworks.com/security-for/zero-trust |
| Symantec Corporation | Symantec Integrated Cyber Defense (ICD) | https://www.symantec.com/theme/integrated-cyber-defense |

*Note: Links are current as of September 22, 2019.*

## 5.4 Defense-in-Depth Model Schema

To help you with planning and documenting your defense-in-depth model, Table 5-13 provides you with a template you can copy to an Excel spreadsheet. Once you have created your spreadsheet, start adding your attack surface layers, and cross map those to the domains, subdomains, and primary components previously discussed in this chapter. Next, enter the specific countermeasures you will use to enforce or support the primary components. Then use Table 5-4 as a legend to identify which NIST CSF category to align to your countermeasures.

**Table 5-14. Defense-in-Depth Model Schema.**

| Attack Surface | Domain | Subdomain | Primary Components | NIST CSF Category | Countermeasures |
|---|---|---|---|---|---|
| Supply chain | GRC | Third-party management | Compliance reporting | Detect | Third-party compliance state reporting dashboard |
| | | | Continuity of supply chain | Recover | Supply chain business continuity plan |
| | | | Risk management | Identify | Third-party risk assessment |
| | | | Security controls agreement | Protect | Third-party cybersecurity controls agreement |
| | | | Supplier incident response | Respond | Third-party incident response plan |

You should strive to identify countermeasures for each NIST CSF category for each primary component. If you were to do this for each of the primary cybersecurity program components identified within this book, you would have over 900 countermeasures defined within your defense-in-depth model. Sounds like a lot and it is. But remember, the devil is in the detail. In my opinion, not documenting your defense-in-depth approach is the number one reason why defense-in-depth fails many companies.

## 5.5 Open Source Software Protection

You may have already noticed that your IT organization has made the strategic shift toward adopting *open source software*. According to a recent market survey by Black Duck Software (Flomenberg, 2016), more than 78% of enterprises run on open source, and fewer than 3% indicate they don't rely on open software in any way. This shift to open source changes how security is applied within the defense-in-depth model. Not only do you need to be concerned about how to protect attack surface components that include open source software, but now many cybersecurity products are based on open source code. Ignoring the security of open source attack surface components can prove to be disastrous. A case in point is the September 2017 announcement by consumer reporting company Equifax, Inc. that a giant cybersecurity breach compromised the personal information of as many as 143 million Americans – almost half the country (O'Brien, 2017).

At the time of this writing, the full investigative report is incomplete; however, Sonatype Inc. the stewards of The Central Repository (https://central.sonatype.org/) of the open source community published its analysis of the cyberattack, essentially laying the blame squarely at the feet of Equifax. According to Sonatype, "Organizations like Equifax are continuously deciding where and how to invest in cybersecurity based on a cost-benefit assessment, but at the end of the day they are ultimately liable for the security of their data and systems" (Weeks, 2017). Equifax, on the other hand, publicly blamed Apache's Struts open source software for its record-breaking security breach. The court of public opinion will ultimately decide if the open source community is responsible for building secure code or if organizations must accept the responsibility to secure the open source code they chose to deploy.

> **Did You Know?**
>
> On July 22, 2019, Equifax agreed to an *up to* $700 million settlement with the Federal Trade commission (FTC) over its 2017 data breach. The court of public opinion as well as the FTC did speak and found Equifax negligent in its cybersecurity practices.
>
> *How would your cybersecurity practices hold up in court?*
>
> **Source:**
> https://www.usatoday.com/story/money/2019/07/22/ftc-equifax-settlement/1793029001/

Many of my colleagues assert that open source software is inherently more secure because of the transparent nature of the way it is developed within an open community. They argue that many eyes are on the code to identify vulnerabilities and bugs. My position is that whether your organization uses commercial off-the-shelf (COTS) or open source software, you must follow proper cybersecurity practices. I have seen many companies lured into a false sense of security by thinking that either their COTS or open source software is more secure than it is. I recommend that you follow the advice in Table 5-9 – specifically the sub-domain of secure software development lifecycle component of software composition analysis – to begin planning for the security of your organization's open source software library. Virtually all aspects of this book can and should be applied to open source.

Here are my top tips for ensuring your open source library is secure:

1. **Adopt DevSecOps:** Ignoring basic blocking and tackling will cause you to lose the cyber war. Open source is introduced in applications development and your cybersecurity should be introduced at the same time.

2. **Identify open source code:** If you can't see it, you can't protect it. Commit to discovering all opensource through composition analysis.
3. **Monitor open source vulnerabilities:** If you let your guard down, you will get overrun. Acquire an alerting capability to provide notifications of new open source vulnerabilities.
4. **Patch vulnerable open source code:** Receive notifications from open source providers of new versions, releases, or patches. Rate each following your risk management approach.
5. **Monitor open source code library:** Continuously monitor open source code security performance, and conduct security training.
6. **Never assume open source code is secure:** Expecting someone else to do your security work is a failed strategy. Trust but verify all open source code.

If you're wondering why I haven't provided you with a *securing open source silver bullet*, the simple answer is that there isn't one. But if you follow the advice in this book and treat open source the same as any component of your attack surface, you just may avoid becoming the next Equifax.

## 5.6 Defense-in-Depth Checklist

To help you with the building of your defensive in depth strategy, I have provided a checklist in Table 5-14. This checklist pulls together the essential steps covered in this chapter in an order that will simplify all that you will need to do to achieve an effective defense-in-depth strategy.

**Table 5-15. Defense-in-Depth Strategy Checklist**

| Step | Activity |
|------|----------|
| 1 | Finalize your attack surface – define the first dimension of your defense-in-depth model. Only select the layers that make sense for your organization. If your program excludes the supply chain, then exclude it from your model. |
| 2 | Adopt NIST CSF – use CSF as your second dimension of your defense-in-depth model. Align your existing cybersecurity countermeasures to each applicable NIST CSF category. Use table 5-4 as your legend. |
| 3 | Create a defense-in-depth schema –use an Excel spreadsheet using the template provided in Table 5-13. |

| Step | Activity |
|------|----------|
| 4 | Align countermeasures – align countermeasures to each category of the NIST CSF. |
| 5 | Document defense-in-depth – build a schema like Table 5-13 to document the defense-in-depth countermeasures. |

## *Summary*

You now have a knowledge set that, frankly, many managers involved in their organization's cybersecurity program do not have. They have not had the benefit of over 30 years of building and maturing a cybersecurity program that you obtained by reading the first five chapters of this book. Think of yourself as having manufactured a fine European race car. But before you take it out on the track, you should learn how to drive it, right?

In the next chapter, I will show you how to operationalize the cybersecurity program that you have designed and built. Chapter 6 will cover everything from documenting your countermeasures in a service catalog to properly staffing the cybersecurity functions. But don't stop short of your journey, Chapter 7 provides you with a host of cybersecurity program design templates that will make your destination one you will remember always.

# References

Chen, P. (1976, March). The entity-relationship model – Toward a unified view of data. *ACM Transactions on Database Systems*, 1(1), 10-36. Retrieved from http://www.comp.nus.edu.sg/~lingtw/papers/tods76.chen.pdf

Flomenberg, J, (2016, June 19). *The next wave in software is open adoption software.* [Blog post] Retrieved from https://techcrunch.com/2016/06/19/the-next-wave-in-software-is-open-adoption-software/

Gemalto. (2018). *2018: Data Privacy and New Regulations Take Center Stage.* Retrieved from https://breachlevelindex.com/request-report

Mitchell, B. (2017, June 9). Understanding the open systems interconnection model? *Lifewire.* Retrieved from https://www.lifewire.com/open-systems-interconnection-model-816290?_ga=2.101929281.1939442934.1495204556-1362401804.1495204

O'Brien, A. (2017, September 8). Giant Equifax data breach: 143 million people could be affected. *CNN Tech.* Retrieved from http://money.cnn.com/2017/09/07/technology/business/equifax-data-breach/index.html

Weeks, D. (2017, September 9). *Struts2 vulnerability cracks Equifax.* [Blog post]. Retrieved from http://blog.sonatype.com/struts2-vulnerability-cracks-equifax

Chase, C. (2018, November). *The Forrester Wave™: Zero Trust eXtended (ZTX) Ecosystem Providers, Q4 2018*. Retrieved from https://www.illumio.com/resource-center/research-report-the-forrester-wave-zero-trust-extended-ecosystem-providers?utm_source=bing&utm_medium=cpc&utm_campaign=Search-NB-Zero_Trust-BMM-Bing-US&utm_term=%2Bzero%20%2Btrust&creative={creative}


The American Council for Technology (ATC). (2019, April). *Zero trust Cybersecurity Current Trends*. Retrieved from https://www.actiac.org/zero-trust-cybersecurity-current-trends

# Self-Study Questions

The following questions will help you build your expertise in designing a cybersecurity program.

1. What is defense-in-Depth?
   A concept coined by the US military to describe the placement of layers of defenses to impede the advancement of a threat.

2. What are the types of defense-in-depth models?
   Box, concentric circles, pyramid and stairs.

3. What is the OSI Security Model?
   A security model which recommends information and asset safeguards in terms of seven layers.

4. What is an active attack?
   An attacker attempting to break into a system by introducing or changing data.

5. Which domain does Business Continuity Management reside?
   Governance, Risk and Compliance Management.

6. What is non-custodial data protection?

> The protection of data held or processed by others.

7. What is the purpose of a malware lab?

> To quarantine, observe and reverse engineer malware to understand how to adjust defensive measure to detect, block or prevent malware from causing damage.

8. What is source code comprehension?

> An application analysis tool that documents how an application functions when no documentation is available. Used for security analysis of legacy applications.

9. What is Digital Rights Management (DRM)?

> The control of the use of digital data restricting its storage, printing, forwarding, and modification.

10. What is the Cloud Security Alliance (CSA) Cloud Controls Matrix?

> A set of controls specifically suited for protecting a cloud computing environment.

# Chapter 6

# Applying Service Management

# to Cybersecurity Programs

Even the best laid plans can come unwound if they are not executed properly. The same is true of your cybersecurity program. You can spend months if not years designing and building the prefect cybersecurity program, but if the program is not properly staffed and operated, your efforts will fall woefully short of expectations. This chapter shows you what is required to properly operate your cybersecurity program from assigning the right staff to implementing the right processes.

### *This chapter will help you to:*

- Understand the importance of adopting a service management approach.
- Know how to implement security into your application development process.
- Identify the proper cybersecurity program roles and responsibilities.
- Learn how to automate and orchestrate cybersecurity program services.

# Chapter 6 Roadmap

 On this last stop you will elevate your cybersecurity program to a higher level of operational efficiency through the application of service management. You will need to make a paradigm shift in thinking and position your cybersecurity countermeasures and processes as services. The baseline for this transformation to service management is Information Technology Service Management (ITSM). Cybersecurity personnel must also be aligned to cybersecurity services

Figure 6.0 shows categories of service management with which to wrap cybersecurity services to improve their operational state. Cybersecurity services can succumb to the same operational disruptions just as any aspect of information technology (IT). Information and assets can only work if they are available and operating correctly. The outcomes of this chapter are designed to apply operational rigor to the infrastructure of the cybersecurity program.

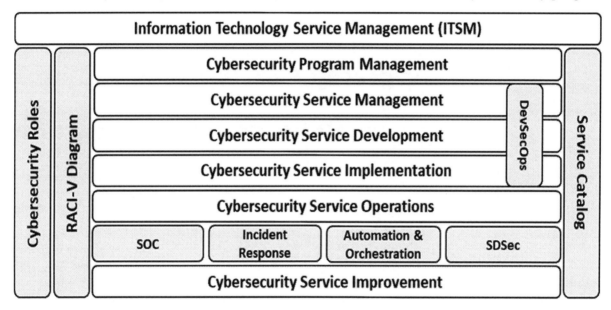

*Figure 6.0. Service Management Reference Architecture*

Each main component (gray) and sub-component of the reference architecture is covered in more detail later in this chapter.

This stop will require you to make quite a few decisions in the face of the substantial number of safeguards you will need to select. I will try to make this decision process a little easier by walking you through the primary purpose of each domain:

- **Step 1: Define Cybersecurity Roles** – Document the roles for each member of the cybersecurity staff. Correct articulation of roles ensures the right people are in the right roles and that they can be held accountable. Roles definition supports training and certifications plans.

- **Step 2: Assign Responsibilities to Activities** – Using the RACI-V diagram assign personnel according to their level of responsibility for a cybersecurity activity. The RACI-V is ideal for co-sharing responsibilities of a control or countermeasure with multiple personnel.

- **Step 3: Adopt DevSecOps** – Integrating application development with operations and security reduces the potential for security flaws to be introduced into production. Arranging for previously disparate operations, development and security personnel to work closely dramatically improves the process of security integration.

- **Step 4: Implement Security Automation and Orchestration (SAO)** – The more automation applied to the security operations function the less chance for human error. SAO can also lead to lower personnel costs by automating the rote tasks normally performed by SOC personnel freeing them up for more important tasks.

- **Step 5: Deploy Software-Defined Security (SDSec)** – Integrating security policies with cybersecurity technologies improves the speed and efficiency of security operations. Polices driven by real time threat intelligence can be used to change configurations and settings on security technology to counter attacks.

- **Step 6: Implement Incident Response** – Incident management is an integral component of security operations. Operations personnel are ideally suited to handle incident response since they are familiar with the technologies required to detect security events and to eradicate threats.

- **Step 7: Document Cybersecurity Services within Service Catalog** – Professionally managing cybersecurity services begins with entries in a service catalog. The service catalog facilitates service customer ordering and provisioning that will reduce the strain on cybersecurity program personnel. All essential attributes of a cybersecurity service are documented within the service catalog. These attributes consist of service description, metrics, billing, support contacts, etc.

Service management is the most discretionary of all aspects of a cybersecurity program. Applying service management to a cybersecurity program is important in the long term as well as contributing to the maturity of the cybersecurity organization. There are two components which can provide significant benefit that you should adopt first, however:

- **Create a RACI-V Diagram** – Using the existing organization chart, assign personnel based on their direct responsibility for countermeasures. Adjust personnel role assignments identified through the process of creating the RACI-V. This will allow you to get maximum effort from your existing staff.

- **Incident Management Program** – Select the top threats and match those to countermeasures identified within this chapter. Based on the assumption of breach, you will require an effective and efficient incident response capability. Creating an incident program should be a top priority.

It will be important that you plan for the operationalization of your cybersecurity program over time. You do not however, need to operationalize every aspect of your program. Begin with the most essential technologies then over an extended period rollout to other technologies.

# 6.1 Information Technology Service Management (ITSM)

<table>
<tr><td>

**Did You Know?**

In 2017, Amazon's S3 system used by over 148 thousand sites suffered a nearly six hour service failure. The cause of the outage was a typo entered by an Amazon technician who was debugging the system at the time. Amazon admitted that implementing better capacity service management would have avoided such a massive disruption.

*Have you deployed service management to avoid wide-spread outages?*

**Source:**
https://fortune.com/2017/03/02/amazon-cloud-outage/

</td></tr>
</table>

Now that your cybersecurity program is designed, you will need to ensure that you operate it with the greatest effectiveness and efficiency. You will need to think of your program as a set of services delivered to protect your organization's assets and information. This is where *information technology service management* (ITSM) comes into play. ITSM is a term given to information technology (IT) activities driven by policies that are enforced by processes and supporting procedures to design, deliver, operate, and control services. IT activities are viewed as services rather than individual systems, applications, or products. Your cybersecurity program essentially becomes a service organization where an appropriate combination of people, processes, and technology combine to deliver a specific service to customers. Your customers are those you protect from cyberattacks. Service management provides several benefits:

- Alignment and focus on customers.
- Higher levels of service effectiveness and efficiency.
- Improved cybersecurity program reputation.
- Lower program cost.
- Predictable, repeatable service outcomes.

## 6.1.1 Brief History of ITSM and ITIL

I am a strong believer in cybersecurity service management, so much so that I became ITIL® v3 Foundation certified. I know I just threw another term at you – Information Technology Infrastructure Library (ITIL) – but trust me it will make sense soon. ITIL is a best practice framework for ITSM. ITIL is a set of detail practices for IT Service Management. ITIL has its origins going back to the 1980s when the British government sought a way to streamline and make more efficient their computer operations. Since July 2013, ITIL has been owned by AXELOS Limited, a joint venture between Capita plc and the Cabinet Office (About AXELOS, 2017). Today, ITIL is a set of five volumes covering over two dozen processes and multiple functions. Many organizations provide service management frameworks or models, but I have chosen to stay with ITIL because it is arguably the world's most recognized framework for ITSM. One of the things I like about ITIL is that you can choose to implement any or all of the practices – adopt and adapt. There is no ITIL principle that states that you must do it a particular way. For example, ITIL provides a nice practice description for financial management – if you have a set of documented practices in place to manage your cybersecurity budget, you are following ITSM. ITIL and ITSM are inexorably linked with ITIL serving as the framework and ITSM serving as the way you implement ITIL within your organization.

> **TIP:** Acquire an ITIL or ITSM certification to enhance your skills in designing and deploying cybersecurity programs. As cybersecurity becomes more integrated with applications and IT infrastructure you will need this skill to remain competent in your field.

# 6.2 Cybersecurity Service Management

Over ten years ago I realized that a significant shortcoming of cybersecurity programs was their lack of service orientation. The programs I had been reviewing all seemed to treat cybersecurity as individualized activities rather than tightly integrated services. In the early 2000s, I went to work for a company that had acquired a managed security service operation. My objective was to take a single security operations center (SOC) and turn it into a market leading security services organization with SOCs strategically placed throughout the world. One of the problems I quickly ran into was a high number of failed firewall rule changes that would bring our customers' networks down. When I began to investigate trouble tickets, I realized that not only were failed firewall rule changes a problem, but also firewall uptime, capacity, and configurations errors were causing their fair share of customer outages. We had dedicated and talented SOC personnel, but they were overworked and had virtually no service management practices in place. By adopting the ITIL service operations process for change evaluation and change management we all but eliminated incorrect firewall rule changes. By following ITIL service design processes for availability management, capacity management, and IT service continuity management, we reduced customer network outages related to failing firewall appliances by over 95%. This is just one of many examples I could cite on the value of adopting cybersecurity service management.

## 6.2.1 Cybersecurity Service Management Approach

There are several ITSM standards that can be used to implement the guidance offered by ITIL. However, I have found a few issues with those approaches mainly because of vague and ambiguous copyright statements, usage licensing, framework ownership, cost, and frankly complexity. Based on these issues and my own preference for open source approaches, I settled on a free standard for ITSM available and funded by the European Commission named FitSM (Federated IT Service Management). FitSM, first available in 2014, is licensed under a Creative Commons Attribution 4.0 International License and is updated regularly. Aside from the free aspect of FitSM, I prefer FitSM for its lightweight approach to ITIL/ITSM. I find that it also translates well in comparison to other service management frameworks such as ITIL, ISO/IEC 20000, Microsoft Operations Framework (MOF), or COBIT's Service Management. This has proved ideal for my clients who wanted to adopt service management but did not want the overhead and cost associated with implementing ITIL, ISO/IEC 20000, MOF, or COBIT.

Using the FitSM framework for service management, I created an adaptation referred to as the CyberSec-SM Model™. Cybersecurity service management is a cornerstone of all the programs I design, assess, or modernize. The CyberSec-SM Model™ declares five operational areas incorporating the FitSM-1: Processes Model, which defines 14 process requirements. The operational domains of the model are based on several phases of my ADDIOI model I covered in Chapter 1. These include design, develop, implement, operate, and improve. Figure 6-1 presents the CyberSec-SM™ Model.

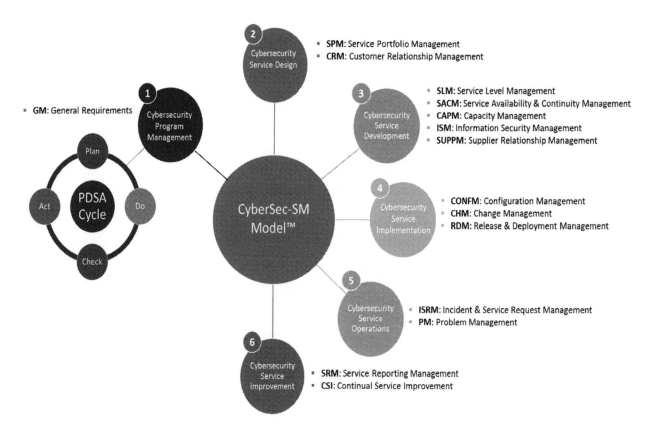

*Figure 6-1. Cybersecurity Service Management Model (CyberSec-SM). (This work is a derivative of "Creative Commons FitSM-1: 14 Processes" by FitSM Working Group, used under CC BY. "CyberSec-SM" is licensed under CC BY Tari Schreider.)*

In the CyberSec-SM Model, I have adapted the FitSM-1 Process Requirements within a cybersecurity program context consisting of the following:

1. **Cybersecurity program general requirements:** Adopt management roles and responsibilities to ensure the cybersecurity program is properly operated according to the William Edwards Deming Plan-Do-Check-Act (PDCA) Cycle. Sixteen general requirements for service management provide the overall guidance necessary for successfully adopting a service management approach to cybersecurity. General service management requirements include:

   o **GR1:** Top management commitment and responsibility – Ensures senior management is actively involved in the design and delivery of cybersecurity services.

      ▪ **GR1.1** – Senior management of an organization is actively involved in the delivery of cybersecurity through evidence of their commitment to planning, implementing, operating, monitoring, reviewing, and improving the cybersecurity management program through adoption of a service management system.

      ▪ **GR1.2** – The cybersecurity program policy manual includes service management policy that describes a commitment to fulfil customer service requirements, service-oriented approach, a process approach, a continual improvement, and overall service management goals of the cybersecurity program.

   o **GR2:** Documentation – Ensures that cybersecurity program services are properly documented to provide predicable repeatable services within target quality levels.

      ▪ **GR2.1** – The overall cybersecurity program service management approach is documented to support effective planning. This documentation must include service management scope, policy, and plan.

      ▪ **GR2.2** – Cybersecurity service process requirements documented for service goals, inputs/outputs, activities, roles and responsibilities, interfaces, policies, and procedures.

      ▪ **GR2.3** – The outputs of all cybersecurity service management processes must be documented, and the execution of key activities of these processes recorded.

      ▪ **GR2.4** – Documentation must be controlled covering creation and approval, communication and distribution, review and versioning, and change tracking.

   o **GR3:** Scope – Ensures service management approach is properly scoped.

      ▪ **GR3.1** - The scope of cybersecurity service management is defined through a scope statement.

   **Note:** The following requirements focus on the PDCA cycle:

   o **GR4:** Planning service management (**"Plan"**) – Ensures a service management plan is created and maintained.

      ▪ **GR4.1** – A service management plan must be created and maintained.

- **GR4.2** – At a minimum, the service management plan needs to include or reference the goals and timing of implementing service management and the related processes. The plan specifies overall roles and responsibilities, required training and awareness activities, and required technology (tools) to support service management.
- **GR4.3** – The service management plan must align to applicable IT and cybersecurity plans.
  - ○ **GR5:** Ensures service management is properly implemented (**"Do"**).
    - **GR5.1** – The service management plan must be implemented.
    - **GR5.2** – Within the scope of service management, the defined service management processes must be followed in practice, and their application, together with the adherence to related policies and procedures, must be enforced.
  - ○ **GR6:** Ensures service management processes are adequately monitored and reviewed (**"Check"**).
    - **GR6.1** – The effectiveness and performance of service management and related processes must be measured and evaluated based on suitable key performance indicators in support of agreed targets.
    - **GR6.2** – Assessments and audits of service management must be conducted to evaluate the level of maturity and compliance.
  - ○ **GR7:** Ensures service management processes are continuously improved (**"Act"**).
    - **GR7.1** – Nonconformities and deviations from targets must be identified and corrective actions must be taken to prevent them from recurring.
    - **GR7.2** – Improvements must be planned and implemented according to the continual service improvement (CSI) management process.
2. **Cybersecurity service design:** Define cybersecurity services to protect assets and information within a service catalog. Manage services as an integrated portfolio identifying owners, features, provisioning process, service prerequisites, and other pertinent information. Portfolio services address customer requirements to protect assets and information with their performance transparent and communicated. Services can be in-house designed or provided by third-party managed security service providers. Process areas include:
   - ○ **PR1 - SPM:** Service portfolio management – Ensures cybersecurity services are properly documented including purpose, features, alignment to compensating controls, and risk treatment. SPM process requirements include:
     - **PR1.1** – A service portfolio must be maintained. All services must be specified as part of the service portfolio.
     - **PR1.2** – Design and transition of new or changed services must be planned.
     - **PR1.3** – Plans for the design and transition of new or changed services must consider timescales, responsibilities, new or changed technology, communication, and service acceptance criteria.

- **PR1.4** – The organizational structure supporting the delivery of services must be identified, including a potential federation structure where third-parties provide cybersecurity services as well as contact points for all parties involved.
  - **PR7 - CRM:** Customer relationship management – Ensures customer expectations are met through the competent delivery of cybersecurity services. Maintain transparent and ongoing relationship with customers to build the program's reputation. CRM process requirements include:
    - **PR7.1** – Service customers shall be identified.
    - **PR7.2** – For each customer, there shall be a designated contact responsible for managing the customer relationship and customer satisfaction.
    - **PR7.3** – Communication mechanisms with customers shall be established.
    - **PR7.4** – Service reviews with the customers shall be conducted at planned intervals.
    - **PR7.5** – Service complaints from customers shall be managed.
    - **PR7.6** – Customer satisfaction shall be managed.
3. **Cybersecurity service development:** Develop cybersecurity services to operate efficiently and effectively within the IT infrastructure. Cybersecurity services will be developed based on declared cybersecurity frameworks or models. Each service will have a defined service level agreement (SLA) including its availability, capacity, and continuity. Services provided by third-party security service providers will be managed through objective supplier management practices. Process areas include:
   - **PR2 - SLM:** Service level management – Ensures that the service levels covering cybersecurity services are specific and measurable. SLAs identified for services need to be actionable where measurements that fall below expectations can be improved by acting. SLAs must be limited to avoid overwhelming customers and SecOps personnel with non-relevant data. SLM process requirements include:
     - **PR2.1** – A service catalogue must be maintained.
     - **PR2.2** – For all services delivered to customers, SLAs must be in place.
     - **PR2.3** – SLAs must be reviewed at planned intervals.
     - **PR2.4** – Service performance must be evaluated against service targets defined in SLAs.
     - **PR2.5** – For supporting services or service components provided by federation members or groups belonging to the same organization as the service provider or external suppliers, operations level agreements (OLAs) and underpinning agreements or underpinning contracts (UA/UCs) must be agreed upon.
     - **PR2.6** – OLAs and UA/UCs must be reviewed at planned intervals.
     - **PR2.7** – Performance of service components must be evaluated against operational targets defined in OLAs and UA/UCs.
   - **PR4 - SACM:** Service availability and continuity management – Ensures cybersecurity services have a high degree of availably of their technical components. Maintenance of services must not adversely affect their availably to

protect assets and information. Recovery of cybersecurity services must occur in a timeline and capability as not to affect the continuous operations of services. SACM process requirements include:

- **PR4.1** – Service availability and continuity requirements shall be identified taking into consideration SLAs.
- **PR4.2** – Service availability and continuity plans shall be created and maintained.
- **PR4.3** – Service availability and continuity planning shall consider measures to reduce the probability and impact of identified availability and continuity risks.
- **PR4.4** - Availability of services and service components shall be monitored.

o **PR5 - CAPM:** Capacity management – Ensures that cybersecurity services have the capacity and scaling ability to handle the volume, velocity, and variety of security event data. Capacity also refers to personnel where adequate resources are available to handle security incidents, security trouble tickets, and cybersecurity service request processing. CAPM process requirements include:

- **PR5.1** – Service capacity and performance requirements shall be identified taking into consideration SLAs.
- **PR5.2** – Capacity plans shall be created and maintained.
- **PR5.3** – Capacity planning shall consider human, technical, and financial resources.
- **PR5.4** – Performance of services and service components shall be monitored to determine the degree of capacity utilization and to identify operational warnings and exceptions.

o **PR6 - ISM:** Information security management – Ensures cybersecurity countermeasures are deployed to provide for the confidentiality, integrity, and accessibility of information and cyber assets. ISM process requirements include:

- **PR6.1** – Information security policies shall be defined.
- **PR6.2** – Physical, technical, and organizational information security controls shall be implemented to reduce the probability and impact of identified information security risks.
- **PR6.3** – Information security policies and controls shall be reviewed at planned intervals.
- **PR6.4** – Information security events and incidents shall be given an appropriate priority and managed accordingly.
- **PR6.5** – Access control, including provisioning of access rights, for information processing systems and services shall be carried out in a consistent manner.

o **PR8 - SUPPM:** Supplier relationship management – Ensures the establishment and maintenance of a healthy relationship with suppliers providing or supporting cybersecurity services. SUPPM process requirements include:

- **PR8.1** – Suppliers shall be identified.

- **PR8.2** – For each supplier, there shall be a designated contact responsible for managing the relationship with the supplier.
- **PR8.3** – Communication mechanisms with suppliers shall be established.
- **PR8.4** – Supplier performance shall be monitored.

4. **Cybersecurity service implementation:** Implement services within the production environment ensuring they are configured correctly and hardened, and promotion to production is approved through a management of change process. Services will be tested for environmental compatibility and security. Process areas consist of:
   o **PR11 - CONFM:** Configuration management – Ensures the establishment and maintenance of a healthy relationship with suppliers supporting the service provider in delivering services to customers. CONFM process requirements include:
      - **PR11.1** – Configuration item (CI) types and relationship types must be defined.
      - **PR11.2** – The level of detail of configuration information recorded must be sufficient to support effective control over CIs.
      - **PR11.3** – Each CI and its relationships with other CIs must be recorded in a configuration management database (CMDB).
      - **PR11.4** – CIs must be controlled and changes to CIs tracked in the CMDB.
      - **PR11.5** – The information stored in the CMDB must be verified at planned intervals.
      - **PR11.6** – Before a new release into a live environment, a configuration baseline of the affected CIs must be taken.
   o **PR12 - CHM:** Change management – Ensures that IT infrastructure changes do not interfere with cybersecurity services and countermeasures. Change also extends to variations in business models, risk landscape, regulatory landscape, etc. CHM process requirements include:
      - **PR12.1** – All changes shall be registered and classified in a consistent manner.
      - **PR12.2** – All changes shall be assessed and approved in a consistent manner.
      - **PR12.3** – All changes shall be subject to a post implementation review and closed in a consistent manner.
      - **PR12.4** – There shall be a definition of emergency changes and a consistent approach to managing them.
      - **PR12.5** – In making decisions on the acceptance of requests for change, the benefits, risks, potential impact to services and customers, and technical feasibility shall be taken into consideration.
      - **PR12.6** – A schedule of changes shall be maintained. It shall contain details of approved changes, and proposed deployment dates, which shall be communicated to interested parties.

- **PR12.7** – For changes of high impact or high risk, the steps required to reverse an unsuccessful change or remedy any negative effects shall be planned and tested.
  - **PR13 - RDM:** Release and deployment management – Ensures that all application and IT software is released to production free of coding errors and security vulnerabilities. Application source code and installation sources of commercial off-the-shelf (COTS) products are protected to prevent tampering. RDM process requirements include:
    - **PR13.1** – A release policy shall be defined.
    - **PR13.2** – The deployment of new or changed services and service components to the live environment shall be planned with all relevant parties including affected customers.
    - **PR13.3** – Releases shall be built and tested prior to being deployed.
    - **PR13.4** – Acceptance criteria for each release shall be agreed with the customers and any other relevant parties. Before deployment the release shall be verified against the agreed acceptance criteria and approved.
    - **PR13.5** – Deployment preparation shall consider steps to be taken in case of unsuccessful deployment to reduce the impact on services and customers.
    - **PR13.6** – Releases shall be evaluated for success or failure.

5. **Cybersecurity service operations:** Operate cybersecurity services according to agreed SLAs, operational level agreements (OLAs), and supplier underpinning agreements (UAs). Prioritize and handle of all cybersecurity incidents. Handle service requests for cybersecurity services such as password resets according to SLAs. Process areas:
   - **PR9 - ISRM:** Incident and service request management – Ensures the logging of cybersecurity incidents and service requests, incident handling, and resolution tracking. Service requests include password resets, risk assessments, etc. ISRM process requirements include:
     - **PR9.1** – All incidents and service requests shall be registered, classified, and prioritized in a consistent manner.
     - **PR9.2** – Prioritization of incidents and service requests shall consider service targets from SLAs.
     - **PR9.3** – Escalation of incidents and service requests shall be carried out in a consistent manner.
     - **PR9.4** – Closure of incidents and service requests shall be carried out in a consistent manner.
     - **PR9.5** – Personnel involved in the incident and service request management process shall have access to relevant information including known errors, workarounds, configuration, and release information.
     - **PR9.6** – Users shall be kept informed of the progress of incidents and service requests they have reported.
     - **PR9.7** – There shall be a definition of major incidents and a consistent approach to managing them.

- **PR10 - PM:** Problem management – Ensures the underlying causes of cyberattacks or cybersecurity service incidents are determined and responded to appropriately. Determining root causes can prevent repetition of events due to issues ranging from incorrectly configured countermeasures to incorrect threat profiles of risk assessments. PM process requirements include:
  - **PR10.1** – Problems must be identified and registered based on analyzing trends on incidents.
  - **PR10.2** – Problems must be investigated to identify actions to resolve them or reduce their impact on the services.
  - **PR10.3** – If a problem is not permanently resolved, a known error must be registered together with actions such as effective workarounds and temporary fixes.
  - **PR10.4** – Up-to-date information on known errors and effective workarounds must be maintained.

6. **Cybersecurity service improvement:** Improve cybersecurity services to raise service maturity levels. Provide regular service performance reporting against agreed upon key performance measures (KPM). Process areas consist of:
   - **PR3 - SRM:** Service reporting management – Ensures management and customers receive regular status of cybersecurity services and countermeasures in terms of key performance measures. Reporting must be timely and relevant and appropriate to the audience. SRM process requirements include:
     - **PR3.1** – Service reports must be specified and agreed with their recipients.
     - **PR3.2** – The specification of each service report must include its identity, purpose, audience, frequency, content, format, and method of delivery.
     - **PR3.3** – Service reports must be produced. Service reporting must include performance against agreed targets, information about significant events, and detected nonconformities.
   - **PR14 - CSI:** Continual service management – Ensures the cybersecurity program improves over time by maturing cybersecurity countermeasures, services, and personnel. Maturity improvements include changes in risk landscape, regulatory requirements, and compensating controls improvements. CSI process requirements include:
     - **PR14.1** – Opportunities for improvement shall be identified and registered.
     - **PR14.2** – Opportunities for improvement shall be evaluated and approved in a consistent manner.

# 6.3 Service Management Catalog

Managing a cybersecurity program like a service organization is essential to the maturity of the program. To exist within an IT organization, cues should be taken from the CIO's playbook. In this case, package your cybersecurity functions and processes as services. Think of a service catalog as a storefront of your cybersecurity services that your customers can acquire. Each service should have the following attributes defined:

- Service name – name of the service registered in the catalog.
- Service description – overview of what the service provides.
- Service owner – name of the owner of the service.
- Billing – cost of the service.
- Delivery manager – person who provides technical support for the service.
- Delivery timeframe – amount of time from order to provisioning of service.
- Service prerequisites – requirements or environment provided by the customer prior to deployment.
- Service targets – key performance indicators used to ensure the service is delivered as designed.
- Service level agreement – guarantees of service delivery.
- Service availability – periods of time service is available.

Service catalogs can be created as Excel spreadsheets or sophisticated web applications. The more sophisticated service catalogs provide online ordering and workflow engines to deploy and the report on the service. Table 6-1 presents sources of service catalogs.

**Table 6-1. Service Catalog Sources**

| Company | Product | URL |
|---------|---------|-----|
| Computer Associates (Broadcom) | Clarity | https://www.ca.com/us/products/ca-service-catalog.html |
| SolarWinds Worldwide, LLC | IT Service Catalog | https://www.solarwinds.com/service-desk/use-cases/service-catalog |
| ServiceNow™ | Service Catalog | https://www.servicenow.com/products/it-service-automation-applications/service-catalog.html |
| Freshworks, Inc. | Smart IT Service Catalogue | https://freshservice.com/service-catalogue-management-software |

*Note: Links are current as of September 22, 2019.*

# 6.4 Cybersecurity Program Personnel

One thing that I have learned over my many years building and managing cybersecurity programs is that you cannot automated your way around poor personnel. You need the right personnel performing the right functions for your cybersecurity program to be successful.

## 6.4.1 Applying the RACI-V Model to Cybersecurity Program Staffing

Ensuring that you have the right personnel in the right positions is the most important aspect of operationalizing a cybersecurity program. I have seen many programs fail because they had either exceptionally talented people doing mundane tasks, or they entrusted poorly trained or unexperienced people with critical program functions. RACI-V is one tool to help you place the right people in the right jobs – people who understand what is expected of them.

Borrowed from the Information Technology Infrastructure Library (ITIL) service management practice, the RACI-V model – **R**esponsible, **A**ccountable, **C**onsulted, **I**nformed, and **V**erifies – is ideally suited to ensure cybersecurity personnel are placed in the right roles with appropriate responsibilities. I define each part of the RACI-V acronym below:

- **Responsible:** Those who do work to achieve the task – multiple resources.
- **Accountable:** The one resource ultimately accountable for the completion of the task.
- **Consulted:** Those whose opinions are sought. Two-way communication).
- **Informed:** Those who are kept up-to-date on progress. One-way communication.
- **Verifies:** The party that checks whether the control meets the acceptance criteria set forth in the product description.

While this model is simple to implement, many managers do not know about it or take the time to utilize it. Table 6-2 is an example of how to set up a RACI-V for your cybersecurity program.

**Table 6-2. RACI-V Diagram**

| Role | Responsible | Accountable | Consulted | Informed | Verifies |
|------|-------------|-------------|-----------|----------|----------|
| Cybersecurity service catalog | Cybersecurity service leads | CISO | SecOps | CIO | CIO |
| Data breach | CIO & CISO | Legal | SecOps | Board of directors | CEO |
| Maturity assessments | CISO | CIO | SecOps | Cybersecurity service leads | Auditing |
| Vulnerability scanning | SecOps | CISO | Network Operations | CIO | Auditing |

I am often asked, "How many people should I have in my cybersecurity program?" Although I would love to have that crystal ball answer, I am rarely able to answer that question without knowing some fundamental aspects of the cybersecurity program. Variables such as the number of security events, number of security technologies, number of third-parties, and others all play a part in estimating a cybersecurity program's staff requirements. The size of your cybersecurity program will drive the number of personnel required. Larger programs can justify a fulltime employee for each role identified; smaller programs will require staff to wear multiple hats. Table 6-3 is an overview of the most common cybersecurity roles and examples of available certifications.

**Table 6-3. Cybersecurity Roles and Responsibilities**

| Role | Overview | Certification |
|---|---|---|
| Application security engineer | An application developer with a significant emphasis developing secure software; understanding of secure coding techniques, application security testing (static, manual and manual), bug bounty programs, and application program interfaces (APIs); and performing application security risk assessments. | • GWEB: GIAC Certified Web Application Defender<br>• CWAPT: Certified Web App Penetration Tester |
| Chief information security officer (CISO) | A senior management position responsible for the entire cybersecurity program and staff. Smaller organizations may require the CISO to have technical hands-on responsibilities as well as overall program management. | • CISM: Certified Information Security Manager<br>• CCISO: Certified Chief Information Security Officer |
| Chief privacy officer | A senior management position responsible for privacy and data security programs to minimize risk and to promote compliance with all applicable laws and regulations in the US and overseas, including the EU General Data Protection Regulation (GDPR). | • CIPP: Certified Information Privacy Professional<br>• CIPT: Certified Information Privacy Technologist<br>• CIPM: Certified Information Privacy Manager |
| Cloud security architect | An architect responsible for the security of cloud service providers (CSPs) – infrastructure, platform, and software as a service (IaaS, PaaS, SaaS) – and cloud-based solutions. Designs security specifications and implements cloud security technologies to protect cloud workload. Oversees security as a service (SECaaS) providers as well as performs security assessments of CSPs. | • CCSK: Certificate of Cloud Security Knowledge<br>• CCSP: Certified Cloud Security Professional |
| Computer security incident response (CERT) specialist | An experienced cyberattack response specialist with deep technical experience in cyber threat hunting, distributed denial of service (DDoS) attacks, malware infection remediation, data breaches, and other cyber incidents. | • ECIH: EC-Council Certified Incident Handler<br>• GCIH: GIAC Certified Incident Handler |

| Role | Overview | Certification |
|------|----------|---------------|
| Cryptography engineer | An engineer with in-depth knowledge of authentication protocols, applied cryptography, public key infrastructure (PKI) and secure sockets layer/transport layer security (SSL/TLS). Uses encryption to secure information or to build security software. Also works as researcher to develop stronger encryption algorithms. | • ECES: EC-Council Certified Encryption Specialist |
| Cyber resiliency manager | A manager responsible for integrating cyber resilience into a cybersecurity program as well as existing management system and processes. Designs plans to minimize damage from a security breach and enables business appropriate response and recovery. | • RESILIA™ Foundation and Practitioner Certifications |
| Cybersecurity architect | An experienced security architect who designs a cybersecurity program referencing authoritative models, frameworks, and standards. Designs reflect architecture principles of The Open Group Architecture Framework (TOGAF) or Zachman Framework. Evaluates cybersecurity technology, mentors staff, and creates roadmaps. | • CNDA: Certified Network Defense Architect<br>• CRTSA: CREST Registered Technical Security Architect |
| Cybersecurity product administrator | An engineer experienced in installing and managing a variety of cybersecurity technologies. Maintains current release levels, tests new functionality, and updates documentation and service catalog entries. | • CISSP: Certified Information Systems Security Professional<br>• Cybersecurity Fundamentals Certificate (CSX) |
| Cybersecurity project manager | A project manager with experience in managing cybersecurity projects and programs. | • CSPM: Certified Security Project Manager<br>• GIAC Certified Project Manager (GCPM) |
| Cybersecurity risk specialist/analyst | An analyst with experience in conducting risk assessments on a wide variety of technologies, applications, and systems. Analyst can identify threats, identify | • CERM: Certified Enterprise Risk Manager®<br>• CRISC: Certified in Risk and Information Systems Control |

| Role | Overview | Certification |
|---|---|---|
| | compensating controls, and calculate a risk score. | |
| Cybersecurity services manager | A technical product manager position responsible for the cybersecurity service catalog. Maintains all pertinent information about cybersecurity technologies and services, licenses, performance reporting, and related budget management. | • ITIL® Foundation Certification<br>• ITIL® Practitioner Certification - IT Service Management |
| Cybersecurity vulnerability analyst | A security specialist who analyzes and assesses vulnerabilities in the infrastructure (software, hardware, networks), investigates available tools and countermeasures to remedy the detected vulnerabilities, and recommends solutions and best practices. Applies security patches to remediate vulnerabilities. | • CVA: Certified Vulnerability Assessor<br>• CompTIA CySA+ |
| DevSecOps engineer | A security specialist with Agile and Waterfall experience using XP, Scrum, Kanban, etc. Integrates application development, IT operations, and security in a continuous process flow. | • DSOE: DevSecOps Engineering<br>• Certified DevSecOps Professional (CDP) |
| Digital forensic analyst | An analyst responsible for providing eDiscovery and digital forensic services. Well versed in preservation of digital records, chain of custody, and use of digital forensics toolkits. Also, able to provide expert witness testimony in data breach cases. | • CCFP: Certified Cyber Forensics Professional<br>• CHFI: Computer Hacking Forensic Investigator |
| Governance, risk, and compliance (GRC) analyst | An analyst who defines and writes cybersecurity policies, researches legal and regulatory compliance requirements, identifies and documents compensating controls and supports, and uses an Enterprise GRC (eGRC) platform to produce program metrics reports and dashboarding. | • CGEIT: Certified in the Governance of Enterprise IT<br>• GRCP: GRC Professional Certification |

| Role | Overview | Certification |
|------|----------|---------------|
| IT Auditor | A manager who plans, leads, and independently performs complex IT audits such as general and application controls, IT governance, enterprise architecture, program management, system development, cloud computing, cybersecurity, data management, and IT standards compliance. | • CISA: Certified Information Systems Auditor<br>• GRCA: GRC Audit Certification |
| Network security engineer | An engineer responsible for the secure design, configuration, implementation, and support of enterprise networks. Focuses on next generation firewalls, IPS/IDS, load balancers, WiFi, RF, VLANs/VPNs, routers, and switches. | • CCNA Security: Cisco Certified Network Associate Security<br>• CCIE Security: Cisco Certified Internetwork Expert Security |
| Penetration tester | An experienced ethical hacker who identifies attack surface vulnerabilities and attempts to exploit them to demonstrate, from a hacker's perceptive, that systems can be compromised. Can play the role of attacker or defender during red team exercises. | • CEH: Certified Ethical Hacker<br>• LPT (Master): Licensed Penetration Tester (Master) |
| Security information and event management (SIEM) engineer | An engineer responsible for evaluating security logs for new technologies, defining how the logs must be parsed to make them usable for detection rules on the SIEM platform, and writing new detection rules. Uses big data platform for deep data mining of indicators of compromise. | • ACSE: AlienVault Certified Security Engineer<br>• McAfee ISCPS - SIEM Certification |
| Security operations (SOC) analyst | An analyst who monitors networks, computers, and applications looking for events and traffic indicators that signal intrusion or indicators of compromise. Triages security alerts and responds according to published protocols. | • CompTIA Security+<br>• Cybrary Security Operations Certification |
| Third-party risk analyst | A risk analyst who performs risk assessments on third-parties, cloud service providers, integration partners, joint ventures, mergers | • CTPRP: Certified Third Party Risk Professional |

| Role | Overview | Certification |
|------|----------|---------------|
| | and acquisition targets, and other entities that could introduce cyber risk to an organization. | |
| Threat intelligence analyst | An analyst responsible for detecting, analyzing and responding to any suspicious cybersecurity activity across business and operational networks as well as actor and campaign attribution, metrics collection, intelligence collection, and distribution. | • CCTA: Certified Counterintelligence Threat Analyst<br>• C\|TIA: Certified Threat Intelligence Analyst |

*Note: Links are current as of September 22, 2019.*

## 6.4.2 Applying the Kanban Method to Cybersecurity Program Staff Workflow

I have found the Kanban Method to be a simple yet highly effective method of getting the most from my cybersecurity operations staff. I borrowed this approach from some application security work I did recently. The word *Kanban* is from the Japanese language and means a billboard where you write your outstanding tasks, of which there are many in managing a cybersecurity program. The concept is that your staff pulls work rather than you push work to them. The Kanban displays the open work tasks, and your cybersecurity staff members pull the tasks that they can complete in the allowed timeframe. Using this approach promotes transparency, competition, collaboration, and focus.

## 6.4.3 Bimodal IT Environments

A few years ago, I read where Gartner observed some organizations were creating two separate organizations within their IT departments to deal with legacy and new applications. The legacy applications and systems were tasked with keeping the lights on and existing revenue streams humming, and the new applications area was concerned with tomorrow. The problem was that IT staff were good at one or the other, but not both. This resulted in what Gartner coined as bimodal IT. You may find yourself in a very similar situation and need to address the security of legacy and emerging applications and systems.

I found myself in just such a situation not long ago. A Fortune 10 company where I was engaged was struggling to basically support two separate security organizations – one legacy InfoSec and the other cybersecurity. They had two separate identity management systems, old and next-generation firewalls and IPS, etc. The staff turnover on the legacy side was high as cybersecurity personnel were stuck using older technology and were not allowed to crossover. The solution I offered was to outsource their legacy InfoSec systems and train their legacy InfoSec staff for their new cybersecurity technologies. The transition did not happen overnight, in fact it took nearly eight months, but it worked. If you find yourself in a bimodal IT environment, think outside the box for a solution.

> **TIP:** Do not develop a false sense of staffing by not counting contractors or support staff provided by managed security service providers (MSSP). You cannot control their availability, tenue, training, or skill sets.

## 6.5 Cybersecurity Operations Center (C-SOC)

A key strategy of operationalizing a cybersecurity program is to create a cybersecurity operations center (C-SOC) where you can consolidate the critical around-the-clock tasks of monitoring, detecting, and responding along with engineering, implementation, and maintenance to effectively protect against external and internal threats. A C-SOC is staffed with highly skilled security personnel whose mission is to continuously monitor and improve your organization's security posture while preventing, detecting, analyzing, and responding to cyber security incidents with the aid of both technology and well-defined processes and procedures. The technology used within the C-SOC can include many of the countermeasures that were outlined in Chapter 5. Primary C-SOC functions require cybersecurity technology to support:

- Advanced persistent threat (APT) monitoring.
- Digital forensics.
- Firewall management.
- Incident response.
- Intrusion detection and prevention.
- Network access control monitoring.
- Network traffic aggregation and visibility.
- Security analytics.
- Security information and event management (SIEM).
- Threat hunting.

> **Did You Know?**
>
> A 2019 Exabeam State of the SOC Report reported that SOC personnel cited keeping up with security alerts as their top technology pain point.
>
> *How have you dealt with SOC your personnel pain points?*
>
> **Source:**
> https://www.msspalert.com/cybersecurity-research/exabeam-2019-state-of-soc-report/

In my career, I have designed, built, and managed nearly 20 security operations centers of one form or another consisting of Cloud-SOCS, Virtual SOCs (V-SOC), and your standard security operations center (SOC). I have assessed the operational effectiveness of many more. My SOC experience includes the US, Japan, Brazil, Sweden, Italy, UK, South Africa, Australia, and other countries. Suffice it to say that when it comes to SOCs, I have pretty much seen everything. I could write a book on SOC design, but within the context of this book, I will focus on operational lessons learned from my SOC experience.

1. **Money won't buy excellence.** I have seen too many organizations write a blank check to build a SOC overnight in response to a data breach. C-SOCs are a delicate balance of people and technology and they must have time to work together to get better. Expect your C-SOC to take two to three years to function efficiently and effectively.

2. **Expect high turnover.** Most of the positions within a C-SOC are rote, tedious, and require working nights and weekends. To reduce turnover, automate the low-level alert triage, adopt a follow-the-sun strategy of staffing the C-SOC where personnel will always work prime business hours, and provide a clear career path for analysts. I have found interns make great C-SOC analysts.

3. **Leverage big data analytics.** C-SOCs inject billions of raw events, you must distill those to a small number of actionable alerts that your limited staff can triage and escalate. You should have an architecture of event filtering, aggregation, and correlation to accomplish this. Considering hiring a data scientist to help set this up.

4. **C-SOCs need to be cool.** If you are asking people to work in the dark on long shift during non-prime business hours, you need to provide them some place cool to work. Do a Google image search on security operations centers and you will quickly see that I am not alone in this opinion. You will need to spend money on the esthetics of the C-SOC. One of my clients actual brought in a Hollywood set designer to help create their C-SOC.

5. **It's all about the process.** C-SOC technology is indispensable, but if you don't have the processes and service management right, your C-SOC will be nothing but a big paperweight.

6. **Tune out the noise.** Organizations tend to make their SOCs very noisy by bringing in intelligence feeds from virtually any available source regardless of the value of the data. I have seen many SOCs with numerous big screens displaying everything from CNN, the Weather Channel to multiple feeds from ISACs. Only feed your C-SOC with actionable information. Remember: Every null event is wasted time that takes your analyst's eye off the ball.

7. **Outsource if the numbers don't add up.** If you cannot properly staff and run your C-SOC within a reasonable operating budget, then it is time for you to consider outsourcing your C-SOC. There are many quality managed security service providers offering SOC that can provide your C-SOC services. A list of top providers is in Appendix A.

## 6.6 Incident Management

Incident management is the operational activity of identifying, analyzing, and correcting cyber incidents and events to prevent a future re-occurrence. Within the context of cybersecurity

---

**Did You Know?**

A 2019 Secureworks® Incident Response Insight Report cites the top three initial access vectors as phishing (33%), credential compromise (25%) and scan and exploit (22%).

*Does your incident repose plan have templates to address these top threat vectors?*

**Source:**
https://www.msspalert.com/cybersecurity-research/exabeam-2019-state-of-soc-report/

---

operations, incidents are handled by an incident response or management team. Incident management is typically closely aligned with the service desk, which is the single point of contact for all users communicating with IT. When a cyber event disrupts IT operations it is essential to restore the service to normal operation as quickly as possible – this is the purpose of incident management. The National Institute of Standards and Technology Special Publication NIST SP 800-61 Revision 2, *Computer Security Incident Handling Guide*, is an excellent resource for structuring your incident response capability.

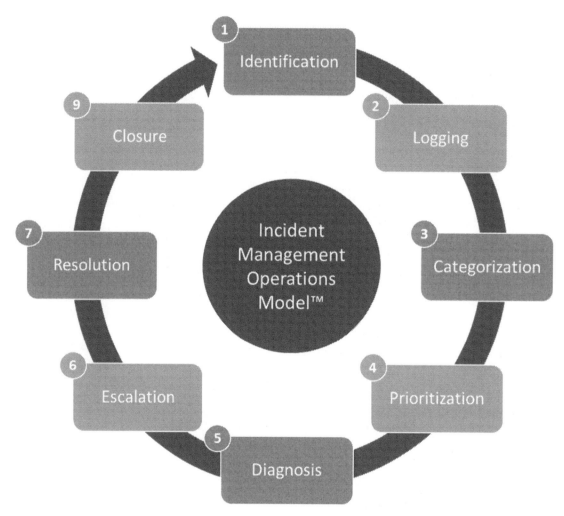

*Figure 6-2. Incident Management Operations Model™. (By Tari Schreider, licensed under a Creative Commons Attribution-Non-Commercial-NoDerivitives 4.0 International License)*

Figure 6-2 is the incident response model I have used throughout many client engagements. Steps in the process include:

- **Identification:** Determine if the report is an incident or request. Only incidents are handled in the model.

- **Logging:** Record login/logout activity, security events of interest and other application or system audit information to a central repository. Maintain a historical account of the activity in a secure logging and monitoring system.
- **Categorization:** Assign a category to the incident to facilitate tracking and normalize reporting. Categories can include network outage, virus, etc.
- **Prioritization:** Incidents should be prioritized as low (service to users can be maintained), medium (few staff affected, workarounds in place) or high (large number of users affected, business interrupted) to trigger respective SLAs.
- **Diagnosis:** Triage of incident and use of troubleshooting techniques.
- **Escalation:** Service desk cannot resolve the incident; escalation to 2$^{nd}$ tier support required.
- **Resolution:** Confirmation incident has been resolved and service restored to the published SLA.
- **Closure:** Documentation of incident complete and incident record is closed.

## 6.6.1 Incident Response Management Products

Managing all the various attributes of risk can be time consuming with many opportunities for error. Fortunately, risk registry tools are available to make this process easier to manage. Most of these tools were originally developed for project management; however, their applicability to cybersecurity is perfect. These tools provide risk dashboards, risk heat maps, and advanced attribute mapping. Table 6-4 provides a list of some of the risk registry tools.

**Table 6-4. Incident Response Management Products**

| Product | Company | URL |
|---|---|---|
| Command Center | Resolver Inc. | http://www.resolver.com/apps/command-center-software/ |
| D3 Security Incident Response Platform | D3 Security | https://d3security.com/solutions/incident-response/ |
| Incident Management Software | SolarWinds Worldwide, LLC | http://www.solarwinds.com/solutions/incident-management-software |
| LogicManager Incident Management Software | LogicManager, Inc. | http://www.logicmanager.com/grc-software/incident-management/ |

| Product | Company | URL |
|---|---|---|
| Remedy Incident and Problem Management | BMC Software, Inc. | http://www.logicmanager.com/grc-software/incident-management/ |

*Note: Links are current as of September 22, 2019.*

**TIP:** Assess the maturity of your organization's incident response capability by using a free incident response maturity assessment produced by CREST (International). The assessment is located at: http://www.crest-approved.org/cyber-security-incident-response-maturity-assessment/index.html

# 6.7 Security Automation and Orchestration (SAO)

Today, a dizzying array of cybersecurity technologies offer the promise of a securer tomorrow. Each one performs their appointed mission of protecting assets and information with aplomb. Layer by layer, one security technology is stacked upon another in the attempt to achieve defense-in-depth. Somehow, however, the bad actors still find a way around our defenses. No wonder CISOs have trouble asking for funding for the next galactic malware cure. Chief financial officers (CFOs) may not say it, but they are thinking, "If you cannot make what we have work together to reduce our risk, we're just throwing good money after bad."

If there were only a way to leverage our growing complexity of desperate cybersecurity technologies and force multiply our limited SecOps personnel with machine agility and speed… There is. The age of automation and orchestration is dawning. Solutions now exist that allow you to automate your cybersecurity playbooks. With an extensible automation and orchestration platform, you can programmatically curate your response to various threat scenarios from your inventory of countermeasures.

Research and Markets published a report in 2019 forecasting the Adaptive Security Market will grow from $4.78 billion in 2019 to $9.62 billion by 2024, at a compound annual growth rate (CAGR) of 15.0%. SOA is an integrated component of the Adaptive Security Market. Some companies jumped on the security automation and orchestration train early by announcing integration partnerships. At my last count, there were over thirty providers of products claiming placement within the security automation and orchestration market. Some claim they are a full automation and orchestration suite while others are carving out narrow niches in areas like policy orchestration or automated incident response.

The promise of automation and orchestration solutions lies in use cases. Depending on your solution, you can improve just about any SecOps function or process. Table 6-5 provides some of the use cases best served by these solutions.

**Table 6-5. SecOps Automation Use Cases**

| Use Case | Rational |
|---|---|
| Alert resolution | Reduce effort to aggregate, correlate, and resolve alerts from multiple sources. |
| Detect and patch | Automate risk scoring of patch advisories, scan for missing patches, and remediate in one continuous motion. |
| Incident response | Execute incident response playbook in real-time. |
| Integrate cybersecurity countermeasures | Automate security technologies to work as a cohesive integrated workflow. |
| Metrics and report consolidation | Reduce time required to chase down metrics, consolidate results, and produce reports. |
| Threat intel fusion | Reduce time and effort to source, analyze, and report on threat intelligence from multiple sources. |

*Note: Links are current as of September 22, 2019.*

If you are waiting for the other shoe to drop, well listen – thud – there it is. Security automation and orchestration solutions are the next best thing to sliced bread, but they are not magic. You must model your processes in advance before you can automate and orchestrate them. These solutions have no idea what you want to accomplish unless you tell them. Remember that adage: "Garbage in, garbage out."

Modeling a process is a 360-degree exercise. You will need to consider people, policies, procedures, processes, products, and proof (metrics). It is only through the union of these domains does automation and orchestration occur.

I know what you are thinking, "If I can get rid of all my SecOps staff through automation and orchestration, I will have a lights-out SecOps." Wait, what? Nice try but it does not work like that. You will still need people. Your goal is to root out the rote tasks of SecOps, freeing up your people to focus on the strategic aspects of your cybersecurity program. While there's s some possibility that you may be able to stave off hiring more staff by addressing the growing skills gap through automation, please do not go into acquiring a security automation and orchestration solution thinking that it will be a way to cut staff.

Sometimes the difference in being compromised or not is a matter of seconds. Security and automation software provide the ability to respond to attacks at machine speed. Designed to execute preset detection protocols, these solutions reduce the dependence on manual intervention. Some of the solutions already come with playbook templates.

Solutions that offer the broadest partner eco system and customizable library of playbooks should be at the top of your evaluation list. However, for a vendor to acquire either, their solution will have had considerable user experience. You will want a company whose product has a reasonable size of customer base (25+) and can provide evidence of automating and orchestrating dozens of security products within the same client.

Security automation and orchestration has been the secret of managed security service providers (MSSP) for years. However, their solutions were mostly hybrids of service management tools or custom code written specifically for their SOCs. Having managed SOCs around the world, I know a thing or two about what goes on behind the scenes. I can also say that some of you are perfect candidates for replacing your expensive MSSP contract through the introduction of an automation and orchestration solution.

Most organizations gravitate to an MSSP because they do not have the people to watch their network around the clock. In addition, when a critical event does happen, most companies still want a call in the middle of the night. What if you could eliminate all the white noise of SecOps, automate your incident response, and receive a call only in times of emergency? It can happen when you implement security automation and orchestration solutions.

I am a huge believer in taking stock of the past to ensure I do not repeat an incident as a future failure. I searched my disaster archives and found an extreme example of an automation blunder that serves as a cautionary tale. In June 2012, Royal Bank of Scotland's (RBS) NatWest and Ulster Bank subsidiaries descended into chaos following a glitch in their software workflow automation product. The outage was so profound it got its own Wikipedia page. During the one-month outage, 1,200 branches had to remain open past normal hours, call center staff was doubled, and millions of customers suffered. The CEO had to forego his bonus because of the fiasco's impact on roughly 20 million customers, and RBS canceled its presence at Wimbledon that year. Game, set, match.

# 6.8 DevSecOps

One of the newest ways to operationalize cybersecurity is to integrate security within your organization's DevOps. Not familiar with DevOps? *DevOps* is a term used to describe the integration of application development with IT operations or the breaking down of the walls that exist between application developers and IT operations personnel. A lack of communications between application developers and IT operations has been a root cause of many security vulnerabilities. The practice of developing applications in a vacuum and then tossing them over to IT operations to run is simply not effective, sustainable, or most importantly, secure. I have found the best way to view DevOps is to think of it as a way for application development teams and IT operations personnel to work together during the entire application development lifecycle from design through development to production. DevOps results in a practice of continuous integration and continuous deployment versus the former big bang approach to launching applications leading to faster and more reliable application development. To learn more about DevOps, I encourage you to check out Ernest Mueller's December 7, 2016 post, *What is DevOps?* at the Agile Admin blog (https://theagileadmin.com/what-is-devops/).

You can embrace the DevOps movement and leverage it to improve the cybersecurity of one of the largest exposure areas of your attack surface: applications. Approached properly, DevOps can significantly improve your organization's cybersecurity practices. One of the main benefits of DevOps is acquiring and acting on application functionality feedback earlier rather than later in the development cycle. This translates to cybersecurity where you can detect application security flaws earlier in the development and deployment phases enabling your organization to respond faster to vulnerabilities. But you will need to understand your organization's DevOps and learn about some of the unique technologies enabling DevOps such as containers and microservices.

DevOps is a disruptive technology that has changed the landscape of application development and operations and now security. Connecting cybersecurity with DevOps integrates security-testing, validation, and monitoring throughout the lifecycle of application development to deployment. By providing application developers with automated cybersecurity tools, placing them in charge of their own destiny, cybersecurity is no longer blamed as the gatekeeper.

In 2012, Gartner introduced the concept of DevSecOps (MacDonald & Head, 2016) creating the linkage between DevOps and security. According to Gartner, by 2019, more than 70% of enterprise DevOps initiatives will have incorporated automated security vulnerability and configuration scanning for open source components and commercial packages, up from less than 10% in 2016. You will want to ensure that you are in the 70% camp and engage cybersecurity with your DevOps efforts.

## 6.8.1 Rugged DevOps

In traditional software development environments, security has always been considered a separate aspect – even an afterthought – but now the two practices have emerged to produce safer software in the form of Rugged DevOps and DevSecOps. Rugged DevOps is an emerging trend that emphasizes a security first approach to every phase of software development. DevSecOps combines traditional DevOps approaches with a more integrated and robust approach to security. These approaches are not mutually exclusive and take slightly different paths toward the same goal of shifting security leftward and continually focusing on it through the production pipeline.

Rugged DevOps takes the traditional view of security teams as an obstacle and turns it upside down, engineering security into all aspects of design and deployment. Instead of security playing the role of traffic cop slowing down progress, a Rugged DevOps approach makes security a kind of police escort, helping the delivery process proceed with speed and safety.

Rugged DevOps starts with creating secure code. In traditional models' code is developed, then penetration testing and automated tools are used to deem the software "safe." Secure code development involves a different approach, where previously separate teams (development, quality assurance, testing, etc.) interact throughout the entire software lifecycle, addressing not just security holes but industry trends and other factors to develop "defensible" code through communication, collaboration, and competition. The Rugged DevOps approach was developed to address problems in the traditional delivery method, which handled security by finding problems in the existing software, reporting them, and fixing them. As production releases come to market with ever increasing speed, this system quickly gets overwhelming, and organizations often resort to building out compliance systems that slow development to a crawl.

The differences between DevSecOps and Rugged DevOps are nearly indistinguishable and in fact have essential melded together in what I have adopted in my model as a hybrid approach. As you can see in Table 6-6, there is little discernable advantage to either approach. I suggest that you follow the DevSecOps Factory Model™ in the following section for the best of both worlds.

**Table 6-6. DevSecOps vs. Rugged DevOps**

| Attribute | DevSecOps | Rugged DevOps |
|---|---|---|
| Credo | DevSecOps Manifesto (http://www.devsecops.org/) | Seven Habits of Rugged DevOps (http://www.devsecops.org/) |
| Focus | Operations-focused. | Developer-focused. |
| Philosophy | Ensure a secure infrastructure. | Ensure secure code. |
| Approach | Service management-oriented security. | Runtime application protection. |
| Roles | Bridge gap between security and operations. | Bridge gap between development and operations. |
| Responsibility | Shared ownership and responsibility for the secure delivery process. | Security escorts developers helping the delivery process proceed with speed and safety. |

*Note: Links are current as of September 22, 2019.*

## 6.8.2 DevSecOps Factory Model™

In early 2016, I was asked by a *Fortune 50* company to design a cybersecurity architecture for their recently adopted Agile application programming initiative. They had switched from Waterfall to Agile and wanted to start with a clean slate regarding cybersecurity. I had designed a good number of application security programs in the past, but this was the first time that I was able to work with a company that wanted the full Monty – application development, service management, and cybersecurity all in one. I was fortunate that they were already converts to service management though their adoption of several ITIL processes. My challenge would be in melding application development with IT operations. Their efforts to accomplish this in their Waterfall days proved problematic resulting in siloed security efforts in application development and IT operations. I knew that if I were to be successful, I needed to change their mindset and ultimately their culture. Once I showed them a model, the client quickly realized that this factory approach was needed. Figure 6-3 is the DevSecOps Factory Model™ I used to visually show an integrated, yet complimentary, approach to securing their applications in their new Agile world.

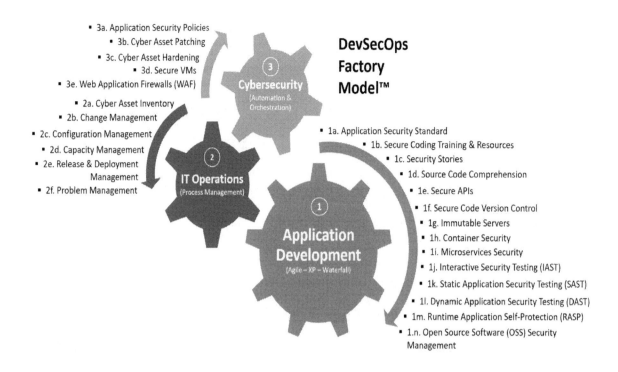

*Figure 6-3. DevSecOps Factory Model™. (By Tari Schreider, licensed under a Creative Commons Attribution-Non-Commercial-NoDerivitives 4.0 International License)*

I have described each of the three factory components below:

i.    **Application development** – One of the contributing failures in securing applications is the discourse that exists between the cybersecurity and application development teams. Lack of trust and lack of communications are two of the main issues that need to be resolved to improve application code security. I rarely encounter a customer that did not feel that cybersecurity was a stumbling block or viewed as "the office of no" when it came to get their applications launched on time. Subsequently, the application development team sought any avenue possible to bypass the cybersecurity team. This is so pervasive that it has become a negative cultural aspect of IT today. Empowering the application development organization to be their own gatekeepers when it comes to securing their applications is one of the first critical steps in adopting DevSecOps.

To accomplish this, the cybersecurity team must relinquish some of its controls over applications and act more as a mentor to the development team. You will need to build a strong partnership with the development team providing them with the tools and expertise for them to build secure applications. I am not advocating stepping away completely, but rather the role of cybersecurity as the provider and verifier. You will provide the necessary resources for the development team to be successful and verify their applications as an independent assessor. The cybersecurity tools you provide the application development team must be on-demand, automated, and integrated to meet the requirements of the DevSecOps Factory Model. Table 6-7 describes the minimum-security consideration of application development prescribed by the model.

**Table 6-7. Security Consideration of Application Development**

| Requirement | Overview | Process Aids |
|---|---|---|
| 1a. Application security standard | Security standards published by recognized authoritative sources on secure coding practices. | • ISO/IEC 27034:2011- Information technology – Security techniques – Application Security<br>• OWASP - Application Security Verification Standard (ASVS) Project<br>• Software Assurance Maturity Model (SAMM) |
| 1b. Secure coding training & resources | Secure coding training and resources to improve the security awareness and capabilities of programmers. | • CERT Secure Coding Publications<br>• Cybrary Secure Coding Training<br>• The Software Assurance Forum for Excellence in Code (SAFECode) |
| 1c. Security stories | Security-focused stories used as acceptance criteria for cybersecurity services. The security stories are non-functional requirements important to the system under development and to the business. | • Agile Software Development: EVIL User Stories<br>• SAFECode Practical Security Stories Template<br>• Security User Stories: Injection Attacks |
| 1d. Source code comprehension | Automatically generate diagrams of source code to understand how an application works when documentation is not available. | • codeBeamer ALM<br>• Doxygen<br>• yEd Graph Editor |
| 1e. Secure application program interfaces (APIs) | End-to-end API management solution for designing, implementing, securing, managing, monitoring, and publishing APIs. Available as a SaaS | • Akana API Management<br>• Axway API Management Plus<br>• Forum Sentry API Security Gateway |

| Requirement | Overview | Process Aids |
|---|---|---|
| | platform, on-premises, and as a hybrid deployment. | |
| 1f. Source code version control | Allows programmers, writers, or project managers to tackle a project from different angles without getting in each other's way and without doing damage that can't be undone. | • Apache™ Subversion<br>• Concurrent Versions System (CVS)<br>• Git<br>• Mercurial |
| 1g. Immutable servers | Servers created from scratch commensurate with each application release. Server state is absolutely known once provisioned and can be replaced or destroyed without creating server disruptions. | • Ansible Tower by Red Hat®<br>• Chef<br>• Packer<br>• Vagrant |
| 1h. Microservices security | Security of application subcomponents, which can be developed separately often providing one specific function such as collections, inventory, or shipping. | • Akana Platform<br>• Anypoint Platform<br>• NGINX Plus |
| 1i. Container security (Docker, Kubernetes, etc.) | Development-to-production lifecycle controls run on-premises, in a cloud. Incudes for securing containerized applications that runtime defense, vulnerability management, access control, etc. | • Aqua Container Security Platform<br>• Black Duck Hub's Docker Container Security Services<br>• Twistlock |
| 1j. Interactive security testing (IAST) – Gray box testing | A hybrid technique combining some of the advantages of SAST with DAST (See 1k and 1l below). Code is instrumented to run in a modified runtime environment where some of the internal details of the application are known. | • AcuSensor<br>• Contrast Assess<br>• Synopsys - Interactive Application Security Testing (IAST) |
| 1k. Static application security testing (SAST) – White box testing | A technique that analyzes the source code or byte code of your software without executing it (as SAST analyses the internal details of a | • Checkmarx Static Code Analysis<br>• WhiteHat Sentinel Source<br>• Veracode Static Analysis |

| Requirement | Overview | Process Aids |
|---|---|---|
| | program). Considered as horizontal code testing. | |
| 1l. Dynamic application security testing (DAST) – Black box testing | A technique that analyzes a running application in the context of its runtime environment from the client to the backend systems. Considered as vertical code testing. | • Appspider<br>• Fortify WebInspect<br>• WhiteHat Sentinel Dynamic |
| 1m. Runtime application self-protection (RASP) | Security software that integrates with an application or its runtime environment during execution and constantly intercepts calls to the application to check their security, permitting those deemed safe and blocking those that could indicate an attack. | • IMMUNIO<br>• Veracode Runtime Protection<br>• Waratek RASP |
| 1n. Open source software (OSS) security management | Detects security vulnerabilities related to the open source components in applications, alerting in real-time throughout the software development lifecycle (SDLC). Informs developers of security issues during open source library searches, providing information on patches or versions without vulnerabilities. | • Black Duck Hub<br>• DejaCode<br>• FlexNet Code Insight<br>• WhiteSource |

*Note: Links are current as of September 22, 2019.*

2. **Service operations** – One of the most overlooked areas of a cybersecurity program is the area of service management. Cybersecurity countermeasures require the same level of service management as any other aspect of IT. In my career, I have witnessed a good number of program failures directly related to a lack of processes and sound IT practices. Take one example of a client I had once that experienced repeated cybersecurity program outages due to failing services. I was hired to perform a complete review of their program. After a few interviews, it didn't take me long to determine that most of their problems were related to lack of service management. When I began to present my findings to the CIO, he stopped me

cold and said, "I doubt you know what you're talking about. Service management has absolutely nothing to do with our issues. Did you even look at our cybersecurity systems?"

Now, having been faced with similar responses, I respectfully asked the CIO if I could have just 15 minutes to explain. He said yes and began typing into his smartphone while I spoke. Despite the CIO's seeming lack of interest, I went on to explain that a failure to perform capacity planning resulted in several issues including logging failures caused by limited audit record storage size and network speed degradation caused by undersized firewall input buffers. I was stopped before I could address the other half dozen service-related issues and was asked to wait while the others in attendance, including the CISO, were asked to leave the meeting. After the others had left, the CIO asked how this could happen when they had an ITIL/ITSM initiative for years. I explained that a series of meeting notes I reviewed documented that the CISO had eschewed the value of ITIL/ITSM saying it was a waste of his team's time. The meeting ended without me knowing what would happen next. The next day the CIO asked me to come in and help fill in for the CISO he had fired. The important point here is that operationalization of cybersecurity matters.

The DevSecOps Factory Model™ includes six primary service management components required to ensure that your cybersecurity services are deployed effectively. You can spend all the money you wish on the latest cybersecurity technology, but if it is not deployed with benefit of service management, it will eventually fail and generally fail hard. Table 6-8 describes the minimum service management processes I believe every cybersecurity program must have.

**Table 6-8. Service Management Requirements**

| Requirement | Overview | Process Aids |
|---|---|---|
| 2a. Cyber asset inventory | An inventory of all cyber assets that comprise the attack surface. Assets include all endpoint devices connected to the network and related software. Applications and third-party services providers connected to the network must be included in the inventory as well. Automated methods of detecting new assets or service providers connected to the network are required. | • Asset Panda's IT Asset Tracking and Management Platform<br>• NIST Interagency Report 7693: Specification for Asset Identification 1.1<br>• PAS Cyber Integrity™ Inventory Management<br>• SDLC Standard Operating Procedure (SOP) 1007 - Asset Management |
| 2b. Change management | Formal management of change process where adds, moves, and changes to cyber assets are planned, tracked, and documented. An automated change management system used by a change management board is a preferred approach. | • ACMP's Standard for Change Management<br>• Intelex's Management of Change Application<br>• Sparta Systems' Change Control Software |
| 2c. Configuration management | Detailed configuration information referred to as configuration items (CIs) maintained on all cyber assets within the attack surface. CI includes cyber asset owner, model and make, serial numbers, firmware version, operating system level, configuration setting, patch level, support contacts, documentation links, and all other pertinent information. Detect out-of-process changes and enforce configuration policies. | • NIST SP 800-128: Guide for Security-Focused Configuration Management of Information Systems<br>• PAS Cyber Integrity™ Configuration Management<br>• SDLC SOP 1003 – Configuration Management<br>• SolarWinds' Network Configuration Manager |
| 2d. Capacity management | View the usage and efficiency of cyber assets supporting cybersecurity services to ensure they have adequate compute, storage, and network resources to function effectively and without interruption. | • BMC's TrueSight Capacity Optimization<br>• Micro Focus (NetIQ)'s PlateSpin Recon<br>• SDLC SOP 1002 – Capacity Management |

| Requirement | Overview | Process Aids |
|---|---|---|
| 2e. Release & deployment management | The planning, scheduling, and control of the build, test, and deployment of cybersecurity service releases. Includes delivery of new functionality required by the business while protecting the integrity of existing services. | • BMC's ITIL® Release and Deployment Management<br>• Rocket Aldon<br>• SDLC SOP 1005 – Release Planning |
| 2f. Problem management | Detection of problems and subsequent diagnosis of problems and implementation of workarounds. Register problems and resolutions in tracking database. | • BMC's ITIL® Problem Management<br>• SDLC SOP 1010 – Site Monitoring and Problem Management |

*Note: Links are current as of September 22, 2019.*

3. **Cybersecurity** – Previously I discussed many types of cybersecurity services and countermeasures that can be used to protect assets and information. This part of the model describes the cybersecurity services that are specific to DevOps, primarily your applications. In DevOps, applications are interactively built in an expedited manner. You can think of this as "build fast, fail fast." This allows you to identify security vulnerabilities early in the development cycle rather than learning about them after the application has been deployed. To identify vulnerabilities as soon as possible, you must have begun by creating application security policies. As a result, you should be prepared to quickly patch application hosts, harden the application hosts to prevent compromises, secure the virtual environment that almost assuredly is used in your DevOps, and deploy web application firewalls to prevent the threats that could not be identified through rapid application development. Table 6-9 describes the specific cybersecurity requirements for DevOps.

**Table 6-9. DevOps Specific Cybersecurity Requirements**

| Requirement | Overview | Process Aids |
|---|---|---|
| 3a. Application security policies | A policy which defines web application security assessments. Web application assessments are performed to identify potential or realized weaknesses because of inadvertent misconfiguration, weak authentication, insufficient error handling, sensitive information leakage, etc. | • SANS' Application Security Policy Templates |
| 3b. Cyber asset patching | A security patch is a change applied to an asset to correct the weakness described by a vulnerability. This corrective action will prevent successful exploitation and remove or mitigate a threat's capability to exploit a specific vulnerability in an asset. | • NIST SP 800-40 Rev 3 Guide to Enterprise Patch Management Technologies<br>• PAS Cyber Integrity™ Patch Management<br>• SolarWinds' Patch Manager |
| 3c. Cyber asset hardening | Process of enhancing server security through a variety of means resulting in a much more secure server operating environment which is due to the advanced security measures that are put in place during the server hardening process. | • Center for Internet Security (CIS) Benchmarks - System Hardening Guides<br>• Open Source Article on Server Hardening Tools<br>• Server Surgeon's Linux Server Hardening |
| 3d. Secure VMs | Virtual machines are the containers in which applications and guest operating systems run. By design, all VMware virtual machines are isolated from one another. This isolation enables multiple virtual machines to run securely while sharing hardware and ensures both their ability to access hardware and their uninterrupted performance. | • ISACA Virtualization Security Checklist<br>• NIST SP 800-125B Secure Virtual Network Configuration for Virtual Machines (VM) Protection |

| Requirement | Overview | Process Aids |
|---|---|---|
| 3e. Web application firewalls (WAF) | Preventive and detective security control solution for web applications reducing the risks of web vulnerabilities exploitation. WAFs prevent simple vectors of the most common web vulnerabilities (such as XSS and SQL injections). | • Barracuda Web Application Firewall<br>• Radware's Cloud WAF Service<br>• WASC OWASP Web Application Firewall Evaluation Criteria Project |

*Note: Links are current as of September 22, 2019.*

# 6.9 Software-Defined Security (SDSec)

Software-Defined Security (SDSec) is a type of cybersecurity model where security policies are implemented, controlled, and managed by software. No longer do hardware constraints and its inherent labor-intensive processes restrict the agility and elasticity of securing assets and information. It is a software-managed, policy-driven and governed cybersecurity where most of the bulk of countermeasures, such as intrusion detection, network segmentation, and access controls, are automated and monitored through a software plane. This ensures that cybersecurity's reach and scalability of the underlying hardware environment move elastically when infrastructure and resources change. Today's IT infrastructure is constantly evolving, with SDSec, data centers, and IT infrastructures which can be moved or migrated between physical and cloud locations without affecting your cybersecurity or governance policies.

There are several key attributes of software-defined security:

1. **Abstraction:** Cybersecurity is abstracted away from physical constructs such as hardening scripts, firewall ports, and network scanners, which are replaced by a set of software controls, in the form of a policy library where specific policy instructions are extracted to address detected threats or risk conditions. Policy instructions automatically configure virtualized or physical assets to protect information. Abstraction is the foundation for establishing common cybersecurity models that can be deployed repeatedly without concern for underlying physical hardware capabilities.

2. **Automation:** SDSec significantly improves the asset deployment. As an asset is deployed or reconfigured, its cybersecurity policy automatically attaches ensuring it has the right security configuration commensurate with its intended use. SDSec eliminates configurations errors, administrator errors, and incorrect or late security patching. SDSec can enforce a policy where no assets move to production without begin properly configured. Role-based controls assure that only properly privileged administrators can make modifications. SDSec automation also means faster response and reaction time to anomalous security events,

instantly alerting and quarantining malware breakouts according to specifications within your cybersecurity policies and standards.

3. **Scalability and flexibility:** Eliminating dependencies on physical hardware to control cybersecurity allows security measures to be deployed on a scale appropriate to your computing environment. This is especially critical for hybrid computing environments where sensitive information is processed across physical, virtual, and cloud platforms. The future of cybersecurity is SDSec for the fundamental reason that cybersecurity policies become elastic and on-demand.

4. **Control orchestration:** SDSec is designed to orchestrate the workings of multiple cybersecurity technologies. For example, should a security policy be extracted from the library where sensitive information is about to be processed, SDSec ensures that a secure network zone is deployed and that intrusion protection and firewall policies for sensitive information are enabled. Additionally, SDSec knows that prior to allowing sensitive information to pass through the network, a PCI DSS network scan must be completed to verify compliance with financial regulations. This all occurs without manual intervention, and automatically in a uniform, integrated process. Unlimited sources of security input such as threat data, vendor patch levels, and control requirements can be accessed to drive your cyberpolicy orchestration engine.

5. **Portability:** In a data center governed by SDSec, assets carry their cybersecurity policies and configurations/settings with them as they move or scale, which is critical in a cloud-enabled IT world. Information security and network operations staff can set security policies and let them run on autopilot.

6. **Visibility:** Cybersecurity policies essentially live within your IT infrastructure, no longer constrained by the limitation of hardware. Today, security policies live in pieces on many different pieces of hardware and software, never communicating, thus creating a chaotic and unmanageable situation. SDSec dramatically improves visibility of network activity by binding all the disparate security configurations, controls, and requirements into a cohesive cybersecurity policy. With SDSec, network administrators and security operations personnel can detect anomalous behavior or malicious payloads that would otherwise be blind to them when using conventional physical security devices and can therefore thwart intruders and protect assets and information with greater accuracy.

These characteristics are unique to SDSec and are difficult and expensive to attain with traditional security appliances. SDSec still has a distance to go to reach full realization, but you will need to account for it in your cybersecurity program design.


# 6.10 Emerging Cybersecurity Technologies


The cybersecurity industry is overdue for a major overhaul in technology and managers of cybersecurity programs need to look several years down the road at emerging technologies to future proof their programs. There is no shortage of companies investing in cybersecurity technologies. Gartner predicts worldwide spending on information security products and services will reach $124B in 2019, growing 8.7% over the $114B invested in 2018. (Columbus, 2019). This is a very attractive market for venture capital companies to invest in emerging technologies. Part of a cybersecurity program manager's role is to keep abreast of emerging technologies. The following are a few technology areas one should keep an eye on.

## 6.10.1 Artificial Intelligence

Artificial intelligence (AI) is emerging as a solution for countering cybersecurity staff shortages and the fast-growing cyber threat. AI is intelligence exhibited by computing machines rather than humans (natural intelligence). The concept is that the machines learn based on programming about patterns and behaviors and then adapt their response to known or emerging conditions. This is an ideal application to apply to cybersecurity. According to CB Insights, over 80 companies are presently using AI to secure information and assets. CB Insights provides an excellent infographic to present the categories of the players in this emerging market. Table 6-10 provides a brief overview of some of the main players in the cybersecurity AI industry.

**Table 6-10. Cybersecurity Artificial Intelligence (AI) Providers**

| Company | Product | AI Approach | URL |
|---|---|---|---|
| BehavioSec | BehavioSense Dashboard | Behavioral biometric intelligence. | https://www.behaviosec.com /behavioral-biometric-solutions/ |
| Cylance | CylancePROTECT ® | Artificial Intelligence to drive real endpoint threat prevention. | https://www.cylance.com/en_us/products/our-products/protect.html |
| Darktrace | Darktrace Threat Visualizer | Real-time, 3D threat notification interface that displays threat alerts and provides a graphical overview of the day-to-day activity of network, | https://www.darktrace.com/products/#darktrace-threat-visualizer |
| LogRhythm, Inc. | LogRhythm UEBA | User and Entity Behavior Analytics (UEBA) platform integration for security infrastructure. | https://logrhythm.com/products/logrhythm-ueba/ |

| Company | Product | AI Approach | URL |
|---------|---------|-------------|-----|
| PatternEx | PatternEx Threat Prediction Platform | Analyst intuition' used to predict existing and emerging cyber-attacks in real time. | https://www.patternex.com/product |
| SentinelOne | SentinelOne Platform | Machine learning and AI to continuously outflank attackers targeting endpoints. | https://www.sentinelone.com/platform/ |
| Shape Security | Shape Solution | Real-time adaptive application defense platform. | https://shapesecurity.com/shape-defense/#overview |
| SS8 | SS8 BreachDetect | Continuous recursive analysis vs. unpredictable AI and machine learning to detect breaches. | https://www.ss8.com/what-we-do/breach-detection/ |
| Vectra | Vectra Cognito™ | Automates the hunt for cyber attackers, shows where they're hiding and tells you what they're doing. | https://vectra.ai/product |
| Zenedge (Oracle) | Zenedge DDoS Mitigation | Machine learning artificial intelligence engine that drives Bot management, WAF, API security, DDoS and Malware protection. | https://www.oracle.com/corporate/acquisitions/zenedge/ |

*Note: Links are current as of September 22, 2019.*

You can expect to see AI incorporated in virtually all mainstay cybersecurity products over the next few years as well as a witness a substantial amount of market consolidation. AI can have a profound impact on improving cybersecurity service management. Be cautious of claims made by vendors and look for solid proven case stories before investing.

## 6.10.2 Augmented Reality (AR)

Adoption of AR in business has been slow with the majority of investment and effort going into the gaming and entertainment industries. There has yet to emerge that one business killer app that proves the viability of AR in business. I believe the cybersecurity industry will provide the killer app. Imagine use cases where a threat analyst uses AR to threat hunt through a virtual representation of an enterprise. AR could also be used to build a truly virtual SOC where SOC personnel would believe they were all in the same room collaborating on threat and incident response. VR in cybersecurity is still a few years from reality, but companies like IBM have been investing in building VR protypes. In 2017, IBM Ireland began developing a prototype VR solution integrating with their IBM QRadar SIEM product. (Hyland & Flood, 2017). In my opinion VR shows great promise in the field of cybersecurity.

## 6.10.3 Blockchain

Blockchain is a disruptive encryption technology that was born from the creation of bitcoin. Blockchain leverages a secure repository to maintain a constantly expanding list of records or blocks, each linked to a previous block. Subsequently, blockchain is inherently resistant to modification by bad actors. Companies like Lockheed Martin was an early adopter of blockchain as part of a cybersecurity product portfolio (Lancaster. 2017). Today companies have launched blockchain-based products to create more secure file repositories, secure digital collaboration, IoT security, etc. The goal of blockchain is to provide organizations with an encryption approach that cannot be circumvented by hackers. Products that incorporate blockchain technology should be carefully considered; however, as a new technology, the viability of the company offering blockchain in their products should be carefully reviewed.

> **Did You Know?**
>
> A threat known as privacy "poisoning," where bad actors load private data, such as names, addresses and credit card numbers, or illegal material, such as child pornography, into a blockchain, places it in conflict with local laws. This type of attack renders blockchain technology unusable.
>
> *Have you evaluated the risk associated with implementing blockchain?*
>
> **Source:**
> https://www.govtech.com/security/Privacy-Poisoning-Cyberattacks-Pose-Risk-to-Blockchain.html

## 6.10.4 Machine Learning (ML)

Machine learning also referred to as deep learning or artificial intelligence is a way for technology to learn from experiences of human decisions. Cybersecurity personnel are mired in basic repetitive tasks that could easily be accomplished by computers. Tasks related to prediction, classification, grouping and response can all benefit from ML. ML is already used in products that detecting abnormalities in network traffic. ML uses historical data to learn how to label everything what deviates from standard network behavior. Leading cybersecurity companies should all have efforts underway on how improving their products through the use of ML.

## 6.11 Cybersecurity Program Operationalization Checklist

To ensure you address all the essential elements of operationalizing your cybersecurity program I have provided a checklist in Table 6-9. Once you have completed each of the activities on the checklist you will have moved your program from design to production allowing you to take full advantage of all your efforts in building your cybersecurity program.

**Table 6-11. Cybersecurity Program Operationalization Checklist**

| Step | Activity |
|------|----------|
| 1 | Adopt a service management approach – operationalize your cybersecurity program according to the service management approach outlined in Section 6.2.1. |
| 2 | Create a service management design checklist to ensure that each cybersecurity service is covered by each of the 14 process requirements. |
| 3 | Create RACI-V diagram – document the roles and responsibilities of program staff using the example in Table 6-1. |
| 4 | Document roles and responsibilities – use Table 6-2 to validate the proper roles and responsibilities as well as certifications of cybersecurity program staff. |
| 5 | Right-size cybersecurity program staff size – carefully scale your program to the right resources. |
| 6 | Automate and orchestrate cybersecurity program processes. |
| 7 | Deploy DevSecOps. |

## Summary

Your journey is nearly complete, Now is the time to pause and enjoy the fruits of your labor to arrive at this point of the book. You have accumulated knowledge equivalent to a lifetime of experience in building a cybersecurity program. You have learned, in a fraction of the time it would normally take, to align your program to the needs of your business, design a program based on true architectural design criteria, identify the real threats and vulnerabilities your organization faces, develop the countermeasures necessary to offset your organization's risk profile, and implement and operate your design according to service management practices.

The next chapter provides a library of design templates that should prove valuable to your efforts to create your cybersecurity program. These documents have evolved over my career and serve me well to this day.

# References

*About AXELOS: Our background.* (2017). Retrieved from https://www.axelos.com/about-axelos

Columbus, L. (2019, June 16). *Top 10 Cybersecurity Companies to Watch In 2019.* Forbes. Retrieved from https://www.forbes.com/sites/louiscolumbus/2019/06/16/top-10-cybersecurity-companies-to-watch-in-2019/#6ee4f2e16022

Hyland, M. & Flood, J. (2017, July 3). *The Emergence of Virtual Reality and Augmented Reality in the Security Operations Center.* Retrieved from https://securityintelligence.com/the-emergence-of-virtual-reality-and-augmented-reality-in-the-security-operations-center/

Lancaster, L. (2017, May 2). *Lockheed Martin bets on blockchain for cybersecurity.* C|Net. Retrieved from https://www.cnet.com/news/lockheed-martin-bets-on-blockchain-for-cybersecurity/

MacDonald, N. & Head, I. (2016, September 30). *DevSecOps: How to seamlessly integrate security into DevOps.* Stamford, CT: Gartner, Inc. Retrieved from https://www.gartner.com/en/documents/3463417/devsecops-how-to-seamlessly-integrate-security-into-devo

# Self-Study Questions

The following questions will help you build your expertise in designing a cybersecurity program.

1. What is the benefit of adopting ITIL/ITSM within a cybersecurity program?
   Applying service management to cybersecurity processes improves the efficiency of security functions in the same manner that IT functions are managed.

2. What are some of the significant benefits to using the FitSM-1: Processes Model?
   It is a free opensource model like ITIL/ITSM that is simpler to deploy.

3. What is a RACI-V?
   A service management tool that outlines who is Responsible, Accountable. Consulted, Informed and Verifies a service task. Facilitates the division of responsibility.

4. What is the role of a Cybersecurity Services Manager?
   A technical product manager position responsible for the cybersecurity service catalog. Maintains all pertinent information about cybersecurity technologies and services, licenses, performance reporting, and related budget management.

5.  What is Kanban?

    *Kanban* is from the Japanese language meaning a billboard where you write your outstanding tasks, of which there are many in managing a cybersecurity program. The concept is that your staff pulls work rather than pushing work to them. The protection of data held or processed by others.

6.  What is a C-SOC?

    A C-SOC is a Cybersecurity Operations Center that serves as a centralized capability to monitor an enterprise, detect abnormal behavior and alert on security events.

7.  What is Security Automation and Orchestration (SOA)?

    A middle layer of software that connects disparate security products and services enabling communications with one another within an integrated workflow. Use cases can be automated to fulfil closed loop security processes such as incident response and security event correlation and automation.

8.  What is DevSecOps?

    An approach to application development where the silos of application development, security and operations are removed. DevSecOps borrows the efficiency of Agile to create a framework where security is integrated into development and operations functions.

9.  What is Software-Defined Security (SDSec)?

    A software-managed, policy-driven and governed cybersecurity approach where most of the bulk of countermeasures, such as intrusion detection, network segmentation, and access controls, are deployed, automated and monitored through a software layer.

10. What is blockchain?

    An encryption method that leverages a secure repository to maintain a constantly expanding list of records or blocks, each linked to a previous block. Subsequently, blockchain is inherently resistant to modification by bad actors.

# Chapter 7

# Cybersecurity Program Design Toolkit

For you to get to this final point in the book you have no doubt wondered about where you go from here. The answer in a word is, *build*. To help you to build your cybersecurity program I have assembled a toolkit of templates I have used over the years to build some of the largest cybersecurity programs in the world. Each of these templates can be customized to fit the requirements of your own design-build program and will serve as essential documents to guide and document how your cybersecurity program will be constructed.

The fundamental reason I developed these templates over the years instead of using those provided for free in TOGAF, for example, is simplicity. If you sample several of the 75+ available technology architectures I mentioned in section 1.2, you will see that many make their design documents freely available. However, I have found most to be overly complex and possibly confusing. I needed something fit for purpose and tailored for a cybersecurity program.

I have presented the documents in a logical order of use, but you are free to use them in any order you choose. My objective is to provide you with tools, not to suggest that every tool must be used.

*This chapter will help you to:*

- Organize your cybersecurity build from a top-down approach, beginning with business alignment and continuing through service catalog implementation.
- Close design gaps before they appear by following a structured approach to cybersecurity architecture.
- Communicate design goals and objectives among cybersecurity program sponsors, stakeholders and contributors.

## 7.1 Overview

I have mentioned throughout this book that building a cybersecurity program begins with establishing a risk profile for an organization. This is also where you will begin using the templates provided in this chapter. To make the process of digesting these templates easier I have organized them in a swim lane diagram. A swim lane diagram is a type of flow chart that organizes related steps in a process.

The 17 templates provided are organized into three swim lanes. The first is baseline: these templates are used to gather the necessary information required before design can begin. Once the baseline documents are completed, you can move to swim lane two, design. The design documents provide the methods by which you specify how the cybersecurity program will function. When you exit the design swim lane you move to the build swim lane. Here you document how the cybersecurity program is built. Once you have exited all three swim lanes the outcome is the completion of your cybersecurity program design guide. Figure 7.1 presents a logical progression of how the design templates should be used.

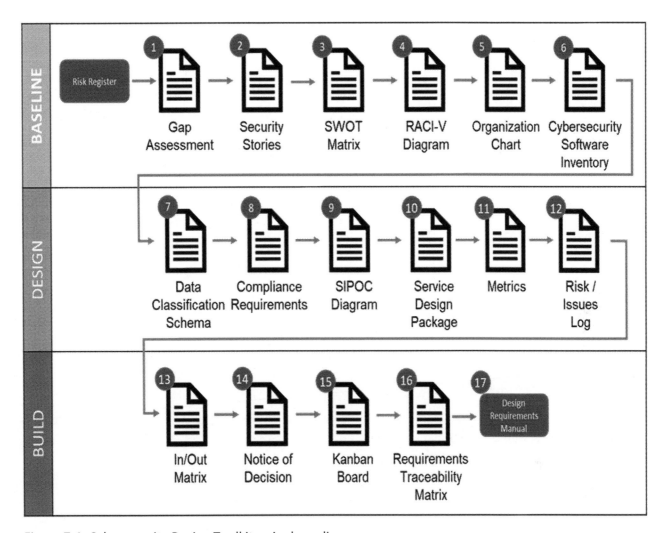

Figure 7-1. Cybersecurity Design Toolkit swim lane diagram.

## 7.2 Gap Assessment

Most of you reading this book will have inherited a cybersecurity program. Few times in our career will we be able to build one from the ground up. Acknowledging this truth is why it is best to begin the building process with an understanding of what you already have to work with. You want to ensure you're not throwing the preverbal baby out with the bath water. This process begins with taking stock in the status of the current cybersecurity program by performing a gap assessment.

A gap assessment compares the present-state cybersecurity program with a desired future state. The future is generally defined by an accepted standard such as ISO 27001 or NIST SP 800-53. Each of these standards are discussed in detail throughout the book. The gap assessment will allow you to focus on building your cybersecurity program around the gaps noted by the assessment. For each gap noted you can create a security story on how you can close the gap.

Table 7-1 shows you how to structure a simple gap assessment. To take it a step further, check out an excellent tool that you can use to conduct a gap assessment. This gap assessment tool can be found at the Federal Financial Institutions Examination Council (FFIEC) web site: https://www.ffiec.gov/cyberassessmenttool.htm.

**Table 7-1. Simple Gap Assessment.**

| | | Cybersecurity Gap Assessment | | | |
|---|---|---|---|---|---|
| ID | Key Control | Current State | Desired Future State | Design Requirements | Risk |
| 010 | Security Policy | Few policies exist, no executive sponsorship. | A.5.1.1 - Policies for Information Security | REQ010 | High |
| 020 | Asset Inventory | No asset inventory exists. | A.8.1.1 - Inventory of Assets | REQ020 | Medium |
| 030 | Privileged Account Management | No privileged account management and monitoring. | A.12.4.3 - Administrator & Operator Logs | REQ030 | High |
| 040 | Encryption | Encryption algorithms used primarily within US. | A.18.1.5 - Regulation of Cryptographic Controls | REQ040 | Low |

# 7.3 Security Stories

Taking a page from Agile development's user stories, crafting security stories to create design parameters can prove to be an effective method to arrive at a business-aligned cybersecurity program. A security story can capture in simplified terms the requirements for how a cybersecurity program should operate. Writing a story is a straightforward process. You provide the who, what and why. For example, *who are we building this for? What are we building? And why are we building it?* and *what value does it provide?*

Let's put this all together to build your first security story. We'll use privileged account access as our first story.

*"As the CISO, I need to ensure that we restrict privileged access within an Active Directory environment to isolate and restrict the use of privileged accounts and reduce the potential of their theft."*

This story would guide the selection and implementation of a privileged access management solution (PAM). Table 7-2 provides the format used to create the security story example presented above.

**Table 7-2. Security Story Inventory**

| Security Stories | | | |
|---|---|---|---|
| **Who** | **What** | **Why** | **Value** |
| CISO | Privileged accounts | Isolate and restrict | Prevent credential theft |
| **Story** | | | |
| As the CISO, I need to ensure that we restrict privileged access within an Active Directory environment to isolate and restrict the use of privileged accounts and reduce the potential of their theft. | | | |
| **Outcome** | | | |
| Implement privileged account management (PAM) solution. | | | |

# 7.4 SWOT Matrix

A SWOT matrix, invented in the 1960s at Stanford Research Institute, is a simple and effective strategic planning technique used to identify **S**trengths, **W**eaknesses, **O**pportunities, and **T**hreats of essentially anything. I have found this to be a pragmatic approach to taking stock in an existing cybersecurity program. During my projects I generally gather key stakeholders to conduct a SWOT working session. I draw a SWOT matrix on a board and walk the cybersecurity program stakeholders through completing each quadrant of the SWOT matrix. Table 7-3 presents a SWOT matrix that can be used as a model to produce a view of what's working, what needs improvement, where opportunities exist and what threatens your cybersecurity program.

**Table 7-3. SWOT Matrix**

| **S**trengths | **W**eaknesses | **O**pportunities | **T**hreats |
|---|---|---|---|
| • Things your cybersecurity program does well<br>• Key cybersecurity staff<br>• Cybersecurity products operating at peak performance<br>• Cybersecurity services fully provisioned | • Cybersecurity services missing<br>• Cybersecurity services requiring improvement<br>• Unfilled key cybersecurity staff positions<br>• Underperforming cybersecurity products<br>• Budget, resource constraints | • Create a unified security control framework<br>• Create a single face to the customer<br>• Reduce cybersecurity program cost through operationalization | • Lack of management commitment<br>• Security culture<br>• Zero-day threats<br>• Competing security agendas |

# 7.5 RACI-V Diagram

Designing a cybersecurity program involves more than just technology layers, it involves aligning the right people to their respective roles and responsibilities to ensure the program functions properly. A key template to accomplish this is a RACI diagram. The acronym RACI stands for **R**esponsible, **A**ccountable, **C**onsulted and **I**nformed. I added the "V" early on in my career to identify who should verify the activities or processes. More information is available on the RACI in Chapter 6. The example RACI-V presented in Table 7-4 is based on ISO 27001 and can be expanded to include more stakeholders as well as ISO 27001 key controls to reflect your company's organizational model. Completing the RACI-V before creating the organization chart will bring clarity to cybersecurity program role assignment

**Table 7-4. RACI-V Diagram**

| Program Components (ISO Clauses) | Program Stakeholders | | | | | | | |
|---|---|---|---|---|---|---|---|---|
| | CISO | SecOps | Security Engineer | Audit | Asset Owner | Legal | HR | Users |
| 5. Information Security Policies | A | R | C | V | C | C | R | I |
| 6. Organizing Information Security | A | R | I | V | C | I | A | I |
| 7. Human Resource Security | R | C | I | V | C | C | A | I |
| 8. Asset Management | R | C | I | V | A | I | I | I |
| 9. Access Control | A | R | R | V | C | I | C | I |
| 10. Cryptography | A | R | R | V | C | I | I | I |
| 11. Physical & Environmental Security | A | C | C | V | C | I | C | I |
| 12. Operations Security | A | R | C | V | C | I | I | I |
| 13. Communications Security | A | C | R | V | C | I | I | I |
| 14. System Acquisition, Development & Maintenance | R | C | C | V | C | C | I | I |
| 15. Supplier Relationships | A | R | C | V | C | C | C | I |
| 16. Information Security Incident Management | A | R | C | V | C | C | C | I |
| 17. Information Security Aspects of Business Continuity Management | R | R | C | V | R | I | C | I |
| 18. Compliance | A | R | C | V | R | C | C | I |

# 7.6 Organization Chart

Now that you have completed the RACI-V, it's time for you to create your cybersecurity program organization chart. Assigning your cybersecurity staff roles is a form of architecture.

Your security staff should align closely to your cybersecurity framework or blueprint. This builds consistency and makes it easier for customers to know who to reach out. Figure 7-2 presents a proposed cybersecurity program organization chart.

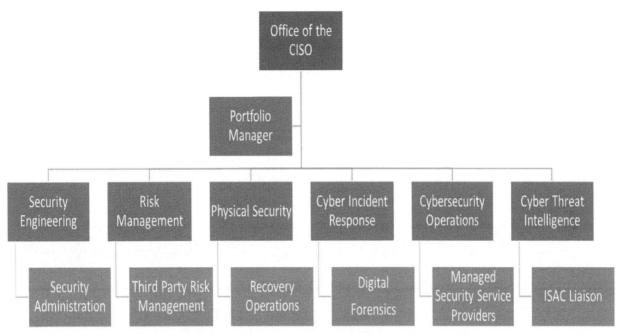

Figure 7-2. Cybersecurity Program Organization Chart.

## 7.7 Cybersecurity Software Inventory

Managing the assets of a cybersecurity program is essential – mapping which products provide which level of protection of data is a core requirement of a defense-in-depth strategy. You can review defense-in-depth in Chapter 5. This mapping is key to designing the cybersecurity program as well as performing a gap assessment. To lay the groundwork for this, you will need to create an inventory. In some organizations, a definitive media library (DML) or secure repository is used to store the authorized versions of software. The DML can also produce inventory reports. To learn more about DMLs, check out the following wiki page at: https://en.wikipedia.org/wiki/Definitive_Media_Library.

**Did You Know?**

EDUCBA, a leading global provider of skill-based education provides a list of 32 important cyber security tools with summaries of how each contributes to protection of enterprises and data.

*Do you have any gaps in your defense-in-depth strategy?*

**Source:** https://www.educba.com/32-most-important-cyber-security-tools/

Table 7-5 presents how to create an inventory of cybersecurity program products or solutions that will be integrated with the cybersecurity program. Many optional categories can be added to the inventory to allow it to be used as a management tool for all solutions and technologies. This would include licensing and maintenance information, owner, service alignment and other important criteria of interest.

**Table 7-5. Cybersecurity Software Inventory**

| Cybersecurity Program Technology & Solutions Inventory | | | | | |
|---|---|---|---|---|---|
| **Product or Solution** | **Provider** | **Product** | **OSI Layer** | **Category** | **ISO 27001 Control** |
| Identity and access management (IDAM) | SailPoint | IdentityIQ | 6. Presentation | Access Control | A.9.1.2 - Access to Networks & Network Services |

To guide you in selecting cybersecurity solutions, reference the OSI Security Model with Countermeasure Examples presented in Chapter 5. This inventory will be used as input to the Service Design Package (SDP) presented later in this chapter.

# 7.8 Data Classification Schema

The core of a cybersecurity program is the protection of data. To ensure that data is properly protected, privacy needs to be considered during the initial design.

Most data privacy laws and regulations require an organization to account for and classify their private data. One regulation is the European General Data Protection Requirement (GDPR). The GDPR requires organizations to create, maintain and classify data of EU citizens it holds or processes. Table 7-6 presents a data classification matrix that can be used to model data privacy protection strategies.

**Did You Know?**

The National Conference of State Legislatures (NCSL) up to date access to all US state and territories data breach laws.

*Have you inventoried all applicable data breach laws?*

Source:
http://www.ncsl.org/research/telecommunications-and-information-technology/security-breach-notification-laws.aspx

**Table 7-6. Data Classification Schema**

| Data Risk Levels | | |
|---|---|---|
| **High Risk** | **Medium Risk** | **Low Risk** |
| Protection of data is mandated by laws and regulations. Loss, damage or alteration, which impacts the confidentiality, integrity, or availability of the data or systems would result in significant adverse impacts. | Data not generally available to the public, or<br><br>the loss of confidentiality, integrity, or availability of the data or system would have a mildly adverse impact. | Data intended for public disclosure, or the loss of confidentiality, integrity, or availability of the data or system would have no adverse impact on safety, finances, or reputation. |
| **Data Examples** | | |
| • Social security number<br>• Date of birth<br>• Driver's license numbers<br>• Passport / Visa numbers<br>• Financial account numbers<br>• Credit / Debit card numbers<br>• Protected Health Information (PHI)<br>• Export controlled information under U.S. laws<br>• Biometric markers<br>• PINs / Passwords | • Employment applications<br>• Employment records<br>• Non-public policies<br>• Manuals<br>• Contracts<br>• Internal memos<br>• Email<br>• Non-public reports<br>• Budgets / financial records<br>• Engineering documents | • Directory information<br>• Policy and procedure manuals designated by the owner as public<br>• Job postings<br>• Information in the public domain |
| **Protection Requirements** | | |
| ▪ Data-in-use required<br>▪ Data-in-transit required<br>▪ Data-at-rest required<br>▪ Only approved third parties<br>▪ Only approved cloud service providers | ▪ Data-in-use recommended<br>▪ Data-in-transit required<br>▪ Data-at-rest required<br>▪ Only approved third parties<br>▪ Only approved cloud service providers | ▪ Data-in-use not required<br>▪ Data-in-transit not required<br>▪ Data-at-rest not required |

## 7.9 Compliance Requirements

The design of your cybersecurity program must consider requirements of legal and regulatory statutes. Many regulations specifically call out security requirements that could alter the course of one or more components of the cybersecurity program. Each identified regulatory requirement should be analyzed to determine if technical requirements are required to adhere to the statute. In the event your organization experiences a data breach and ends up in court defending how it protected breached data, proving you classified data properly will be a critical element of your defense. Table 7-7 outlines how to decompose a statute to reveal the technical requirements that should be considered in the cybersecurity program design.

**Table 7-7. Compliance Requirements**

| Regulation | Stipulation | Technology Component | Design Requirement |
|---|---|---|---|
| Tennessee Senate Bill 2005 (S.B. 2005) | (i) unencrypted computerized data or (ii) encrypted computerized data and the encryption key | Requires compliance with Federal Information Processing Standard (FIPS) 140-2. | Base encryption solution on upcoming revised FIPS 140-3 – 05.01.2019 standard. Requires strong controls over encryption strength and key management. |
| Payment Card Industry (PCI Data Security Standard (DSS) 3.2 | (8.3) Multi-factor authentication. | Requires multi-factor authentication for non-console access to computers and systems handling cardholder data, and remote access to the cardholder data environment (CDE). | Deploy a data access solution the uses at least two of the three authentication factors as described in PCI DSS Requirement 8.2. Factors include password/PIN/secret answers, token device or smartcard, and biometric. |

## 7.10 SIPOC Diagram

One of the lesser used documents in the design of a cybersecurity program is a SIPOC diagram. SIPOC stands for **S**uppliers, **I**nputs, **P**rocess, **O**utputs, and **C**ustomers. It serves as a tool to visualize a cybersecurity process from beginning to end. SIPOC is often used in Information Technology Infrastructure Library (ITIL) or Six Sigma projects. I have found that when you're looking to operationalize a cybersecurity program its best to reference ITIL or Six Sigma.

Service management is discussed in depth in Chapter 6. Table 7-8 shows how to complete a SIPOC using data loss prevention as the solution. Using a SIPOC does add complexity to the process and is not required for all services, just the services you may be unclear.

**Table 7-8. SIPOC Diagram**

| Data Loss Prevention (DLP) Service | | | | |
|---|---|---|---|---|
| **S**uppliers | **I**nputs | **P**rocesses | **O**utputs | **C**ustomers |
| Who supplies the process input? | What inputs are required? | What are the major steps in the process? | What are the process outputs? | Who receives the outputs? |
| Company that produces or provides a cybersecurity product or service. | Inputs are discrete items such as a goods, services, or information that are consumed by the process. | Series of steps where an Input converts to an output. | Outcomes from the result of a **Process**. | Customer that receives the cybersecurity services. |
| Cloud-based cybersecurity service provider. | • Data classification schema.<br>• Confidential documents. | • Monitor network egress points for exfiltration of confidential documents.<br>• Scan enterprise for unauthorized possession of classified documents. | • Discovery and protection of confidential information wherever stored in the enterprise.<br>• Prevent confidential information from exiting the network, gateway or endpoint.<br>• Enforcement of data privacy policies. | MS Exchange users. |

# 7.11 Service Design Package (SDP)

A Service Design Package (SDP) is an ITIL process that defines how to create a service throughout its lifecycle from creation to retirement. All the information required to deliver a cybersecurity service is captured in an SDP. The SDP specifies the requirements from the viewpoint of the customer rather than the cybersecurity program. SDPs are used to create the cybersecurity catalog. The customer view helps with describing the service in non-security jargon. Figure 7-9 presents how to complete an SDP. Whether you use an excel spreadsheet or a commercial security catalog you should create an SDP for every service the cybersecurity program.

**Table 7-9. Service Design Package**

| Cybersecurity Service Design Package | |
|---|---|
| Service Name | Data Loss Prevention (DLP) Service |
| Service Class | Data protection and privacy |
| Description | DLP is a software-based solution that protects sensitive data against unauthorized access, use, sharing, or other egress. The DLP solution also controls which data end users may transfer. |
| Customers | All MS Exchange user accounts. |
| Service Owner | Jim Doe |
| Service Manager | Jane Doe |
| Functional Requirements | The DLP solution provides:<br><br>• Discovery and protection of confidential information wherever stored in the enterprise.<br>• Prevention confidential information from exiting the network, gateway or endpoint.<br>• Enforcement of data privacy policies. |
| Cost | $3.25 per user. Billed monthly internal chargeback. |
| Service level Agreement (SLA) | The DLP service provides coverage based on 99.999% solution availability. |
| Support Contact | John Doe – 555.555.5555 |

## 7.12 Metrics

Metrics are essential to managing a cybersecurity program. However, for them to be effective they need to be simple to explain, easy to calculate, expressed as a number or percentage and lend themselves to benchmarking. They should also be expressed as a unit of measure such as defects, hours, incidents, etc. Table 7-10 provides examples of risk metrics.

**Table 7-10. Cybersecurity Program Risk Metrics**

| Cybersecurity Program Metrics | | | | | |
| --- | --- | --- | --- | --- | --- |
| No. | Metric | Measure | Target Base | Achieved | Score |
| M010 | Percentage of laptops for full disk encryption deployed | Percentage of Privileged Accounts | 1200 | 1165 | 97.08% |
| M020 | Percentage of User Accounts Reviewed for User Account Privilege Changes. | Percentage of User Accounts Reviewed | 120 | 120 | 100.00% |
| M030 | Percentage of Server Log Files Reviewed for Malicious Activity. | Percentage of Logs | 450 | 375 | 83.33% |
| M040 | Percentage of assets registered in attack surface. | Percentage of Assets | 7055 | 7030 | 99.64% |

An excellent guide to developing metrics is NISTIR 7564 – Directions in Security Metrics Research found at: https://csrc.nist.gov/publications/detail/nistir/7564/final.

# 7.13 Risk/Issue Log

A risk/issue log is a way to document risks and issues as well as identify contingencies or resolutions in the development of a cybersecurity program. The risk aspect of the log can be a simple list or spreadsheet to forecast potential problems that could arise and how you would address those problems. It can also be used to log issues that occur during the design and build swim lanes. An issue is something that has already come up in your project and requires timely resolution. You can also use the log to prioritize risks and issues to facilitate assigning resources and resolving them in a timely manner to thwart any project delays.

You would use the log to document *any* roadblock or unintended impact that directly affects your project's timeline or performance. Table 7-11 provides an example of how to complete a risk/issue log.

**Table 7-11. Risk/Issue Log**

| ID | Risk or Issue | Likelihood | Impact | Contingency / Resolution | Risk Owner | Type |
|----|---------------|------------|--------|--------------------------|------------|------|
| 01 | Cybersecurity program technology providers don't pass purchasing requirements. | Likely | High | Select secondary provider of cybersecurity program products. | CISO | Risk |
| 02 | Security administrator for Security and Information Event Management (SIEM) platform on medical. | Occurred | Medium | Contract for SIEM contractor to fill in during medical leave. | SecOps | Issue |

## 7.14 In/Out Matrix

An important step in building a cybersecurity program is to clarify what is changing. The Six Sigma approach to process improvement leverages a tool called the In/Out matrix. I have found this tool valuable to the cybersecurity program design process. By identifying what is going to be reused or replaced as well as being able to clearly and succinctly communicate this to program sponsors and stakeholders, the In/Out matrix creates transparency in the design process. The In/Out diagram is a companion document to the cybersecurity program gap assessment. The In/Out document provides a forum for deciding on program components that can be saved or discarded as well as documenting changes that need to be made.

Table 7-12 is an example of how to complete an In/Out matrix. Create as many line items as necessary to document what is changing in the cybersecurity program.

**Table 7-12. In/Out Matrix**

| Program Component | In | Out |
|-------------------|-----|-----|
| Security Operations | Managed Security Service Provider (MSSP) | Inhouse Security Event & Incident Monitoring |
| Risk Management | NIST SP 800-53 r5 | NIST SP 800-53 r4 |
| Governance | CISO Dashboard | Monthly Word-based reports. |

## 7.15 Notice of Decision (NoD)

During the design and build of a cybersecurity program many decisions are made that potentially alter the original design. Looking back on the why and who of decisions months after a decision has been made can be nearly impossible. Documenting these decisions is critical; to facilitate this, a NoD is recommended. Table 7-13 provides an example of how to complete a NoD.

**Table 7-13. Notice of Decision (NoD)**

<table>
<tr><th colspan="6">Notice of Decision Matrix</th></tr>
<tr><th>Decision ID</th><th>Background</th><th>Decision</th><th>Date</th><th>Approvers</th><th>Decision</th></tr>
<tr><td>NOD010</td><td>Four separate vulnerability scanning solutions are in use.</td><td>A single platform will be used to perform vulnerability scanning.</td><td>07.25.19</td><td>▪ CISO<br>▪ Steering Committee</td><td>Approved</td></tr>
<tr><td>NOD020</td><td>Adopt NIST SP 800-53 v5 vs. V4.</td><td>Keep current with cybersecurity program framework reference document.</td><td>07.26.19</td><td>▪ CISO</td><td>Approved</td></tr>
<tr><td>NOD030</td><td>Convert cybersecurity program framework from NIST 800-53 to ISO 27001.</td><td>Replace NIST framework with ISO 27001.</td><td>07.26.19</td><td>▪ CIO</td><td>Unapproved</td></tr>
</table>

# 7.16 Kanban Board

During my many projects I observed project team members who wanted to work on aspects of a cybersecurity program outside of their core competency as a way of growing their skill set. I also witnessed that project team members could take on more work tasks if they knew they were available. During an Agile development class, I learned of an Agile project management technique used to motivate project team members through healthy competition and to speed up projects. This technique was called a Kanban board. Kanban is a Japanese word meaning visual signal. The idea is to make work activities and accountability visual. This is accomplished by visibly posting work tasks and their status.

A Kanban board is a visual way to project work activities in various stages including scheduled, in process or completed. A Kanban board doesn't need to be elaborate; it can simply be sticky notes on a wall or a whiteboard. or electronic board. Figure 7-3 presents how to setup a Kanban board.

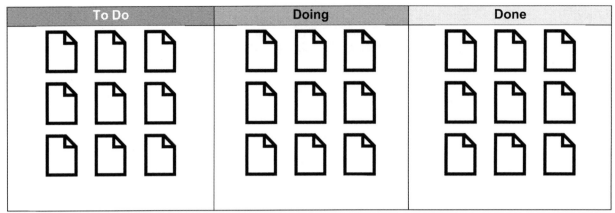

Figure 7-3. Kanban Board.

## 7.17 Requirements Traceability Matrix (RTM)

One of the main problems in commissioning a cybersecurity program is validating that the original business and functional requirements actually made it into the program before going live. For example, if you interview several stakeholders and each explains the need to leverage security to the reduce onboarding time of partners, the stakeholders will expect that their requirements have been addressed. If you cannot show them within the program their wishes have been addressed, you risk losing valuable stakeholders.

One way to do this is to use a Requirements Traceability Matrix (RTM). An RTM is a document linking design requirements to the expected outcomes of the cybersecurity program. Each entry in the RTM will have a unique identifier to facilitate tracking, a documented business and/or functional requirement and the priority of the requirement. Priorities include requirements that must be included, requirements that should be included and requirements that are optional. Table 7-14 show how to complete an RTM.

336

**Table 7-14. Requirements Traceability Matrix (RTM)**

| Req ID | Business Requirement | Functional Requirement | Priority | Owner |
|--------|----------------------|------------------------|----------|-------|
| REQ010 | Eliminate ambiguous assumptions regarding asset protection. | Publish and maintain a comprehensive InfoSec Program Policy Manual. | Must | CISO |
| REQ020 | Align assets to owner to instill risk ownership. | Implement an asset inventory system. | Should | IT Manager |
| REQ030 | Improve privileged account management and monitoring. | Implement Privileged Account Management (PAM) solution. | Must | SecOps |
| REQ040 | Reduce the amount of time to onboard a new service provider. | Revise risk assessment template. | Optional | GRC |

# 7.18 Design Requirements Manual (DRM)

A Design Requirements Guide (DRM) is used to document the requirements, standards and technical criteria of a cybersecurity program. The templates in this chapter as well as information provided elsewhere in the book provide the basis of the DRM. The DRM will serve as the *as built* documentation for the program. You can include a copy of the reference cybersecurity standard, frameworks, models, blueprints and other documentation that documents how the cybersecurity program was built.

### *Summary*

Your education in designing and building a cybersecurity program has come to an end, now it's time to apply what you have learned. This book should serve as your reference guide that you refer to often. If you come to a point where you are stumped, you can always reread the applicable portions of the book to refresh or reinvigorate your thought process. Throughout the book there are many callouts and tips with additional information you can review as well. There are also hundreds of sources of products and solutions that can be used to create your cybersecurity program.

## *Looking Forward*

What we wouldn't give to have a crystal ball to gaze into the future and see where our career will take us next. How will the landscape of cybersecurity be shaped by emerging threats or advances in cybersecurity technologies? Much has happened since 1972 when a man named Bob Thomas launched the first hacker inspired virus, which was a simple program that moved across ARPANET (predecessor to the Internet) printing the message "I'm the Creeper Catch Me if You Can" on Digital Equipment Corporation (DEC) Tenex paper readout terminals. Mr. Thomas also wrote the first anti-virus program that chased Creeper down and deleted it. (SentinalOne, 2019).

A lot has transpired in the last 47 years. Billions of dollars have been spent on cybersecurity technology, yet we never quite feel like we have gained the upper hand on hackers. Attacks against organizations seem to be more brazen and egregious up to and including causing 60 percent of small businesses to fold within six months of a cyberattack (Galvin, 2018). On a global scale data breaches are estimated to cost organizations upwards of a trillion dollars annually.

What role will you play in the future of cybersecurity? Will you be the one who stops your company from going out of business? Will you create the next disruptive cybersecurity technology? Or will you save lives by preventing a ransomware attack from bringing a hospital or police department to its technology knees?

One thing is certain: you must keep pace with the rapidity of this industry you choose to become part of. You must be like a shark, constantly moving for if you stay still, you will sink. I have heard from readers of this book that it has not only made their life easier, but that it also inspired them. My hope is that you become inspired and live your best cybersecurity life!

# References

Nirgan, S. (2017, October 16). *Cybercrime Damages $6 Trillion By 2021*. Cybersecurity Ventures. Retrieved from https://cybersecurityventures.com/hackerpocalypse-cybercrime-report-2016/

SentinalOne. (2019, February 10). *The History Of Cyber Security — Everything You Ever Wanted To Know*. Retrieved from https://www.sentinelone.com/blog/history-of-cyber-security/

Galvin, H. (2018, May 7). 60 Percent of Small Businesses Fold Within 6 Months of a Cyber Attack. Here's How to Protect Yourself. *Inc*. Retrieved from https://www.inc.com/joe-galvin/60-percent-of-small-businesses-fold-within-6-months-of-a-cyber-attack-heres-how-to-protect-yourself.html

# Self-Study Questions

The following questions will help you build your expertise in establishing a foundation of governance.

1.  What is NCATS?
    > National Cybersecurity Assessments and Technical Services (NCATS). A free cybersecurity assessment tool provided by U.S. CERT.

2.  What is a RACI-V?
    > A diagram that allows you to assign who is Responsible, Accountable, Consulted, Informed or Verifies aspects or components of a cybersecurity program.

3.  Which international data privacy law requires a data classification schema?
    > The General Data Protection Regulation (GDPR).

4.  Where can you obtain current information on US data breach laws?
    > The National Conference of State Legislatures (NCSL).

5.  What is the primary purpose of ab NoD?
    > To document critical or important decisions regarding the cybersecurity program.

6.  What is the benefit of using an In/Out matrix?
    > Clearly and concisely show what is changing in the cybersecurity program. Compares what is out and what is in.

7.  What is a Kanban board?
    > A visualization of tasks that project team members can self-select to improve the performance and timeliness of projects tasks.

8. What is the value of an RTM?

Having the ability to prove to stakeholders their requirements have been included in the cybersecurity program. Provides a direct correlation to a business requirement with a program capability.

9. What percentage of small businesses go out of business following a cyberattack?

Sixty percent.

10. Who created the first computer virus?

Bob Thomas in 1972

# Appendix A

# Useful Checklists and Information

Key performance measures (KPMs) are an invaluable way to gauge the overall effectiveness of your cybersecurity program. Too many KPMs can work just the opposite, bogging your organization down with meaningless statistics. Table A-1 shows the minimum KPMs that I require of my own programs to assess the health of a cybersecurity program quickly. **(Note: Links in all tables in Appendix A are current as of July 8, 2019. The author does not endorse any of the products presented.)**

Creating actionable security metrics is crucial to tracking the success of a cybersecurity program. Table A-1 provides examples of key metrics that can be used to model a library of metrics for a cybersecurity program.

**Table A-1. Sample Cybersecurity Program Key Performance Measures (KPM)**

| Measurement | Measurement Insight | Performance | Goal Guidance |
|---|---|---|---|
| Sensitive Document Exfiltration Containment. | How many sensitive documents are sent externally by employees? | Number of sensitive documents captured by data loss prevention (DLP) solution. | The average number of lost or stolen records is 24,615 according to Ponemon Cost of Data Breach 2019 Study. |

| Measurement | Measurement Insight | Performance | Goal Guidance |
|---|---|---|---|
| Data Breach Detection and Response Time | How quickly can we detect and respond to a data breach? | Average time to data breach discovery and response. | Average number of days to detect a data breach is 197 Days according to 2019 Ponemon Cost of a Data Breach Study. |
| Open High-Risk Assessment or Audit Findings | Are there any open high-risk assessment or audit findings that remain untreated? | Zero-tolerance for open high-risk findings. | Treatment of audit findings or receipt of a waiving within published audit guidelines. |
| IT Security Budget in Comparison to Total IT Budget | How much do we spend on cybersecurity compared to the total IT budget? | Cybersecurity budget as a percentage of IT budget. | An average of eight percent of an IT budget is spent on cybersecurity according to PwC report. |
| Email Phishing Attacks Susceptibility | How many employees cannot recognize a phishing attack? | Percentage of employee who fail phishing email simulation test. | 25% of employee fail to spot a phishing attempt coming from a suspicious email according to a 2016 State of Privacy and Security Awareness Report. |
| Security Incidents Detected by Automation, Controls and Practices | How are our cybersecurity investments paying off? | Percentage of incidents detected by controls and countermeasures vs. external sources. | Only 31% of intrusions are detected internally. 69% of notifications come from law enforcement, customers or third parties according to a Mandiant® report. |
| Unpatched IT infrastructure (patch latency) vulnerable to compromise. | How effective is out patch management program? | Percentage of servers remaining unpatched after seven days of a vendor's patch release. | Companies leave vulnerabilities unpatched for up to 120 days, according Kenna Security's Remediation Gap Report. |
| Third Party Service Provider Security | How secure are the third parties we conduct business? | Percentage of third parties with valid security assessments on file. | Twenty percent of verified security breaches of healthcare organizations involved third party associates according to OCR's Wall of Shame. |

*Note*: Links are current as of September 22, 2019.

Gathering threat information is one thing, harnessing the power of the data is another. Threat fusion platforms integrate many different threat sources and perform detailed analysis through the fusing of that data into threat views and levering advanced machine learning capabilities. Table A-2 shows some of the platforms available in this emerging cybersecurity area.

**Table A-2. Threat Fusion Platforms**

| Platform | Company | Website |
|---|---|---|
| Cyber Fusion Centers (CFCs) | Kudelski Security | https://www.kudelskisecurity.com/services/managed-security/threat-intelligence-and-monitoring |
| Cyjax Threat Intelligence Platform | Cyjax Limited | https://www.cyjax.com/ |
| EclecticIQ Fusion Center | EclecticIQ BV | https://www.eclecticiq.com/fusion-center |
| Exterro Fusion Platform | Exterro, Inc. | https://www.exterro.com/e-discovery-software/fusion-platform/ |
| Fusion Server | Lucidworks | https://lucidworks.com/products/fusion-server/ |
| Portfolio of Advanced Fusion Solutions | Vital Intelligence Group | http://vital-int.com/ |

*Note: Links are current as of September 22, 2019.*

Improving your cybersecurity program requires an attention to detail in methods and practices. To determine the improvement of your cybersecurity program fairly and uniformly, a maturity model is required. Table A-3 describes several maturity models that can be applied to various aspects of your cybersecurity program.

**Table A-3. Cybersecurity Maturity Models**

| Model | Source | Website |
|-------|--------|---------|
| Buildings Cybersecurity Capability Maturity Model (B-C2M2) | US Department of Energy (DOE) | https://bc2m2.pnnl.gov/ |
| Cyber Security Incident Response Maturity Assessment | CREST International | http://www.crest-approved.org/cyber-security-incident-response-maturity-assessment/index.html |
| FFIEC Cybersecurity Maturity | Federal Financial Institutions Examination Council (FFIEC) | https://www.ffiec.gov/pdf/cybersecurity/FFIEC_CAT_CS_Maturity_June_2015_PDF2_c.pdf |
| Information Governance Maturity Model | ARMA International | https://iapp.org/media/presentations/12Summit/S12_Information_Asset_Management%20_HANDOUT.pdf |
| Information Maturity Model (IMM) | Meta Group | http://mike2.openmethodology.org/wiki/Information_Maturity_Model |
| Security Operations Maturity Architecture (SOMA) | Institute for Security and Open Methodologies (ISECOM) | http://www.isecom.org/research/soma.html |
| The Community Cyber Security Maturity Model | The Center for Infrastructure Assurance and Security | http://cias.utsa.edu/the-ccsmm.html |

*Note: Links are current as of September 22, 2019.*

Policy management software is an essential component for automating a cybersecurity program. Table A-4 provides a curated list of my top policy management products that I maintain for my own client engagements.

## Table A-4. Policy Management Software

| Product | Company | Website |
|---|---|---|
| 360factors | 360factors | www.360factors.com |
| AC Policy Manager | CFM Partners | http://acpolicymanager.com/ |
| Bizmanualz OnPolicy | Bizmanualz | www.bizmanualz.com |
| DynamicPolicy | Zequel Technologies | http://dynamicpolicy.com/ |
| Information Shield | Information Shield, Inc. | https://informationshield.com |
| Instant IT policy Creation Wizard! | InstantSecurityPolicy.com | http://www.instantsecuritypolicy.com |
| MetaCompliance | MetaCompliance | www.metacompliance.com/ |
| Policy Manager | Convercent | https://www.convercent.com/products/policy-manager |
| Policy Manager Software | PolicyStat | https://www.icontracts.com/policy-management/ |
| PolicyHub | Hitec Laboratories | www.hiteclabs.com |
| policyIQ | policyIQ | www.policyiq.com |
| PowerDMS | PowerDMS | www.powerdms.com |

*Note: Links are current as of September 22, 2019.*

Table A-5 provides a curated list of my top 20 governance, risk, and compliance (GRC) program software products that I maintain for my own client engagements.

**Table A-5. Governance, Risk, and Compliance (GRC) Program Software Products**

| Product | Company | Website |
|---|---|---|
| AchieverPlus | Sword Achiever | http://www.sword-achiever.com/solutions/products/ |
| AdaptiveGRC | C&F | www.adaptivegrc.com |
| BWise GRC Platform | NasdaqBWise | http://www.bwise.com/ |
| Enablon Risk Management Suite | Enablon | http://enablon.com |
| GRC Solutions | StandardFusion | https://www.standardfusion.com/ |
| HOPEX GRC Solutions | MEGA International | http://www.mega.com/en/product/governance-risk-compliance |
| Integrated GRC Solutions | DoubleCheck, LLC. | http://www.doublechecksoftware.com/ |
| LogicManager | LogicManager | http://www.logicmanager.com/ |
| MetricStream GRC Platform | MetricStream | http://www.metricstream.com |
| OneSumX GRC | Wolters Kluwer Financial Services, Inc. | http://www.wolterskluwerfs.com |
| OpenPages GRC Platform | IBM | https://www.ibm.com/us-en/marketplace/openpages-it-governance?mhq=openpages&mhsrc=ibmsearch_p |
| ProcessGene GRC Software Suite | ProcessGene Ltd. | http://processgene.com/ |

| Product | Company | Website |
|---|---|---|
| Resolver's Compliance App | Resolver Inc. | http://www.resolver.com/apps/compliance-software/ |
| RSA Archer® eGRC Platform | EMC/RSA | https://www.rsa.com/en-us/products/integrated-risk-management/archer-platform |
| Rsam eGRC Platform | ACL Services Ltd. dba Galvanize | https://www.wegalvanize.com/it-risk-management/ |
| SAS® Enterprise GRC | SAS Institute Inc. | https://www.sas.com/en_us/software/risk-management/enterprise-grc.html |
| ServiceNow Governance, Risk, and Compliance (GRC) | ServiceNow | https://www.servicenow.com/products/governance-risk-and-compliance.html |

*Note: Links are current as of September 22, 2019.*

Locating the vulnerabilities within your attack surface is essential to protecting your organization's assets and information: you cannot protect against something you do not know exists. The vulnerability scanners listed in Table A-6 will help you find the hidden vulnerabilities within your attack surface.

**Table A-6. Vulnerability Scanning Solutions**

| Solution | Company | Website |
|---|---|---|
| Arachni – Web Application Security Scanner Framework | Sarosys LLC | http://www.arachni-scanner.com/ |
| GFI Lan Guard | GFI Software | https://www.gfi.com/products-and-solutions/network-security-solutions/gfi-languard |
| Lynis Enterprise Suite | CISOfy | https://cisofy.com/lynis/ |
| Nessus® Professional NP™ | Tenable™ | https://www.tenable.com/products/nessus-vulnerability-scanner |
| Network Detective | RapidFire Tools | https://www.rapidfiretools.com/products/network-detective/ |
| Network Mapper (Nmap) | NMAP.org | https://nmap.org/ |
| Open Vulnerability Assessment System (OpenVAS) | Greenbone Networks | http://www.openvas.org/ |
| Qualys Vulnerability Management | Qualys, Inc. | https://www.qualys.com/suite/vulnerability-management/?_ga=2.51663081.171679008.1498045248-978778524.1498045248 |
| Retina Network Security Scanner | BeyondTrust | https://www.beyondtrust.com/products/retina-cs/ |

*Note: Links are current as of September 22, 2019.*

Keeping your assets properly patched is one of the top countermeasures an organization can utilize to protect its assets from compromise. The security patch management solutions in Table A-7 offer a wide array of capabilities to patch all your vulnerable assets automatically.

**Table A-7. Security Patch Management Solutions**

| Solution | Company | Website |
|---|---|---|
| Cloud Management Suite - IT Patch Management | Verismic. | https://www.cloudmanagementsuite.com/patch-management/ |
| ConnectWise Automate | ConnectWise, Inc. | https://www.connectwise.com/software/automate |
| Dameware Patch Manager | SolarWinds Worldwide, LLC. | http://www.dameware.com/patch-manager |
| Kaseya® VSA™ Patch Management | Kaseya Limited | http://www.kaseya.com/products/vsa-feature/patch-management |
| Lumension® Patch and Remediation | Lumension Security, Inc. | https://www.lumension.com/vulnerability-management/patch-management-software/overview.aspx |
| Miradore Patch Management | Miradore Ltd | https://www.miradore.com/patch-management/ |
| Patch Connect Plus | Zoho Corp. | https://www.manageengine.com/patch-management/?MEtab |
| SolarWinds® Patch Manager | SolarWinds Worldwide, LLC. | http://www.solarwinds.com/patch-manager |
| SysAid Patch Management | SysAid Technologies Ltd. | https://www.sysaid.com/it-service-management-software/it-asset-management/patch-management |

*Note: Links are current as of September 22, 2019.*

If you have decided to move toward the next-generation of security patching, the following list of virtual patching solutions are available to help you reach that goal. Table A-8 provides a partial list of virtual patching solutions.

**Table A-8. Virtual Patching Solutions**

| Product or Service | Company | Website |
|---|---|---|
| Airlock Suite | Ergon Informatik AG | https://www.airlock.com/en/solutions/techies/#virtual-patching |
| McAfee Database Security | McAfee, LLC | https://www.mcafee.com/us/resources/misc/infographic-case-for-virtual-patching.pdf |
| Virtual PatchingGoCodes | Trend Micro, Inc. | http://apac.trendmicro.com/cloud-content/us/pdfs/business/sb_virtual-patching.pdf |
| Virtual Patching | Waratek | https://www.waratek.com/solutions/virtual-patching/ |
| Virtual Patching Solutions | Honeywell International Inc. | https://www.honeywellprocess.com/library/marketing/whitepapers/VirtualPatchingWhitePaper.pdf |

*Note: Links are current as of September 22, 2019.*

IT asset management products are invaluable in identify an attack surface. Table A-9 provides a curated list of my network discovery products that I maintain for my own client engagements.

**Table A-9. IT Asset Management Products**

| Product | Company | Website |
|---|---|---|
| AssetStudio for Enterprise SAM | Certero | http://www.certero.com/products/assetstudio-for-enterprise-sam/ |
| Freshservice. Inc. | Freshdesk | https://freshservice.com/ |
| GoCodes Asset Management | GoCodes, Inc. | http://it-asset-tracking.gocodes.com/ |
| Samanage IT Asset Management | Samanage Ltd. | https://www.samanage.com/ |
| ServiceNow Asset Management | ServiceNow | https://www.servicenow.com/products/it-service-automation-applications/asset-management.html |

*Note: Links are current as of September 22, 2019.*

Tracking down Shadow IT within your organization will help you identify a threat vector that often goes undetected by anyone besides hackers. The cloud access security broker (CASB) products in Table A-10 are uniquely designed to track and manage the risk of Shadow IT.

**Table A-10. Cloud Access Security Broker (CASB) Solutions**

| Product | Company | Website |
|---|---|---|
| Adallom | Microsoft | https://www.microsoft.com/en-us/cloud-platform/cloud-app-security |
| CirroSecure (Aperture™ SaaS Security Service) | Palo Alto Networks | https://www.crunchbase.com/organization/cirrosecure |
| Cloud Access Monitor | Managed Methods | https://managedmethods.com/products/cloud-access-monitor/ |
| Cloud Access Security Broker | Bitglass, Inc. | https://www.bitglass.com/ |
| Cloud Application Visibility & Control | Zscaler | https://www.zscaler.com/products/cloud-app-visibility-and-control |
| Cloud Security Broker (CSB) | CipherCloud | https://www.ciphercloud.com/ |
| CloudLock | Cisco | https://www.cloudlock.com/solutions/ |
| Elastica | Symantec + Bluecoat | https://www.elastica.net/shadow-it/ |
| Netskope Shadow IT | Netskope | https://www.netskope.com/solutions/shadow-it/ |
| Palerra LORIC™ | Oracle | http://palerra.com/platform/loric-discovery/ |
| Forcepoint CASB (Cloud Access Security Broker) | Forcepoint by Raytheon | https://www.forcepoint.com/skyfence-customer-transition |

*Note: Links are current as of September 22, 2019.*

Reliable, actionable intelligence is essential to guide the deployment of your cybersecurity program's countermeasures. Obtaining that information internally can prove to be time consuming and costly. The threat intelligence services listed in Table A-11 can greatly enhance your cybersecurity program threat intelligence capability.

**Table A-11. Threat Intelligence Services**

| Platform | Company | Website |
|---|---|---|
| Advisory Services | Flashpoint | https://www.flashpoint-intel.com/solutions/#advisory_services |
| Application and Threat Intelligence | Ixia | https://www.ixiacom.com/products/application-and-threat-intelligence-subscription |
| CAWS Cyber Threat Protection Platform | NSS Labs | https://www.g2.com/products/caws-cyber-threat-protection-platform/reviews |
| Cyber Threat Intelligence | Control Risks Group Holdings Ltd | https://www.controlrisks.com/en/services/security-risk/cyber-security-services/cyber-threat-intelligence |
| DeepSight™ Intelligence | Symantec Corporation | https://www.symantec.com/services/cyber-security-services/deepsight-intelligence |
| Digital Shadows SearchLight™ | Digital Shadows Ltd | https://www.digitalshadows.com/digital-shadows-searchlight/ |
| Falcon Intelligence | CrowdStrike | https://www.crowdstrike.com/products/falcon-intelligence/ |
| iDefense Security Intelligence Services | Accenture | https://www.accenture.com/us-en/service-idefense-security-intelligence |
| INTEL471 | Intel 471 Inc. | http://intel471.com/ |

| Platform | Company | Website |
|---|---|---|
| iSIGHT Intelligence Subscriptions | FireEye, Inc. | https://www.fireeye.com/products/isight-cyber-threat-intelligence-subscriptions.html |
| Kaspersky Security Intelligence Services | Kaspersky Lab | https://usa.kaspersky.com/enterprise-security/intelligence-services |
| NSFOCUS Threat Intelligence Subscription Service | NSFOCUS | https://nsfocusglobal.com/products/threat-intelligence-ti/ |
| Proofpoint ET Intelligence | Proofpoint, Inc. | https://www.proofpoint.com/us/products/et-intelligence |
| QuickThreat® | Centripetal Networks | https://www.centripetalnetworks.com/how-it-works.php |
| SurfWatch Threat Analyst | SurfWatch Labs, Inc. | https://www.surfwatchlabs.com/threat-intelligence-products/threat-analyst |
| Threat Intelligence Services | LookingGlass Cyber Threat Intelligence Group | https://www.lookingglasscyber.com/products/threat-intelligence-services/ |
| ThreatConnect | ThreatConnect, Inc. | https://www.threatconnect.com/products/ |
| ThreatQ | ThreatQuotient, Inc. | https://www.threatq.com/ |
| ThreatStream | ANOMALI | https://www.anomali.com/ |

*Note*: *Links are current as of September 22, 2019.*

To help you benchmark your cybersecurity program against studies and to research the causes of data breaches, I have curated a list in Table A-12 of what I find to be the most insightful data breach and threat reports for your analysis.

## Table A-12. Data Breach and Threats Reports

| Report | Source | Pages | Summary |
|---|---|---|---|
| 2019 Cyber Security Risk Report | Aon | 26 | Exploration of eight specific risk organization face today. |
| 2019 Data Breach Litigation Report | Bryan Cave Leighton Paisner LLP | 23 | Analysis of Federal class action data breach litigation initiated between January 1, 2017 December 31, 2018. |
| 2019 BAE Systems Incident Response Report | BAE Systems | 16 | Survey of information security professionals to determine their organizations' readiness and ability to recover from a data compromise. |
| 2019 Global Incident Response Threat Report | CarbonBlack | 16 | Report aggregating qualitative and quantitative input from 40 Carbon Black IR partners, which offer actionable intelligence for business and technology leaders, fueled by analysis of the newest threats and expert insights on how to stop them. |
| 2019 M-Trends Report | FireEye, Inc. | 76 | Latest trends revealed through FireEye incident response investigations by FireEye Mandiant. These include evolving APT activity in various regions, phishing risks during mergers and acquisitions. |
| 2019 Thales Data Threat Report | Thales eSecurity | 32 | Report is based on a survey of over 1200 senior security executives from around the world with influence over IT and data security. |
| 2019 Insider Threat Report | Verizon | 71 | Analysis of thousands of data breach incidents. |

| Report | Source | Pages | Summary |
|---|---|---|---|
| 2019 Internet Security Threat Report | Symantec Corporation | 61 | Exhaustive research is informed by 123 million sensors recording thousands of threat events every second from 157 countries and territories. |
| 2018: Data Privacy and New Regulations Take Center Stage | Gemalto NV | 16 | Extensive information about data breaches worldwide, using sources such as Internet searches, news articles and analyses and other resources. The data gathered is then aggregated into the Index, a database. |
| 2018 Cost of a Data Breach | Ponemon Institute LLC | 47 | Results of 2,200 interviews of security and IT executives on their data breach experiences. |
| 2018 Credential Spill Report | Shape Security | 40 | Key findings from credential spills reported in 2018 that show how stolen credentials are used in credential attacks worldwide. |

*Note: Links are current as of September 22, 2019.*

If you decide to outsource some or a portion of your cybersecurity countermeasures, the MSSPs in Table A-13 offer a rich set of security services for your consideration. For a comprehensive list, check out https://www.msspalert.com/top100/list-2018/10/.

**Table A-13. Managed Security Service Providers (MSSP)**

| Company | Key Services | Website |
|---|---|---|
| Atos<br><br>• 14 - SOCs | • McAfee® Active Response (MAR)<br>• McAfee® Advanced Threat Defense (ATD)<br>• McAfee® Data Exchange Layer (DXL)<br>• McAfee® Endpoint Security<br>• McAfee® Enterprise Security Manager (SIEM)<br>• McAfee® Threat Intelligence Exchange (TIE) | https://atos.net/en/solutions/cyber-security/managed-security-services |
| BAE Systems<br><br>• 5 SOCs | • Complete Security Monitoring (CSM)<br>• Managed Detection and Response (MDR)<br>• Security Device Management (SDM)<br>• Security Event Monitoring (SEM) | http://www.baesystems.com/en-us/capability/managed-security-services |
| CenturyLink® MSS 2.0<br><br>• 4 – SOCs | • Device Management<br>• Incident Response and Recovery<br>• Network and Cloud Based Security<br>• Threat Intelligence and Predictive Analytics | http://www.centurylink.com/business/enterprise/managed-services/managed-security.html |
| DXC Technology (CSC and HPE)<br><br>• 11- SOCs | • Managed Firewall Service<br>• Managed IDS/IPS Service<br>• Managed SIEM Service | https://www.dxc.technology/security |
| IBM® Managed Security Services<br><br>• 5 - SOCs | • Firewall Management<br>• Intelligent Log Management on Cloud<br>• Intrusion Detection / Prevention Management<br>• Managed Database Security<br>• Unified Threat Management | https://www.ibm.com/security/services/managed-security-services/ |
| NTT Security<br><br>• 6 - SOCs | • AWS Monitoring<br>• ActiveGuard Portal<br>• Next Generation Firewall Monitoring<br>• IDS/IPS Monitoring<br>• Realtime Malware Detection<br>• Log Analysis | http://www.nttcomsecurity.com/us/services/managed-security-services/ |
| SecureWorks®<br><br>• 5 - SOCs | • Advanced Malware Protection and Detection (AMPD)<br>• Counter Threat Platform™ (CTP)<br>• Managed Firewall<br>• Managed IDS/IPS | https://www.secureworks.com/capabilities/managed-security |

| Company | Key Services | Website |
|---|---|---|
| | • Managed iSensor IPS<br>• Palo Alto Next Generation Firewalls | |
| Symantec Managed Security Services<br><br>• 6 – SOCs | • Advanced Threat Monitoring<br>• DeepSight Intelligence<br>• Incident Response Services<br>• Symantec Global Intelligence Network | https://www.symantec.com/services/cyber-security-services/managed-security-services |
| Trustwave Managed Security Services (Singtel Group)<br><br>• 9 - SOCs | • Compliance Management<br>• Threat Management<br>• Vulnerability Management | https://www.trustwave.com/Services/Managed-Security/ |
| Unisys Managed Security Services<br><br>• 8 - SOCs | • Governance Risk & Compliance (GRC)<br>• Managed Identity and Access Management Services<br>• Managed Security Information and Event Management (SIEM)<br>• Security Device Management (SDM) | http://www.unisys.com/offerings/security-solutions/managed-security-services |
| Verizon Managed Security Services<br><br>• 9 - SOCs | • Advanced Threat Detection<br>• Device Health Monitoring and Management<br>• Identity and access management services | http://www.verizonenterprise.com/products/security/security-monitoring-operations/ |

*Note: Links are current as of September 22, 2019.*

In an increasingly sophisticated threat landscape, automating and orchestrating your cybersecurity program will be essential to leverage limited human resources and financial investment. Products in Table A-14 provide capabilities for you to automate and orchestrate your cybersecurity program.

**Table A-14. Cybersecurity Automation and Orchestration Solutions**

| Product | Company | Website |
|---|---|---|
| CyberSponse Platform | CyberSponse, Inc. | https://cybersponse.com/ |

| Product | Company | Website |
|---|---|---|
| Demisto Enterprise | Demisto | https://www.demisto.com/ |
| Gemini Manage | Gemini Data Inc | https://www.geminidata.com/products/gemini-manage/ |
| IncMan | DFLabs SPA | https://www.dflabs.com/ |
| Intelligent Incident Response and Orchestration | Resolve Systems | https://www.resolvesystems.com/ |
| Komand Security Orchestration & Automation Platform | Rapid7 | https://www.komand.com/ |
| Phantom Security Orchestration | Splunk, Inc. | https://www.phantom.us/ |
| Process Orchestrator | Cisco Systems | http://www.cisco.com/c/en/us/products/cloud-systems-management/process-orchestrator/index.html |
| Security Intelligence Platform | Exabeam | https://www.exabeam.com/info/security-management-resources/?gclid=COfxqcOJ79ICFUs7gQod59EGXg |
| Security Orchestrator | FireEye, Inc. | https://www.fireeye.com/products/security-orchestrator.html |
| Swimlane LLC | Swimlane LLC | https://swimlane.com/solution/ |
| ThreatNexus™ Orchestration Engine | Siemplify | https://www.siemplify.co/security-orchestration-automation/ |

| Product | Company | Website |
|---|---|---|
| Tufin Orchestration Suite | Tufin Orchestration Suite | https://www.tufin.com/tufin-orchestration-suite/ |

*Note: Links are current as of September 22, 2019.*

Table A-15 presents the top cybersecurity blogs you can use to stay abreast of data breaches as well as emerging cybersecurity trends and products.

**Table A-15. Cybersecurity Blogs**

| Blog | Overview | Website |
|---|---|---|
| Dark Reading | Breaking news and analysis on attacks, breaches and vulnerabilities, as well as strategies for protecting enterprise data. | www.darkreading.com |
| The Guardian – Data & Computer Security | Known for quality articles on world news, Guardian offers a section dedicated to information security for companies and individuals. | www.theguardian.com/technology/data-computer-security |
| Krebs on Security | A daily blog dedicated to investigative stories on cybercrime and computer security. | www.krebsonsecurity.com |
| Naked Security | Threat newsroom with warnings of kinds of bad computer threats, | http://www.nakedsecurity.com/ |
| Threatpost | Independent news site which is a leading source of information about IT and business security. | www.threatpost.com |

*Note: Links are current as of September 22, 2019.*

Magazines in Table A-16 present sources of cybersecurity news that you can use to stay abreast of data breaches, products and industry news.

**Table A-16 Cybersecurity Magazines**

| Magazine | Overview | Website |
|---|---|---|
| Brilliance Security Magazine | Illuminating the intersection of physical and cyber security. We scour the web, blogosphere, and social media to bring you timely and relevant security industry news. | http://brilliancesecuritymagazine.com/ |
| Cyber Defense Magazine | Cyber Defense Magazine is by ethical, honest, passionate information security professionals for IT Security professionals. Our mission is to share cutting edge knowledge, real world stories and awards on the best ideas, products and services in the information technology industry. | www.cyberdefensemagazine.com |
| Cybercrime Magazine | Page ONE for the global cyber economy, and a trusted source for cybersecurity facts, figures, and statistics. Cybercrime Magazine by Cybersecurity Ventures provides research and reports on cybercrime costs, cybersecurity market size and spending forecasts, cybersecurity jobs & more. | www.cybersecurityventures.com |
| **SC Magazine** | SC Media UK is a dedicated IT security publication having served the IT security industry for over 20 years and arms information security professionals with the in-depth, unbiased business and technical information they need to tackle the countless security challenges they face and establish risk management and compliance postures that underpin overall business strategies. | www.scmagazineuk.com |
| Security Magazine | The magazine features news, comprehensive analysis, cutting-edge features, and contributions from thought leaders, that are nothing like the ordinary. | https://www.securitymagazine.com/topics/2236-cyber-security-news |

*Note: Links are current as of September 22, 2019.*

Cyber threats listed in Table A-17 represent the top threats should most concern organizations. Threats are presented alphabetically to avoid anyone subverting their own threat likelihood analysis.

## Table A-17 Top Cyber Threats

| Threat | Overview |
|---|---|
| Advanced Persistent Threats (APT) | An attack where hackers who infiltrate a network using sophisticated tactics undetected and deposit code designed to exfiltrate information is known as an Advanced Persistent Threat (APT). The attackers take an extended period to steal login credentials in order to elevate their privileges to seek out more confidential and sensitive information. |
| Cloud Service Provider Compromises | Tens of millions of records have been leaked or stolen from cloud service providers. Off-the-shelf tools on the web allow attackers to identify misconfigured cloud resources and launch an attack. |
| Internet of Things (IoT) Botnet DDoS Attacks | Hackers access IoT devices using them as a launching platform for DDoS attacks. These compromised IoT devices are remotely directed through Command and Control (C&C) networks. |
| Phishing Attacks | Providers of anti-phishing systems report their systems are triggered hundreds of millions of times a year. With the number of phishing attacks growing every year, this is a significant threat. Phishing attacks have been at the core of many of the most significant cyberattacks the past five years. |
| Ransomware | Thousands of ransomware attacks occur every day, and published reports estimate a ransomware attack occurs every minute of the day. Several media outlets have even reported that well over $1 billion dollars in ransoms have been paid to date. |
| Zero-Day or Forever-Day Exploits | Zero-day attacks occur when a software or hardware vulnerability is exploited before developers either know of the vulnerability or have an opportunity to create a patch. Zero days can also exist when bad actors create and release exploitive malware.<br><br>Forever-day attacks are known security vulnerabilities that have never been patched. Results for both are essentially the same. |
| Supply Chain Third-Party Attacks | Hackers have learned that one of the easiest paths to infiltrate a target is through their supply chain. Some of the most egregious cyberattacks have come through previously trusted third parties. |

*Note: Links are current as of September 22, 2019.*

# Index

*Figures and tables are indicated by f and t following the page number.*

# Credits

**Kristen Noakes-Fry, ABCI,** is Executive Editor at Rothstein Associates Inc. Previously, she was a Research Director, Information Security and Risk Group, for Gartner, Inc.; Associate Editor at Datapro (McGraw-Hill), where she was responsible for Datapro Reports on Information Security; and Associate Professor of English at Atlantic Cape College in New Jersey. She holds an M.A. from New York University and a B.A. from Russell Sage College.

**Cover Design and Graphics:**   Sheila Kwiatek, Flower Grafix

**eBook Design & Processing:**   Donna Luther, Metadata Prime

**Philip Jan Rothstein, FBCI,** is President of Rothstein Associates Inc., a management consultancy he founded in 1984 as a pioneer in the disciplines of Business Continuity and Disaster Recovery. He is also the Executive Publisher of Rothstein Publishing.

**Glyn Davies** is Chief Marketing Officer of Rothstein Associates Inc. He has held this position since 2013. Glyn has previously held executive level positions in Sales, Marketing and Editorial at several multinational publishing companies and currently resides in California.

**Rothstein Publishing** is your premier source of books and learning materials about Business Resilience, including Crisis Management, Business Continuity, Disaster Recovery, Emergency Management, Security, Cybersecurity and Risk Management, as well as related fields including Root Cause Analysis and Critical Infrastructure. Our industry-leading authors provide current, actionable knowledge, solutions, and tools you can put in practice immediately. Rothstein Publishing remains true to the decades-long commitment of Rothstein Associates, which is to prepare you and your organization to protect, preserve, and recover what is most important: your people, facilities, assets, and reputation.

info@rothstein.com
www.rothstein.com

# About the Author

**Tari Schreider** is a distinguished technologist and nationally known expert in the fields of cybersecurity, risk management, and disaster recovery. He was formerly Chief Security Architect at Hewlett-Packard Enterprise and National Practice Director for Security and Disaster Recovery at Sprint E|Solutions. Schreider is an instructor for EC-Council where he teaches advanced CISO certification and risk management courses.

Schreider has designed and implemented complex cybersecurity programs including a red team penetration testing program for one of the world's largest oil and gas companies, an NERC CIP compliance program for one of Canada's largest electric utility companies, an integrated security control management program for one of the largest 911 systems in the US and designed a cybersecurity service architecture for one of the largest retailers in the US. He has advised organizations worldwide including Brazil, China, India and South Africa on how to improve their cybersecurity programs.

Schreider implemented a virtual Security Operations Center network with vSOCs located in the US, Brazil, Italy, Japan, Sweden, and the US. He was also responsible for creating the first Information Sharing and Analysis Center in collaboration with the Information Technology Association of America (IT-ISCA). His earliest disaster recovery experiences included assisting companies affected during the 1992 Los Angeles riots and 1993 World Trade Center bombing. His most unique experience came during the Gulf War helping a New York financial institution recover after becoming separated from its data center in Kuwait.

Schreider has appeared on ABC News, CNN, CNBC, NPR, and has had numerous articles printed in security and business magazines, including *Business Week, New York Times, SC Magazine, The Wall Street Journal* and many others. He is the author of *The Manager's Guide to Cybersecurity Law* (Rothstein Publishing, 2017) and is a co-author of the US patent Method for Analyzing Risk.

He studied Criminal Justice at the College of Social & Behavioral Sciences at the University of Phoenix and holds the following certifications in security and disaster recovery:

- American College of Forensic Examiners, CHS-III
- Certified CISO (C|CISO)
- Certified in Risk and Information Systems Control (CRISC)
- ITIL® v3 Foundation Certified
- System Security Certified Practitioner (SSCP)
- Member of the Business Continuity Institute (MBCI)
- University of Richmond – Master Certified Recovery Planner (MCRP)

# CYBERSECURITY LAW:
# ESSENTIALS FOR TODAY'S BUSINESS
# (2nd EDITION)

By Tari Schreider C|CISO, CRISC, ITIL® Foundation, MCRP, SSCP

## NEW 2nd EDITION FOR 2020

A thoroughly updated revision of this successful title will be available in early 2020 in print, ePub and eBook formats, reflecting the very latest developments in cybersecurity law, regulations and standards.

In today's litigious business world, cyber-related matters could land you in court. As a computer security professional, you are protecting your data, but are you protecting your company? While you know industry standards and regulations, you may not be a legal expert. Fortunately, in a few hours of reading, rather than months of classroom study, Tari Schreider's *CYBERSECURITY LAW: ESSENTIALS FOR TODAY'S BUSINESS (2nd EDITION)* lets you integrate legal issues into your cybersecurity program.

## NEW IN THE 2nd EDITION

- A complete Cybercrime Taxonomy.
- Over 30 "call out" boxes
- Revised Fourth Amendment Rights and Digital Evidence.
- New Inclusion of the General Data Protection Regulation (GDPR).
- Update on Children's Online Privacy Protection Act (COPPA)
- Detailed coverage of enforcement actions.
- An update on HIPAA enforcement actions.
- New coverage of Cybercrime on Tribal Lands.
- A thorough update on state data breach laws.

- Expanded coverage of the Gramm-Leach-Bliley Act (GLBA).
- Data privacy updates on the G7.
- Updated international data privacy and protection laws.
- Cybersecurity whistleblower protections.
- Digital assistant (Alexa, Siri, etc.) privacy considerations.
- Cybercrime extradition updates.
- Coverage of recent Supreme Court rulings and opinions update.
- Numerous Self-study questions and exercises.

Print ISBN – 9781944480561
EPub ISBN – 9781944480578
PDF eBook ISBN – 9781944480585
https://www.rothstein.com/product/guide-to-cybersecurity-law/

Made in the USA
Columbia, SC
23 July 2021